The Cross-Platform Prep Course

Welcome to the Cross-Platform Prep Course Edition! McGraw-Hill Education's multi-platform course gives you a variety of tools to raise your scores and get in to the school of your choice. Whether you're studying at home, the library, or on-the-go, you can find practice content in the format you need—print, online, or mobile.

Print Book

This print book gives you the tools you need to ace the test. In its pages you'll find smart test-taking strategies, in-depth reviews of key topics, and ample practice questions and tests. See the Welcome section of your book for a step-by-step guide to its features.

Online Platform

The Cross-Platform Prep Course's online platform gives you additional study and practice content that you can access *anytime, anywhere.* You can create a personalized study plan based on your test date that sets daily goals to keep you on track. Integrated lessons provide important review of key topics. Practice questions, exams, and flashcards give you the practice you need to build test-taking confidence. The game center is filled with challenging games that allow you to practice your new skills in a fun and engaging way. You can interact with other test-takers in the discussion section and gain valuable peer support.

Getting Started

To get started, open your account on the online platform:

Go to www.xplatform.mhprofessional.com

↓

Enter your access code, which you can find on the inside back cover of your book

↓

Provide your name and e-mail address to open your account and create a password

↓

Click "Start Studying" to enter the platform

It's as simple as that. You're ready to start studying online.

Your Personalized Study Plan

First, select your test date on the calendar, and you're on your way to creating your personalized study plan. Your study plan will help you stay organized and on track and will guide you through the course in the most efficient way. It is tailored to *your* schedule and features daily tasks that are broken down into manageable goals. You can adjust your end date at any time and your daily tasks will be reorganized into an updated plan.

You can track your progress in real time on the Study Plan Dashboard. The Today's Knowledge Goal progress bar gives you up-to-the-minute feedback on your daily goal. Fulfilling this is the most efficient way to work through the entire course. You can get an instant view of where you stand in the entire course with the Study Plan Progress bar.

If you need to exit the program before completing a task, you can return to the Study Plan Dashboard at any time. Just click the Study Task icon and you can automatically pick up where you left off.

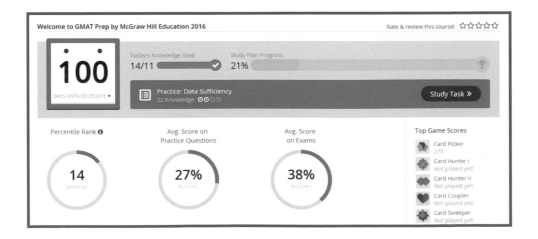

Practice Tests

One of the first tasks in your personalized study plan is to take the Diagnostic Test. At the end of the test, a detailed evaluation of your strengths and weaknesses shows the areas where you need to focus most. You can review your practice test results either by the question category to see broad trends or question-by-question for a more in-depth look.

The full-length tests are designed to simulate the real thing. Try to simulate actual testing conditions and be sure you set aside enough time to complete the full-length test. You'll learn to pace yourself so that you can get the best possible score on test day.

Full Length Test 1						Reset Test
Question Review **Category Scores**						Review All
	#	✓	Preview (Click to toggle full preview)	Time	Difficulty	
38% Correct	246	✓	Direction : For the following question, select the best of the answer choices given. There are few things worse for a new parent...	0 min 13 sec	Unrated	Review
	247	✗	Direction : For the following question, select the best of the answer choices given. Charlie's Chainsaw Company has reason to be...	0 min 31 sec	Unrated	Review
	248	✗	Direction : For the following question, select the best of the answer choices given. A dog enthusiast took home two puppies from...	0 min 9 sec	Unrated	Review
Questions Taken 93 of 93	249	✓	Direction : For the following question, select the best of the answer choices given. Paleontologists hypothesize that modern bi...	0 min 12 sec	Unrated	Review
Avg. Answer Time 0 min 19 sec	250	✓	Direction : For the following question, select the best of the answer choices given. Bob and Linda are tired of the freezing co...	0 min 13 sec	Unrated	Review
Avg. Correct Answer Time 0 min 23 sec	251	✗	Direction : For the following question, select the best of the answer choices given. Although many people would not believe it, ...	0 min 13 sec	Unrated	Review
Avg. Incorrect Answer Time 0 min 16 sec	252	✓	Direction : The following question present a sentence, part of which or all of which is underlined. Beneath the sentence, you will find five w...	0 min 26 sec	Unrated	Review
	253	✓	Direction : The following question present a sentence, part of which or all of which is underlined. Beneath the sentence, you will find five w...	0 min 37 sec	Unrated	Review
	254	✓	Direction :The following question present a sentence, part of which or all of which is underlined. Beneath the sentence, you will find five wa...	0 min 19 sec	Unrated	Review

Lessons

The lessons in the online platform are divided into manageable pieces that let you build knowledge and confidence in a progressive way. They cover the full range of topics that appear on your test.

After you complete a lesson, mark your confidence level. (You must indicate a confidence level in order to count your progress and move on to the next task.) You can also filter the lessons by confidence levels to see the areas you have mastered and those that you might need to revisit.

> *Use the bookmark feature to easily refer back to a concept or leave a note to remember your thoughts or questions about a particular topic.*

Practice Questions

All of the practice questions are based on real-life exams and simulate the test-taking experience. The Review Answer gives you immediate feedback on your answer. Each question includes a rationale that explains why the correct answer is right and the others are wrong. To explore any topic further, you can find detailed explanations by clicking the "Help me learn about this topic" link.

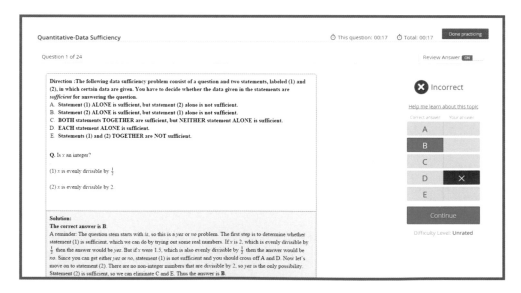

You can go to the Practice Dashboard to find an overview of your performance in the different categories and sub-categories.

Dashboard

Visit the dashboard to see personalized information on your progress and performance. The Percentile Rank icon shows your position relative to all the other students enrolled in the course. You can also find information on your average scores in practice questions and exams.

A detailed overview of your strengths and weaknesses shows your proficiency in a category based on your answers and difficulty of the questions. By viewing your strengths and weaknesses, you can focus your study on your weaker spots.

Flashcards

Hundreds of flashcards are perfect for learning key terms quickly, and the interactive format gives you immediate feedback. You can filter the cards by category and confidence level for a more organized approach. Or, you can shuffle them up for a challenge.

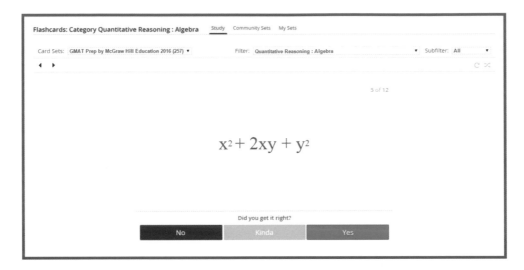

Another way to customize the flashcards is to create your own sets. You can keep these private or share or them with the public. Subscribe to Community Sets to access sets from other students preparing for the same exam.

Game Center

Play a game in the Game Center to test your knowledge of key concepts in a challenging but fun environment. Up the difficulty level and complete the games quickly to build the highest score. Be sure to check the leaderboard to see who's on top.

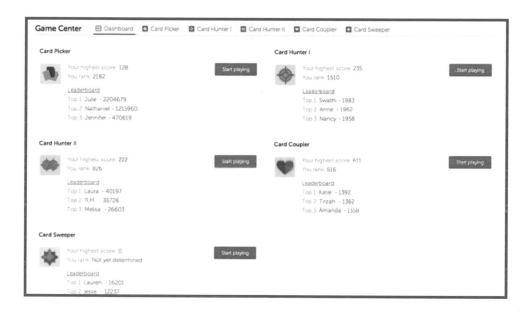

Social Community

Interact with other students who are preparing for your test. Start a discussion, reply to a post, or even upload files to share. You can search the archives for common topics or start your own private discussion with friends.

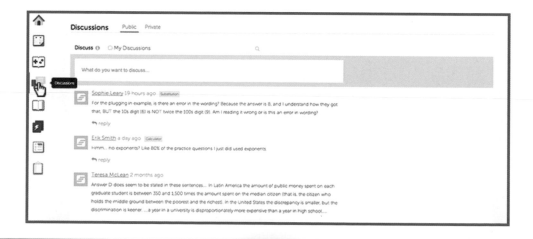

Mobile App

The companion mobile app lets you toggle between the online platform and your mobile device without missing a beat. Whether you access the course online or on your smartphone or tablet, you'll pick up exactly where you left off.

Go to the iTunes or Google Play stores and search "BenchPrep Companion" to download the companion iOS or Android app. Enter your e-mail address and the same password you created for the online platform to open your account.

Now, let's get started!

ELITE STUDENT EDITION

5 STEPS TO A 5

AP English Language

2018

Barbara L. Murphy
Estelle M. Rankin

McGraw Hill Education

New York   Chicago   San Francisco   Athens   London   Madrid
Mexico City   Milan   New Delhi   Singapore   Sydney   Toronto

1 2 3 4 5 6 7 8 9   LHS   22 21 20 19 18 17 (Cross-Platform Prep Course only)
  2 3 4 5 6 7 8 9   LHS   22 21 20 19 18   (Elite Student Edition)

ISBN   978-1-259-86231-1 (Cross-Platform Prep Course only)
MHID   1-259-86231-3

e-ISBN 978-1-259-86232-8 (Cross-Platform Prep Course only)
e-MHID   1-259-86232-1

ISBN   978-1-259-86228-1 (Elite Student Edition)
MHID   1-259-86228-3

e-ISBN 978-1-259-86229-8 (Elite Student Edition)
e-MHID   1-259-86229-1

The series editor for this book was Grace Freedson and the project editor was Del Franz.

AP, Advanced Placement Program, and *College Board* are registered trademarks of the College Board, which was not involved in the production of, and does not endorse, this product.

McGraw-Hill Education products are available at special quantity discounts to use as premiums and sales promotions or for use in corporate training programs. To contact a representative, please visit the Contact Us pages at www.mhprofessional.com.

CONTENTS

STEP 4   Review the Knowledge You Need to Score High

STEP 5 **Build Your Test-Taking Confidence**

ELITE STUDENT EDITION

5 Minutes to a 5
180 Activities and Questions in 5 Minutes a Day   245

PREFACE

Welcome to our latest revised AP English Language class. As we said in the earlier versions of this book, we are, first and foremost, teachers who have taught Advanced Placement to literally thousands of students who successfully took the AP exam. With this guide, we hope to share with you what we know, as well as what we have learned from our own students.

We see you as a student in our class—only quieter! Our philosophy has always been NOT to teach only for the AP test. Instead, our goal is to develop those insights, appreciations, and skills that lead to advanced levels of facility with a wide range of texts. These are the same skills that will enable you to do well on the AP English Language exam. Our aim is to remove your anxiety and to improve your comfort level with the test. We believe that you are already motivated to succeed; otherwise, you would not have come this far. And, obviously, you would not have purchased this prep book.

Because you are already in an AP English class, this book is going to supplement your course readings, analysis, and writing. We are going to give you the opportunity to practice processes and techniques that we know from experience REALLY WORK! If you apply the techniques and processes presented in this book, we are confident you can succeed both in the course and on the exam.

We have listened to comments and suggestions from both instructors and students of AP English Language. Keeping their thoughts in mind, this revised text has more interactive activities and practice to help hone those skills needed to do well in class and on the AP English Language exam. In addition, there are special review questions and activities related to specific chapters that McGraw-Hill has available on its website devoted to the 5 Steps series. There you can test how well you have internalized the material in the chapter.

Let's begin.

ACKNOWLEDGMENTS

Our love and appreciation to Leah and Allan for their constant support and encouragement. Special thanks to our professional mentors who have guided us throughout our careers: Steven Piorkowski and Howard Damon. To the following for their support and suggestions: Diane Antonucci, Jodi Rice, Margaret Cross Rice, Pat Kelley, Stephanie Tidwell, and Sandi Forsythe—thank you.

The authors want to acknowledge the participation, insights, and feedback provided us by the following colleagues and students:

East Islip High School:
  Teacher: Marge Grossgold
  Students: Kyle Hill, Jamie Ray

Garden City High School:
  Teachers: Mary Watts, Ed Schmeider
  Students: Alexandra Wertis, Michael Marino

Jericho High School:
  Teachers: Diane Antonucci, Patricia Gulitti
  Students: Vikas Anand, Jenna Butner, Shinae Lee, Josh Levine, Boyang Li, Anish
          Mashettiwar, Erica Ross, Sherli Yeroushalmi, Qi Yu

Kings Park High School:
  Teacher: Jeanne Palm
  Students: Fred Langer, Stephanie Kersling, Janet Lee

Moro Bay High School:
  Teacher: Michelle Dowell
  Students: Katey Maruska, Heather Spellacy

Roslyn High School:
  Student: Jenna Kahn

Wellington High School:
  Teacher: Margaret Cross Rice
  Student: Annaliesa Copan

Also, our thanks to Yale University students Danielle Tumminio and Jilian Cabot Fletcher. We'd also like to acknowledge the collaborative and inventive participants in the 2006–2015 AP English Language Institutes held at Goucher College, Molloy College, in Lewes, Delaware; and in Philadelphia, Pennsylvania, for their contributions and constructive comments.

Barbara L. Murphy taught AP Language and other college-level courses at Jericho High School for more than 26 years. She has been a reader of the AP Language and Composition exam since 1993 and is a consultant for the College Board's AP Language and Composition, for which she has conducted workshops, conferences, and Summer Institutes. She is currently on the faculty of Syracuse University's Project Advance in English.

After earning her B.A. from Duquesne University and her M.A. from the University of Pittsburgh, Ms. Murphy did her doctoral course work at Columbia University. She also holds professional certifications in still photography and motion picture production and is one of the founding members of the women's film company Ishtar Films.

Estelle M. Rankin taught AP Literature at Jericho High School for more than 25 years. She was honored with the AP Literature Teacher of the Year award by the College Board in 1996. She also received the Long Island Teacher of the Year award in 1990. She was the recipient of the Cornell University Presidential Scholars' Award and has been recognized by the C.W. Post Master Teachers Program.

Ms. Rankin earned her B.A. from Adelphi University and her M.A. from Hofstra University. She has pursued further graduate work in the field of creative studies at Queens College and Brooklyn College.

She has done extensive work in the research and development of film, drama, and creative writing curricula, SAT prep, and the new NYS Regents benchmarks for English, and has participated in numerous AP Literature conferences and workshops. Ms. Rankin is currently a College Board consultant for pre-AP and AP English. Her finest teachers were her parents, Edward and Sylvia Stern.

Ms. Murphy and Ms. Rankin are also the coauthors of McGraw-Hill's *5 Steps to a 5: AP English Literature*, *Writing the AP English Essay*, and *Writing an Outstanding College Application Essay*.

Cartoon by Jim Sizemore used with permission of Cartoon Stock Ltd. (www.Cartoon Stock.com).

Editorial cartoon by Chris Britt used with permission of the cartoonist.

Editorial cartoon by Clay Bennett © 2006 *The Christian Science Monitor* (www.csmonitor .com). All rights reserved.

Editorial cartoon by Jeff Koterba/*Omaha World-Herald*.

"Eminent Domain," excerpt from *60 Minutes*, July 4, 2004. Reprinted by permission of CBS News Archives.

From *In Cold Blood* by Truman Capote, copyright © by Truman Capote and renewed 1993 by Alan U. Schwartz. Used by permission of Random House, Inc.

From "Introduction," *The Best Essays of 1988*. Reprinted by permission of Russell & Volkening as agents for the author. Copyright © 1988 by Annie Dillard.

From "States Curbing Right to Seize Private Houses," by John Broder from the *New York Times* on the Web © The New York Times Company. Reprinted with permission.

From "The Case for Flag-Burning. . .," an editorial published June 27, 2006. Copyright © 2006 *Los Angeles Times*. Reprinted with permission.

From *What Is Marriage For?* by E. J. Graff. Copyright © 1999. Reprinted by permission of Beacon Press, Boston.

Jencks, Christopher. From a review and discussion of *American Dream: Three Women, Ten Kids, and a Nation's Drive to End Welfare* appearing in *The New York Review of Books*, December 15, 2005. Reprinted with permission from *The New York Review of Books*. Copyright © 2005 NYREV, Inc.

Lapham, Lewis. Excerpt from *Money and Class in America: Notes and Observations on Our Civil Religion*. Copyright © 1988 by Lewis Lapham. Reprinted by permission.

Lindberg, Todd. "The Star Spangled Banner." Copyright © 2006 The Washington Times LLC. This reprint does not constitute or imply any endorsement or sponsorship of any product, service, company or organization.

O'Neill, Jesse. From *The Golden Ghetto: The Psychology of Affluence*. Copyright © 1997 The Affluenza Project. Reprinted by permission.

Sekula, Allen. "Reading an Archive." From *Blasted Allegories*. Copyright © 1987 by MIT. Used by permission of the publisher, MIT Press.

"The Voice of the Story, the Story as Voice," an excerpt from "Reading Blind"; first appeared in *The Best American Short Stories 1989* © 1989 O.W. Toad, Ltd.

INTRODUCTION: THE FIVE-STEP PROGRAM

Some Basics

Reading

We believe that reading should be an exciting interaction between you and the writer. You must bring your own context to the experience, and you must feel comfortable reaching for and exploring ideas. You are an adventurer on a journey of exploration, and we act as your guides. We set the itinerary, but you will set your own pace. You can feel free to "stop and smell the roses" or to explore new territory.

The Journey

On any journey, each traveler sees something different on new horizons. So, too, each student is free to personalize his or her own literary experience, provided he or she tries at all times to strive for excellence and accuracy.

Critical Thinking

There are no tricks to critical thinking. Those who claim to guarantee you a 5 by using gimmicks are doing you a disservice. No one can guarantee a 5. However, the reading and writing skills you will review, practice, and master will give you the very best chance to do your very best. You will have the opportunity to learn, to practice, and to master the critical thinking processes that can empower you to achieve your highest score.

Philosophy of This Book: In the Beginning . . .

This is an important concept for us, because we believe that if you focus on the beginning, the rest will fall into place. When you purchased this book and decided to work your way through it, you were beginning your journey to the AP English Language and Composition exam. We will be with you every step of the way.

Why This Book?

We believe we have something unique to offer you. For more than 25 years we have addressed the needs of AP students just like you, and we have been fortunate to learn from these students. Therefore, the contents of this book reflect genuine student concerns and needs. This is a student-oriented book. We will not overwhelm you with pompous language, mislead you with inaccurate information and tasks, or lull you into a false sense of confidence through cutesy shortcuts. We stand behind every suggestion, process, and question we present. There is no "busywork" in this book.

We know you will not do every activity we suggest. Therefore, think of this text as a resource and guide to accompany you on your AP English Language and Composition exam journey throughout the year. This book is designed to serve many purposes. It will:

- clarify requirements for the AP English Language and Composition exam;
- provide you with test practice;

- show you models and rubrics on which you can model and evaluate your own work;
- anticipate and answer your questions;
- enrich your understanding and appreciation of the writing process;
- help you pace yourself; and
- make you aware of the Five Steps to Mastering the AP English Language and Composition exam.

Organization of the Book

We know that your primary concern is information about the AP English Language and Composition exam; therefore, we begin at the beginning with an overview of the AP exam in general. We then introduce you to the Diagnostic/Master exam we use throughout the book to show you the "ins and outs" of an AP test. In separate chapters, you will become familiar with both sections of the exam. We lead you through the multiple-choice questions and how to go about answering them, and we take you through the essay questions and approaches to writing these essays.

Because you must be fluent in the language and the process of composition, synthesis, and analysis, we provide a full comprehensive review part in analysis, synthesis, and argument. This review is not a mere listing of terms and concepts. Rather, it is a series of practices that will hone your analytical and writing skills. However, do not fear. You will find terms and concepts clearly delineated within their contexts. We will also provide you with annotated suggestions for high-interest readings for analysis, synthesis, and argument.

After carefully working your way through Chapters 4 through 10, you may wish to go to McGraw-Hill's *5 Step* series website which provides review, reinforcement, and enrichment questions that refer to the skills covered in each chapter. You can compare your response(s) with what we provide on the website for this book: **www.mhpracticeplus.com**

A separate section of this book contains the practice exams. Here is where you will test your own skills. You may be sure that the selections included in each exam are on an AP level. The multiple-choice questions provide practice with types of questions asked on AP exams. The essay questions are designed to cover the techniques and terms required by the AP exam. The free-response essays are both challenging and specific, but broad enough to suit all curricula. After taking each exam, you can check yourself against the explanations of every multiple-choice question and the ratings of the sample student essays.

The final part is one you should not pass over. It contains a glossary of terms, a bibliography of works that may be of importance to you, and a list of websites related to the AP English Language and Composition exam.

Introduction to the Five-Step Preparation Program

The Five-Step Preparation Program is a powerful tool designed to provide you with the best possible skills, strategies, and practice to help lead you to that perfect 5 on the AP English Language and Composition exam administered each May to more than 250,000 high school students. Each of the five steps will provide you with the opportunity to get closer and closer to the 5, which is the "Holy Grail" to all AP students.

Step 1: Set Up Your Study Program
- Month-by-month: September through May
- The calendar year: January through May
- Basic training: the 4 to 6 weeks before the exam

Step 2: Determine Your Test Readiness

- A comprehensive review of the exam
- One "Diagnostic/Master exam" you will go through step by step and question by question to build your confidence level
- Explanation of multiple-choice answers

Step 3: Develop Strategies for Success

- Learn about the test itself
- Learn to read multiple-choice questions
- Learn how to answer multiple-choice questions, including whether or not to guess
- Learn how to deconstruct the essay prompts
- Learn how to plan the essay

Step 4: Review the Knowledge You Need to Score High

- A comprehensive review of analysis and argument
- Practice activities that will hone your skills in close reading
- Practice activities in critical thinking
- Practice activities in critical/analytical/argumentative writing

Step 5: Build Your Test-Taking Confidence

- The opportunity to take a Diagnostic/Master exam
- Time management techniques/skills
- Two practice exams that test how well-honed your skills are
- Rubrics for self-evaluation

Finally, at the back of the book you'll find additional resources to aid your preparation. These include:

- Glossary of terms
- Bibliography for further reading
- Websites related to the AP English Language exam

The Graphics Used in This Book

To emphasize particular skills and strategies, we use several icons throughout this book. An icon in the margin will alert you that you should pay particular attention to the accompanying text. We use three icons:

 This icon points out a very important concept or fact that you should not pass over.

 This icon calls your attention to a problem-solving strategy that you may want to try.

 This icon indicates a tip that you might find useful.

In addition, **bold** and **<u>bold underlined</u>** words indicate terms included in the Glossary.

Scattered throughout the book are marginal notes and numerous shaded boxes. We urge you to pay close attention to them because they can provide tips, hints, strategies, and further explanations to help you reach your full potential.

STEP 1

Set Up Your Study Program

CHAPTER 1

What You Need to Know About the AP English Language and Composition Exam

IN THIS CHAPTER

Summary: Information about the AP English Language and Composition exam and its scoring.

Key Ideas

✪ Learn answers to frequently asked questions.
✪ Learn how your final score is calculated.
✪ Learn tips for successfully taking the exam.

Background on the AP English Language and Composition Exam

What Is the AP Program?

The Advanced Placement program was begun by the College Board in 1955 to construct standard achievement exams that would allow highly motivated high school students the opportunity to be awarded advanced placement as freshmen in colleges and universities in the United States. Today, there are more than 37 courses and exams with over two million students from every state in the nation, and from foreign countries, taking the annual exams in May.

As is obvious, the AP programs are designed for high school students who want to take college-level courses. In our case, the AP English Language and Composition course and exam are designed to involve high school students in college-level English studies in both the use and structure of language and composition.

Who Writes the AP English Language and Composition Exam?

According to the College Board, the AP Comp exam is created by a group of college and high school English instructors called the "AP Development Committee." Their job is to ensure that the annual AP Comp exam reflects what is being taught and studied in college-level English classes at the high schools.

This committee writes a large number of multiple-choice questions that are pretested and evaluated for clarity, appropriateness, and range of possible answers. The committee also generates a pool of essay questions, pretests them, and chooses those questions that best represent the full range of the scoring scale to allow the AP readers to evaluate the essays equitably.

It is important to remember that the AP English Language and Composition exam is thoroughly evaluated after it is administered each year. This way, the College Board can use the results to make course suggestions and to plan future tests.

What Are the AP Scores and Who Receives Them?

Once you have taken the exam and it has been scored, your test will be given one of five numbers by the College Board.

- 5 indicates you are extremely well qualified.
- 4 indicates you are well qualified.
- 3 indicates you are qualified.
- 2 indicates you are possibly qualified.
- 1 indicates you are not qualified to receive college credit.

Your score is reported first to your college or university, second to your high school, and third to you. All the reporting is usually completed by the middle to end of July.

Reasons for Taking the AP English Language and Composition Exam

Why Would I Want to Take the AP English Language and Composition Exam?

Good question. Why put yourself through a year of intensive study, pressure, stress, and preparation? To be honest, only you can answer that question. However, over the years, our students have indicated to us that there are several reasons why they were willing to take the risk and to put in the effort.

- For personal satisfaction
- To compare themselves with other students across the nation
- Because colleges look favorably on the applications of students who elect to enroll in AP courses
- To receive college credit or advanced standing at their colleges or universities

- A love of the subject
- So the family will be proud of them

There are plenty of other reasons, but hopefully, no matter what the other reasons might be, the top reason for your enrolling in the AP English Language and Composition course and taking the exam in May is to feel good about yourself and the challenges you have met.

What You Need to Know About the AP English Language and Composition Exam

If I Don't Take an AP Composition Course, Can I Still Take the AP English Language and Composition Exam?

Yes. Although the AP English Language and Composition exam is designed for the student who has had a year's course in AP English Language and Composition, there are high schools that do not offer this type of course, and the students in these high schools have also done well on the exam. However, if your high school does offer an AP Composition course, by all means take advantage of it and the structured background it will provide you.

How Is the AP English Language and Composition Exam Organized?

The exam has two parts and is scheduled to last 3 hours and 15 minutes. The first section is a set of multiple-choice questions based on a series of prose passages. You will have 1 hour to complete this part of the test. The second section of the exam is a 2-hour and 15-minute essay writing segment consisting of three different essays: analysis, argument, and synthesis. According to the College Board's **AP English Language and Composition Exam Instructions**, the 15-minute reading period in Section II is recommended, not required. Students are strongly encouraged to use the reading period to read the questions and sources and plan their responses. They may begin writing their responses during that time if they choose to do so. However, our advice is to use this time for careful reading.

After you complete the multiple-choice section, you will hand in your test booklet and scan sheet, and you will be given a brief break. Note that you will not be able to return to the multiple-choice questions when you return to the examination room.

Must I Check the Box at the End of the Essay Booklet That Allows the AP People to Use My Essays as Samples for Research?

No. This is simply a way for the College Board to make certain that it has your permission if it decides to use one or more of your essays as a model. The readers of your essays pay no attention to whether or not that box is checked. Checking the box will not affect your grade either.

How Is My AP English Language and Composition Exam Scored?

Let's look at the basics first. The multiple-choice section counts for 45% of your total score, and the essay section counts for 55%. Next comes a four-part calculation: the raw scoring of the multiple-choice section, the raw scoring of the essay section, the calculation of the composite score, and the conversion of the composite score into the AP grade of 5, 4, 3, 2, or 1.

How Is the Multiple-Choice Section Scored?

The scan sheet with your answers is run through a computer that counts the number of correct answers. Questions left blank and questions answered incorrectly are treated the same and get no points. There is no longer a "guessing penalty," which formerly involved the deduction of a fraction of a point for answering a question but getting it wrong.

How Is My Essay Section Scored?

Each of your essays is read by a different, trained AP reader called a "faculty consultant." The AP/College Board people have developed a highly successful training program for its readers, together with many opportunities for checks and double checks of essays to ensure a fair and equitable reading of each essay.

The scoring guides are carefully developed by the chief faculty consultant, question leader, table leaders, and content experts. All faculty consultants are then trained to read and score just **one** essay question on the exam. They become experts in that one essay question. No one knows the identity of any writer. The identification numbers and names are covered, and the exam booklets are randomly distributed to the readers in packets of 25 randomly chosen essays. Table leaders and the question leader review samples of each reader's scores to ensure quality standards are constant.

Each essay is scored as 9, 8, 7, 6, 5, 4, 3, 2, or 1, plus 0, with 9 the highest possible score. Once your essay is rated from 9 to 1, the next set of calculations is completed. Here, if there are 27 possible points divided into 55% of the total possible score, each point awarded is given a value of 3.055. The formula would look something like this:

$$(\text{pts.} \times 3.055) + (\text{pts.} \times 3.055) + (\text{pts.} \times 3.055) = \text{essay raw score}$$

Essay 1   Essay 2   Essay 3

How Do They Calculate My Composite Score?

You need to do a little math here: 150 is the total composite score for the AP English Language and Composition test. Fifty-five percent of this score is the essay section; that equals 82.5 points. Forty-five percent of the composite score is the multiple-choice section, which equals 67.5 points. Each of your three essays is scored on a 9-point scale; therefore, each point is worth 3.055. You would divide the number of multiple-choice questions by 67.5. For example, if there were 55 questions, each point of the raw score would be multiplied by 1.227. If you add together the raw scores of each of the two sections, you will have a composite score. We provide a little practice with this process in the two practice exams in this book.

How Is My Composite Score Turned into the Grade Reported to My College?

Remember that the total composite scores needed to earn a 5, 4, 3, 2, or 1 differ each year. This is determined by a committee of AP/College Board/ETS directors, experts, and statisticians. The score is based on such items as:

- AP distribution over the past three years
- Comparability studies
- Observations of the chief faculty consultant
- Frequency distributions of scores on each section and the essays
- Average scores on each exam section and essays

However, over the years a trend can be observed that indicates the number of points required to achieve a specific score.

- 150–100 points = 5
- 99–86 = 4
- 85–67 = 3

2 and 1 fall below this range. You do not want to go there.

What Should I Bring to the Exam?

- Several pencils
- A good eraser
- Several BLACK pens (black ink is easier on the eyes)
- A watch
- Something to drink—water is best
- A quiet snack, such as Life Savers
- Tissues

Are There Additional Recommendations?

- Allow plenty of time to get to the test site.
- Wear comfortable clothing.
- Eat a light breakfast or lunch.
- Remind yourself that you are well prepared and that the test is an enjoyable challenge and a chance to share your knowledge. Be proud of yourself! You worked hard all year. Now is your time to shine.

Is There Anything Special I Should Do the Night Before the Exam?

We certainly don't advocate last-minute cramming, and, if you've been following the guidelines, you won't have to. However, there may be a slight value to some last minute review. Spend the night before the exam relaxing with family or friends. Watch a movie; play a game; gab on the telephone, blog, or Twitter; and then find a quiet spot. While you're unwinding, flip through your own notebook and review sheets. By now, you're bound to be ready to drift off to sleep. Pleasant dreams.

CHAPTER 2

How to Plan Your Time

IN THIS CHAPTER

Summary: Assess your own study patterns and preparation plans.

Key Ideas

✪ Explore three approaches.

✪ Choose a calendar that works for you.

Three Approaches to Prepare for the AP English Language and Composition Exam

No one knows your study habits, likes, and dislikes better than you. You are the only one who can decide which approach you want and/or need to adopt to prepare for the AP English Language and Composition exam. Look at the brief profiles below. These may help you to place yourself in a particular prep mode.

You are a full-year prep student (Approach A) if:

1. You like to plan for a vacation or the prom a year in advance.
2. You never think of missing a practice session, whether it's for your favorite sport, musical instrument, or activity.
3. You like detailed planning and everything in its place.
4. You feel you must be thoroughly prepared.
5. You hate surprises.
6. You are always early for appointments.

You are a one-semester prep student (Approach B) if:

1. You begin to plan for your vacation or the prom 4 to 5 months before the event.
2. You are willing to plan ahead to feel comfortable in stressful situations, but are okay with skipping some details.
3. You feel more comfortable when you know what to expect, but a surprise or two does not floor you.
4. You are always on time for appointments.

You are a 4- to 6-week prep student (Approach C) if:

1. You accept or find a date for the prom a week before the big day.
2. You work best under pressure and close deadlines.
3. You feel very confident with the skills and background you've learned in your AP English Language and Composition class.
4. You decided late in the year to take the exam.
5. You like surprises.
6. You feel okay if you arrive 10 to 15 minutes late for an appointment.

CALENDARS FOR PREPARING FOR THE AP ENGLISH LANGUAGE AND COMPOSITION EXAM

Calendar for Approach A:
Yearlong Preparation for the AP English Language and Composition Exam

 Although its primary purpose is to prepare you for the AP English Language and Composition exam you will take in May, this book can enrich your study of language and composition, your analytical skills, and your writing skills.

SEPTEMBER–OCTOBER (Check off the activities as you complete them.)

_____ Determine into which student mode you would place yourself.

_____ Carefully read the Introduction and Chapter 1.

_____ Pay very close attention to the "Walk Through" the Diagnostic/Master exam.

_____ Get on the Web and take a look at the AP website(s).

_____ Skim the Comprehensive Review section. (These areas will be part of your yearlong preparation.)

_____ Buy a highlighter.

_____ Flip through the entire book. Break the book in. Write in it. Highlight it.

_____ Get a clear picture of what your own school's AP English Language curriculum is.

_____ Review the Bibliography and establish a pattern of outside reading.

_____ Begin to use this book as a resource.

NOVEMBER (The first 10 weeks have elapsed.)

_____ Write the argumentative essay in the Diagnostic/Master exam.

_____ Compare your essay with the sample student essays.

_____ Refer to Chapters 6 and 9 on the argumentative essay.

_____ Take five of our prompts and write solid opening paragraphs.

DECEMBER

_____ Maintain notes on literary works studied in and out of class.

_____ Refine analytical skills (see Chapters 5 and 8).

_____ Write one of the two analytical essays in the Diagnostic/Master exam. (This will depend on the organization of your own curriculum.)

_____ Compare your essay with the sample student essays.

JANUARY (20 weeks have now elapsed.)

_____ Write the synthesis essay in the Diagnostic/Master exam. (This will depend on your previous choice.)

_____ Compare your essay with the sample student essays.

_____ Refer to Chapters 7 and 10 on the synthesis essay.

FEBRUARY

_____ Take the multiple-choice section of the Diagnostic/Master exam.

_____ Carefully go over the explanations of the answers to the questions.

_____ Score yourself honestly.

_____ Make a note of terms and concepts and types of questions that give you trouble.

_____ Review troublesome terms by checking the Glossary.

MARCH (30 weeks have now elapsed.)

_____ Form a study group.

_____ Choose a selection you have studied in class and create an essay question to go with it, or you can use one of our suggested prompts.

_____ Choose a passage from a current editorial and create an essay question to go with it, or you can choose one of our suggested prompts.

_____ Write one of the analytical essays.

_____ Write one of the synthesis essays.

_____ Compare essays and rate them with your study group. (Use our rubrics.)

APRIL

_____ Take Practice Exam 1 in the first week of April.

_____ Evaluate your strengths and weaknesses.

_____ Study appropriate chapters to correct weaknesses.

_____ Practice creating multiple-choice questions of different types with your study group.

_____ Develop and review worksheets for and with your study group.

MAY—First two weeks (THIS IS IT!)

_____ Highlight only those things in the Glossary about which you are still unsure. Ask your teacher for clarification. Study!

_____ Write at least three times a week under timed conditions.

_____ Take Practice Exam 2.

_____ Score yourself.

_____ Give yourself a pat on the back for how much you have learned and improved over the past nine months.

_____ Go to the movies. Call a friend.

_____ Get a good night's sleep. Fall asleep knowing you are well prepared.

GOOD LUCK ON THE TEST!

Calendar for Approach B:
Semester-Long Preparation for the AP English Language and Composition Exam

The following calendar assumes that you have completed one semester of language and composition and will use those skills you have been practicing to prepare you for the May exam. You still have plenty of time to supplement your course work by taking our study recommendations, maintaining literary notations, doing outside readings, and so forth. We divide the next 16 weeks into a workable program of preparation for you.

JANUARY–FEBRUARY (Check off the activities as you complete them.)

_____ Carefully read the Introduction and Chapter 1.

_____ Write the three essays on the Diagnostic/Master exam.

_____ Compare your essays with the sample student essays.

_____ Complete the multiple-choice section of the Diagnostic/Master exam.

_____ Carefully go over the answers and explanations of the answers.

_____ Take a close look at the Bibliography for suggestions regarding possible outside readings.

MARCH (10 weeks to go)

_____ Form a study group.

_____ Choose a favorite essay or excerpt from a book and create an essay question to go with it, or you can use one of our suggested prompts.

_____ Choose a prose passage or essay and create an essay question to go with it, or you can choose one of our suggested prompts.

_____ Write one of the analytical essays.

_____ Write one of the synthesis essays.

_____ Compare essays and rate them with your study group. (Use our rubrics.)

APRIL

_____ Take Practice Exam 1 in the first week of April.

_____ Evaluate your strengths and weaknesses.

_____ Study appropriate chapters to correct weaknesses.

_____ Practice creating multiple-choice questions of different types with your study group.

_____ Develop and review worksheets for and with your study group.

MAY—First two weeks (THIS IS IT!)

_____ Highlight only those things in the Glossary about which you are still unsure. Ask your teacher for clarification. Study!

_____ Write at least three times a week under timed conditions.

_____ Take Practice Exam 2.

_____ Score yourself.

_____ Give yourself a pat on the back for how much you have learned and improved over the past nine months.

_____ Go to the movies. Call a friend.

_____ Get a good night's sleep. Fall asleep knowing you are well prepared.

GOOD LUCK ON THE TEST!

Calendar for Approach C:
4- to 6-Week Preparation for the AP English Language and Composition Exam

 At this point, we assume that you have been developing your argumentative, analytical, and writing skills in your English class for more than six months. You will, therefore, use this book primarily as a specific guide to the AP English Language and Composition exam. Remember, there is a solid review section in this book, to which you should refer.

Given the time constraints, now is not the time to try to expand your AP curriculum. Rather, it is the time to limit and refine what you already do know.

APRIL

_____ Skim the Introduction and Chapter 1.

_____ Carefully go over the "Rapid Review" sections of Chapters 5 through 10.

_____ Strengthen, clarify, and correct your weak areas after taking the Diagnostic/Master exam.

_____ Write a minimum of three sample opening paragraphs for each of the three types of essays.

_____ Write a minimum of two timed essays for each type of essay on the exam.

_____ Complete Practice Exam 1.

_____ Score yourself and analyze your errors.

_____ Refer to the appropriate chapters to correct weaknesses.

_____ Refer to the Bibliography.

_____ If you feel unfamiliar with specific forms of discourse, refer to the list of suggested appropriate works.

_____ Develop a weekly study group to hear each other's essays and discuss writing.

_____ Skim and highlight the Glossary.

MAY—First two weeks (THIS IS IT!)

_____ Complete Practice Exam 2.

_____ Score yourself and analyze your errors.

_____ Refer to the appropriate chapters to correct weaknesses.

_____ Go to the movies. Call a friend.

_____ Get a good night's sleep. Fall asleep knowing you are well prepared.

GOOD LUCK ON THE TEST!

"One of the first steps to success on the AP exam is knowing your own study habits."
—Margaret R., AP Language teacher

STEP **3**

Develop Strategies for Success

CHAPTER 4

Section I of the Exam— The Multiple-Choice Questions

IN THIS CHAPTER

Summary: Become comfortable with the multiple-choice section of the exam. If you know what to expect, you can prepare.

Key Ideas

✪ Prepare yourself for the multiple-choice section of the exam.
✪ Review the types of multiple-choice questions asked on the exam.
✪ Learn strategies for approaching the multiple-choice questions.
✪ Score yourself by checking the answer key and explanations for the multiple-choice section of the Diagnostic/Master exam.

Introduction to the Multiple-Choice Section of the Exam

Multiple choice? Multiple guess? Multiple anxiety? It's been our experience that the day after the exam finds students bemoaning the difficulties and uncertainties of Section I of the AP English Language and Composition exam.

"It's unfair."

"I didn't understand a word of the third reading."

"Was that in English?"

"Did you get four Ds in a row for the last reading?"

"I just closed my eyes and pointed."

Is it really possible to avoid these and other exam woes? We hope that by following along with us in this chapter, you will begin to feel a bit more familiar with the world of multiple-choice questions and, thereby, become a little more comfortable with the multiple-choice section of the exam.

What Is It About the Multiple-Choice Questions That Causes Such Anxiety?

Basically, a multiple-choice literature question is a flawed method of gauging understanding. Why? Because, by its very nature, a multiple-choice question forces you to play a cat-and-mouse game with the test maker, who demands that you concentrate on items that are incorrect before you can choose what is correct. We know, however, that complex literary works have a richness that allows for ambiguity. In the exam mode, you are expected to match someone else's reading of a work with your choice of answers. This is what often causes the student to feel that the multiple-choice section is unfair. And, perhaps, to a degree, it is. But, get with the program! It's a necessary evil. So, our advice to you is to accept the difficulties and limitations of Section I and to move on.

"You know, when my teacher required us to make up multiple-choice questions that came from the AP prompts we wrote essays on, I really became more confident about how to answer these types of questions on the exam."
—Samantha T., AP student

This said, it's wise to develop a strategy for success. Once again, practice is the key to this success.

You've answered all types of multiple-choice questions during your career as a student. The test-taking skills you have learned in your social studies, math, and science classes may also apply to this specific situation.

A word in defense of the test makers is in order here. The test is designed to allow you to shine, NOT to be humiliated. To that end, the people who design the multiple-choice questions take their job seriously and take pride in their product. You will not find "cutesy" questions, and they will not play games with you. What they will do is present several valid options in response to a challenging and appropriate question. These questions are designed to separate the knowledgeable, perceptive, and thoughtful reader from the superficial and impulsive one.

What Should I Expect in Section I?

For this first section of the AP English Language and Composition exam, you are allotted 1 hour to answer between 45 and 60 objective questions on four to five prose passages. The selections come from works of nonfiction and are from different time periods, of different styles, and of different purposes. In other words, you will not find two essays by Thoreau in the multiple-choice section of the same test.

At least one of the readings will contain some type of citation, attribution, footnote, and so on. You will be expected to be able to determine HOW this citation, etc., is employed by the author to further his purpose. You will NOT be asked about specific formats such as MLA or APA.

These are NOT easy readings. They are representative of the college-level work you have been doing throughout the year. You will be expected to:

- follow sophisticated syntax;
- respond to diction;
- be comfortable with upper-level vocabulary;
- be familiar with rhetorical terminology;
- make inferences;
- be sensitive to irony and tone;
- recognize components of organization and style;
- be familiar with modes of discourse and rhetorical strategies; and
- recognize how information contained in citations contributes to the author's purpose.

THE GOOD NEWS IS . . . the selection is self-contained. If it is about the Irish Potato Famine, you will NOT be at a disadvantage if you know nothing about Irish history. Frequently, there will be biblical references in a selection. This is especially true of works from an earlier time period. You are expected to be aware of basic allusions to biblical and mythological works often found in literary texts, but the passage will never require you to have any particular religious background.

DO NOT LET THE SUBJECT MATTER OF A PASSAGE THROW YOU. Strong analytical skills will work on any passage.

How Should I Begin to Work with Section I?

Take no more than a minute and thumb through the exam, looking for the following:

- The length of the selections
- The time periods or writing styles, if you can recognize them
- The number of questions asked
- A quick idea of the type of questions

This brief skimming of the test will put your mind into gear, because you will be aware of what is expected of you.

How Should I Proceed Through This Section of the Exam?

Timing is important. Always maintain an awareness of the time. Wear a watch. (Some students like to put it directly in front of them on the desk.) Remember, this is not your first encounter with the multiple-choice section of the test. You've probably been practicing timed exams in class; in addition, this book provides you with three timed experiences. We're sure you will notice improvements as you progress through the timed practice activities.

Depending on the particular passage, you may take less or more time on a particular passage, but know when to move on. The test DOES NOT become more difficult as it progresses; therefore, you will want to give yourself the opportunity to answer each set of questions.

Work at a pace of about one question per minute. Every question is worth the same number of points, so don't get bogged down on those that involve multiple tasks. Don't panic if a question is beyond you. Remember, it will probably be beyond a great number of the other students taking the exam. There has to be a bar that determines the 5s and 4s for this exam. Just do your best.

Reading the text carefully is a must. Begin at the beginning and work your way through.

Most people read just with their eyes. We want you to slow down and to read with your senses of sight, sound, and touch.

- Underline, circle, and annotate the text.
- Read closely, paying attention to punctuation, syntax, diction, pacing, and organization.
- Read as if you were reading the passage aloud to an audience, emphasizing meaning and intent.
- As corny as it may seem, hear those words in your head.
- This technique may seem childish, but it works. Using your finger as a pointer, underscore the line as you are reading it aloud in your head. This forces you to slow down and to really notice the text. This will be helpful when you have to refer to the passage.
- Use all of the information given to you about the passage, such as title, author, date of publication, and footnotes.
- Be aware of organizational and rhetorical devices and techniques.

> *"Even though it's time-consuming, I find it invaluable to take class time to accurately simulate exam conditions."*
> —Cynthia N.,
> AP teacher

- Quickly skim the questions stems, ignoring the choices. This will give you an idea as to what is expected of you as a reader of the given text.
- Be aware of thematic lines and be sensitive to details that could be material for multiple-choice questions.

> You can practice these techniques anytime. Take any work and read it aloud. Time yourself. A good rate is about 1½ minutes per page.

Types of Multiple-Choice Questions

Is the Structure the Same for All of the Multiple-Choice Questions?

No. There are several basic patterns that the AP test makers employ. These include:

1. The *straightforward question*.
   - The passage is an example of
     C. a contrast/comparison essay
   - The pronoun "it" refers to
     B. his gait

2. The question that refers you to specific lines and asks you to *draw a conclusion* or *interpret*.
   - Lines 52–57 serve to
     A. reinforce the author's thesis

3. The ALL . . . <u>EXCEPT</u> *question* requires more time, because it demands that you consider every possibility.
   - The AP English Language and Composition exam is all of the following <u>except</u>
     A. It is given in May of each year.
     B. It is open to high school seniors.
     C. It is published in the *New York Times*.
     D. It is used as a qualifier for college credit.
     E. It is a 3-hour test.

4. The question that asks you to *make an inference or to abstract a concept not directly stated in the passage*.
   - In "Letter from a Birmingham Jail," the reader can infer that the speaker is
     E. religious

5. The footnote question: This is the question that requires you to abstract, interpret, or apply information contained in footnotes attached to passages.
   - The purpose of the footnote is to
     A. cite a primary source
     B. verify the writer's assertions
     C. direct the reader to other sources
     D. cite a secondary source
     E. provide the writer's additional commentary

What Kinds of Questions Should I Expect on the Exam?

The multiple-choice questions center on form and content. Naturally, the test makers are assessing your understanding of the meaning of the selection as well as your ability to draw inferences and perceive implications based on the given work. They also want to know if you understand HOW an author develops his or her ideas.

The questions, therefore, will be *factual, technical, analytical,* and *inferential.* The brief chart below illustrates the types of key words/phrases in these four categories you can expect to encounter.

Note: DO NOT MEMORIZE THESE TABLES. Likewise, do not panic if a word or phrase is not familiar to you. You may or may not encounter any or all of these words or phrases on any given exam. You can, however, count on meeting up with many of these in our practice exams in this book.

FACTUAL	TECHNICAL	ANALYTICAL	INFERENTIAL
Words refer to	Sentence structure	Rhetorical strategy	Effect of diction
Allusions	Style	Shift in development	Tone
Antecedents	Grammatical purpose	Rhetorical stance	Inferences
Pronoun referents	Dominant technique	Style	Effect of description
	Imagery	Metaphor	Effect of last paragraph
	Point of view	Contrast	Effect on reader
	Organization of passage	Comparison	Narrator's attitude
		Cause/effect	Image suggests
	Narrative progress of passage	Argument	Effect of detail
		Description	Author implies
	Conflict	Narration	Author most concerned with
	Irony	Specific–general	Symbol
	Function of . . .	General–specific	
		How something is characterized	
		Imagery	
		Passage is primarily concerned with	
		Function of . . .	

A WORD ABOUT JARGON: Jargon refers to words unique to a specific subject. A common language is important for communication, and there must be agreement on the basic meanings of terms. Although it is important to know the universal language of a subject, it is also important that you NOT limit the scope of your thinking to a brief definition. All of the terms used in the above chart are categorized only for easy reference. They also work in many other contexts. In other words, THINK OUTSIDE OF THE BOX.

Scoring the Multiple-Choice Section

How Does the Scoring of the Multiple-Choice Section Work?

Multiple-choice scores are based solely on the number of questions answered correctly. Therefore, it is to your advantage to answer ALL of the multiple-choice questions. Your chances of guessing the correct answer improve if you skillfully apply the process of elimination to narrow the choices.

Strategies for Answering the Multiple-Choice Questions

As observed earlier, you've been answering multiple-choice questions most of your academic life, and you've probably figured out ways to deal with them. There may, however, be some points you have not considered that will be helpful for this particular exam.

"One of my biggest challenges in preparing for the exam was to learn not to jump to conclusions when I was doing the multiple-choice questions."
—Samantha S., AP student

General Guidelines

- Work in order. We like this approach for several reasons:
  — It's clear.
  — You will not lose your place on the scan sheet.
  — There may be a logic to working sequentially which will help you to answer previous questions. BUT, this is your call. If you are more comfortable moving around the exam, do so.
- Write on the exam booklet. Mark it up. Make it yours. Interact with the test.
- Do not spend too much time on any one question.
- Do not be misled by the length or appearance of a selection. There is no correlation between this and the difficulty of the questions.
- Don't fight the question or the passage. You may know other information about the subject of the text or a question. It's irrelevant. Work within the given context.
- Consider all the choices in a given question. This will guard against your jumping to a false conclusion. It helps you to slow down and to look closely at each possibility. You may find that your first choice was not the best or most appropriate one.
- Maintain an open mind as you answer subsequent questions in a series. Sometimes a later question will contradict an answer to a previous one. Reconsider both. Likewise, even the phrasing of a question may point to an answer in a previous question.
- Remember that all parts of an answer must be correct.
- When in doubt, go back to the text.

Specific Techniques

- <u>Process of Elimination</u>—This is the primary tool, except for direct knowledge of the answer.
  1. Read the five choices.
  2. If no choice immediately strikes you as correct, you can
     — eliminate any which are obviously wrong;
     — eliminate those choices which are too narrow or too broad;
     — eliminate illogical choices;
     — eliminate answers which are synonymous;
     — eliminate answers which cancel each other out.
  3. If two answers are close,
     — find the one general enough to contain all aspects of the question
     OR
     — find the one limited enough to be the detail the question is seeking.

- <u>Substitution/Fill In the Blank</u>
  1. Rephrase the question, leaving a blank where the answer should go.
  2. Use each of the choices to fill in the blank until you find the one that is the best fit.

- <u>Using Context</u>
  1. Use this technique when the question directs you to specific lines, words, or phrases.
  2. Locate the given word, phrase, or sentence and read the sentence before and after the section of the text to which the question refers. Often this provides the information or clues you need to make your choice.

- <u>Anticipation</u>
  As you read the passage for the first time, mark any details and ideas that you would ask a question about. You may second-guess the test makers this way.

- <u>Intuition/The Educated Guess</u>
  You have a wealth of skills and knowledge in your language and composition subconscious. A question or a choice may trigger a "remembrance of things past." This can be the basis for your educated guess. Have the confidence to use the educated guess as a valid technique. Trust your own resources.

> ### A Survival Plan
>
> If time is running out and you haven't finished the last selection,
>
> 1. Scan the remaining questions and look for:
>   — the shortest questions; and/or
>   — the questions that point you to a line.
>
> These two types of questions are relatively easy to work with and to verify.
>
> 2. Look for specific detail/definition questions.
>
> 3. Look for self-contained questions.
>   "The jail sentence was a bitter winter for his plan" is an example of
>   C. an analogy.
>
> You did not have to go to the passage to answer this question.

Some Thoughts About Guessing

You can't be hurt by making educated guesses based on a careful reading of the selection. Be smart. Understand that you need to come to this exam well prepared. You must have a foundation of knowledge and skills. You cannot guess through the entire exam and expect to do well.

This is not Lotto. This book is not about how to "beat the exam." We want to maximize the skills you already have. There is an inherent integrity in this exam and your participation in it. With this in mind, when there is no other direction open to you, it is perfectly fine to make an educated guess.

Is There Anything Special I Should Know About Preparing for the Multiple-Choice Questions?

After you have finished with the Diagnostic/Master exam, you will be familiar with the format and types of questions asked on the AP English Language and Composition exam. However, just practicing answering multiple-choice questions on specific works will not give you a complete understanding of this questioning process. We suggest the following to hone your multiple-choice skills with prose multiple-choice questions.

- Choose a challenging passage from a full-length prose work or a self-contained essay, plus choose another that contains documentation/citations. (Take a close look at your science and social studies texts for examples.)
- Read the selection a couple of times and create several multiple-choice questions about specific sections of the selection.
  — Make certain the section is self-contained and complex.
  — Choose a speech, a philosophical passage, an essay, an editorial, a letter, a preface or epilogue, a significant passage from a chapter, or a news article.
- Refer to the chart given earlier in this chapter for suggested language and type.
- Administer your miniquiz to a classmate, study group, or class.
- Evaluate your results.
- Repeat this process through several different works during your preparation for the exam. The selections can certainly come from those you are studying in class.
- Create a variety of question types.

DIAGNOSTIC/MASTER EXAM
ADVANCED PLACEMENT ENGLISH LANGUAGE
AND COMPOSITION

Section I

Total Time–1 hour

Carefully read the following passages and answer the accompanying questions.

Questions 1–12 are based on the following passage from "Samuel Johnson on Pope," which appeared in *The Lives of the English Poets* (1779–1781).

The person of Pope is well known not to have been formed by the nicest model. He has compared himself to a spider and, by another, is described as protuberant behind and before. He is said to have been beautiful in his infancy, but he was of a constitution feeble and weak. As bodies of a tender frame are easily distorted, his deformity was probably in part the effect of his application. But his face was not displeasing, and his   5
eyes were animated and vivid.

By natural deformity, or accidental distortion, his vital functions were so much disordered, that his life was a "long disease."

He sometimes condescended to be jocular with servants or inferiors; but by no merriment, either of others or his own, was he ever seen excited to laughter.   10

Of his domestic character frugality was a part eminently remarkable. Having determined not to be dependent, he determined not to be in want, and, therefore, wisely and magnanimously rejected all temptations to expense unsuitable to his fortune.

The great topic of his ridicule is poverty; the crimes with which he reproaches his antagonists are their debts and their want of a dinner. He seems to be of an opinion not   15
very uncommon in the world, that to want money is to want everything.

He professed to have learned his poetry from Dryden, whom he praised through his whole life with unvaried liberality; and perhaps his character may receive some illustration, if he be compared with his master.

Integrity of understanding and nicety of discernment were not allotted in a less   20
proportion to Dryden than to Pope. But Dryden never desired to apply all the judgment that he had. He wrote merely for the people. When he pleased others, he contented himself. He never attempted to mend what he must have known to be faulty. He wrote with little consideration and, once it had passed the press, ejected it from his mind.

Pope was not content to satisfy; he desired to excel, and, therefore, always endeavored   25
to do his best. Pope did not court the candor, but dared the judgment of his reader, and, expecting no indulgence from others, he showed none to himself. He examined lines and words with minute and punctilious observation, and he retouched every part with diligence, until he had nothing left to be forgiven.

Poetry was not the sole praise of either; for both excelled likewise in prose. The   30
style of Dryden is capricious and varied; that of Pope is cautious and uniform. Dryden observes the motions of his own mind; Pope constrains his mind to his own rules of composition. Dryden's page is a natural field, diversified by the exuberance of abundant vegetation. Pope's is a velvet lawn, shaven by the scythe, and leveled by the roller.

If the flights of Dryden are higher, Pope continues longer on the wing. If of Dryden's   35
fire the blaze is brighter, of Pope's the heat is more regular and constant. Dryden is read with frequent astonishment, and Pope with perpetual delight.

1. The passage is primarily a(n)
   A. character sketch of Pope
   B. discussion of poetic style
   C. criticism of Dryden
   D. model for future poets
   E. opportunity for the writer to show off his own skills

2. The passage discusses a contrast among all of the following except
   A. prose and poetry
   B. Pope and Dryden
   C. body and mind
   D. poverty and wealth
   E. body and soul

3. "If the flights" (35) means
   A. Pope's writing will outlast Dryden's
   B. both Pope and Dryden are equal
   C. Pope is not idealistic
   D. Pope is more wordy
   E. Pope is not as bright as Dryden

4. The character of Pope is developed by all of the following except:
   A. examples
   B. comparison
   C. contrast
   D. satire
   E. description

5. According to the passage, Pope and Dryden are
   A. rivals
   B. equally intelligent
   C. outdated
   D. equally physically attractive
   E. in debt

6. From the passage, the reader may infer that Pope
   A. was extravagant
   B. was a man of the people
   C. was jealous of Dryden
   D. had a desire to be popular
   E. had a bitter, satirical nature

7. The tone of the passage is
   A. informal and affectionate
   B. formal and objective
   C. condescending and paternalistic
   D. laudatory and reverent
   E. critical and negative

8. Lines 20–24 indicate that Dryden was what type of writer?
   A. one who labored over his thoughts
   B. one who wrote only for himself
   C. one who wrote only for the critics
   D. one who wrote to please Pope
   E. one who did not revise

9. Using the context of lines 27–29, "punctilious" means
   A. precise
   B. timely
   C. cursory
   D. scholarly
   E. philosophical

10. In the context of the passage, "until he had nothing left to be forgiven" (29) means
    A. Pope outraged his readers
    B. Pope suffered from writer's block
    C. Pope exhausted his subject matter
    D. Pope's prose was revised to perfection
    E. Pope cared about the opinions of his readers

11. "Shaven" and "leveled" in line 34 indicate that Pope's style of writing was
    A. natural
    B. richly ornamented
    C. highly controlled
    D. mechanical
    E. analytical

12. Based on a close reading of the final paragraph of the passage, the reader could infer that the author
    A. looks on both writers equally
    B. prefers the work of Pope
    C. sees the two writers as inferior to his own writing style
    D. indicates no preference
    E. prefers the work of Dryden

Questions 13–23 are based on the following excerpt from Charlotte Perkins Gilman's "Politics and Warfare," which appears in *The Man-Made World: Our Androcentric Culture* (1911).

There are many today who hold that politics need not be at all connected with warfare; and others who hold that politics is warfare from start to finish.   1

The inextricable confusion of politics and warfare is part of the stumbling block in the minds of men. As they see it, a nation is primarily a fighting organization; and its principal business is offensive and defensive warfare; therefore the ultimatum with which they oppose the demand for political equality—"women cannot fight, therefore they cannot vote."   2

Fighting, when all is said, is to them the real business of life; not to be able to fight is to be quite out of the running; and ability to solve our growing mass of public problems; questions of health, of education, of morals, of economics; weighs naught against the ability to kill.   3

This naïve assumption of supreme value in a process never of the first importance; and increasingly injurious as society progresses, would be laughable if it were not for its evil effects. It acts and reacts upon us to our hurt. Positively, we see the ill effects already touched on; the evils not only of active war, but of the spirit and methods of war; idealized, inculcated, and practiced in other social processes. It tends to make each man-managed nation an actual or potential fighting organization, and to give us, instead of civilized peace, that "balance of power" which is like the counted time in the prize ring—only a rest between combats.   4

It leaves the weaker nations to be "conquered" and "annexed" just as they used to be; with "preferential tariffs" instead of tribute. It forces upon each the burden of armament; upon many the dreaded conscription; and continually lowers the world's resources in money and in life.   5

Similarly in politics, it adds to the legitimate expenses of governing the illegitimate expenses of fighting; and must needs have a "spoils system" by which to pay its mercenaries.   6

In carrying out the public policies the wheels of state are continually clogged by the "opposition"; always an opposition on one side or the other; and this slow wiggling uneven progress, through shorn victories and straggling concessions, is held to be the proper and only political method.   7

"Women do not understand politics," we are told; "Women do not care for politics"; "Women are unfitted for politics."   8

It is frankly inconceivable, from the androcentric viewpoint, that nations can live in peace together, and be friendly and serviceable as persons are. It is inconceivable also, that, in the management of a nation, honesty, efficiency, wisdom, experience and love could work out good results without any element of combat.   9

The "ultimate resort" is still to arms. "The will of the majority" is only respected on account of the guns of the majority. We have but a partial civilization, heavily modified to sex—the male sex.   10

13. The author's main purpose in the passage is to
A. argue for women being drafted
B. criticize colonialism

present a pacifist philosophy
criticize the male-dominated society
protest tariffs

14. In paragraph 2, the author maintains that men support their position on equality for women based upon which of the following approaches?
    A. begging the question
    B. a syllogism using a faulty premise
    C. an appeal to emotion
    D. circular reasoning
    E. an *ad hoc* argument

15. Using textual clues, one can conclude that "androcentric" most probably means
    A. robot-centered
    B. world-centered
    C. female-centered
    D. self-centered
    E. male-centered

16. In addition to indicating a direct quotation, the author uses quotation marks to indicate
    A. the jargon of politics and warfare
    B. the coining of a phrase
    C. a definition
    D. the author's scholarship
    E. that the author does not take responsibility for her words

17. In paragraph 4, "increasingly injurious as society progresses" is reinforced by all of the following except:
    A. "ill effects already touched on" [paragraph 4]
    B. "active war" [paragraph 4]
    C. "weaker nations to be 'conquered' and 'annexed'" [paragraph 5]
    D. "illegitimate expenses of fighting" [paragraph 6]
    E. "Women do not understand politics" [paragraph 8]

18. According to the author, men view the primary purpose of government to be
    A. educating the people
    B. solving the "mass of public problems"
    C. obtaining as much power as possible
    D. economics
    E. health

19. The argument shifts from a discussion of warfare to a discussion of politics in the first sentence of which of the following paragraphs?
    A. paragraph 4
    B. paragraph 5
    C. paragraph 6
    D. paragraph 7
    E. paragraph 9

20. The tone of the passage is best described as
    A. ambivalent
    B. reverent
    C. condescending
    D. accusatory
    E. indifferent

21. The style of the passage can best be described as
    A. poetic and emotional
    B. editorial and analytical
    C. mocking and self-serving
    D. preaching and moralistic
    E. authoritative and pretentious

22. To present her argument, Gilman primarily uses which of the following rhetorical strategies?
    A. process
    B. definition
    C. cause and effect
    D. narration
    E. description

23. "It," as used in paragraphs 4, 5, and 6, only refers to
    A. "Fighting is to them the real business of life" [paragraph 3]
    B. "evil effects" [paragraph 4]
    C. "man-managed nation" [paragraph 4]
    D. "preferential tariffs" [paragraph 5]
    E. "spoils system" [paragraph 6]

Questions 24–33 are based on the following speech, "On the Death of Martin Luther King, Jr." by Robert F. Kennedy.

1. I have bad news for you, for all of our fellow citizens, and people who love peace all over the world, and that is that Martin Luther King was shot and killed tonight.

2. Martin Luther King dedicated his life to love and to justice for his fellow human beings, and he died because of that effort.

3. In this difficult day, in this difficult time for the United States, it is perhaps well to ask what kind of a nation we are and what direction we want to move in, for those of you who are black—considering the evidence there evidently is that there were white people who were responsible—you can be filled with bitterness, with hatred, and a desire for revenge. We can move in that direction as a country, in great polarization—black people amongst black, white people amongst white, filled with hatred toward one another.

4. Or we can make an effort, as Martin Luther King did, to understand and to comprehend, and to replace that violence, that stain of bloodshed that has spread across our land, with an effort to understand with compassion and love.

5. For those of you who are black and are tempted to be filled with hatred and distrust at the injustice of such an act, against all white people, I can only say that I feel in my own heart the same kind of feeling. I had a member of my family killed, [and] he was killed by a white man. But we have to make an effort in the United States, we have to make an effort to understand, to go beyond these rather difficult times.

6. My favorite poet was Aeschylus. He wrote: "In our sleep, pain which cannot forget falls drop by drop upon the heart until, in our own despair, against our will, comes wisdom through the awful grace of God."

7. What we need in the United States is not division; what we need in the United States is not hatred; what we need in the United States is not violence or lawlessness but love and wisdom, and compassion toward one another and a feeling of justice toward those who still suffer within our country, whether they be white or black.

8. So I shall ask you tonight to return home, to say a prayer for the family of Martin Luther King, that's true, but more importantly to say a prayer for our own country, which all of us love—a prayer for understanding and that compassion of which I spoke.

9. We can do well in this country. We will have difficult times. We've had difficult times in the past. We will have difficult times in the future. It is not the end of violence; it is not the end of lawlessness; it is not the end of disorder.

10. But the vast majority of white people and the vast majority of black people in this country want to live together, want to improve the quality of our life, and want justice for all human beings who abide in our land.

11. Let us dedicate ourselves to what the Greeks wrote so many years ago: to tame the savageness of man and to make gentle the life of this world.

12. Let us dedicate ourselves to that, and say a prayer for our country and for our people.

24. The primary purpose of RFK's speech is most probably to
A. inform the people of the event
B. praise the accomplishments of Martin Luther King, Jr.
C. offer condolences to King's family
D. call for calm and unity between blacks and whites
E. offer condolences to the black community at large

25. Which of the following paragraphs does not contain examples of parallel structure?
   A. paragraph 3 beginning with "In this difficult . . ."
   B. paragraph 6 beginning with "My favorite poet . . ."
   C. paragraph 7 beginning with "What we need . . ."
   D. paragraph 9 beginning with "We can do well . . ."
   E. paragraph 10 beginning with "But the vast majority . . ."

26. Paragraph 5 contains an example of
   A. understatement
   B. figurative language
   C. sarcasm
   D. logical fallacy
   E. analogous example

27. The tone of the speech can best be described as
   A. elevated and conciliatory
   B. angry and inflammatory
   C. formal and detached
   D. informal and emotional
   E. accusatory and bitter

28. To avoid having his speech incite violence, RFK employs all of the following techniques except
   A. constantly repeating King's name and his desire for unity between races
   B. stressing the possible consequences of a violent response
   C. an ethical appeal based on the power of religion
   D. classical allusions
   E. emphasizing a common bond between himself and his audience

29. All of the following paragraphs give support to the inference that RFK expected violence to follow the assassination except:
   A. paragraph 3 beginning with "In this difficult day . . ."
   B. paragraph 4 beginning with "Or we can . . ."
   C. paragraph 6 beginning with "My favorite . . ."
   D. paragraph 7 beginning with "What we need . . ."
   E. paragraph 9 beginning with "We can do well . . ."

30. RFK most probably chose to refer to the Greeks in paragraph 11 for all of the following reasons except:
   A. to impress the audience with his scholarship
   B. to concisely restate the theme of the speech
   C. to provide a healing thought for the people to remember
   D. to elevate the level of discourse
   E. to reinforce the ideals of democracy with which the Greeks are associated

31. Paragraphs 7 and 8 are constructed around which of the following rhetorical strategies?
   A. analysis
   B. definition
   C. narration
   D. process
   E. cause and effect

32. The quotation given in paragraph 6 can best be restated as
   A. the process of healing is inevitable
   B. time heals all wounds
   C. sleep numbs those in pain
   D. God is the source of humankind's grief
   E. sleep is the only escape from pain

33. All of the following are effects of the repetition in paragraphs 11 and 12 except that it
   A. links the speaker with the audience
   B. refers to paragraph 2 and King's dedication
   C. emphasizes dedication so that the audience will remember it
   D. reinforces the tribute to Martin Luther King, Jr.
   E. elevates the occasion to one which is worthy of honor

Questions 34–44 are based on the following letter.

Albert Einstein
Old Grove Road
Nassau Point
Peconic, New York
August 2, 1939

F. D. Roosevelt,
President of the United States,
White House
Washington, D.C.

Sir:

1   Some recent work by E. Fermi and L. Szilard, which has been communicated to me in manuscript, leads me to expect that the element uranium may be turned into a new and important source of energy in the immediate future. Certain aspects of the situation which has [sic] arisen seem to call for watchfulness and, if necessary, quick action on the part of the Administration. I believe therefore that it is my duty to bring to your attention the following facts and recommendations:

2   In the course of the last four months it has been made probable—through the work of Joliot in France as well as Fermi and Szilard in America—that it may become possible to set up a new nuclear chain reaction in a large mass of uranium, by which vast amounts of power and large quantities of new radium-like elements would be generated. Now it appears almost certain that this could be achieved in the immediate future.

3   This new phenomenon would also lead to the construction of bombs, and it is conceivable—though much less certain—that extremely powerful bombs of a new type may thus be constructed. A single bomb of this type, carried by boat and exploded in a port, might very well destroy the whole port together with some of the surrounding territory. However, such bombs might very well prove to be too heavy for transportation by air.

4   The United States has only very poor ores of uranium in moderate quantities. There is some good ore in Canada and the former Czechoslovakia, while the most important source of uranium is Belgian Congo.

5   In view of this situation you may think it desirable to have some permanent contact maintained between the Administration and the group of physicists working on chain reactions in America. One possible way of achieving this might be for you to entrust with this task a person who has your confidence and who could perhaps serve in an official capacity. His task might comprise the following:

a) to approach Government Departments, keep them informed of the further development and put forward recommendations for Government action;

b) giving particular attention to the problem of securing a supply of uranium ore for the United States;

c) to speed up the experimental work, which is at present being carried on within the limits of the budgets of University laboratories, by providing funds, if such funds be required, through his contacts with private persons who are willing to make contributions for this cause, and perhaps also by obtaining the co-operation of industrial laboratories which have the necessary equipment.

I understand that Germany has actually stopped the sale of uranium from the Czechoslovakian mines which she has taken over. That she should have taken such early action might perhaps be understood on the ground that the son of the German Under-Secretary of State, von Weizacker, is attached to the Kaiser-Wilhelm-Institut in Berlin where some of the American work on uranium is now being repeated.

Yours very truly,
Albert Einstein

34. In both paragraphs 2 and 3, Einstein makes use of the dash
  A. to emphasize the words set off
  B. as an exception to the point immediately before it
  C. to sound more scholarly and formal
  D. as an informal aside to what was said previously
  E. to summarize

35. The omission of a cordial opening and identification of the credentials of the writer imply all of the following <u>except</u>:
  A. Einstein expects his name alone will identify him
  B. Einstein assumes that the information he presents is compelling enough to command a response
  C. Einstein believes himself too busy and important to waste time on pleasantries
  D. As a scientist, Einstein was accustomed to having the facts speak for themselves
  E. They've had previous contact

36. The purpose of the listing in paragraph 5 is to
  A. secure Einstein's role as Roosevelt's "permanent contact"
  B. suggest a plan of necessary action to ensure American security
  C. increase research funding for further nuclear experimentation
  D. end scientific research leading to the construction of nuclear bombs
  E. send a letter of warning to Germany

37. Einstein's attitude can best be described as
  A. confrontational
  B. deferential
  C. cautionary
  D. complacent
  E. antagonistic

38. Einstein's first paragraph suggests all of the following <u>except</u>:
  A. FDR is not staying abreast of important scientific developments
  B. Einstein is concerned about how the administration is handling the new developments in uranium research
  C. Einstein is concerned that the administration may be unaware of important developments in the scientific community
  D. Einstein is an authority in the use of uranium
  E. FDR is familiar with the work of Fermi and Szilard

39. Which of the following best identifies Einstein's primary mode of discourse in his letter to FDR?
  A. narration
  B. process
  C. analysis
  D. persuasion
  E. exposition

40. To illustrate the gravity of the situation, Einstein uses all of the following <u>except</u>:
  A. "call for watchfulness" [paragraph 1]
  B. "it is my duty" [paragraph 1]
  C. "appears almost certain" [paragraph 2]
  D. "in the immediate future" [paragraph 2]
  E. "obtaining the co-operation" [paragraph 5]

41. Einstein understates the urgency of developing "chain reactions" in America
  A. with the repetition of the words *might* and *may*
  B. by excluding a fatalistic prediction
  C. by mentioning "other countries repeating America's work"
  D. with the phrase "though much less certain"
  E. all of the above

42. To persuade Roosevelt to consider his recommendations, Einstein uses all of the following approaches <u>except</u>:
 A. discussions with other members of the scientific community
 B. appeals to fear
 C. presentation of evidence
 D. making predictions
 E. offering a plan

43. In his letter, Einstein's own assumptions are all of the following <u>except</u>:
 A. his interpretation of the manuscript is accessible
 B. his reputation as a scientist lends weight to his opinion
 C. his plan can be implemented quietly

 D. his urgency concerning the situation is apparent
 E. Germany recognizes the urgency of the situation

44. After a careful reading of the letter, which of the following inferences is *not* <u>valid</u>?
 A. Einstein understood the urgency of addressing the nuclear problem.
 B. Einstein assumed FDR would react to the letter.
 C. Einstein viewed the private sector as a means of circumventing a possible governmental impasse.
 D. The Germans could have possibly misunderstood the significance of this scientific discovery.
 E. Einstein is suspicious of German espionage.

Questions 45–56 are based on the following passage entitled "Reading an Archive," by Allan Sekula, which appeared in *Blasted Allegories*, a collection of contemporary essays and short stories, published by MIT Press in 1987.

. . . The widespread use of photographs as historical illustrations suggests that significant events are those which can be pictured, and thus history takes on the character of *spectacle*.[7] But this pictorial spectacle is a kind of rerun, since it depends on prior spectacles for its supposedly "raw" material.[8] Since the 1920s, the picture press, along with the apparatuses of a corporate public relations, publicity, advertising, and   5
government propaganda, have contributed to a regularized flow of images: of disasters, wars, revolutions, new products, celebrities, political leaders, official ceremonies, public appearances, and so on. For a historian to use such pictures without remarking on these initial uses is naïve at best, and cynical at worst. What would it mean to construct a pictorial history of postwar coal mining in Cape Breton by using pictures from a   10
company public relations archive without calling attention to the bias inherent in that source? What present interests might be served by such an oversight?
     The viewer of standard pictorial histories loses any ground in the present from which to make critical evaluations. In retrieving a loose succession of fragmentary glimpses of the past, the spectator is flung into a condition of imaginary temporal   15
and geographical mobility. In this dislocated and disoriented state, the only coherence offered is that provided by the constantly shifting position of the camera, which provides the spectator with a kind of powerless omniscience. Thus, the spectator comes to identify with the technical apparatus, with the authoritative institution of photography. In the face of this authority, all other forms of telling and remembering   20
begin to fade. But the machine establishes the truth, not by logical argument, but by providing an experience. This experience characteristically veers between nostalgia, horror, and an overriding sense of the exoticism of the past, its irretrievable otherness for the viewer in the present. Ultimately, then, when photographs are uncritically presented as historical documents, they are transformed into aesthetic objects. Accordingly, the   25

pretense to historical understanding remains, although that understanding has been replaced by aesthetic experience.[9]

But what of our second option? Suppose we abandoned all pretense to historical explanation, and treated these photographs as artworks of one sort or another? This book would then be an inventory of aesthetic achievement and/or an offering for disinterested aesthetic perusal. The reader may well have been prepared for these likelihoods by the simple fact that this book has been published by a press with a history of exclusive concern with the contemporary vanguard art of the United States and Western Europe (and, to a lesser extent, Canada). Further, as I've already suggested, in a more fundamental way, the very removal of these photographs from their initial contexts invites aestheticism.

I can imagine two ways of converting these photographs into "works of art," both a bit absurd, but neither without ample precedent in the current fever to assimilate photography into the discourse and market of the fine arts. The first path follows the traditional logic of romanticism, in its incessant search for aesthetic origins in a coherent and controlling authorial "voice." The second path might be labeled "post-romantic" and privileges the subjectivity of the collector, connoisseur, and viewer over that of any specific author. This latter mode of reception treats photographs as "found objects." Both strategies can be found in current photographic discourse; often they are intertwined in a single book, exhibition, or magazine or journal article. The former tends to predominate, largely because of the continuing need to validate photography as a fine art, which requires an incessant appeal to the myth of authorship in order to wrest photography away from its reputation as a servile and mechanical medium. Photography needs to be won and rewon repeatedly for the ideology of romanticism to take hold.[10]

30

35

40

45

50

---

[7] See Guy DeBord, *La société du spectacle* (Paris: Editions Buchat-Chastel, 1967): unauthorized translation, *Society of the Spectacle* (Detroit: Black and Red, 1970: rev. ed. 1977).

[8] We might think here of the reliance, by the executive branch of the United States government, on "photo opportunities." For a discussion of an unrelated example, see Susan Sontag's dissection of Leni Reifenstahl's alibi that *Triumph of the Will* was merely an innocent documentary of the orchestrated-for-cinema 1934 Nuremberg Rally of the National Socialists. Sontag quotes Reifenstahl: "Everything is genuine. . . . It is *history—pure history.*" Susan Sontag, "Fascinating Fascism," *New York Review of Books* 22, no. 1 (February 1975); reprinted in *Under the Sign of Saturn* (New York: Farrar, Straus, & Giroux, 1980), p. 82.

[9] Two recent books counter this prevailing tendency in "visual history" by directing attention to the power relationships behind the making of pictures: Craig Heron, Shea Hoffmitz, Wayne Roberts, and Robert Storey, *All that Our Hands Have Done: A Pictorial History of the Hamilton Workers* (Oakville, Ontario: Mosaic Press, 1981), and Sarah Graham-Brown, *Palestinians and Their Society, 1880–1946* (London: Quartet Books, 1980).

[10] In the first category are books that discover unsung commercial photographers: e.g., Mike Disfarmer, *Disfarmer: The Heber Springs Portraits*, text by Julia Scully (Danbury, N.H.: Addison House, 1976). In the second category are books that testify to the aesthetic sense of the collector: e.g., Sam Wagstaff, *A Book of Photographs from the Collection of Sam Wagstaff* (New York: Gray Press, 1978).

---

45. The first sentence (lines 1–3) does all of the following, <u>except</u>
   A. to indicate that material appears in this essay prior to this section
   B. to indicate scholarly research
   C. to indicate a cause/effect relationship
   D. to state the thesis of the piece
   E. to establish that the essay is based on the opinion of the author

46. The word *oversight* in line 12 refers to
   A. "pictures from a company public relations archive" (10–11)
   B. "without calling attention to the bias" (11)
   C. "construct a pictorial history" (9–10)
   D. "coal mining in Cape Breton" (10)
   E. "present interests" (12)

CHAPTER 5

Introduction to the Analysis Essay

IN THIS CHAPTER

Summary: Complete explanation of the analysis essay and its purpose as it is presented on the AP English Language exam.

Key Ideas

✪ Learn the types of analysis prompts you might encounter on the AP English Language exam.
✪ Learn about the rubrics and rating of the AP English Language essay.
✪ Learn the basics of reading and notating a given passage.
✪ Learn the basics of constructing your response to the prompt.
✪ Examine student models that respond to the diagnostic exam's analysis essay prompt.
✪ Learn how the rubrics were used to rate the student sample essays.

After your brief break, you will be given your free-response booklet that contains all three prompts: synthesis, analysis, and argument. You should spend the initial 15 minutes carefully reading each of the sources provided and planning your response to the synthesis prompt. The remaining 120 minutes are for you to compose your three essays.

On the cover of the booklet you will find the breakdown of the three essays and the time suggested for each.

Section II

Total Time—2¼ hours

Number of questions—3

Percent of total grade—55

Each question counts one-third of the total section score.

Note: After the 15 minute reading period, you will have a total of 2 hours to write, which you may divide any way you choose. However, each essay carries the same weight, so do <u>NOT</u> spend an inappropriate amount of time on any one question.

The next step is to quickly turn the pages of the packet and skim the given selections. This should take you less than a minute.

Some Basics

Just What Is an AP English Language Analysis Essay?

Generally, the student is presented with a prose passage that can be drawn from various genres and time periods. Although the specific tasks asked of the student may vary from year to year, they will involve the analysis of language, including **rhetorical strategies**. (If you are in doubt about the meaning of the underlined terms, make certain to refer to the Glossary and the Comprehensive Review section.)

> You may be extremely lucky and find a familiar piece by a familiar author. This certainly can enhance your comfort level. But, don't try to plug into the question everything you know about that author or selection if it does not exactly fit the prompt. Likewise, do not be rattled if you are unfamiliar with the work. <u>You will be familiar with the approaches necessary to analyze it</u>. Remember, this exam reaches thousands of students, many of whom will be in a similar situation and equally anxious. Be confident that you are thoroughly prepared to tackle these tasks and have fun doing so.

What Is the Purpose of the Analysis Essay?

The College Board wants to determine your facility with reading, understanding, and analyzing challenging texts. They also want to assess how well you manipulate language to communicate your written analysis of a specific topic to a mature audience. **The level of your writing should be a direct reflection of your critical thinking.**

AP is looking for connections between analysis and the passage. For example, when you find an image, identify it and connect it to the prompt. Don't just list items as you locate them.

"Doing close readings of editorial columns in newspapers and magazines is a real help to my students as they prepare to attack both multiple-choice questions and analysis essays."
—Chris S.,
  AP teacher

Types of Analysis Essay Prompts

What Kinds of Questions Are Asked in the Analysis Essay?

Let's look at a few of the TYPES of questions that have been asked on the AP English Language and Composition exam in the past. These types may seem more familiar to you if you see them in the form of prompts.

- Analyze an author's view on a specific subject.
- Analyze rhetorical devices used by an author to achieve his or her purpose.
- Analyze rhetorical elements in a passage and their effects.
- Analyze the author's tone and how the author conveys this tone.
- Compare and/or contrast two passages with regard to style, purpose, or tone.
- Analyze the author's purpose and how he or she achieves it.
- Analyze some of the ways an author re-creates a real or imagined experience.
- Analyze how an author presents him or herself in the passage.
- Discuss the intended and/or probable effect of a passage.

You should be prepared to write an essay based on any of these prompts. Practice. Practice. Practice. Anticipate questions. Keep a running list of the kinds of questions your teacher asks.

It's good to remember that the tasks demanded of you by the question remain constant. What changes is the source material on which you base your response to the question. Therefore, your familiarity with the terms and processes related to the types of questions is crucial.

Don't be thrown by the complexity of the passage. *You* choose the references you want to incorporate into your essay. So, even if you haven't understood everything, you *can* write an intelligent essay—AS LONG AS YOU ADDRESS THE PROMPT and refer to the parts of the passage you do understand.

Watch for overconfidence when you see what you believe to be an easy question with an easy passage. You are going to have to work harder to find the nuances in the text that will allow you to write a mature essay.

Rating the Analysis Essay

How Do the AP Readers Rate My Essay?

It's important to understand just what it is that goes into rating your essay. This is called a **rubric**, but don't let that word frighten you. A rubric is just a fancy, professional word that simply means the **rating standards that are set and used by the people who read the essays**. These standards are fairly consistent, no matter what the given prompt might be. The only primary change is in the citing of the specifics in a particular prompt.

As experienced readers of AP exams, let us assure you that the readers are trained to *reward* those things you do well in addressing the question. They are NOT looking to punish you. They are aware of the time constraints and read your essay just as your own instructor would read the first draft of an essay you wrote on a 40-minute exam. These readers do look forward to reading an interesting, insightful, and well-constructed essay.

So, let's take a look at these rubrics.

Remember: PROMPT is another word for QUESTION.

A **9** essay has all the qualities of an 8 essay, and the writing style is especially <u>impressive</u>, as is the analysis of the specifics related to the prompt and the text.

An **8** essay will <u>effectively</u> and <u>cohesively</u> address the prompt. It will analyze and/or argue the elements called for in the question. In addition, it will do so using appropriate evidence from the given text. The essay will also show the writer's ability to control language well.

A **7** essay has all the properties of a 6, only with a <u>more complete</u>, well-developed analysis/argument or a more mature writing style.

A **6** essay <u>adequately</u> addresses the prompt. The analysis and/or argument is on target and makes use of appropriate specifics from the text. However, these elements are less fully developed than scores in the 7, 8, and 9 range. The writer's ideas are expressed with clarity, but the writing may have a few errors in syntax and/or diction.

A **5** essay demonstrates that the writer <u>understands the prompt</u>. The analysis/argument is generally understandable but is limited or uneven. The writer's ideas are expressed clearly with a few errors in syntax or diction.

A **4** essay is <u>not an adequate response</u> to the prompt. The writer's analysis/argument of the text indicates a misunderstanding, an oversimplification, or a misrepresentation of the given passage. The writer may use evidence which is inappropriate or insufficient to support the analysis/argument.

A **3** essay is a lower 4, because it is <u>even less effective</u> in addressing the prompt. It is also less mature in its syntax and organization.

A **2** essay indicates <u>little success in speaking to the prompt</u>. The writer may misread the question, only summarize the passage, fail to develop the required analysis/argument, or simply ignore the prompt and write about another topic. The writing may also lack organization and control of language and syntax. (***Note*: No matter how good the summary, it will never rate more than a 2.**)

A **1** essay is a lower 2, because it is even <u>more simplistic, disorganized</u>, and <u>lacking in control of language</u>.

"Throughout the year, I have students mimic the styles of various authors. We then present the pieces to the class, which tries to identify the author being imitated. Through this process, the students become more cognizant of what makes up style, tone, syntax, and diction."
—Denise C., AP teacher

> REMEMBER, THIS ESSAY IS REALLY A FIRST DRAFT. THE READERS KNOW THIS AND APPROACH EACH ESSAY KEEPING THIS IN MIND.

Timing and Planning the Analysis Essay

Just How Should I Plan to Spend My Time Writing This Type of Essay?

Remember, timing is crucial. With that in mind, here's a workable strategy:

- 1–3 minutes reading and working the prompt.
- 5 minutes reading and making marginal notes regarding the passage.
  — Try to isolate two references that strike you. This may give you your opening and closing.
- 10 minutes preparing to write. (Choose one or two of these methods with which you're comfortable.)
  — Highlighting
  — Marginal mapping
  — Charts or key word/one word/line number outlining
- 20 minutes writing your essay, based on your preparation.
- 3 minutes proofreading.

Working the Prompt

> For the purposes of this text, highlighting refers to any annotative technique, including underlining, circling, marginal notes, or using colored markers. The AP exam does NOT permit the use of highlighters, but this technique is valuable in other circumstances.

How Should I Go About Reading the Prompt?

To really bring the answer home to you, we are going to deconstruct a prompt for you right now. (This is the same question that is in the Diagnostic/Master exam you first saw in the introduction to this book.)

You should plan to spend 1–3 minutes carefully reading the question. This gives you time to really digest what the question is asking you to do.

Here's the prompt:

The following paragraphs are from the opening of Truman Capote's *In Cold Blood*. After carefully reading the excerpt, compose a well-written essay that analyzes how Capote uses rhetorical strategies to convey his characterization of Holcomb and its citizens.

> In the margin, note what time you should be finished with this essay. For example, the test starts at 1:00. You write 1:40 in the margin. Time to move on.

Here are three reasons why you do a 1–3 minute careful analysis of the prompt.

1. Once you know what is expected, you will read in a more directed manner.
2. Once you internalize the question, you will be sensitive to those details that will apply.
3. Once you know all the facets that must be addressed, you will be able to write a complete essay demonstrating adherence to the topic.

> TOPIC ADHERENCE, WHICH MEANS STICKING TO THE QUESTION, IS A KEY STRATEGY FOR ACHIEVING A HIGH SCORE.

DO THIS NOW.
Highlight, circle, or underline the essential terms and elements in the prompt.

(Time yourself) How long did it take you? _____

(Don't worry if it took you longer than 1–3 minutes with this first attempt. You will be practicing this technique throughout this review, and it will become almost second nature to you.)

Compare our highlighting of the prompt with yours.

The following paragraphs are from the **opening** of **Truman Capote's *In Cold Blood***. After carefully reading the excerpt, compose a well-written essay that <u>analyzes how Capote uses rhetorical strategies to convey</u> his <u>characterization of Holcomb and its citizens</u>.

In this prompt, anything else you may have highlighted is extraneous.

Note: You are free to choose your own selection of techniques, strategies, and devices. Not only must you identify appropriate rhetorical strategies, etc., you must also indicate the effect of each strategy you choose to discuss. If you only identify strategies without discussing their effects, your essay will be incomplete.

Review terms related to elements of style and techniques and methods of analysis.

> Sometimes the incidental data given in the prompt, such as the title of the work, the author, the date of publication, the genre, etc., can prove helpful.

Reading and Notating the Passage

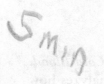

Finally, READ THE PASSAGE. Depending on your style and comfort level, choose one of these approaches to your **close reading**.

1. A. Read quickly to get the gist of the passage.
   B. Reread, using the highlighting and marginal notes approach discussed in this chapter.

2. A. Read slowly, using highlighting and marginal notes.
   B. Reread to confirm that you have caught the full impact of the passage.

Note: In both approaches, you MUST highlight and make marginal notes. There is no way to avoid this. Ignore what you don't immediately understand. It may become clear to you after reading the passage. Practice. Practice. Concentrate on those parts of the passage that apply to what you highlighted in the prompt.

There are many ways to read and analyze any given passage. You have to choose what to use and which specifics to include for support.

Don't be rattled if there is leftover material.

We've reproduced the passage for you below so that you can practice both the reading and the process of deconstructing the text. Use highlighting, arrows, circles, underlining, notes, numbers, whatever you need to make the connections clear to you.

DO THIS NOW.
Spend between 8 and 10 minutes "working the material."
DO NOT SKIP THIS STEP. It is time well spent and is a key to the high score essay.

Excerpt from the opening of *In Cold Blood*

The village of Holcomb stands on the high wheat plains of western Kansas, a lonesome area that other Kansans call "out there." Some seventy miles east of the Colorado border, the countryside, with its hard blue skies and desert-clear air, has an atmosphere that is rather more Far Western than Middle West. The local accent is barbed with a prairie twang, a ranch-hand nasalness, and the men, many of them, wear narrow frontier trousers, Stetsons, and high-heeled boots with pointed toes. The land is flat, and the views are awesomely extensive; horses, herds of cattle, a white cluster of grain elevators rising as gracefully as Greek temples are visible long before a traveler reaches them.

Holcomb, too, can be seen from great distances. Not that there is much to see—simply an aimless congregation of buildings divided in the center by the main-line tracks of the Santa Fe Railroad, a haphazard hamlet bounded on the south by a brown stretch of the Arkansas (pronounced "Ar-kan-sas") River, on the north by a highway, Route 50, and on the east and west by prairie lands and wheat fields. After rain, or when snowfalls thaw, the streets, unnamed, unshaded, unpaved, turn from the thickest dust into the direst mud. At one end of the town stands a stark old stucco structure, the roof of which supports an electric sign—Dance—but the dancing has ceased and the advertisement has been dark for several years. Nearby is another building with an irrelevant sign, this one in flaking gold on a dirty window—HOLCOMB BANK. The bank closed in 1933, and it is one of the town's two "apartment houses," the second being a ramshackle mansion known, because a good part of the local school's faculty lives there, as the Teacherage. But the majority of Holcomb's homes are one-story frame affairs, with front porches.

Down by the depot, the postmistress, a gaunt woman who wears a rawhide jacket and denims and cowboy boots, presides over a falling-apart post office. The depot, itself, with its peeling sulphur-colored paint, is equally melancholy; the Chief, the Super Chief, the El Capitan go by every day, but these celebrated expresses never pause there. No passenger trains do—only an occasional freight. Up on the highway, there are two filling stations, one of which doubles as a meagerly supplied grocery store, while the other does extra duty as a cafe—Hartman's Cafe, where Mrs. Hartman, the proprietress, dispenses sandwiches, coffee, soft drinks, and 3.2 beer. (Holcomb, like all the rest of Kansas, is "dry.")

And that, really, is all. Unless you include, as one must, the Holcomb School, a good-looking establishment, which reveals a circumstance that the appearance of the community otherwise camouflages: that the parents who send their children to this modern and ably staffed "consolidated" school—the grades go from kindergarten through senior high, and a fleet of buses transport the students, of which there are usually around three hundred and sixty, from as far as sixteen miles away—are, in general, a prosperous people. . . . The farm ranchers in Finney County, of which Holcomb is a part, have done well; money has been made not from farming alone but also from the exploitation of plentiful natural-gas resources, and its acquisition is reflected in the new school, the comfortable interiors of the farmhouses, the steep and swollen grain elevators.

Until one morning in mid-November of 1959, few Americans—in fact, few Kansans—had ever heard of Holcomb. Like the waters of the river, like the motorists on the highway, and like the yellow trains streaking down the Santa Fe tracks, drama in the shape of exceptional happenings, had never stopped there. The inhabitants of the village, numbering two hundred and seventy, were satisfied that this should be so, quite content to exist inside ordinary life . . .

Now, compare your reading notes with what we've done. Yours may vary from ours, but the results of your note taking should be similar in scope.

Notice that, in the sample, we have used a kind of shorthand for our notations. Rather than repeating the specific elements or points each time they are found in the text, we have numbered the major points.

1 = Something old West and insignificant about Holcomb
2 = The starkness of the town
3 = People reflecting the setting
4 = Contrast between first three paragraphs and the last two

This saves precious time. All you need do is list the categories and number each. Then, as you go through the text, number specifics that support these categories.

Excerpt from the opening of *In Cold Blood*

The village of Holcomb stands on the high wheat plains of western Kansas, a lonesome area that other Kansans call "out there." Some seventy miles east of the Colorado border, the countryside, with its hard blue skies and desert-clear air, has an atmosphere that is rather more Far Western than Middle West. The local accent is barbed with a prairie twang, a ranch-hand nasalness, and the men, many of them, wear narrow frontier trousers, Stetsons, and high-heeled boots with pointed toes. The land is flat, and the views are awesomely extensive; horses, herds of cattle, a white cluster of grain elevators rising as gracefully as Greek temples are visible long before a traveler reaches them.

Holcomb, too, can be seen from great distances. Not that there is much to see—simply an aimless congregation of buildings divided in the center by the main-line tracks of the Santa Fe Railroad, a haphazard hamlet bounded on the south by a brown stretch of the Arkansas (pronounced "Ar-kan-sas") River, on the north by a highway, Route 50, and on the east and west by prairie lands and wheat fields. After rain, or when snowfalls thaw, the streets, unnamed, unshaded, unpaved, turn from the thickest dust into the direst mud. At one end of the town stands a stark old stucco structure, the roof of which supports an electric sign—Dance—but the dancing has ceased and the advertisement has been dark for several years. Nearby is another building with an irrelevant sign, this one in flaking gold on a dirty window—HOLCOMB BANK. The bank closed in 1933, and it is one of the town's two "apartment houses," the second being a ramshackle mansion known, because a good part of the local school's faculty lives there, as the Teacherage. But the majority of Holcomb's homes are one-story frame affairs, with front porches.

Down by the depot, the postmistress, a gaunt woman who wears a rawhide jacket and denims and cowboy boots, presides over a falling-apart post office. The depot, itself, with its peeling sulphur-colored paint, is equally melancholy; the Chief, the Super Chief, the El Capitan go by every day, but these celebrated expresses never pause there. No passenger trains do—only an occasional freight. Up on the highway, there are two filling stations, one of which doubles as a meagerly supplied grocery store, while the other does extra duty as a cafe—Hartman's Cafe, where Mrs. Hartman, the proprietress, dispenses sandwiches, coffee, soft drinks, and 3.2 beer. (Holcomb, like all the rest of Kansas, is "dry.")

And that, really, is all. Unless you include, as one must, the Holcomb School, a good-looking⁴ establishment, which reveals a circumstance that the appearance of the community otherwise camouflages:⁴ that the parents who send their children to this modern⁴ and ably staffed "consolidated" school—the grades go from kindergarten through senior high, and a fleet of buses transport the students, of which there are usually around three hundred and sixty, from as far as sixteen miles away—are, in general, a prosperous people.⁴ . . . The farm ranchers in Finney County, of which Holcomb is a part, have done well;⁴ money has been made not from farming alone but also from the exploitation of plentiful natural-gas resources, and its acquisition is reflected in the new school, the comfortable interiors of the farmhouses, the steep and swollen grain elevators.⁴

Until one morning in mid-November of 1959, few Americans—in fact, few Kansans—had ever heard of Holcomb. Like the waters of the river, like the motorists on the highway, and like the yellow trains streaking down the Sante Fe tracks, drama in the shape of exceptional happenings, had never stopped there. The inhabitants of the village, numbering two hundred and seventy, were satisfied that this should be so, quite content to exist inside ordinary life . . .

Developing the Opening Paragraph

After you have marked your passage, review the prompt. Now, choose the elements you are able to identify and analyze those that support Capote's view. To demonstrate, we have chosen structure, tone, and selection of detail.

Now, it's time to write. Your opening statement is the one that catches the eye of the reader and sets the expectation and tone of your essay. Spend time on your first paragraph to maximize your score. A suggested approach is to relate a direct reference from the passage to the topic. Make certain that the topic is very clear to the reader. This reinforces the idea that you fully understand what is expected of you and what you will communicate to the reader. As always, identify both the text and its author in this first paragraph.

Now, you try it. Write your own first paragraph for this prompt. Write quickly, referring to your notes. Let's check what you've written:

- Have you included author, title?
- Have you addressed "Capote's view of Holcomb"?
- Have you specifically mentioned the elements you will refer to in your essay?

Here are four sample opening paragraphs that address each of the above criteria:

A

In the opening of *In Cold Blood*, Truman Capote presents a picture of the town of Holcomb, Kansas. Through structure, selection of detail, and a detached tone, he makes it clear that he views Holcomb as dull and ordinary.

B

Holcomb, Kansas. Holcomb, Kansas. Even the sound of the place is boring and uninteresting. Moreover, Truman Capote seems to agree with this in his opening to *In Cold Blood*. I, too, would be inclined to pass by this sleepy, bland, and undistinguished hamlet. This view is developed through the author's tone, structure, and selection of detail.

C

"Like the waters of the river, like the motorists on the highway, and like the yellow trains streaking down the Sante Fe tracks, drama in the shape of exceptional happenings, had never stopped here." This is the town of Holcomb, Kansas. Using a reportorial tone, specific structure, and selection of detail, Capote introduces the reader to this unremarkable town in the opening of *In Cold Blood*.

D

In Cold Blood is a very appropriate title, because Capote presents a cold and unemotional view of Holcomb, Kansas. His tone, structure, and selection of detail create a distant and detached picture of this desolate farm community.

Each of these opening paragraphs is an acceptable beginning to this AP English Language and Composition exam essay. Look at what each of the paragraphs has in common:

- Each has identified the title and author.
- Each has stated which stylistic elements will be used.
- Each has stated the purpose of analyzing these elements.

However, observe what is different about the opening paragraphs.

- **Sample A** restates the question without elaborating. It is to the point and correct, but it does not really pique the reader's interest. (Use this type of opening if you feel unsure or uncomfortable with the prompt.)
- **Sample B** reflects a writer who really has a voice. He or she has already determined Capote's view and indicates that he or she understands how this view is created.
- **Sample C** immediately places the reader into the passage by referring specifically to it.
- **Sample D** reveals a mature, confident writer who is unafraid to make his or her own voice heard.

Note: There are many other types of opening paragraphs that could also do the job. Into which of the above samples could your opening paragraph be classified?

Writing the Body of the Essay

What Should I Include in the Body of This Analysis Essay?

1. Obviously, this is where you present *your* analysis and the points you want to make that are related to the prompt.

2. Adhere to the question.

3. Use specific references and details from the passage.
   - Don't always paraphrase the original. Refer directly to it.
   - Place quotation marks around those words/phrases you extract from the passage.

4. Use "connective tissue" in your essay to establish adherence to the question.
- Use the repetition of key ideas in the prompt and in your opening paragraph.
- Try using "echo words" (that is, synonyms: *town/village/hamlet*; *bland/ordinary/ undistinguished*).
- Use transitions between paragraphs (see Chapter 8).

To understand the process, carefully read the sample paragraphs below. Each develops one of the elements asked for in the prompt. Notice the specific references and the "connective tissue." Details that do not apply to the prompt are ignored.

A
This paragraph develops **tone.**

Throughout the passage, Capote maintains a tone that resembles a detached reporter who is an observer of a scene. Although the impact of the passage is seeing Holcomb in a less than positive light, the author rarely uses judgmental terminology or statements. In describing the town, he uses words such as "float," "haphazard," "unnamed," "unshaded," "unpaved." Individuals are painted with an objective brush showing them in "denim," "Stetsons," and "cowboy boots." Capote maintains his panning camera angle when he writes of the buildings and the surrounding farmland. This matter-of-fact approach is slightly altered when he begins to portray the townspeople as a whole when he uses such words as "prosperous people," "comfortable interiors," and "have done well." His objective tone, interestingly enough, does exactly what he says the folks of Holcomb do. He "camouflages" his attitude toward the reality of the place and time.

B
This paragraph develops **structure.**

Capote organizes his passage spatially. He brings his reader from "great distances" to the periphery of the village with its borders of "main-line tracks" and roads, river and fields, to the heart of the town and its "unnamed, unshaded, unpaved" streets. As the reader journeys through the stark village, he or she is led eventually from the outskirts to the town's seemingly one bright spot—the prosperous Holcomb school. Capote develops our interest in the school by contrasting it with the bleak and lonely aspects of the first three paragraphs. He shifts our view with the word "unless" and focuses on the positive aspects of the town. Holcomb "has done well" despite its forbidding description. The passage could end now, except that Capote chooses to develop his next paragraph with the words, "until one morning," thus taking the reader on another journey, one of foreshadowing and implication. Something other than wheat is on the horizon.

C
This paragraph develops selection of **detail.**

In selecting his details, Capote presents a multilayered Holcomb, Kansas. The town is first presented as stark and ordinary. It is a "lonesome area" with "hard blue skies," where "the land is flat" and the buildings are an "aimless congregation." The ordinary qualities of the village are reinforced by his references to the "unnamed" streets, "one-story frame" houses, and the fact that "celebrated expresses never pause there" (i.e., the "Chief, the Super Chief, the El Capitan"). Details portray the citizens of Holcomb in the same light. Ranch hands speak with "barbed" and nasal "twangs." They wear the stereotypical "cowboy" uniform and so does the "gaunt" postmistress in her "rawhide jacket." Once this description is established, the author contrasts it with an unexpected view of the town. He now deals with the appearance of Holcomb's "camouflages," the "modern" school, the "prosperous people," the "comfortable interiors," and the "swollen grain elevators." If Capote chooses to illuminate this contrast, does it indicate more to come?

> Study Group: Approach a subject in a joint manner. After you've deconstructed the prompt, have each person write a paragraph on a separate area of the question. Come together and discuss. You'll be amazed how much fun this is, because the work will carry you away. This is a chance to explore very exciting ideas.

We urge you to spend more time developing the body paragraphs rather than worrying about a concluding paragraph, especially one beginning with "*In conclusion,*" or "*In summary.*" To be honest, in such a brief essay, the reader can remember what you have already stated. It is not necessary to repeat yourself in a summary final paragraph.

If you want to make a final statement, try to link your ideas to a particularly effective line or image from the passage. (It's a good thing.)

> Look at the last line of Sample **B** on structure.
>
> *Something other than wheat is on the horizon.*
>
> Or, look at the last line of Sample **C** on selection of detail.
>
> *If Capote chooses to illuminate this contrast, does it indicate more to come?*
>
> Each of these two final sentences would be just fine as a conclusion to the essay. A conclusion does not have to be a paragraph. It can be the writer's final remark/observation in a sentence or two.

DO THIS NOW.

Write the body of your essay. Time yourself.

When you write the body of your essay, take only 15–20 minutes.

Find a way to time yourself, and try your best to finish within that time frame.

Because this is practice, don't panic if you can't complete your essay within the given 20 minutes. You will become more and more comfortable with the tasks presented to you as you gain more experience with this type of question.

Refer to the Comprehensive Review section in Step 4 of this book on developing the body of an AP Language and Composition essay.

NOTE: Sharing your writing with members of your class or study group will allow you and all of the participants to gain more experience and more of a comfort zone with requirements and possibilities.

Sample Student Essays

Here are two actual student essays with comments on each.

Student Sample A

Truly successful authors have the ability to convey their view of a place without actually saying it, to portray a landscape in a certain light simply by describing it. In the provided excerpt taken from the opening paragraphs of <u>In Cold Blood</u>, Truman

1

Capote does just this. Through his use of stylistic elements such as selection of detail, imagery, and figurative language, Capote reveals his own solemn and mysterious view of Holcomb, Kansas, while setting the stage for an imminent change.

Beginning in the first line of the passage, Capote selects the most boring details   2
of life in the small town in order to portray its solemnity. He draws attention to the physical isolation of Holcomb by referring to it as the place that "other Kansans call 'out there.'" In addition, he speaks of the parameters of the small town, pointing out that it is enclosed on all sides by rivers, prairies, and wheat fields. He describes the town as remote and unaffected, desolate and boring, continually mentioning the old, peeling paint and "irrelevant signs" that dot the landscape. Capote also gives the village a feeling of laziness in his writing, describing it as an "aimless congregation of buildings" and a "haphazard hamlet." He obviously feels that the town lacks liveliness, that it is bland and unchanging, simple and average. Almost looking down on the village and its inhabitants, the author characterizes the people in broad categories and focuses on their outward appearances and superficial similarities instead of delving more deeply into their abilities or livelihoods. This reveals that he views the people and their surroundings as one-dimensional and simplistic. The idea that he may summarize an entire town, generalize about its people and not be far from the truth, contributes greatly to Capote's solemn view of Holcomb. One gets the feelings from the author's selection of detail that he wishes there was something more interesting, deeper, to share with his audience, and is disappointed by the cursory nature in which he must approach the description of such a melancholy place.

In addition to including the most boring of details, Capote uses a great deal of   3
imagery to describe the town and its residents. Focusing mostly on visual appeal, he describes the "sulphur-colored paint" and "flaking gold" to reveal the town's atrophying appearance and has been status. Portraying the area as one that has seen better days, Capote writes about the "old stucco structure" that no longer holds dances, the crumbling post office, and the bank that now fails to serve its original purpose. Combining visual imagery with hints of desolation and obsoleteness, Capote attempts to reveal the gray and boring nature of the town through its appearance. He does not, however, rely only on visual details; in describing the local accent as "barbed with a prairie twang," he uses both auditory and visual appeal to make one imagine a ranch-hand's tone of voice and pattern of speech as he describes the monotonous events of his farming days. The "hard blue skies and desert-clear air" contribute to a feeling of emptiness, an emotional vacancy that seems omnipresent in the small town. Finally, even "the steep and swollen grain elevators" that represent the town's prosperity are seen in a solemn and mysterious light, as Capote makes certain to mention that the townspeople camouflage this abundance without explaining why they choose to do so.

Capote also uses a great deal of figurative language and contrasts to portray the   4
small town as solemn and dead, yet somewhat mysterious. The area's intrigue lies more in its paradoxes than in its appearance, more in what Capote fails to explain than what he discusses. With the simile, "a white cluster of grain elevators rising as gracefully as

Greek temples," he almost points toward a happy, prosperous side of the town for the first and perhaps only time in this passage. Not long after this sentence, however, the author describes the streets as "unnamed, unshaded, unpaved," returning to his description of the village as desolate and empty, so destroyed that it is almost primitive.

This is not the only contrast of Capote's opening paragraphs; it seems the entire passage paints the town as quiet and simple only so that it may shock us with what is to come. The author uses personification at the end of the passage, stating that "drama . . . had never stopped there." The position of these words, just after he discusses the positive aspects of the school and its students' families, results in yet another contrast, another mysterious solemnity. Finally, in the last paragraph of this excerpt, when Capote writes "until one morning . . . few . . . had ever heard of Holcomb," the reader becomes aware that the solemn nature of this town is about to change. It becomes clear that the reader has been somewhat set up by Capote, made to view the town in the same way the author does, so that we may then realize the shock of the approaching aberration. 5

Through his use of stylistic elements, Capote builds the perfect scenery for the setting of a murder, the perfect simple town waiting for a complicated twist, a faded flower or ghost town that has surely seen better days. By the end of the passage, he has already warned the reader that everything he has stated about Holcomb is about to change, that the quiet and solitude, the blandness of the small town, may soon be replaced by very different descriptions. 6

Student Sample B

Holcomb, Kansas, a village containing two hundred and seventy inhabitants, has skipped over the drama of life, according to Truman Capote. The square town is described spatially with houses, rivers, fields of wheat, stations, a bank, and a school. In Truman Capote's In Cold Blood, an image of the town of Holcomb is presented through precise types of diction, syntax, imagery, and tone. 1

In order to convey a Western dialect used in Holcomb, Capote refers to the town as, "out there," and addresses the pronunciation of the Arkansas River with an informative, "Ar-kan-sas." Throughout the town there are quite a few signs which transmit the ghostliness present there. For example, "—Dance—but the dancing has ceased and the advertisement has been dark for several years," and "HOLCOMB BANK," which is later on discussed as being closed down, demonstrate the vacantness of the town. To create a better concept of the land itself, Capote uses alliterative devices and an allusion when he states, "horses, herds of cattle, a white cluster of grain elevators rising as gracefully as Greek temples are visible long before a traveler reaches them." This magnifies the field-like setting, and some of the town's old remnants of massive buildings. Altogether, the author's utilization of diction devices greatly personifies the town. 2

Although not a glaring feature of the excerpt, the sentence structure plays an important role in developing the author's viewpoint. He predominantly utilizes compound sentences, and complex with some prepositional phrases. The use of parallel 3 structures such as, "Like the waters of the river, like the motorists on the highway, and like the yellow trains streaking down the Sante Fe tracks . . ." greatly adds to the monotony of the town. "(Holcomb, like all the rest of Kansas, is 'dry'.)" is one of the numerous similes found throughout the passage that create a sense of vacancy within the town.

Capote's use of all of these literary devices envelope the reader into picturing what Holcomb looks like, a worn out, rustic town filled with "grain elevators," or fields and fields of wheat. The reference to the grain and wheat exemplifies the daily activities that occur in the town. After all of the rural descriptions, a vision of the school is given, as it "camouflages" into the mix. Reading about all of the emptiness of the town, then envisioning a school that is the pride of the town provides insight into the type of people the inhabitants of Holcomb are. For example, they are described as, "in general, a prosperous people." Overall, a precise and objective image of the town, along with the townspeople is certainly focused on in the passage.

Encompassing all of the author's literary, stylistic approaches, one is able to "hear" a voice or tone in the reading. A feeling of desolation, weariness, and loneliness should be derived from reading about this town, and a sense of rejuvenation is experienced toward the closing of the excerpt due to descriptions of the school. In exemplifying that the town has pride in one area, which is education, it leaves the reader with a sense of hope in the town and in its inhabitants. A strong voice toward Holcomb of its rugged, run down, and exhausted institutions is present.

Truman Capote's excerpt from <u>In Cold Blood</u>, which objectively describes Holcomb, a town in Kansas, is profoundly written because of its abundance of allusions, alliteration, imagery, and particular syntax utilized. Capote's detailing enables one to envision what the town looks like because of spatial and in depth descriptions.

Rating the Essays

Let's Take a Look at a Set of Rubrics for This Analysis Essay

By the way, if you want to see actual AP rubrics as used in a recent AP English Language and Composition exam, log onto the College Board website at www.collegeboard.org/ap.

As you probably know, essays are rated on a 9–1 scale, with 9 being the highest and 1 the lowest. Because we are not there with you to rate your essay personally and to respond to your style and approach, we are going to list the criteria for high-, middle-, and low-range papers. These criteria are based on our experience with rubrics and reading AP Literature essays.

A **HIGH** range essay can be a 9, an 8, or a high-end 7. **MIDDLE** refers to essays in the 7 to 5 range, and the **LOW** scoring essays are rated 4 to 1.

High-Range Essay (9, 8, 7)

- Indicates complete understanding of the prompt
- Integrates the analysis of Capote's view of Holcomb with his tone
- Explores the implications of the contrasts within the excerpt

- Identifies and analyzes rhetorical elements, such as imagery, diction, structure, selection of detail
- Cites specific references to the passage
- Illustrates and supports the points being made
- Is clear, well-organized, and coherent
- Reflects the ability to manipulate language at an advanced level
- Contains, if any, only minor errors/flaws

Note: A 7 essay rated in the high range makes the jump from the middle range because of its more mature style and perception.

Mid-Range Essay (7, 6, 5)

- Refers accurately to the prompt
- Refers accurately to the stylistic elements used by Capote
- Provides a less thorough analysis of the development of Capote's view of Holcomb than the higher-rated paper
- Is less adept at linking techniques to the purpose of the passage
- Demonstrates writing that is adequate to convey the writer's intent
- May not be sensitive to the contrasts in the excerpts and their implications

Note:
- The 7 paper demonstrates a more consistent command of college-level writing than does the 5 or 6 essay.
- A 5 paper does the minimum required by the prompt. It relies on generalizations and sketchy analysis. It is often sidetracked by plot and the references may be limited or simplistic.

Low-Range Essay (4, 3, 2, 1)

- Does not respond adequately to the prompt
- Demonstrates insufficient and/or inaccurate understanding of the passage
- Does not link rhetorical elements to Capote's view of Holcomb
- Underdevelops and/or inaccurately analyzes the development of Capote's view of Holcomb
- Fails to demonstrate an understanding of Capote's tone
- Demonstrates weak control of the elements of diction, syntax, and organization

Note:
- The mid- to high-range essays identify rhetorical strategies PLUS the purpose/effect of the strategies
- A 4 or 3 essay may do no more than paraphrase sections of the passage rather than analyze Capote's view of Holcomb.
- A 2 essay may merely summarize the passage.
  (NO MATTER HOW WELL WRITTEN, A SUMMARY CAN NEVER EARN MORE THAN A 2.)
- A 1–2 essay indicates a major lack of understanding and control. It fails to comprehend the prompt and/or the passage. It may also indicate severe writing problems.

Student Essay A

This is a **high-range** paper for the following reasons:

- It is on task.
- It indicates complete understanding of the prompt and the passage.
- It uses mature diction [paragraph 1: "Capote reveals . . . imminent change"], [paragraph 2: "Capote also gives . . . simplistic"], [paragraph 3: "the hard blue skies . . . to do so"].
- It integrates references to support the thesis of the essay [paragraph 2: "Capote also gives . . . hamlet"], [paragraph 3: "Focusing . . . has-been status"], [paragraph 4: "with the simile . . . passage"].
- It grasps subtleties and implications [paragraph 1: "Capote reveals . . . change"], [paragraph 2: "One gets . . . place"], [paragraph 4: "The area's . . . discusses"], [paragraph 6: "By the end . . . descriptions"].
- It introduces specifics in a sophisticated manner [paragraph 3: "He does not . . . farming days"], [paragraph 5: "The author . . . solemnity"].
- It uses good "connective tissue" [paragraphs 2 and 3: "in addition"], [paragraph 4: "Capote also uses . . ."], [paragraph 5: "This is not the only contrast . . ."].
- It creates original and insightful comments [paragraph 2: "one gets . . . melancholy place"], [paragraph 3: "He does not . . . farming days"].
- It presents a conclusion that introduces unique observations and brings the reader directly to what may follow this passage.

This is a high-range essay that indicates a writer who "gets it"—who clearly understands the passage and the prompt and who can present ideas in a mature, controlled voice.

Student Essay B

This is a **mid-range** essay for the following reasons:

- It sets up an introduction that indicates the writer's understanding of the prompt.
- It cites appropriate specifics, but often does not adequately integrate these into the analysis [paragraph 2: "In order . . . present there"], [paragraph 3, sentence 2].
- It uses frequently awkward diction and syntax [first line of paragraph 2], [last sentence of paragraph 2], [all of paragraph 5].
- It demonstrates good topic adherence.
- It reveals a facility with stylistic analysis [paragraph 2: "To create . . . reaches them"], [paragraph 3, sentence 3].
- It presents a conclusion that does not add anything to the impact of the essay.

This mid-range paper indicates a writer who understands both the prompt and the process of analysis. However, the essay does not address the subtle, underlying purpose of the passage and ignores the foreshadowing and contrast. The writer's frequently awkward and disconnected diction and syntax prevent it from achieving the level of the high-range essays.

Now It's Your Turn

STRATEGY

1. Try a little reverse psychology. Now that you are thoroughly familiar with this passage, construct two or three alternate AP level prompts. (Walk a little in the examiner's shoes.) This will help you gain insight into the very process of test-making.

2. Find other examples of descriptions of setting you can analyze in the same way as you did with the Capote excerpt. You might want to investigate works by John Steinbeck, Joan Didion, Peter Matthiessen, and, certainly, Sebastian Jung's *The Perfect Storm*.

Other Types of Analysis Essays

Are There Other Types of Analysis Questions on the Exam?

You bet. Another analysis prompt you can expect on the exam asks the student to analyze the author's intended effect on the reader and how the author re-creates an experience. Still another type is comparison and contrast. This prompt can be based on either a fiction or a nonfiction passage.

What Am I Expected to Do When Asked to Identify the Author's Intended Effect on the Reader?

No one can ever know what an author intended, unless you could personally approach the writer and ask, "Tell me, just exactly what did you intend the effect to be on your reader when you wrote this passage?" And, we all know that this is not a possibility for 999 out of 1,000 authors. This said, keep the following in mind.

The AP Comp test makers obviously believe that there is a clear, definite effect on the reader; otherwise, they would not be asking you to identify it. When writing about effect, think about your **personal** reaction to the text. While reading it, or as a result of reading it, how do you *feel* (happy, sad, angry, amused, perplexed, uplifted, motivated, informed, inspired, "connected"—you get the idea)?

What Should I Try to Include in My Essay When I'm Asked to Analyze How an Author Re-creates an Experience?

Think about this. Have you ever tried to re-create your own personal experience for your friends, your family, or your teacher? Ask yourself what you did to ensure that your listeners would really feel as if they were actually there. Were you trying to be humorous or serious? You chose what you would say to introduce this experience, didn't you? Did you set up the scene with descriptions of the setting, the people? Did you tell them why you were there? What kind of details did you choose to include? Why those, and not others? What kind of language did you use? (You were quite aware that your audience responds to certain kinds of language manipulation.) Did you center the tale on yourself, the action, a person, or group of people? Did you emphasize actions, reactions, dialogue? Did you tell the story in chronological order, or did you move back and forth in time? Did you interject personal comments? Did you tell the story so that the listeners felt a part of the experience or set apart from it? Did you emote or try to remain aloof?

Get the picture? This is the type of questioning that should be part of your process of analysis when asked how an author re-creates an experience.

What Do I Do About the Comparison and Contrast Essay?

The comparison and contrast essay is not difficult, but it demands that you have organizational control over your material. First, carefully read the prompt and understand what you are being asked to compare and contrast. With this in mind, carefully read and annotate each of the given texts, looking for major points to support and illustrate your thesis. Next, decide on the structure you want to use to present your points:

- Point by point
- Subject by subject
- A combination of both of the preceding

"Working the Prompt"

As you did with the previous essay, the very first thing you must do is to read and deconstruct the prompt carefully. What follows is a sample prompt that you could find in the essay section of the exam.

- Plan to spend 1–3 minutes carefully reading the question.
- After this initial reading, highlight the essential terms and elements of the prompt.

Carefully read the following excerpt from Louisa May Alcott's nonfiction narrative *Hospital Sketches* (1863). In a well-written essay, analyze how Alcott develops her argument concerning human compassion in a time of war.

Time yourself. How long did it take you? _____
Compare your highlighting of the prompt with ours.

Carefully read the following excerpt from **Louisa May Alcott's nonfiction narrative** *Hospital Sketches* (1863). In a well-written essay, **analyze how Alcott develops her argument concerning human compassion in a time of war.**

Notice that the prompt asks you to do TWO things. You must identify Alcott's argument AND analyze how the author constructs her argument. If you address only one of these areas, your essay will be incomplete, no matter how well written it is.

Review terms and strategies related to purpose, effect, organization.

Follow the process for reading the passage we illustrated for you in the first section of this chapter. Remember, you are going to do a close reading that requires you to highlight and make marginal notes (glosses) that refer you to the section of the prompt that this citation illustrates.

DO THIS NOW.
Spend between 8 and 10 minutes "working the material."
Do not skip this step. It is key to scoring well on the essay.

"Death of a Soldier"

As I went on my hospital rounds with Dr. P., I happened to ask which man in the room suffered most. He glanced at John. "Every breath he draws is like a stab; for the ball pierced the left lung and broke a rib. The poor lad must lie on his wounded back or suffocate." [1]

"You don't mean he must die, doctor?" [2]

"There's not the slightest hope for him." [3]

I could have sat down on the spot and cried heartily, if I had not learned the wisdom of bottling up one's tears for leisure moments. The army needed men like John, earnest, brave, and faithful; fighting for liberty and justice with both heart and hand. [4]

John sat with bent head, hands folded on his knee, and no outward sign of suffering, till, looking nearer, I saw great tears roll down and drop upon the floor. It was a new sight there; for, though I had seen many suffer, some swore, some groaned, most endured silently, but none wept. Yet it did not seem weak, only very touching, and straightway my fear vanished, my heart opened wide and took him in. Gathering the bent head in my arms, as freely as if he had been a little child, I said, "Let me help you bear it, John." [5]

Never, on any human countenance, have I seen so swift and beautiful a look of gratitude, surprise and comfort. He whispered, "Thank you, m'am, this is right good! I didn't like to be a trouble; you seemed so busy . . ." [6]

I bathed his face, brushed his bonny brown hair, set all things smooth about him. While doing this, he watched me with the satisfied expression I so liked to see. He spoke so hopefully when there was no hope. "This is my first battle; do they think it's going to be my last?" [7]

It was the hardest question I had ever been called upon to answer; doubly hard with those clear eyes fixed upon mine. "I'm afraid they do, John." [8]

He seemed a little startled at first, pondered over the fateful fact a moment, then shook his head. "I'm afraid, but it's difficult to believe all at once. I'm so strong it don't seem possible for such a little wound to kill me." And then he said, "I'm a little sorry I wasn't wounded in front; it looks cowardly to be hit in the back, but I obeyed orders." [9]

John was dying. Even while he spoke, over his face I saw a gray veil falling that no human hand can lift. I sat down by him, wiped drops from his forehead, stirred the air about him with a slow wave of a fan, and waited to help him die. For hours he suffered dumbly, without a moment's murmuring: his limbs grew cold, his face damp, his lips white, and again and again he tore the covering off his breast, as if the lightest weight added to his agony. [10]

One by one, the other men woke, and round the room appeared a circle of pale faces and watchful eyes, full of awe and pity; for, though a stranger, John was beloved by all. "Old boy, how are you?" faltered one. "Can I say or do anything for you anywheres?" whispered another. [11]

"Take my things home, and tell them that I did my best." [12]

He died then; though the heavy breaths still tore their way up for a little longer, they were but the waves of an ebbing tide that beat unfelt against the wreck. He never spoke again, but to the end held my hand close, so close that when he was asleep at last, I could not draw it away. Dan, another patient, helped me, warning me as he did so that it was unsafe for dead and living flesh to lie so long together. But though my hand was strangely cold and stiff, and four white marks remained across its back, even when warmth and color had returned elsewhere, I could not but be glad that, through its touch, the presence of human sympathy, perhaps, had lightened that hard hour. [13]

When they had made him ready for the grave, I stood looking at him. The lovely 14
expression which so often beautifies dead faces soon replaced marks of pain. The ward
master handed me a letter, saying it had come the night before but was forgot. It was
John's letter, come just an hour too late to gladden the eyes that had longed for it so
eagerly.

Symbol

After I had cut some brown locks for his mother, and taken off the ring to send her, 15
I kissed this good son for her sake, and laid the letter in his hand. Then I left him, glad
to have known so genuine a man, and carrying with me an enduring memory of a brave
Virginia blacksmith, as he lay serenely waiting for the dawn of that long day which
knows no night.

resurrection

Now, compare your reading notes with ours. As we said earlier, your notes may vary
from ours, but the results should be similar in scope.

focus/subject?

"**Death** of a **Soldier**"

simile
details

As I went on my **hospital** rounds with Dr. P., I happened to ask 1
which man in the room **suffered most**. He glanced at John. "Every
breath he draws **is like a stab**; for the ball **pierced** the left lung and
broke a rib. The poor lad **must** lie on his **wounded back** or **suffocate**."

dialogue
"You don't mean he must die, doctor?" 2
Pity/inevitable death
"There's not the slightest hope for him." 3
too busy to cry
I **could have** sat down on the spot and **cried** heartily, if I had not 4
learned the wisdom of **bottling up one's tears for leisure moments**.

(emotional appeal to
Americans who can
empathize with John)
The army needed men **like John, earnest, brave, and faithful;**
fighting for liberty and justice with both heart and hand.

prayer?
He has time to cry;
she not
//

John sat with **bent head**, **hands folded** on his knee, and no outward 5
sign of suffering, till, looking nearer, **I saw great tears** roll down and
drop upon the floor. It was a new sight there; for, though I had seen
many suffer, some swore, some groaned, most endured silently,
but none wept. Yet it did not seem weak, only **very touching**, and
straightway my fear vanished, my heart opened wide and took him in.

simile
Dialogue—begin to
identify with nurse
Gathering the **bent head** in my arms, as freely **as if he had been a little**
child, I said, "**Let me help you bear it, John**."

Never, on any human countenance, have I seen so swift and 6
beautiful a look of gratitude, surprise and comfort. He whispered,

dialogue = real John
//
"Thank you, m'am, this is right good! I didn't like to be a trouble; you
seemed so busy . . ."

I bathed his face, brushed his bonny brown hair, set all things 7
smooth about him. While doing this, he watched me with the satisfied
expression I so liked to see. He spoke so hopefully when there was no
dialogue
hope. "This is my first battle; do they think it's going to be my last?"

It was the hardest question I had ever been called upon to answer; 8
doubly hard with those **clear eyes fixed upon mine**. "I'm afraid they
dialogue
do, John."

He seemed a little startled at first, pondered over the fateful fact a
moment, then shook his head. "I'm afraid, but it's difficult to believe all
at once. I'm so strong it don't seem possible for such a little wound to kill
me." And then he said, "I'm a little sorry I wasn't wounded in front; it
looks cowardly to be hit in the back, but I obeyed orders."

9

*(Dialogue—real
insight into character)*

short metaphor

imagery

[**John was dying.**] Even while he spoke, over his face I saw a gray veil
falling that no human hand can lift. I sat down by him, **wiped drops**
from his forehead, stirred the air about him with a **slow wave of a fan**,
and waited to help him die. For hours he suffered dumbly, without a
moment's murmuring: his **limbs grew cold**, **his face damp**, his **lips
white**, and again and again he **tore the covering off his breast**, as if the
lightest weight added to his agony.

10

imagery

how to think

One by one, the other men woke, and round the room appeared
a **circle of pale faces and watchful eyes**, **full of awe and pity**; for,
though a stranger, **John was beloved** by all. "Old boy, how are you?"
faltered one. "Can I say or do anything for you anywheres?" whispered
another.

11

dialogue

dialogue-character

"Take my things home, and tell them that I did my best."

12

obj. short

[**He died then**]; though the heavy breaths still tore their way up for
a little longer, they were but the **waves of an ebbing tide that beat
unfelt against the wreck**. He never spoke again, but to the end held
my hand close, so close that when he was asleep at last, I could not
draw it away. Dan, another patient, helped me, warning me as he did
so that it was unsafe for dead and living flesh to lie so long together.
But though my hand was strangely cold and stiff, and four white marks
remained across its back, even when warmth and color had returned
elsewhere, I could not but be glad that, through its touch, the presence
of human sympathy, **perhaps, had lightened that hard hour**.

13

metaphor

lasting physical effect

*(reinforces her pur-
pose as a nurse)*

When they had made him ready for the grave, I stood looking at
him. The lovely expression which so often beautifies dead faces soon
replaced marks of pain. The ward master handed me a letter, saying it
had come the night before but was forgot. **It was John's letter, come
just an hour too late to gladden the eyes that had longed for it so
eagerly**.

14

*(ironic detail—
sentimental)*

*nurse's role
how to think
of John*

After I had cut some brown locks for his mother, and taken off
the ring to send her, I kissed this good son for her sake, and laid the
letter in his hand. Then I left him, glad to have known **so genuine a
man**, and carrying with me an enduring memory of a brave Virginia
blacksmith, as he lay serenely **waiting for the dawn of that long day
which knows no night**.

15

beautiful metaphor

The Opening Paragraph

Remember, your opening paragraph is going to set the subject and tone of your entire essay.
Make certain that your reader knows precisely where you intend to take him or her. This
clarity of purpose will give your reader confidence in what you have to present. Some of the
questions you should ask yourself about your opening paragraph include.

- Have you cited the author and title?
- Have you identified the author's intended effect on the reader?
- Have you specifically mentioned which strategies, devices, or elements you will consider in your analysis of Alcott's re-creation of her experience?

Remember, this information can be provided to your reader in may different ways. You can be direct or inventive. Whatever you choose to do, be confident and clear.

Below are four sample opening paragraphs that address the prompt for the Louisa May Alcott analysis essay.

We recognized many areas we could develop in this analysis essay. Pacing is obvious in this brief narrative. Alcott tells of her experience in chronological order and uses a combination of short, direct sentences to balance longer, figurative ones. We could have just concentrated on dialogue, but we chose to include it with our discussion of selection of detail, diction, imagery, and tone.

Sample A

In Hospital Sketches, Louisa May Alcott presents a sentimental retelling of an episode she experienced as a Civil War nurse. As she tells of her encounter with a dying soldier, Alcott uses details, imagery, and diction to make her reader emotionally identify with her and her subject. These strategies and devices evoke a sentimental and sorrowful response in the reader.

Sample B

"John was dying." Such a direct statement for such a tragic and moving event. But, Louisa May Alcott does more than just objectively present a medical report of the death of a Civil War soldier in Hospital Sketches. Rather, through diction, selection of details, imagery, and tone, Alcott emotionally involves her reader in this sentimental re-creation of one young blacksmith's death.

Sample C

War is hell. But, occasionally an angel of mercy on a mission braves the horror to save a lost soul. Louisa May Alcott, a Civil War nurse, was such an angel—and perhaps her presence helped the troubled soul of a dying blacksmith reach the rewards of heaven he so deserved. Through imagery, diction, selection of detail, and tone, Alcott allows her readers to join her in this sentimental and awe-inspiring narrative from Hospital Sketches.

Sample D

My only previous connection with Louisa May Alcott was with Little Women. What a very different scene she presents in her story from Hospital Sketches. The reader is made to come face to face with the death of a wounded Civil War soldier as he is tended by a most caring nurse. This moving and sentimental narrative is developed through imagery, diction, selection of detail, and tone.

Although each of these opening paragraphs is different, each does the expected job of an introductory AP Comp analysis essay.

- Each cites the author and title.
- Each identifies the author's intended effect on the reader.
- Each states which strategies/devices will be discussed in the analysis of Alcott's narrative.

Let's take a look at what is different about each of these introductory paragraphs.

- **Sample A** restates the prompt directly. It is to the point without elaboration, but it enables the reader to immediately know the focus of the essay.
- **Sample B** uses a direct quotation from the text to grab the reader's attention. It is obvious that this is a writer who understands how language operates.
- **Sample C** imposes a personal viewpoint immediately and establishes a metaphor that will most likely be the unifying structure of the essay.
- **Sample D** makes reference to one of Alcott's other works as the scene is being set. The writer does not spend any additional time referring to the other work. It merely provides a kind of "stepping-stone" for both the writer and the reader.

Into which of the above samples could your opening paragraph be classified?

Writing the Body of the Essay

What Should I Include in the Body of This Analysis Essay?

Your strategy here should be the same as on the previous essay:

1. Present *your* analysis and your prompt-related points.
2. Adhere to the question.
3. Use specific references and details from the passage.
4. Use connective tissue—repetition, "echo words," and transitions—to establish coherence.

For more detail, refer back to the first discussion of this subject, earlier in this chapter.

To understand the process, carefully read the sample paragraphs below. Each develops one of the elements asked for in the prompt and cited in the introductory paragraph. Notice the specific references and the "connective tissue." Also notice that details that do not apply to the Alcott prompt are ignored.

This Paragraph Develops Diction

Throughout her account, Alcott's diction manipulates emotional responses in her readers. Words such as "earnest," "brave" and "faithful" establish John as a soldier worthy of sympathy, while "liberty and justice" rally the reader to his side with their patriotic connotations. Once the reader is involved, Alcott directs the tragic scene with words intended to bring forth more negative emotional responses: "suffering, tears, groans, and wept" emphasize John's pain. Yet, when the author says, "very touching," "fear vanished," and "my heart opened wide," the reader also wants to help John bear his pain. Alcott balances the negative side of death by using words that will make the reader more at ease during this uncomfortable passage. "Beautiful, gratitude and comfort" relax the reader and allow him to feel good about Alcott and her caregiving. Then, her direction changes as the young man is dying. He is now "cold, damp, white, and in agony." When the reader's heart is breaking, Alcott chooses words to lift the moment. The other men are "full of awe and pity," like the reader. In this way, the diction unites the reader, John, and Alcott. She makes certain that her concluding choices are comforting and positive. The "hard hour" has been "lightened." His expression is now "lovely and beautiful."

This Paragraph Develops Selection of Details

Louisa May Alcott chooses very special details to include in her development of scene and character. Dialogue is one of these details which provides tangible insights into the character of John. The immediacy and reality of John's inevitable death is brought straightforwardly home to the reader in paragraphs 2 and 3. "You don't mean he must die, doctor?" "There's not the slightest hope for him." John's politeness and unassuming personality are observed when we hear him respond to the nurse in paragraph 6. And, his youth and sense of honor are heartbreakingly presented in the dialogue in paragraph 7 and the end of paragraph 9. This sense of duty and honor is reinforced with his last words, ". . . tell them that I did my best." Selection of details also help the reader to understand and feel the horror of war and its casualties. The pain and coldness of death is almost brutally punctuated in paragraph 5, where Alcott chooses to emphasize others not crying while John does. Alcott chooses to tell us about the letter from John's mother that was not delivered until after his death to add more pathos and irony to an already tragic scene. And, to select the detail of her placing this letter into the dead soldier's hands prior to his burial heightens the reader's emotional involvement.

This Paragraph Develops Imagery

It might be easy to become dulled to pain in a war hospital filled with dying men. To prevent this and to personalize the experience, Alcott uses imagery to re-create the events of John's death. The reader can feel that "every breath he draws is like a stab." The image of suffocation tightens our throats as we read about his pain, but we, like Alcott, must learn to "bottle up our tears" as we envision through her simile the nurse as mother and soldier as child. The metaphor of "a gray veil falling that no human hand can lift" softens the death of the soldier while heightening the finality. The concluding metaphor reassures the reader of salvation as she, the writer, allows John into the "dawn of that long day which knows no night."

This Paragraph Develops Tone

As a result of her selection of details, diction, and imagery, Louisa May Alcott creates a scene with a predominant tone of sorrow. Re-creating the death scene of this young soldier, the author chooses those details that emphasize that pain and sorrow, both in herself and in her patient. She chooses to tell of the undelivered letter prior to the soldier's death, which further reinforces the reader's sense of sorrow and pity. Words like "suffering," "wept," "cold," "white," "in agony," help to convey and evoke sadness in the reader. And, the piteous situation is further developed when John's face is described as "lovely and beautiful" after his death. Imagery is also employed to create this tone of sorrow or sadness. Images of suffering, loss, and grief throughout, together with the final metaphor of "a gray veil falling that no human hand can lift," sadly portray the passing of this young Virginian blacksmith into eternity.

DO THIS NOW.

- Write the body of your essay. Time yourself.
- Allow 15–20 minutes to write your body paragraphs.

Here are two actual student essays with comments on each.

Student A

Louisa May Alcott experiences the worst part of war—suffering. Each day brings her 1
in contact with new bloodied men brought in on stretchers, and only a few walk out. She
has to live with their souls on her mind. One soldier, John, is described as a "brave" young
man who fought for "liberty and justice." But, he is suffering. Alcott writes with an
emotional tone about this soldier whom she helps "live" through his final moments. She
obviously retells this story so that her readers can begin to understand the anguish of war.

This chronologically organized story spans two hours, from life to the end of life. It 2
is said that no man should die alone, and Alcott helps this young man to die with the
comfort of one who cares for him. Alcott's diction includes adjectives to describe his
slow drift towards heaven with words like "his limbs grew cold, his face damp, his lips
white . . ." These characteristics added together with the metaphorically imposed "gray
veil" all lead up to his death. John's last words, "tell them that I did my best," symbolize
both his life and his death. From then on, he said nothing and waited to enter his next
life. Though he dies, Alcott hangs on as if trying to keep him from leaving. When
she finally lets him go, four white marks stay on her hand, symbolizing John's lasting
presence.

". . . Many suffer, some swore, some groaned, most endured silently, but none wept." 3
However, John was the exception. He let his emotions go, and his pain was answered
by a caring nurse. Alcott appeals to the reader's emotions with such words as "crying,"
"suffering," "pity," and "awe," that express the extremes of feeling present in the hospital
ward. A man in pain, about to die, should be pitied, especially when his life is about to
be cut short. All his childhood dreams are to go unfulfilled. It is a waste of a "genuine
man." Alcott uses this not only to tell of her experiences in war, but also to clarify for her
reader the devastation of war. Alcott's balanced sentences enhance her story. In paragraph
7, John says, "This is my first battle; do they think it's going to be my last?" Alcott
uses this question to illustrate the shock soldiers feel when faced with death. How can
anyone believe a doctor who tells him he is dying. This shock, on the part of the soldier
illustrates the human horror of war—people die!

Alcott also uses irony to emphasize the sadness of this boy's death. Just an hour after 4
he passes on, another doctor brings in a letter for John. It is just too late. If he had seen it,
maybe it would have put one last sparkle in his eyes before he shut them forever.

The ending of the passage summarizes the entire experience of so many of those who 5
fought in the Civil War. Here was a young man who was very human. He was an average
boy from Virginia who worked as a blacksmith. He had had a regular life and a regular
job until this terrible war. That was when this regular life ceased to exist: John's and pre–
Civil War America.

Having witnessed this young soldier waiting for the "dawn of that long day which 6
knows no night," people should cry and be awe struck at the consequences of war.

Student B

In this excerpt from <u>Hospital Sketches</u> by Louisa May Alcott, she constructs her story to deeply move the reader by re-creating her personal experience as a nurse. Alcott's rhetorical strategies, including diction, imagery and selection of details, help to emphasize the pain and the sorrow which filled the U.S. Army hospital.

A reason why Alcott's excerpt was very successful in helping the reader understand the atmosphere during the Civil War is through her choice of words. The repetition of "hope," reveals that although she and John hoped that he would survive, it was inevitable that he would die, for he had been deeply hurt. Alcott reveals her sympathy and care for this man named John by asking the doctor how long he has to live. She also helps us understand that during the war precious lives were taken away. "The army needed men like John, earnest, brave, and faithful." Alcott even reveals to her readers that having this companionship with John wasn't an easy job. She would have to answer heartbreaking questions, such as "Do they think it's going to be my last?" Telling a person that they won't live for long may be one of the hardest jobs Alcott may have had.

In addition to Alcott's diction, the details which she presents for her readers give the story an even more melancholy effect. She doesn't simply just state how many men were injured or how they were injured. Rather, she writes about her short encounter with the man named John. "John sat with bent head . . . and no outward sign of suffering, till . . . I saw great tears roll down and drop upon the floor." It's like this simple example shows the sadness and grief felt by this young man who was brave and fought for liberty. She reveals the soft side of a soldier. Alcott re-creates her experience by presenting the details of her relationship with John. "I sat down by him, wiped drops from his forehead, stirred the air . . . waited to help him die." She even displays the gradual physical change of the dying human body. "His limbs grew cold, his face damp, his lips white . . ." She also includes a small conversation between John and another injured man who, although a stranger, still had pity and sympathy for him. She also appeals to emotion by adding his mother in the story. She, as a friend, cuts his hair and kisses him for her instead at the grave.

Furthermore, the use of imagery also added to the re-creation of the Civil War scene. She describes John's pain as "every breath he draws is like a stab; for the ball pierced the left lung and broke a rib." With this quotation, it is evident that his pain was great. Alcott also shows the slow deterioration of John. "I saw a gray veil falling that no human hand can lift." This reveals that John's death is inevitable and there was nothing any human could do, but she could play the role of a friend. Alcott also displays the strength of John, how he wished to live, as "heavy breaths still tore their way up for a little longer."

Alcott describes her experience of the Civil War by telling a personal story. She reveals great love and generosity for John. Through this, it helps us understand the true power of human companionship.

Rubrics for Alcott Essay

As we said previously in this chapter, you can view actual AP English Language and Composition rubrics by logging on to the College Board website.

High-Range Essay (9, 8, 7)

- Indicates a complete understanding of the prompt
- Clearly identifies and illustrates the author's intended effect on the reader
- Presents various rhetorical strategies, devices, and elements used by the author to re-create her experience
- Clear, well-organized, and coherent
- Demonstrates a mature writing style
- Thoroughly cites specific references from the text to illustrate and support points being made
- Minor errors/flaws, if any

Note: A 7 essay which is rated in the high range makes the jump from the mid-range because of its more mature style and perception.

Mid-Range Essay (7, 6, 5)

- The mid to high range essays identify rhetorical strategies PLUS the purpose/effect of the strategies
- Refers accurately to the prompt
- Refers accurately to the author's intended effect on the reader
- Presents a less thorough analysis of how Alcott re-creates her experience than the higher-rated essays
- Is less adept at linking strategies and devices to the creation of effect or re-creation of the experience
- Demonstrates writing that is adequate to convey Alcott's assertion
- May not be sensitive to the more subtle strategies employed by Alcott
- A few errors/flaws may be present

Note:
- The 7 paper demonstrates a more consistent command of college-level writing than does the 5 or 6 essay.
- A 5 paper does the minimum required by the prompt. It relies on generalizations and sketchy analysis. It is often sidetracked by plot, and the references may be limited or simplistic.

Low-Range Essay (4, 3, 2, 1)

- Does not respond adequately to the prompt
- Demonstrates insufficient and/or inadequate understanding of the passage and prompt
- Does not clearly identify the author's intended effect on the reader or does not illustrate or supply support for the intended effect
- Underdevelops and/or inaccurately analyzes Alcott's re-creation of her experience
- Demonstrates weak control of the elements of diction, syntax, and organization

Note: A 4 or 3 essay may do no more than paraphrase sections of the passage. A 2 essay may merely summarize the passage. (NO MATTER HOW WELL WRITTEN, A SUMMARY CAN NEVER EARN MORE THAN A 2.)

A 1–2 essay indicates a major lack of understanding and control. It fails to comprehend the prompt and/or the passage. It may also indicate severe writing problems.

Rubrics for Student A Essay

This is a high-range essay for the following reasons:

- Indication of a mature writer [paragraph 2, sentence 3], [paragraph 3, sentences 2 and 3]
- Clear understanding of the author's intended effect on the reader and applies it to a larger context [last paragraph]
- Strong integration of textual support with rhetorical strategies [paragraph 4], [paragraph 5, sentence 1]
- Strong topic adherence and connective tissue
- Interesting and appropriate insights derived from the text [last paragraph]

This high-range essay is well organized, with a strong, mature voice that has a clear point of view together with a well-developed analysis.

Rubrics for Student B Essay

This is a mid-range essay for the following reasons:

- Identifies the intended effect on the reader [paragraph 1, sentence 1], [paragraph 3, sentence 1]
- Adequately develops cited textual references
- Shows understanding of rhetorical devices [paragraph 4]
- Good transitions ("connective tissue")
- Frequently uses awkward syntax [paragraph 2, last 3 sentences], [paragraph 3, last 2 sentences]
- Minor technical errors, such as apostrophes and commas

This mid-range essay is indicative of a writer who understands the text and the prompt. The student is able to choose the obvious rhetorical strategies and devices and relate them to Alcott's purpose with less fully developed analysis in comparison with the high-range papers.

Rapid Review

- Analysis is the study of rhetorical strategies.
- Your writing reflects your critical thinking.
- Review the types of analysis questions asked on previous exams.
- Always address the prompt.
- Review the rubrics to understand the rating system.
- Remember, the essay on the exam is a first draft.
- Follow a timing strategy for writing the exam essay.
- Carefully analyze the prompt.
- Practice topic adherence.
- Employ close reading and highlighting of the given passage.
- "Work" the material.
- Write your essay and check against models.
- Use echo words.
- Form a study group.
- Read sample essays and rubrics.
- Score your own essays.

CHAPTER 6

Introduction to the Argumentative Essay

IN THIS CHAPTER

Summary: Examination of the argumentative essay and its purpose as it is presented in the AP English Language exam.

Key Ideas

✪ Learn to take a position/stand on a situation given in the argumentative prompt.

✪ Familiarize yourself with strategies to support your position.

✪ Learn the basics of constructing the argumentative essay in response to the AP English Language prompt.

Some Basics

The second type of essay on the Advanced English Language exam is the argumentative essay. Many students believe it to be the easiest of the three essays to write. Unfortunately, too many students spend too little time in the actual planning of this essay and, as a result, present an underdeveloped, illogical, or off-topic piece. Although there is a great deal of latitude given for the response to the prompt, the argumentative essay demands careful reading and planning.

What Does the Argumentative Essay Require of Me?

Basically, you need to do three things

- understand the nature of the position presented in the prompt
- develop a position in response to the prompt
- clearly and logically support your claim

What Does It Mean to Develop a Position?

Basically, this is a "So, what do YOU think?" prompt. You are asked to carefully read a passage or statement and to consider your own thoughts and where you stand on the issue. You are NOT being asked to confront the writer or speaker of the given text.

Timing and Planning the Essay

How Should I Approach the Writing of My Argumentative Essay?

Before beginning to actually write the essay, you need to do some quick planning. You could brainstorm a list of ideas, construct a chart, or create an outline. Whatever it is, you MUST find a way to allow yourself to think through the issue and your position.

Once I've Chosen My Position on the Given Issue, How Do I Go About Supporting It?

Remember that you've been taught how to write an argument throughout your school years, and you've even studied it in detail in your AP Comp course this year. Here is a brief overview of the kinds of support/evidence you could include to bolster your argument:

— facts/statistics	— needed definitions	— anecdotes
— details	— recognition of	— contrast and comparison
— quotations	the opposition	— cause and effect
— dialogue	— examples	— appeal to authority

Just make certain to choose the strategy or strategies that are most familiar to you and with which you feel most comfortable. Don't try to "con" your reader or pad your essay with irrelevancies.

Does It Matter What Tone I Take in My Argumentative Essay?

The College Board and the AP Comp readers are open to a wide range of approaches. You can choose to be informal and personal, formal and objective, or even humorous and irreverent, and anything in between. Just be certain that your choice is appropriate for your purpose.

Will I Be Penalized for Taking an Unpopular, Unexpected, Irreverent, or Bizarre Position on the Given Issue?

As long as you are addressing the prompt and appropriately supporting your position, there is no danger of your losing points on your essay because you've decided to take a different approach. Your essay is graded for process and mastery and manipulation of language, not for how close you come to the viewpoint of your reader.

How Should I Plan to Spend My Time Writing the Argumentative Essay?

Learning to budget your time is a skill that can be most helpful in writing the successful essay. The following is a sample timeline for you to consider:

- 1–3 minutes reading and working the prompt
- 3 minutes deciding on a position
- 5–10 minutes planning the support of your position
- 20 minutes writing the essay
- 3 minutes proofreading

Working the Prompt

Before beginning to write, you MUST spend some time carefully reading and deconstructing the prompt. (We call this "working the prompt.") Your success depends upon your clearly understanding what is expected of you.

Below is the prompt of the third essay on the Diagnostic/Master exam.

> In his famous "Vast Wasteland" address to the National Association of Broadcasters in May of 1961, Newton Minow, the Chairman of the Federal Communications Commission, spoke about the power of television to influence the taste, knowledge, and opinions of its viewers around the world. Carefully read the following, paying close attention to how timely it is today, especially in light of the Internet, smart phones, social media, and digital games, etc.
>
> Minow ended his speech warning that "The power of instantaneous sight and sound is without precedent in mankind's history. This is an awesome power. It has limitless capabilities for good—and for evil. And it carries with it awesome responsibilities—responsibilities which you and [the government] cannot escape . . ."
>
> Using your own knowledge and your own experiences or reading, write a carefully constructed essay in which you present and support your position of Minnow's ideas about mass media and technology.

DO THIS NOW.
Highlight the essential elements of the prompt.
(Time yourself.) How long did it take you? _____
Compare your highlighting of the prompt with ours.

> In his famous "**Vast Wasteland**" address to the **National Association of Broadcasters** in May of **1961**, **Newton Minow**, the **Chairman of the Federal Communications Commission**, spoke about the **power of television to influence the taste, knowledge, and opinions of its viewers around the world**. Carefully read the following, paying close attention to how **timely** it is today, especially in light of the worldwide **Internet**.
>
> Minow ended his speech **warning** that "**The power of instantaneous sight and sound is without precedent in mankind's history**. This is an **awesome power**. It has **limitless capabilities for good—and for evil**. And it carries with it **awesome responsibilities**—responsibilities which **you and [the government] cannot escape** . . ."

Using your **own knowledge** and your **own experiences** or **reading**, write a carefully constructed essay that **defends, challenges, or qualifies Minow's ideas**.

For this prompt, anything else you may have highlighted is extraneous.

> The prompt asks the student to defend, challenge, or qualify Minow's ideas. Notice that it does NOT state "all," "some," or a "specific number." Therefore, the student has freedom of choice. (This is similar to the "such as" instructions in other prompts.)

Developing the Opening Paragraph

NOW, BEGIN TO PLAN YOUR ESSAY.

Write your introductory paragraph. Make certain to

- refer specifically to the prompt; and
- clearly state your position on the given issue.

The following are three sample opening paragraphs.

A

I agree with Newton Minow's assertion to the National Association of Broadcasters that "The power of instantaneous sight and sound is . . . an awesome power . . . [with] capabilities for good—and for evil." However, I disagree with his placing the responsibility for this power squarely in the hands of the broadcasters and the government.

B

Imagine—you have limitless capabilities for good and evil—you, not Superman, can control the world with your super powers. And, what are your powers? Do you have x-ray vision, morphability, immortality? NO, you have the most awesome power ever devised—you can instantaneously influence the taste, knowledge, and opinions of mankind around the world. You are Supernet! and you have a super headache because you agree with Newton Minow, who warned the National Association of Broadcasters in 1961 that "You have an awesome responsibility."

C

Nowhere is the awesome power for good and evil of modern technology more clearly seen than in the Internet's pervasiveness and influence. Newton Minow was right on target in 1961 when he warned the National Association of Broadcasters that the power of TV has "limitless capabilities for good—and for evil."

Each of these opening paragraphs does the job required of an introduction to an argumentative essay on the AP English Language and Composition exam.

- Each cites the speaker and the occasion.
- Each clearly states the writer's position on the given issue.

Let's look at what is different about each of the paragraphs.

Sample A qualifies the assertion presented by Minow. The writer agrees with the potential of the power but disagrees about who should take responsibility.

Sample B agrees with Minow's position but treats the assertion in a lighthearted fashion. The reader can expect a humorous and possibly irreverent tone in the essay.

Sample C indicates a writer who has obviously decided to limit the area of the argument to that of the Internet and has chosen to agree with Minow.

Note: Given the subject matter, this prompt does not lend itself easily to a negative position. However, if a creative thinker and writer were to assert such a viewpoint, it would not be penalized.

Which of the above samples is similar to your opening paragraph? Are there any changes you would make in yours?

Developing the Body of the Essay

DO THIS NOW.

— Plan the body of your argumentative essay.

A sample strategy for planning the Minow essay follows. After carefully reading and deconstructing the prompt, we decided to use Minow's own three-part warning to the NAB. We brainstormed for ideas that could be linked to each of the categories. (Remember, ideas about how to organize or approach your essay can sometimes be found in the excerpt itself.)

GOOD	**EVIL**	**RESPONSIBILITY**
— education	— promote hate	— laws
— warning of dangers	— distort reality	— censorship
— recognition of heroes	— help terrorists	— self-censorship
— involvement in humankind's achievements	— invasion of privacy	— prior restraint
	— threats to national security	— 1st Amendment
— instant communications with family and friends		— 4th Amendment
	— create mass hysteria	— financial gain
		— copyrights
— medical care	— exploit children	— parental control
— links to the world for the the disabled, elderly, isolated	— fraud	— v-chip
	— conspiracy	— personal checks and balances
	— subvert elections	
— entertainment	— brainwashing	

Once you've completed your initial planning, in our case brainstorming, you must choose those specific items you will be best able to use to support and develop your argument. We limited ours to the following.

GOOD	**EVIL**	**RESPONSIBILITY**
— instant communications	— promote hate	— personal checks and balances
— medical treatment	— exploit children	— laws
— entertainment	— create mass hysteria	

This type of chart will provide you as a writer with a structure for your presentation. You are now ready to write the body of your essay based on your carefully considered choices.

Below are three sample body paragraphs which are based on the chart on page 100.

Body Paragraph on "Good"

One of the most rewarding applications of the Internet is its ability to provide instant communication between friends and family. A grandmother-to-be in New York is able to share in the moment by moment experience of her daughter's pregnancy and her granddaughter Daisy's birth in California through e-mail, scanned photos and quick videos. Likewise, the ability to instantly communicate with others may have saved the life of a doctor stranded at the South Pole. Her contact with medical resources and experts via the Internet enabled her to undergo surgery and treatment for breast cancer. Research and innovations in medical treatment are now available to those around the world via the "Net." Similarly, the ability for instant communication enables millions to enjoy concerts, sports events, theatrical presentations and other cultural activities without ever having to leave home. These wonderful benefits are all because of the fabulous and awesome technological creation—the Internet.

Body Paragraph on "Evil"

The other side of the mass communication coin has the face of evil on it. The Internet offers hate mongers unlimited access to anyone with a connection to the World Wide Web. Groups like the Neo Nazis can spread their hate messages to susceptible minds via bright, entertaining and engaging websites. What looks like a simple, fun game can easily reinforce the group's hate-filled philosophy to unsuspecting browsers. With the potential for millions of "hits" each week, it does not take a rocket scientist to perceive the danger here. This danger is also present with the minds and bodies of curious and vulnerable young people. Because of its easy access and easy production, "kiddie porn" is both possible and available via the Internet and the films any number of porn sites offer for downloading with the mere click of a keyboard key. Through contacts made through e-mail and/or chat rooms on the Net, children can be easily fooled and led to contact those who would abuse their bodies and minds for a quick profit or cheap thrill. With instantaneous messaging, whether real or imagined, positive or negative, a single person or group can set into motion mass hysteria just by warning of an impending disaster, such as a flood, fire, bomb, poison, and so on. There are obviously many more possibilities floating out there in the ethernet. These are just three of the evil ones.

Body Paragraph on "Responsibility"

Just as there is the potential for both good and evil with regard to mass communication, so too is there the potential for both beneficial and destructive strategies related to responsibilities. The most powerful regulator of our responsibility as individuals is our finger and its power to press a button or double click on a key and to "just say no." With this slight pressure, we are able to exert monumental pressure on those who produce programs, websites, photos, documents, etc., which we find unacceptable. Who better to tell us what to watch, what to do, and what to think? All too often many people prefer to abdicate their personal responsibility and give that power to either the government or the communication industry. We must never forget that dictators target the control and censorship of mass media as the first step in the total control of the minds and hearts of the populace. The laws, which we as citizens of a democracy look to, must never impinge upon our First and Fourth Amendment rights. Each of us has the right of free speech, and each of us has the right to privacy. None of us has the right to harm others or to limit the rights of others; why, then, would we give that right to the communication industry or to the government?

> Regarding a concluding paragraph, our advice is to spend your time in planning and writing the body of your essay rather than worrying about a concluding paragraph. With a brief essay, you can be certain that your reader can remember what you've already said, so there is no need to summarize your major points or to repeat the prompt. If you feel you must have a concluding statement/remark, by all means do so. But, make certain it is a FINAL remark that is of interest and is appropriate to your purpose. You may want to use the last sentence of your last body paragraph as your concluding comment. For example, the final sentences in the first and third sample body paragraphs could be used as the conclusion to the essay.

DO THIS NOW.
Spend about 20 minutes writing the body of your essay. Make certain that your essay follows your plan.

Sample Student Essays

The following are two sample student essays.

Student A

When Newton Minow ended his speech in May, 1961, he warned that, "The power of instantaneous sight and sound is without precedent . . . [and] it has limitless capabilities for good—and for evil." I wholeheartedly agree with both Minow's position about modern technology, especially about how it relates to the Internet today and the responsibility facing its users.   1

Scene One—Pre-1980's. Big project. Long haul to the library, gazing despondently until your eyes resemble those of a zombie. Too many books, too little time, in short, just TOO much. Scene Two—mid-1990's. A two-foot walk to the computer, and Voila! All the information you'd ever need is at your fingertips. The Internet has truly revolutionized how people can obtain their information. Now, more than ever, it is easier and quicker to access all types of information from "Exactly what IS that fungus growing on my toe?" to "What are the names of every major river system in the continental United States?" The plethora of information enables people to almost cease the burdensome trip to the library and halt the overwhelming feelings of dread they find as they stare blankly at a stack of books. With the schedule of the typical American today, there's hardly enough time to breathe, nevermind attempting to fit that hour-long trip to the library in the time frame. With the birth of the Internet, people with access to a computer can locate information faster than ever. But, how are we to judge the acceptability of that information?   2

The awesome power of these new technological inventions, such as computers and the Internet, do not always produce, however, grade-A products. People have begun to utilize the Internet to recruit new cult members, to teach people how to build bombs,   3 to teach hate. Basically, anything and everything evil can be posted on the "Net." Scene Three. Mr. Parker, a 75-year-old man from rural Indiana is in severe pain with abdominal cramps. Instead of attempting a two-hour drive to the nearest hospital, he makes it to his computer, logs on to the Internet in hopes of finding out what is wrong with him and in hopes of finding a quick remedy. Following the www's advice, he treats himself for stomach pain. Scene Four. Poor Mr. Parker dies hours later of acute appendicitis.

The Internet has the power to give birth to both good and evil. Today, as our society becomes more and more advanced, we rely more and more on anything that promises to make our busy lives less hectic. The easy way out, it seems, is always the right way in. Call it our American laziness, or call it our penchant to make learning easier, either way you slice it, the Internet has the potential for both positive and negative effects on society. Our responsibility is to find ways to exhibit our ability to distinguish between that which is beneficial and that which is destructive. 4

Student B

In his now famous address to the National Association of Broadcasters in May, 1961, FCC chairman Newton Minow spoke of the unprecedented power that those who control television's programming have over the American public, and how the mass media should be controlled and censored by the government, for it could wield awesome amounts of either good or evil. This assertion, that "television is a vast wasteland" rings true throughout the modern history of American society, especially in light of the global Internet. 1

There is no doubt that television has greatly altered the very psyche of Americans countless times since Minow's speech. From patriotic events like Neil Armstrong's first step on the moon and the "miracle on the ice" American victory over the Soviet Union in the 1980 Olympic hockey semi-finals, to historical events like Tiananmen Square, the assassination of JFK, and the fall of the Berlin Wall. Television has provided Americans with triumph—the Persian Gulf War—and tragedy—the Columbine massacre. Most importantly, however, it is entertainment for the masses, and is affordable to the point that 95% of Americans watch at least once a week, and this is where it goes awry. 2

Americans, due to the overwhelming economic prosperity and technological revolution of the last forty years, have become slovenly. We can get almost anywhere in the world within 24 hours via airplane and expect to be waited on while flying there. We drive to work everyday. We have every type of cuisine imaginable less than twenty minutes away, contrasting with several countries which don't have food, period. We have secure incomes, capital growth, and all of the material comforts of the day. We have the Internet, the new mass media which allows for anyone to learn about anything at anytime, anywhere. We are inactive, obese, materialistic, boring people, and television has adapted itself to fit our collective personas. Or possibly, we changed for television. 3

The nightly news is filled with images of death, suffering, pain, agony, misery, and other horrors that we gobble up because we as middle-class Americans have an infinitesimal chance of ever seeing it. The most popular TV shows are either irreverent comedies like "Seinfeld" and "Friends" with no actual cultural impact, or worse game shows like "Weakest Link" or "Survivor" that reward, in pride and prizes, ruthlessness, emotional warfare, and pointless competition that reinforces those attributes in the 30 million viewers they get every Monday and Wednesday night. The sensationalistic television programming caters to every evil desire we have, so it makes them grow inside us and want more, making us fervent to tune in next week for the next fantastic episode. God forbid they show a rerun.   4

Television has become a wasteland, and it's turning Western culture into one, too.   5
One has to believe Newton Minow knew what he was talking about. In a classic quote from <u>Catch-22</u>, Joseph Heller writes that "There was a general consensus that the platitudes of Americanism were horsesh-t." I wholeheartedly agree.

Rating the Essays

High-Range Essays (9, 8)

- Correctly identifies Minow's position regarding the power of television and other forms of mass communication
- Effectively presents a position about Minow's own ideas
- Clear writer's voice
- Successfully defends his or her position
- Presents carefully reasoned arguments making appropriate reference to specific examples from personal experience
- Clear and effective organization
- Effectively manipulates language
- Few, if any, syntactical errors

Mid-Range Essays (7, 6, 5)

- Correctly identifies Minow's position and attitude about television and mass communications
- Understands the demands of the prompt
- Clearly states a position with regard to that of Minow
- Presents a generally adequate argument that makes use of appropriate examples
- Ideas clearly stated
- Less well-developed than the high-range essays
- A few lapses in diction and/or syntax

Low-Range Essays (4, 3, 2, 1)

- Inadequate response to the prompt
- Misunderstands, oversimplifies, or misrepresents Minow's position
- Insufficient or inappropriate examples used to develop the writer's position
- Lack of mature control of the elements of essay writing

For this argumentative essay, almost all of the writers understood that Minow was commenting on the power of television and were able to comment on the timeliness of his assertions. In their essays, student writers attempted to distinguish between good and bad effects of modern technology, especially the Internet, and many illustrated their claims with fine examples of the power of this technology. They recognized the potential for inciting violence, for learning, for conformity, and for influencing political opinions and outcomes. The majority only touched upon power and influence, but the high-range essays recognized the subtlety of the responsibility of television and the Internet.

Most, if not all, student writers agreed with Minow, but few offered any real examination of the need for responsibility with regard to the advances in technology. Some were cautious about First Amendment rights, and a few saw the government as the chief "overseer."

Student A

This is a high-range essay for the following reasons:

- a strong, mature voice willing to be creative as well as analytical;
- clear statement about the writer's position on Minow's assertion;
- overall structure clearly defined through "scenes";
- original illustrations and details to support writer's position;
- tight focus;
- mature vocabulary and sentence structure; and
- brief response to Minow's challenge about responsibility regarding the media.

This high-range essay, although brief, does the work of a mature, clear, and responsive writer. The assertion and support for it are well organized and developed in a very clear writer's voice.

Student B

This is a mid-range essay for the following reasons:

- evidence that the writer understood the question and prompt;
- indication of a writer's voice;
- does not connect all parts of the essay, especially in paragraph 3, with the topic;
- includes interesting and varied details and examples to support the thesis;
- some obviously incorrect assumptions [paragraph 4, sentence 2];
- a few problems with diction and syntax [fragment in paragraph 4, sentence 2]; ["slovenly" in paragraph 3, sentence 1], ["fervent" in paragraph 4, next to last sentence];
- an interesting style and content; and
- does not really address the responsibility issue.

This mid-range essay indicates a writer who is a risk taker and intellectually curious. At times, the writer's enthusiasm seems to get in the way of a clear focus.

Rapid Review

- Create an argument.
  - understand the position or assertion
  - agree, disagree, or qualify
  - take a position, relate to an idea
  - support your point of view

- Work the prompt.
  — read and deconstruct the assignment
  — highlight
- Plan the essay.
- Address the opposition.
- Allow for final remarks.
- Write the essay.
- Read the sample essays and rubrics.
- Score your own essay.

CHAPTER 7

Introduction to the Synthesis Essay

IN THIS CHAPTER

Summary: An introduction to the synthesis essay and its purpose as it is presented on the AP English Language exam.

Key Ideas
✪ Learn how the synthesis essay differs from the argumentative and analysis essays.
✪ Learn the process of dealing with many texts.
✪ Learn the strategies that can be used to incorporate specific texts into your essay.
✪ Learn the basics for constructing your response to the synthesis prompt.

Some Basics

What Is the Synthesis Essay on the Exam Like?

Basically, the student is presented with an introduction to and a description of an issue that has varying viewpoints associated with it. Accompanying this is a selection of sources that address the topic. These sources can be written texts that could include nonfiction, fiction, poetry, or even drama, as well as visual texts, such as photos, charts, artwork, cartoons, and so forth.

After carefully reading and annotating the sources, the student is required to respond to the given prompt with an essay that incorporates and synthesizes at least THREE of the sources in support of his position on the subject.

What Is the Purpose of the Synthesis Essay?

The College Board wants to determine how well the student can do the following:

- Read critically
- Understand texts
- Analyze texts
- Develop a position on a given topic
- Support a position on a given topic
- Support a position with appropriate evidence from outside sources
- Incorporate outside sources into the texts of the essay
- Cite sources used in the essay

The synthesis essay is a chance to demonstrate your ability to develop a "researched idea," using not only your personal viewpoint, but also the viewpoints of others. This essay is a reflection of your critical reading, thinking, and writing skills.

The Prompt

The first time you see a synthesis prompt, you may feel overwhelmed. After all, it's quite complex: three paragraphs long and several outside sources. Don't panic. Just begin at the beginning, and take it step by step.

The first step is to READ THE PROMPT!!!

- No, don't just skim it.
- Yes, read it word for word.
- Underline important words, phrases, instructions.
- Don't assume anything.

As an example of how to deal with a synthesis prompt, let's carefully read and annotate the eminent domain prompt from the diagnostic/master exam

A recent <u>Supreme Court decision</u> has provoked much <u>debate about private property rights (eminent domain)</u>. In it the court ruled that the city of <u>New London was within the bounds of the *Constitution* when it condemned private property for use in a redevelopment plan</u>. This ruling is an <u>example of the classic debate between individual rights vs. the greater good</u>.

Carefully read the following sources, including any introductory information. Then, in an essay that <u>synthesizes at least three of the sources for support</u>, take a <u>position on the claim that the governmental taking of property from one private owner to give to another to further economic development constitutes permissible "public use" under the Fifth Amendment.</u>

Make certain to <u>take a position</u> and that your <u>essay centers on your argument</u>. Use the <u>sources to support your reasoning</u>; <u>avoid simply summarizing</u> the sources. You may <u>refer to the sources by their letters</u> (Source A, Source B, etc.) <u>or by the identifiers</u> given in the parentheses.

Source A (U.S. Constitution)
Source B (60 Minutes)
Source C (Kelo decision)
Source D (Koterba, political cartoon)
Source E (Broder)
Source F (Britt, political cartoon)
Source G (CNN and American Survey)

1. Note the organization of the prompt.
   - The first paragraph gives important background information in order to establish context. This first paragraph will **always** provide background.
   - The second paragraph is the actual assignment – what are you required to do. The second paragraph is the true "meat" of the prompt. It **will change** with each new synthesis prompt you encounter.
   - The third paragraph provides instruction about how to construct your argument. This third paragraph will **always** provide organization information.
   - Each source is given a LETTER. The names of authors, etc. are given in parentheses.
2. Underline the important words and/or phrases. (We've already done that for you.) Note that ignoring any of the underlined words or phrases could seriously threaten your argument. That's what *important* means in this situation.
3. If you follow these two steps, you will have a working understanding of what is expected of you in this particular situation. If you have time, you might even want to write your assignment in ONE sentence. If you can do this, you really understand what your job is.

What Kinds of Synthesis Essays Can I Expect?

The synthesis essay has two primary approaches.

The first kind of synthesis essay is one you're probably familiar with. This is the essay in which you develop your thesis and support it with specific examples from appropriate sources. You could develop this type of synthesis essay using any of the rhetorical strategies, such as:

- Compare and contrast
- Cause and effect
- Analysis

The second kind of synthesis essay presents an argument. Here, you take a position on a particular topic and support this position with appropriate outside sources, while indicating the weaknesses of other viewpoints.

You should be ready to write either of these two types of synthesis essays. **Given the nature of the AP Language exam, however, it is more likely that you will be presented with a synthesis essay prompt that requires a response in the form of an argument**.

The important thing is to practice composing both types of synthesis essays. Practice. Practice. Being familiar and comfortable with the synthesis process is the crucial factor.

> Don't be put off by the length and/or complexity of the introduction to the subject and the prompt. Remember, you are the one who will choose your position on the topic. And you are the one who chooses which sources to incorporate into your essay.
>
> You can do this—AS LONG AS YOU ADDRESS THE PROMPT AND INCORPORATE AND CITE THE REQUIRED NUMBER OF SOURCES.

How Is the Synthesis Essay Rated?

As with the other essays on the AP Language exam, the synthesis essay is rated on a 9-point scale that is based on the AP Reader's evaluation of this first draft of an essay written in approximately 40 minutes. Here is a sample rubric for the synthesis essay.

A **9** essay has all the qualities of an 8 essay, and the <u>writing style</u> is especially <u>impressive</u>, as is the analysis and integration of the specifics related to the given topic and the given sources.

An **8** essay <u>effectively</u> and <u>cohesively</u> addresses the prompt. It clearly takes a position on the given topic and supports the claim using carefully integrated and appropriate evidence, including at least three of the given sources. The essay will also show the writer's <u>ability to control language</u>.

A **7** essay has all the properties of a 6, only with a <u>more complete</u>, well-developed, and integrated argument or a more mature writing style.

A **6** essay <u>adequately</u> addresses the prompt. The claim is on the given topic and integrates, as well as makes use of, appropriate evidence, including at least three references from the given sources. These elements are less fully integrated and/or developed than scores in the 7, 8, or 9 range. The writer's ideas are expressed with clarity, but the writing may have a few errors in syntax and/or diction.

A **5** essay demonstrates that the writer <u>understands the prompt</u>. The argument/claim/position about the given topic is generally understandable, but the development and/or integration of appropriate evidence and at least three of the given sources are limited, strained, or uneven. The writer's ideas are expressed clearly with a few errors in syntax or diction.

A **4** essay is <u>not an adequate response</u> to the prompt. The writer's argument indicates a misunderstanding, an oversimplification, or a misrepresentation of the assigned task. The writer may use evidence that is inappropriate or insufficient to support the argument, or use fewer than three of the given sources. The writing presents the writer's ideas, but it may indicate immaturity of style and control.

A **3** essay is a lower 4 because it is <u>even less effective</u> in addressing the question. It is also less mature in its syntax and organization.

A **2** essay indicates <u>little success in speaking to the prompt</u>. The writer may misread the question, only summarize the given sources, fail to develop the required argument, or simply ignore the prompt and write about another topic. The writing may also lack organization and control of language and syntax. (***Note***: **No matter how well written, a summary will never rate more than a 2.**)

A **1** essay is a lower 2 because it is even <u>more simplistic</u>, <u>disorganized</u>, and <u>lacking in control of language</u>.

Timing and Planning the Synthesis Essay

Before Writing

Before you begin to write your essay, you need to perform an important series of tasks. <u>**The first among these tasks is to wisely use the allotted, prewriting 15 minutes of reading time.**</u>

- Read ALL three of the prompts
- Deconstruct the synthesis prompt
- Read and annotate each of the given texts related to the synthesis prompt
- Decide how you will address the synthesis prompt

The second of these tasks is to be aware of the timing of writing your essay. You've been told to open the test booklet and begin to write. Now what? Well, you've already read each of the three prompts and decided what position you're going to take on the synthesis essay. Here's what we recommend as a timeline for writing the synthesis essay:

- 5 to 6 minutes going back to the texts and deciding which you will use in your essay
- 8 to 10 minutes planning the support of your position
- 20 minutes writing the essay
- 3 to 4 minutes checking to make certain you've included at least the minimum number of sources and correctly cited each of them
- 3 minutes proofreading

Working the Prompt

> As with the analysis and argument essays, you MUST spend time carefully reading and deconstructing the prompt. This entails your carefully reading and looking for key words, phrases, and other information that make your task clear. DO NOT FORGET TO READ ANY INTRODUCTORY MATERIAL PROVIDED. The introduction will set up the situation and give you any needed background information. Plan to spend about three minutes <u>carefully reading both the introduction and the assignment</u>, and highlighting the important terms and elements of the prompt.
>
> The following is the prompt from the Diagnostic Master exam.

A recent Supreme Court decision has provoked much debate about private property rights. In this decision, the court ruled that the city of New London was within the bounds of the *U.S. Constitution* when it condemned private property for use in a redevelopment plan. This ruling is an example of the classic debate between individual rights versus the greater good.

Carefully read the following sources, including any introductory information. **Then, in an essay that synthesizes at least three of the sources for support, take a position that supports, opposes, or qualifies the claim that the government taking property from one private owner to give to another for the creation of further economic development constitutes a permissible "public use" under the Fifth Amendment.**

Make certain that you take a position and that the essay centers on your argument. Use the sources to support your reasoning; avoid simply summarizing the sources. You may refer to the sources by their letters (Source A, Source B, etc.) or by the identifiers in the parentheses below.

- Source A (*U.S. Constitution*)
- Source B (*60 Minutes*)
- Source C (*Kelo* decision)
- Source D (Koterba, political cartoon)
- Source E (Broder)
- Source F (Britt, political cartoon)
- Source G (CNN and American Survey)

DO THIS NOW.
Time yourself for this activity.

Highlight the essential elements of the prompt.

How long did it take you? _____

Compare your highlighting with ours.

A recent Supreme Court decision has provoked much debate about private property rights. In it, the court ruled that the city of New London was within the bounds of the *U.S. Constitution* when it condemned private property for use in a redevelopment plan. This ruling is an example of the classic debate between individual rights versus the greater good.

Carefully read the following sources, including any introductory information. **Then, in an essay that synthesizes at least three of the sources for support, take a position that supports, opposes, or qualifies the claim that the government taking property from one private owner to give to another for the creation of further economic development constitutes a permissible "public use" under the Fifth Amendment.**

Make certain that you take a position and that the essay centers on your argument. Use the sources to support your reasoning; avoid simply summarizing the sources. You may refer to the sources by their letters (Source A, Source B, etc.) or by the identifiers in the parentheses below.

- Source A (*U.S. Constitution*)
- Source B (*60 Minutes*)
- Source C (*Kelo* decision)
- Source D (Koterba, political cartoon)
- Source E (Broder)
- Source F (Britt, political cartoon)
- Source G (CNN and American Survey)

Notice we have highlighted or underlined the essential parts of both the introduction and the prompt itself. All other words and phrases are nonessential.

> We now know a debate is centering around private property rights and public use for the greater good. We know the U.S. Supreme Court recently handed down a ruling supporting the principle of eminent domain, and we know we must take a position on this debate. And, lastly, we know we must choose at least three of the seven given sources.

Developing the Opening Paragraph

Now that you are aware of what is expected of you, you can begin to plan your essay.

> Before beginning the actual writing, we recommend you jot down a few notes about HOW you are going to present your material. There is no need to construct a formal outline. Simply create a brief listing of the major points you want to include and the order in which you will present them.

DO THIS NOW.

I have decided to use the following sources in my essay:

Source ___ A ___ B ___ C ___ D ___ E ___ F ___ G

When creating the opening paragraph, most student writers feel more in control if they:

— refer specifically to the prompt and/or introduction
— clearly state their position on the given topic

Now is the time to write your opening paragraph.

DO THIS NOW.

The position I'm going to take on this issue is _____ support _____ oppose _____ qualify.
    The following are three sample introductory paragraphs.

A

Payday. As usual, the line at the bank drive-thru is a mile long, so Joe Citizen just sits and listens to the radio. This paycheck is especially important to him because it is the final payment on his castle—his home. Mr. Smith has a family waiting back at home for him. Even his dog will be happy to see Joe walk through the door. What Joe Citizen and his family don't know is this: waiting for Joe is a notice from his local government, a letter notifying him that his home and property are being taken, using the right of eminent domain. One has to ask, "Is this fair?" I think not.

B

Every time that my grandparents visit, I have to vacate my bedroom, so they can have a room of their own during their visit. It's always a painful few days because I'm locked out of the room that I've decorated, the room that holds all of my things; it's the room that's "mine." As my mother always says, "It's for the good of the family." But, no matter how much I feel deprived, I always know that I'll have it back in a few days. However, the results would be different if she applied the principle of "eminent domain." I would lose my room permanently, and it would be turned into a real guest room. I would not be a happy family member.

C

Today there is a wide-ranging debate about the individual's right to possess and protect his private property and the right of the government to seize a person's home and land needed for redevelopment that would benefit the entire community. Even though the principle of eminent domain is granted to the government in the *U.S. Constitution*'s Fifth Amendment, it should be used only in the most extreme circumstances.

Each of the previous opening paragraphs could be used to begin the synthesis essay demanded of the eminent domain prompt.

— Each introduces the subject and its context.
— Each clearly indicates the writer's position on the issue.

Let's examine these paragraphs.

Sample A clearly states a position in opposition to eminent domain. This writer tries to place his opinion in the context of a generic man and his family. This brief paragraph begins to indicate the writer's voice. By answering the rhetorical question, the writer emphatically declares a position.

Sample B uses personal experience to present an opposing opinion. By placing the general concept of eminent domain in the context of a very personal experience, the reader hears a real voice that defends private property rights with some exceptions.

Sample C presents an objective statement of the subject and its context. There is no indication of the personal in this introduction, and the reader can expect the objectivity to continue as the writer develops his qualifying essay.

Which of these introductory paragraphs is similar to yours? Are there any changes you would make in your opening? If so, what are they?

Developing the Body of the Essay

DO THIS NOW.

— Plan the body of your synthesis essay.

<u>Take a close look at the planning our writer did for this synthesis essay.</u>

Position on issue: qualifying position on eminent domain

Sources to use: (See the sources in the Diagnostic Master exam, pages 30–34.)

✔ Source A (*U.S. Constitution*)
Source B (*60 Minutes*)
✔ Source C (*Kelo* decision)
Source D (Koterba, political cartoon)
✔ Source E (Broder)
Source F (Britt, political cartoon)
✔ Source G (CNN and American Survey)

Points to make:

1. The *Kelo* decision + the Fifth Amendment = right of eminent domain. Empathize with private property owners.
2. *60 Minutes* interview to support negative idea of what happens when eminent domain takes private property.
3. Get into the idea of the greater good. Use *60 Minutes* interview with the mayor and the Broder points about the need for urban development to help blighted areas.
4. Use the *Washington Times* survey to support my position of leaning toward those who oppose this type of use of eminent domain.

   With these points in mind, our writer is now ready to compose the body of the synthesis essay.

Body Paragraph Based on Point 1 (*Kelo* + Fifth Amendment)

Because of this experience, I can empathize with the home owners affected by the recent 5:4 Supreme Court decision *Kelo v. New London* that cited a section of the Fifth Amendment to the *U.S. Constitution* that states, "nor shall private property be taken for public use, without just compensation" (Source A). The Court ruled that New London, Connecticut, was within its constitutional rights to take private property and give it to another private individual in order to further the economic development of the city (Source C).

- Uses a transition to refer to the opening paragraph
- States empathy with those affected by the *Kelo* decision and summarizes both the case and the Fifth Amendment
- Appropriately cites the sources as directed in the prompt

Body Paragraph Based on Point 2 (*60 Minutes* interview + negative attitude)

Contrary to what the Court sees as "permissible public use" (Source C), I believe that a government taking a person's home or business away and allowing another private individual or company to take it over goes against the idea of our private property rights. A good example of this is the situation in Lakewood, Ohio, where the mayor wants to condemn a retired couple's home in order to make way for a privately owned, high-end condominium and shopping mall. As Jim Saleet said in his interview with *60 Minutes*, "The bottom line is this is morally wrong . . . This is our home . . . We're not blighted. . . . This is a close-knit, beautiful neighborhood" (Source B). The Saleets, who have paid off their mortgage, should be allowed to remain there as long as they want and pass it on to their children. Here, individual rights should prevail.

- Uses the transition device of repeating a phrase from the previous paragraph
- Maintains the personal with *I*
- Backs up personal position with the *60 Minutes* interview of the Saleets
- Appropriately cites the sources as directed in the prompt

Body Paragraph on Point 3 (Qualifying + Broder + *60 Minutes* and mayor)

However, I must also take into consideration the need for cities and states to improve troubled urban areas and clear blighted sections with new construction, tax revenues, and jobs (Source E). If governments are blocked from arranging for needed improvements and income, decline of cities and other areas could result. For example, the mayor of Lakewood, Ohio, Madeleine Cain, claims that the city cannot make it without more tax money coming in. As she sees it, Lakewood needs more money to provide required services. "This is about Lakewood's future. Lakewood cannot survive without a strengthened tax base," Mayor Cain told *60 Minutes* (Source B). Here, it sounds like the greater good should prevail.

- Introduces ambivalence with the transitional word "however"
- Uses both the Broder source and the mayor's words from the *60 Minutes* interview to illustrate and support the qualifying position
- Appropriately cites the sources as directed in the prompt

Body Paragraph Based on Point 3 (Qualifying + Broder)

Legal experts disagree about which of the two positions is the better one. Scott Bullock of the Institute for Justice sees the principle of eminent domain as an important one for government planning and building, but not for private development (Source E). On the other hand, John Echeverria, the executive director of the Georgetown Environmental Law and Policy Institute, sees a danger in legislators going to the extreme in the opposite direction and limiting essential powers of government. "The extremist position is a prescription for economic decline for many metropolitan areas around the country" (Source F).

- Transition created by referring to "the two positions"
- Uses the Broder source to give an overview of both sides of the issue
- Appropriately cites the sources as directed in the prompt and names authorities cited in the source material

> *Note:* This is just one example of the many ways this synthesis essay could be planned and developed. The important thing to remember is YOU MUST PLAN BEFORE YOU WRITE.

DO THIS NOW.

Spend about 20 minutes writing the body of your essay. Make certain that your essay follows your plan and that you cite your sources.

Writing the Conclusion

Now that you've written the intro and body paragraphs, you can't just drop your pen or leave your laptop and walk away. You need to end your essay with a final remark. This concluding idea is the last pertinent thought you want your reader to remember concerning the significance of the issue.

> ATTENTION. ATTENTION. Avoid final paragraphs that are merely summaries. This is not a lengthy, complicated presentation. Your reader can remember what you've said in the previous paragraphs.

DO THIS NOW.

Spend about five minutes quickly writing the concluding paragraph. Keep in mind what you said in your introduction and what you developed as your major points in the body of your essay.

Now, take a look at our three sample conclusions.

In the case of this synthesis essay, you'll recall that our writer wanted to make four major points. The body paragraphs developed three of those ideas. What to do with the fourth: "Use the *Washington Times* survey to support my position of leaning toward those who oppose this type of eminent domain."

Our writer realizes this could be an important source to solidify the qualifying position, and it brings both sides of the argument together.

The decision is made. Use Source G to develop the concluding paragraph. The following are three sample conclusions that make use of the survey.

A

It seems that there is no right position in all circumstances. According to a *Washington Times* survey, 60% of the American public is against local governments having the power to seize private homes and businesses (Source G). However, there may be times when the greater good has to win the toss.

B

Finally, 60% of the responders to a *Washington Times*/CNN survey opposed the right of eminent domain to local governments. Even though this may seem to be the most compelling position on this issue, there are going to be special circumstances when the greater good trumps private ownership.

C

Ultimately, I have to agree with the large majority of people who responded to recent polls conducted by both the *Washington Times* and CNN. When asked if local governments should be able to take over private homes and businesses, over 60% said "no" (Source G). But, I will have to be open to the possibility that public use and the greater good may, in some cases, be the only viable solution to a complicated problem.

Which of these concluding paragraphs is similar to yours? Are there any changes you would make in your ending? If so, what are they?

Sample Synthesis Essay from the Master Exam

The following is the complete essay that our writer developed for the eminent domain synthesis prompt, which is found in the Master exam.

Every time that my grandparents visit, I have to vacate my bedroom so that they can have a room of their own during their visit. It's always a painful few days because I'm locked out of the room that I've decorated, the room that holds all of my things; it's the room that's "mine." As my mother always says, "It's for the good of the family." But, no matter how much I feel deprived, I always know that I'll have it back in a few days. However, the results would be different if she applied the principle of "eminent domain." I would lose my room permanently, and it would be turned into a real guest room. I would not be a happy family member.

Because of this experience, I can empathize with the home owners affected by the recent 5:4 Supreme Court decision *Kelo v. New London* that cited a section of the Fifth Amendment to the *U.S. Constitution* that states, "nor shall private property be taken for public use, without just compensation" (Source A). The Court ruled that New London, Connecticut, was within its constitutional rights to take private property and give it to another private individual in order to further the economic development of the city (Source C).

Contrary to what the Court sees as "permissible public use" (Source C), I believe that a government taking a person's home or business away and allowing another private individual or company to take it over goes against the idea of our private property rights. A good example of this is the situation in Lakewood, Ohio, where the mayor wants to condemn a retired couple's home in order to make way for a privately owned, high-end condominium and shopping mall. As Jim Saleet said in his interview with *60 Minutes*, "The bottom line is this is morally wrong . . . This is our home . . . We're not blighted. . . . This is a close-knit, beautiful neighborhood" (Source B). The Saleets, who have paid off their mortgage, should be allowed to remain there as long as they want and pass it on to their children. Here, individual rights should prevail.

However, I must also take into consideration the need for cities and states to improve troubled urban areas and clear blighted sections with new construction, tax revenues, and jobs (Source E). If governments are blocked from arranging for needed improvements and income, decline of cities and other areas could result. For example, the mayor of Lakewood, Ohio, Madeleine Cain, claims that the city cannot make it without more tax money coming in. As she sees it, Lakewood needs more money to provide required services. "This is about Lakewood's future. Lakewood cannot survive without a strengthened tax base," Mayor Cain told *60 Minutes* (Source B). Here, it sounds like the greater good should prevail.

Legal experts disagree about which of the two positions is the better one. Scott Bullock of the Institute for Justice sees the principle of eminent domain as an important one for government planning and building, but not for private development (Source E). On the other hand, John Echeverria, the executive director of the Georgetown Environmental Law and Policy Institute, sees a danger in legislators going to the extreme in the opposite direction and limiting essential powers of government. "The extremist position is a prescription for economic decline for many metropolitan areas around the country" (Source E).

Ultimately, I have to agree with the large majority of people who responded to recent polls conducted by both the *Washington Times* and CNN. When asked if local governments should be able to take over private homes and businesses, over 60% said "no" (Source G). But, I will have to be open to the possibility that public use and the greater good may, in some cases, be the only viable solution to a complicated problem.

Rubric for Eminent Domain Synthesis Essay

A **9** essay has all the qualities of an 8 essay, and the <u>writing style</u> is especially <u>impressive</u>, as is the analysis and integration of the specifics related to eminent domain and the given sources.

An **8** essay <u>effectively</u> and <u>cohesively</u> addresses the prompt. It clearly takes a position on eminent domain and supports the argument using carefully integrated and appropriate evidence, including at least three of the given sources. The essay will also show the writer's <u>ability to control language</u>.

A **7** essay has all the properties of a 6 essay, only with a <u>more complete</u>, well-developed, and integrated argument or a more mature writing style.

A **6** essay <u>adequately</u> addresses the prompt. The argument is on eminent domain and integrates, as well as makes use of, appropriate evidence, including at least three references from the given sources. These elements are less fully integrated and/or developed than scores in the 7, 8, or 9 range. The writer's ideas are expressed with clarity, but the writing may have a few errors in syntax and/or diction.

A **5** essay demonstrates that the writer <u>understands the prompt</u>. The argument/claim/ position about eminent domain is generally understandable, but the development and/or integration of appropriate evidence and at least three of the given sources are limited or uneven. The writer's ideas are expressed clearly with a few errors in syntax or diction.

A **4** essay is <u>not an adequate response</u> to the prompt. The writer's argument indicates a misunderstanding, an oversimplification, or a misrepresentation of the assigned task. The writer may use evidence that is inappropriate or insufficient to support the argument or may use fewer than three of the given sources. The writing presents the writer's ideas, but may indicate immaturity of style and control.

A **3** essay is a lower 4 because it is <u>even less effective</u> in addressing the question. It is also less mature in its syntax and organization.

A **2** essay indicates <u>little success in speaking to the prompt</u>. The writer may misread the question, only summarize the given sources, fail to develop the required argument, or simply ignore the prompt and write about another topic. The writing may also lack organization and control of language and syntax. (***Note:*** **No matter how well written, a summary will never rate more than a 2.**)

A **1** essay is a lower 2 because it is even <u>more simplistic</u>, <u>disorganized</u>, and <u>lacking in control of language</u>.

Sample Student Essays

Student A

Eminent domain. Two little words that strike fear in the hearts of homeowners all over the country. But what exactly is it anyway? Eminent domain is the power of the government to take privately owned property away for "public use" as long as the original owners are given "fair" compensation for it. (Source A) However, the more the

1

government exercises this power given to it by the Fifth Amendment, the more the public feels the need to curtail it.

I agree with those opposing this governmental sledge hammer. My parents own their own house and have spent much of their lives paying off the mortgage, and now it is finally ours. I would never want to give it away—just compensation or not. The same appears to be true for Jim and Joanne Saleet who live in Lakewood, Ohio, who in a *60 Minutes* interview described their feelings about their mayor, Madeleine Cain, deciding to invoke this right of eminent domain. The mayor's reason for seizing this house that the Saleets "plan to spend the rest of their days [in] and pass on to their grandchildren" is not to build a needed highway or a hospital. NO, it is to build a high-end shopping mall (Source B). This is hardly justifiable—the neighborhood being seized is just your basic middle class suburbia—much like the house you most likely live in. Much like the house 80% of America lives in.

Since the Saleets, their neighbors in Scenic Park don't want to leave, the mayor has labeled Scenic Park, ironically enough, as "blighted." This has created a negative picture of the area in the public's mind. Jim Saleet told *60 Minutes*, "You don't know how humiliating this is to have people tell you, 'You live in a blighted area,' and how degrading this is. . . . This is an area that we absolutely love." (Source B) The intent of the new classier condos and mall is to raise Lakewood's property tax revenues, but so far, by calling the area "blighted," all they have done is to lower the reputation of Scenic Park. As Mr. Saleet said, "This is morally wrong, what they're doing here. This is our home." (Source B)

Some might say, "Well, this is just one small town example with just one guy's opinion." This is hardly so. In a CNN commissioned survey of 177,987 voters, 66% of those who responded said that local government should never be able to seize homes and businesses. Only 33% said it should be permitted for public use, and only a measly 1% voted to allow eminent domain for private economic development. (Source G)

Cities have claimed that invoking the right of eminent domain is being done to further "the greater good." And, yet, as the CNN survey shows, the masses who are supposedly benefiting from it either are not feeling this greater good or just plain don't appreciate it. In either case, something tells me that if most people are not happy about a situation something ought to be done about it. (We are still living in a democracy aren't we?)

Some have tried to stop it. But, the Supreme Court ruled on February 22, 2005, in the case of *Kelo v. City of New London* that "the governmental taking of property from one private owner to give to another in furtherance of economic development constitutes a permissible 'public use' under the Fifth Amendment." (Source C) This decision not only went against what the vast majority of the public feels, but it also was made with a very narrow margin of 5:4. This is because the Fifth Amendment doesn't state any specifics regarding what public use is, only that the owner of the property seized must be duly compensated.

The Supreme Court's narrow margin of votes demonstrates how heavily disputed this topic is. The public feels that their individual rights are being infringed upon—and I'm on their side.

Student B

The debate over government's authority over private property and the seizing of it has been heard ever since the creation of the Constitution. For over two hundred years, both federal and local governments alike have been taking private property for public use (with compensation): a power known as eminent domain. While government officials have used this right to help build public services such as roads and railroad tracks, they have also used this power under the label of "economic development" to benefit private corporations that build these projects.

Government should be allowed to take private property only for the creation of public goods and services. This right is stated in the Fifth Amendment of the Constitution, which deals with the issue of private property rights (Source A). However, the term "public use" is ambiguous and is open for much interpretation. Eminent domain should be used to build services like roads and schools. As the nation grows, and new economic centers develop, there is a need for the creation of new roads. The land for these roads needs to be taken from somewhere, and often times the only option is to take land from private owners. A similar situation arises when towns need to build new schools because of growing population pressures. Scott G. Bullock of the Institute for Justice concurs when he says, "It [eminent domain] has an important but limited role in government planning and the building of roads, parks, and public buildings" (Source E).

Although the Supreme Court in *Kelo v. New London* ruled that eminent domain can be used to seize private property to sell to private buyers for economic development that would benefit a needy area (Source C), the results of this power can cause unnecessary displacement and pain for the individuals whose homes are part of this "buy out." The Saleets of Lakewood, Ohio, present one example of this situation. This couple has been living in their home for 38 years and feels that the government is morally wrong in trying to evict them from their house in order to create high priced condos and shopping malls. The area in question is not a run down locale; therefore, it doesn't need renovation. The mayor of Lakewood claims the city needs money, and that the "area can be used for a higher and better use" (Source B).

However, it can also be argued that there is always room for improvement when it comes to the use of land, especially because of the ever changing needs and desires of people and governments. The United States was built on the principle of capitalism and private enterprise. It is not run with a planned economy as communist nations are. Therefore, the economy should be allowed to take its own course without government interference. The invisible hand of the free market guiding the economy has led and will continue to lead to better outcomes for the entire society.

Additionally, because the government is run by the people and for the benefit of the people, the public's opinion should be taken into consideration. In a recent CNN poll, only 1% indicated that it affirms the right of eminent domain for private economic development. While the poll doesn't display everyone's opinion, it is a good indicator of the attitudes of American citizens (Source G).

Clearly, eminent domain shouldn't be invoked for economic development by   6
private developers. It should be limited to the construction of public services. However,
this debate over property rights, and in a sense, individual rights versus the greater
good, will continue for years to come as the conditions and outlooks of the American
people change.

Rating the Essays

Student A
This is a high-range essay for the following reasons:

- Opening forcefully catches the reader's attention and immediately identifies the subject
- Brings the reader into the conversation with the rhetorical question
- Presents a brief overview of both sides of the debate
- Integrates sources smoothly into the text of the essay
- Uses proper citations
- Utilizes transitions
- Exhibits control of language, for example: parallel structure, punctuation, parenthetical statements, and diction
- Recognizes the opposite position—"Some might say . . ."
- Employs irony to comment on textual material
- Incorporates not only sources, but also provides pertinent comments to develop the argument
- Presents a succinct and straightforward final point
- Presents a true voice

Student B
This is a mid-range essay for the following reasons:

- Clearly takes a position on the issue
- Uses appropriate evidence
- Clearly incorporates sources into the text
- Cites the opposition (paragraph 4)
- Presents a personal opinion (paragraph 4)
- Develops a clear organizational pattern
- Uses good transitions
- Develops a final paragraph that makes a clear statement
- Uses a matter-of-fact voice
- Accomplishes the task demanded by the prompt

Rapid Review

- Read ALL information in the prompt.
- Carefully read and annotate the prompt and the given texts.
- Choose your position on the issue.
- Choose suitable texts from among those given to support your position (choose at least three).
- Plan your essay.
- Write your essay in the allotted time.
- Check your essay to make certain you have cited your sources.
- Proofread.

STEP 4

Review the Knowledge You Need to Score High

CHAPTER 8

Comprehensive Review—Analysis

IN THIS CHAPTER

Summary: Examine structure, purpose, and style as evidenced in the modes of discourse

Key Ideas

✪ Learn the language of analysis and how to use it.

✪ Acquaint yourself with rhetorical strategies.

✪ Learn how selection of detail, subject matter, diction, and syntax contribute to style.

✪ Learn how topic adherence and connective tissue unify your essay.

✪ Understand the difference between active and passive voice.

Some Basics

What Is ANALYSIS?

For the AP English Language exam student, the definition of *analysis* is quite specific. It means that *you* are going to take apart a particular passage and divide it into its basic components for the purpose of examining how the writer develops his or her subject.

Are There Different Types of Analysis?

For the AP English Language exam, the *different types of analysis* include the analysis of structure, purpose, and style.

What Is *DISCOURSE*?

Discourse simply means "conversation." For the writer, this "conversation" takes place between the text and the reader. To communicate with the reader, the writer uses a particular method or combination of methods to make his or her idea(s) clear to the reader.

What Is *RHETORIC*?

Don't let professional jargon throw you. Rhetoric is basically an umbrella term for *all* of the strategies, modes, and devices a writer can employ to allow the reader to easily accept and understand his or her point of view.

What Is a *MODE OF DISCOURSE*?

Here's another piece of the lingo puzzle that you need not fear. Prose can be divided into FOUR primary categories. They are:

1. EXPOSITION: illustrates a point
2. NARRATION: tells a story
3. DESCRIPTION: creates a sensory image
4. ARGUMENTATION: takes a position on an issue and defends it

These are generally referred to as the *modes of discourse*. You should be able to distinguish among them but, do not become bogged down in worrying about these classes. They will be obvious to you. Being familiar with the professional terminology of this course is a way of beginning to develop a common vocabulary needed to discuss writing.

What Are *RHETORICAL STRATEGIES*?

Rhetorical strategies include example, contrast and comparison, definition, cause and effect, process, analysis/division, and classification. The writer may also employ descriptive and narrative strategies. These are the basic approaches a writer uses to tell a story, explain a point, describe a situation, or argue a position. (Modes of discourse, for those in the know.)

What Is the Analysis of *RHETORICAL STRUCTURE*?

Regardless of the length of a passage, the writer will employ one or more strategies to develop the purpose of the piece. Your job is to:

- Carefully read the passage
- Recognize and identify strategies used in the passage
- Determine how these strategies are utilized in the development of the author's purpose

After this, it is up to you to use your own rhetorical strategies to present the points you want to illustrate in your analysis. Remember, your primary purpose is to analyze the passage. In so doing, you will probably employ one or more of the rhetorical strategies, such as example, cause and effect, or contrast and comparison.

There Is So Much to Know, How Can I Prepare Myself for the Exam?

First, don't panic. You're in an AP English Language course, and you will have a year to become prepared. The work of this course centers on developing those analytical skills required by the AP English Language exam. In this chapter, we are going to provide you with a brief overview of the different rhetorical strategies. For each rhetorical strategy, we will do the following:

- define the term;
- cite examples;
- provide practice with analysis; and
- offer suggestions for writing your own AP essays using that strategy.

Rhetorical Strategies

Example

Definition: <u>Example</u> is a specific event, person, or detail of an idea cited and/or developed to support or illustrate a thesis or topic.

Here is an excerpt from Jane Jacobs's "A Good Neighborhood" that uses examples.

> *Perhaps I can best explain this subtle but all-important balance between people's desire for essential privacy and their wish to have differing degrees of contact with people in terms of the stores where people leave keys for their friends. In our family, we tell friends to pick up the key at the delicatessen across the street. Joe Cornacchia, who keeps the delicatessen, usually has a dozen or so keys at a time for handing out like this. He has a special drawer for them.*
>
> *Around on the other side of our block, people leave their keys at a Spanish grocery. On the other side of Joe's block, people leave them at a candy store. Down a block they leave them at the coffee shop, and a few hundred feet around the corner from that, in a barber shop. Around one corner from two fashionable blocks of town houses and apartments in the Upper East Side, people leave their keys in a butcher shop and a bookshop; around another corner they leave them in a cleaner's and a drug store. In unfashionable East Harlem, keys are left with at least one florist, in bakeries, in luncheonettes, in Spanish and Italian groceries.*

Practice with Analysis

1. Underline the thesis statement.

2. The topic/subject of the passage is _____.

3. The purpose of the passage is to _____.

4. Does the passage contain an extended example? _____

5. The passage contains how many examples? _____

6. Briefly list the examples. _____

7. The organization is ___ chronological ___ spatial ___ least to most important ___ most to least important.

Remarks About the Passage

This informative passage uses a lengthy list of examples to indicate informally the relationship between people and businesses in a neighborhood. There is no single extended example, but rather a series of more than eight examples.

It's a good idea to actually mark up the passage as you answer the analysis questions. It will give you practice and help this process to become second nature to you.

Contrast/Comparison

Definition: <u>Contrast/comparison</u> is a method of presenting similarities and differences between or among at least two persons, places, things, ideas, etc. The contrast/comparison essay may be organized in several ways including:

- Subject by subject—Subject A is discussed in its entirety and is followed by a full discussion of Subject B.
- Point by point—A major point related to Subject A is examined and is immediately followed with a corresponding point in Subject B.
- Combination—In a longer essay, the writer may employ both of the preceding strategies.

Here is an example of a passage that uses contrast/comparison from W. H. Auden's "Work, Labor, and Play."

> *Between labor and play stands work. A man is a worker if he is personally interested in the job which society pays him to do; and that which society views as necessary labor, is from his own point of view voluntary play. Whether a job is to be classified as labor or work depends, not on the job itself, but on the tastes of the individual who undertakes it. The difference does not, for example, coincide with the difference between a manual and a mental job; a gardener or a cobbler may be a worker; a bank clerk, a laborer. Which a man is can be seen from his attitude toward leisure. To a worker, leisure means simply the hours he needs to relax and rest in order to work efficiently. He is therefore more likely to take too little leisure than too much; workers die of coronaries and forget their wives' birthdays. To the laborer, on the other hand, leisure means freedom from compulsion, so that it is natural for him to imagine that the fewer hours he has to spend laboring, the more hours he is free to play, the better.*

Practice with Analysis

1. The topic/subject of the passage is _____.

2. Underline the thesis statement.

3. The purpose of the passage is to _____.

4. The items being compared/contrasted are _____.

5. One example of a comparison in the passage is _____.

6. One example of contrast in the passage is _____.

7. The pattern of development is ____ opposing ____ alternating.

8. The organization is ____ subject to subject ____ point by point ____ combination.

Remarks About the Passage

As with most of your AP contrast/comparison selections, the emphasis is on distinction and contrast. In this passage, the author uses a pattern of alternating points that develops the contrast between work, labor, and leisure.

Cause and Effect

Definition: <u>Cause and effect</u> establishes a relationship: B is the result of A. The cause-and-effect essay can emphasize the cause or the effect, or can treat both equally. It can detail a single cause with many effects, or several causes with a single effect, or any combination.

The organization can present the cause or the effect first. All of this depends upon the intent of the writer. Depending on his or her purpose, the writer can choose to present the most important idea in the beginning, middle, or end. The author can also choose from myriad strategies to develop the cause and effect, such as:

- facts
- statistics
- authorities
- anecdotes
- cases
- real or imagined scenarios

It should be noted that, in some cases, the successful writer of a cause-and-effect essay anticipates and addresses reader objections and/or questions.

Here is an example of a passage using cause and effect from Thomas Hobbes's "Of the Natural Condition of Mankind" (1651).

> *From this equality of ability arises equality of hope in the attaining of our ends. And therefore if any two men desire the same thing, which nevertheless they cannot both enjoy, they become enemies; and in the way to their end (which is principally their own conservation, and sometimes their delectation only), endeavor to destroy or subdue one another. And from hence it comes to pass that where an invader has no more fear than another man's single power, if one plant, sow, build, or possess a convenient seat, others may probably be expected to come prepared with forces united to dispossess and deprive him, not only of the fruit of his labor, but also of his life, or liberty. And the invader again is in like danger of another.*

Practice with Analysis

1. Underline the thesis statement.

2. The topic/subject of the passage is _____.

3. The purpose of the passage is to _____.

4. List the causes. _____

5. List the effects. _____

6. The emphasis is on ____ cause ____ effect ____ causes ____ effects.

7. The passage makes use of ____ statistics ____ facts ____ authorities ____ anecdotes ____ cases ____ real/imaginary scenarios.

Remarks About the Passage

The entire focus of this paragraph is on the singular result of one person's envy for the possessions of another. If both cannot possess it, envy ensues, which leads to dispossession and/or violence.

Classification

Definition: Classification separates items into major categories and details the characteristics of each group and why each member of that group is placed within the category. It is possible to divide the categories into subgroups. The principle of classification should be made clear to the reader. (This is the umbrella term under which everything fits.)

Here is a passage that makes use of classification from Jane Howard's "All Happy Clans Are Alike."

> . . . *If blood and roots don't do the job, then we must look to water and branches, and sort ourselves into new constellations, new families.*
>
> *These new families, to borrow the terminology of an African tribe (the Bangwa of the Cameroons), may consist either of friends of the road, ascribed by chance, or friends of the heart, achieved by choice. Ascribed friends are those we happen to go to school with, work with, or live near. They know where we went last weekend and whether we still have a cold. Just being around gives them a provisional importance in our lives, and us in theirs. Maybe they will still matter to us when we or they move away; quite likely they won't. Six months or two years will probably erase each from the other's thoughts, unless by some chance they and we have become friends of the heart. . . . [Those] will steer each other through enough seasons and weathers so that sooner or later it crosses our minds that one of us . . . must one day mourn the other.*

Practice with Analysis

1. The topic/subject of the passage is _____.

2. Underline the thesis statement.

3. The purpose of the passage is to _____.

4. Identify the principle of division/classification. _____

5. List the main subgroups. _____

6. Cite the major characteristic(s) of each subgroup. _____

Remarks About the Passage

This passage briefly details two classes of friends, one by chance and the other by choice. The thesis given at the beginning of the excerpt is stated in general terms that lead the reader to the specific classifications.

Process

Definition: <u>Process</u> is simply "how to" do something or how something is done. Process can have one of two purposes. It can either give instructions or inform the reader about how something is done. It is important to understand that a clear process presentation must be in chronological order. In other words, the writer leads the reader step by step, from beginning to end, through the process. A clear process essay will define necessary terms and will cite any precautions if needed.

Here is a passage that makes use of process from L. Rust Hills's "How to Care for and About Ashtrays."

> *To clean ashtrays the right way, proceed as follows. Take a metal or plastic or wooden (but never a basket) wastebasket in your left hand, and a paper towel in your right. Approach the ashtray that is to be cleaned. Put the wastebasket down on the floor, and with your released left hand pick up the ashtray and dump its contents of cigarette ends, spent matches, and loose ashes (nothing else should be in an ashtray!) into the wastebasket. Then, still holding the ashtray over the basket, rub gently with the paper towel at any of the few stains or spots that may remain. Then put the ashtray carefully back into its place, pick up the wastebasket again, and approach the next ashtray to be cleaned. It should never be necessary to wash an ashtray, if it is kept clean and dry.*

Throughout its whole lifetime in a well-ordered household, an ashtray need never travel more than three feet from where it belongs, and never be out of place at all for more than thirty seconds.

Practice with Analysis

1. Underline the thesis.

2. What is the topic/subject? _____

3. The general purpose is to ____ give specific directions ____ be informative.

4. List the major steps given in the selection. _____

5. Is the essay in chronological order? ____ yes ____ no

6. List any words that are defined. _____

7. Were there any other words that should have been defined? _____

_____

8. List any precautions given. _____

9. The process presented is ____ clear ____ unclear ____ complete ____ incomplete.

Remarks About the Passage

The formal tone of such a menial process makes this small paragraph a bit humorous. Its clearly developed ashtray cleaning process is quite complete and needs no added definitions nor precautions.

Definition

Definition: Definition identifies the class to which a specific term belongs and those characteristics which make it different from all the other items in that class. There are several types of definitions: physical, historical, emotional, psychological, and relationship(s) to others.

An essay of definition can be developed using any of the rhetorical strategies, and the writer should decide whether to be serious or humorous.

Here is a passage that uses definition.

BUGDUST

The dinner was fine, the play funny; let's hope my drive home will easily top off a relaxing and rewarding evening. What a surprise! Brightly perched on my car's windshield is a yellow ticket which not so brightly announces that I am being fined $50.00 for an expired parking meter. Grabbing the thing and choking it, I exclaim, "Bugdust!"

Now, let's be honest. This ticket is neither an insect, nor is it dirt. So, am I blind, ignorant or just plain crazy? I hope none of the above. The expletive, "Bugdust," is my personal substitute for the ever-popular, overused and vulgar, four letter curses. My background forces me to avoid these common, rude and inappropriate four letter words. And, heaven only knows that over the years I've had many occasions where I would have loved to use them. For much of my young life, when I found myself in a situation which cried out for some sort of exclamation, I usually reverted to RATS! or CRUMB! Really harsh curses, huh? However, years ago I came upon a substitute by sheer accident.

I was helping out in the kitchen at my sorority house. While chopping onions, I accidentally slipped and cut my thumb quite badly. I really needed a way to express my surprise, pain, and fear. Nothing inside my head would allow me to scream the usual expletives words. (By the way, I sincerely believe that a good deal of money spent on psychotherapy could have been saved had I been able to "just say IT.") In that nanosecond, I wanted, I demanded that my mind come up with something—anything—that I could use. My mind obviously obeyed and began working at a frantic pace. "I hate insects; I hate housework." My mind works in strange ways; it's really warped. (Hmm, that's a word I should also define.) Put two abominable conditions together. Voila! Murf's rule = one new expression = BUGDUST. What a mind!

The people around me during the birth of this little word-gem said, "What the *@#?! does that mean?" I had to stop for a second. They were right. What did it mean? It was not the incinerated remains of a roach colony. It was not the unkempt environs of a roach motel. It was a way for me to say that I was monumentally angry. It was also a way for me to say I was hurting. It was original and ME.

Years have passed. And, so today . . .

It's 15°; it's snowing and icy; I'm cold. Let's shop. I join the rest of the universe at the supermarket. Heaven only knows one needs rice crispy treats in the house when it snows. What I don't need is the keys locked in my car. BUGDUST!

I'm doing 7 mph behind a 1965 Volkswagen Beetle being driven by its original owner. I miss the green light. I'm late for my dental appointment. BUGDUST!

And, into cyberspace . . . My computer just crashed. BUGDUST!

Practice with Analysis

1. Underline the thesis.

2. The topic/subject is _____.

3. The purpose is to _____.

4. The attitude of the writer is ____ serious ____ humorous.

5. To what class does the word being defined belong? _____

6. List the major rhetorical strategies used. _____

7. The definition is ____ historical ____ physical ____ emotional ____ psychological ____ relationship(s) to others.

8. Do you, as a reader, have an understanding of the definition presented? _____

9. Briefly state your understanding of the term. _____

Remarks About the Passage

The topic of the essay is the definition of the expletive *bugdust*. The thesis is the fifth sentence of the second paragraph. The primary purpose is to humorously narrate the invention of the word "bugdust." The rhetorical strategies used throughout the essay are example [paragraph 1] and anecdote [paragraphs 3 and 4]. The definition of *bugdust* is primarily emotional [last two sentences in paragraph 3 and the last two sentences in paragraph 4].

Now it's your turn. Write a paragraph that defines a favorite word that is special or unique to you or your friends or family. Choose an attitude and go for it. When finished, ask yourself the same analytical questions you asked for the sample essay.

Narration

Definition: <u>Narration</u> is nothing more than storytelling. There is a beginning, a middle, and an end. Moreover, there's a point to it—a reason for recounting the story that becomes clear to the reader. There should be a focus to the story as well. For example, your point might be that lying gets you into trouble. To illustrate this, you might focus on an anecdote about the repercussions of a specific lie you told your parents. Narration requires a specific point of view, such as:

- 1st person
- 3rd person omniscient
- 3rd person objective
- Stream of consciousness

A narrative generally revolves around a primary tension and employs character, plot, and setting. The point the author is trying to make corresponds to the literary term *theme.* The development of a narrative may be extended and fully developed or brief to support or illustrate the subject of an essay.

The following excerpt from "Death of a Soldier" by Louisa May Alcott is an example of a narrative.

> *John was dying. Even while he spoke, over his face I saw a gray veil falling that no human hand can lift. I sat down by him, wiped drops from his forehead, stirred the air about him with a slow wave of a fan, and waited to help him die. For hours he suffered dumbly, without a moment's murmuring: his limbs grew cold, his face damp, his lips white, and again and again he tore the covering off his breast, as if the lightest weight added to his agony.*
>
> *One by one, the other men woke, and round the hospital ward appeared a circle of pale faces and watchful eyes, full of awe and pity; for, though a stranger, John was beloved by all. "Old boy, how are you?" faltered one. "Can I say or do anything for you anywheres?" whispered another.*
>
> *"Take my things home, and tell them that I did my best."*

Practice with Analysis

1. The topic/subject is _____.

2. The purpose is to _____.

3. The focus is _____.

4. The point of view is ____ first person ____ third person objective ____ third person omniscient ____ stream of consciousness.

5. The setting is _____.

6. The main character(s) is/are _____.

7. The gist of the plot is _____.

8. List the sequence of the major events (beginning, middle, end)

   _____

   _____

Remarks About the Passage

This brief excerpt is enough of a story to allow you to identify the basic narrative elements. Employing the first person point of view, Alcott provides a beginning, middle, and ending to this episode that occurs in a hospital ward. Focusing on the boy's death, the author illustrates the quality of John's character.

Description

Definition: <u>Description</u> is writing that appeals to the senses. It can be objective, which is scientific or clinical, or it can be impressionistic, which tries to involve the reader's emotions or feelings. Description can also be direct or indirect, and the organization can be as follows:

- Chronological
- Spatial
- Emphasizing the most important detail
- Emphasizing the most noticeable detail

To create his or her description, the writer can employ any or all of the following literary devices:

- Analogy
- Concrete, specific words
- Appeal to the senses
- Personification
- Hyperbole
- Contrast and comparison
- Onomatopoeia
- Other figurative language

The following excerpt from Charles Dickens's *Bleak House* uses description.

> *Fog everywhere. Fog up the river, where it flows among green aits and meadows; fog down the river, where it rolls defiled among tiers of shipping and waterside pollutions of a great (and dirty) city. Fog on the Essex marshes, fog on the heights, fog creeping into the cabooses of [coal barges]. Fog lying out on the yards, and hovering in the rigging of great ships; fog drooping on the gunwales of barges and small boats. Fog in the eyes and throats of ancient Greenwich pensioners, wheezing by the firesides of their wards; fog in the stem and bowl of the afternoon pipe of the wrathful skipper, down in his close cabin; fog cruelly pinching the toes and fingers of his shivering little 'prentice boy on deck. Chance people on the bridges peeping over the parapets into a nether sky of fog, with fog all round them, as if they were up in a balloon, and hanging in the misty clouds.*

Practice with Analysis

1. Underline the thesis.

2. The topic/subject of the passage is _____.

3. The description is ____ objective ____ impressionistic.

4. The passage contains examples of

   - ____ analogy, ex. _____
   - ____ concrete words, ex. _____
   - ____ imagery, ex. _____

- ___ contrast/comparison, ex. _____
- ___ personification, ex. _____
- ___ onomatopoeia, ex. _____
- ___ other figurative language, ex. _____

5. The intended effect is to _____.

Remarks About the Passage

In its appeal to the senses, this loaded passage about fog contains about every descriptive device possible to re-create the almost palpable scene for the reader.

About Style

> *Note:* Although the style is a designated component of AP English Literature, it is impossible to analyze an author's presentation and purpose without discussing the many elements associated with what we call style.

What Is Style?

Ask yourself a question—What is the difference between two comedians who are familiar to you? They may both be funny, but in different ways. What makes one comedian's humor different from the other's is his distinctive style.

Consider the following:

- Subject matter
- Language (diction)
- Pacing
- Selection of detail
- Presentation—body language
- Attitude toward the material
- Attitude toward the audience

This is what we call style. You do this all the time. You know Jennifer Lopez has a different style than does Adele.

If we were to give you two literary passages, you could probably tell which was written by Hemingway and which was written by Dickens. How would you know? Simple; you would use the same principles you considered with the two comedians:

- Subject matter
- Selection of detail
- Point of view
- Diction
- Figurative language/imagery
- Attitude
- Tone
- Pacing/syntax
- Organization

See how easy it is? The AP English Language and Composition exam expects you to be able to recognize and to explain how these elements function in a given passage.

How Do I Talk About Style?

You need to understand and to refer to some basic writing terms and devices. These include subject matter, selection of detail, organization, point of view, diction, syntax, language, attitude, and tone.

What follows is a brief review of each of these *elements of style*. In this review, we define each device, cite examples, and provide practice for you. (In addition, we have incorporated suggested readings and writing for you.)

Subject Matter and Selection of Detail

Since these two are dependent on each other, let's look at them together. Unlike the poor, beleaguered AP Comp student who is assigned a topic, each author makes a conscious decision about what he or she will write. (In most instances, so do you.) It is not hit or miss. The author wants to make a point about his or her subject and makes numerous conscious decisions about which details to include and which to exclude. Here's an example. Two students are asked to write about hamburgers. One is a vegetarian, and one is a hamburger fanatic. You've already mentally categorized the details each would choose to include in making his or her points about hamburgers. Got it? Selection of detail is part of style.

Note: Many authors become associated with a particular type of subject matter: for example, Mario Puzo with organized crime (*The Godfather*), Steven King with horror and suspense (*The Shining*), Upton Sinclair with muckraking (*The Jungle*). This, then, becomes part of their recognized style.

Think about a couple of your favorite writers, rock groups, singers, comedians, and so on and list their primary subjects and selection of details.

Organization

The way in which a writer presents his or her ideas to the reader is termed *organization*. You do this every day. For example, look at your locker. How are your books, jacket, gym clothes, lunch, and other things arranged in it? If someone else were to open it, what conclusion would that person draw about you? This is your personal organization. The same can apply to a writer and his or her work. Let's review a few favorite patterns of organization.

Writers can organize their thoughts in many different ways, including:

- Chronological
- Spatial
- Specific to general
- General to specific
- Least to most important
- Most to least important
- Flashback or fast-forward
- Contrast/comparison
- Cause/effect

As with your locker, an outside viewer—known here as the reader—responds to the writer's organizational patterns. Keep these approaches in mind when analyzing style. (You might want to make marginal notes on some of your readings as practice.)

Point of View

Point of view is the method the author utilizes to tell the story. It is the vantage point from which the narrative is told. You've had practice with this in both reading and writing. For AP Language purposes, here are a few examples:

- *First person:* The narrator is the story's protagonist. (I went to the store.)
  Here is an example from Charles Dickens's *The Personal History of David Copperfield.*

  > Whether I shall turn out to be the hero of my own life, or whether that station will be held by anybody else, these pages must show. To begin my life with the beginning of my life, I record that I was born (as I have been informed and believe) on a Friday, at twelve o'clock at night. It was remarked that the clock began to strike, and I began to cry, simultaneously.

- *Third person objective:* The narrator is an onlooker reporting the story. (She went to the store.)
  Here is an example from Sinclair Lewis's *Elmer Gantry.*

  > Elmer Gantry was drunk. He was eloquently drunk, lovingly and pugnaciously drunk. He leaned against the bar of the Old Home Sample Room, the most gilded and urbane saloon in Cato, Missouri, and requested the bartender to join him in "The Good Old Summer time," the waltz of the day.

- *Third person omniscient:* The narrator reports the story and provides information that the character(s) is unaware of. (She went to the store unaware that in three minutes she would meet her unknown mother selling apples on the corner.)
  Here is an example from Evan S. Connell's *Mrs. Bridge.*

  > Her first name was India—she was never able to get used to it. It seemed to her that her parents must have been thinking of someone else when they named her. Or were they hoping for another sort of daughter? As a child she was often on the point of inquiring, but time passed, and she never did.

- *Stream of consciousness:* This is a narrative technique that places the reader in the mind and thought process of the narrator, no matter how random and spontaneous that may be (e.g., James Joyce's *Ulysses*).
  Here is an example from William Faulkner's *As I Lay Dying.*

  > I dont know what I am. I dont know if I am or not. Jewel knows who he is, because he does not know that he does not know whether he is or not. He cannot empty himself because he is not what he is and he is what he is not. Beyond the unlamped wall I can hear the rain shaping the wagon that is ours . . . And then I must be, or I could not empty myself for sleep in a strange room. And so if I am not emptied yet, I am is.

- *Interior monologue:* This technique reflects the inner thoughts of the character.

Diction

Diction, also termed *word choice*, refers to the conscious selection of words to further the author's purpose. Once again, place yourself in the writer's position. How would you describe your date last weekend to your parents? Your peers? Yourself? We're guessing you used different words (and selection of details) for each audience. And, may we say, "good choice."

That personal note out of the way, a writer searches for the most appropriate, evocative, or precise word or phrase to convey his or her intent. The author is sensitive to denotation, connotation, and symbolic aspects of language choices.

<u>Diction is placing the right word in the right place.</u> It is a deliberate technique to further the author's purpose or intent. Diction builds throughout a piece so that ideas, tone, or attitude are continually reinforced. You should be able to identify and link examples of specific diction to the ideas, purpose, tone, or intent of the passage.

Let's Try Another

Here is the bare-bones outline of a paragraph.

> *Jonathan I. was a thin guy. He seemed to be smart when he spoke. He didn't smile, and he looked like he was really feeling down.*

Here's how Oliver Sachs actually wrote his paragraph in *The Case of the Colorblind Painter* about one of his patients.

> *When we first saw him, on April 13, 1986, Jonathan I. was a tall, gaunt man, showing obvious recent weight loss. He spoke intelligently and well, both analytically and vividly, but in a soft and rather lifeless voice. He rarely smiled; he was manifestly depressed. We got a sense of inner pain, fear, and tension, held in with difficulty beneath his civilized discourse.*

Now you highlight those changes in words/phrases that transform the tone and effect of the passage.

In this brief paragraph that describes Oliver Sachs's first meeting with his subject, we can easily see the effect of diction. Jonathan is not just thin. He is a series: *tall* and *gaunt* and, most importantly, showing *obvious* signs of *recent weight loss*. This begins to set the reader up for the possibility that Mr. I. is not well. Using *soft* and *rather lifeless* to describe his voice further strengthens the impression of a man who is ill. Sachs calmly lists what he sees and draws conclusions from these details which allow him to state that Jonathan is *manifestly depressed*.

See how the diction enriches the paragraph. Here, the reader begins to get a feeling for Sachs's patient.

> When writing your essay write, "Diction IS . . . " or "An example of Salinger's diction IS . . . ." Avoid saying, "Salinger *uses* diction." It is a little point, but it is one that indicates a mature writer is at work.

Figurative Language and Imagery

Imagery is the written creation of sensory experience achieved through the use of figurative language. Figurative language includes the following:

- Analogy
- Sensory description
- Poetic devices, which include:
  — metaphor
  — simile
  — hyperbole
  — onomatopoeia

— personification
— oxymoron
— metonymy
— synecdoche
— alliteration
— assonance
— consonance

As an example, here is a passage excerpted from Thoreau's *Walden*, Chapter 4, "Sounds."

> *I watch the passage of the morning cars with the same feeling that I do the rising of the sun, which is hardly more regular. Their train of clouds stretching far behind and rising higher and higher, going to heaven while the cars are going to Boston, conceals the sun for a minute and casts my distant field into the shade, a celestial train beside which the petty train of cars which hugs the earth is but the barb of the spear. The stabler of the iron horse was up early this winter morning by the light of the stars amid the mountains, to fodder and harness his steed. Fire, too, was awakened thus early to put the vital heat in him and get him off. If the enterprise were as innocent as it is early! If the snow lies deep, they strap on his snowshoes, and, with the giant plow, plow a furrow from the mountains to the seaboard, in which the cars, like a following drill-barrow, sprinkle all the restless men and floating merchandise in the country for seed. All day the fire-steed flies over the country, stopping only that his master may rest, and I am awakened by his tramp and defiant snort at midnight, when in some remote glen in the woods he fronts the elements incased in ice and snow; and he will reach his stall only with the morning star, to start once more on his travels without rest or slumber. Or perchance, at evening, I hear him in his stable blowing off the superfluous energy of the day, that he may calm his nerves and cool his liver and brain for a few hours of iron slumber. If the enterprise were as heroic and commanding as it is protracted and unwearied!*

Can you recognize the different examples of figurative language used in this paragraph? List several now.

Syntax

Risking your closing the book, we are going to use the dreaded "G" word—*grammar*. Grammar refers to the function of words and their uses and relationship in a sentence. Syntax is the grammatical structure of sentences. Without syntax, there is no clear communication. It is the responsibility of the author to manipulate language so that his or her purpose and intent are clear to the reader.

Note: When we refer to syntax in the context of rhetorical analysis, we are not speaking of grammatical correctness, but rather of the deliberate sentence structure the author chooses to make his or her desired point.

We assume that you are already familiar with the basics of sentence structure and are able to recognize and clearly construct:

- phrases;
- clauses;
- basic sentence types: declarative, interrogative, imperative, exclamatory;
- simple sentences;
- compound sentences;
- complex sentences;
- compound–complex sentences;

- periodic sentence;
- cumulative sentence; and
- rhetorical question.

We also assume that you have a good working knowledge of:

- punctuation,
- spelling, and
- paragraphing.

If you are in doubt about any of these, refer to the English handbook section of your composition textbooks. We also recommend *The Elements of Style* by Strunk and White. And, don't forget, your teacher is your major resource who can provide you with information and practice. Be honest with yourself. If you need help, get it early in the term.

Carefully read the following passage for *more practice with syntax.*

> *It struck eight. Bella waited. Nobody came.*
> *She sat down on a gilt chair at the head of the stairs, looked steadily before her with her blank, blue eyes. In the hall, in the cloakroom, in the supper-room, the hired footmen looked at one another with knowing winks. "What does the old girl expect? No one'll have finished dinner before ten."*
>
> — (*Mr. Loveday's Little Outing*; "Bella Gave a Party," Evelyn Waugh, 1936)

Did you notice the following syntactical elements and their effects in this selection?

- Short declarative sentences
  — Repetitiveness is like the ticking of a clock
  — Immediately introduces tension
- Simple declarative sentence beginning with subject/verbs
  — Parallel structure with phrases beginning with *in*
  — Pacing: clock ticking away time, uncaring
- Periodic sentence draws attention to the setting rather than the footmen
- Ends with a rhetorical question: reader drawn into the tension

You can see from just a brief analysis of the sentence structure of this passage that syntax plays an important role in the creation of character, setting, and tension.

> We recommend that you choose brief passages from works which you study in your AP Comp class and practice this process on them throughout the year.

Here is a sentence structure activity you can use to review creating sentences using coordination and subordination.

Consider the following set of sentences.

I write.
I have a writing problem.
The problem is wordiness.
This tendency leads me somewhere.
It leads me to my writing awkward sentences.
These sentences confuse my readers.
I must edit my writing.
I must be very careful.

Rewrite this set of simple sentences THREE different ways, with each new sentence containing ALL of the information given. Each new sentence is to emphasize a different simple sentence (main clause) given in the original set. Bracket the clause you are emphasizing in each new sentence.

> You might wish to work on this type of activity throughout the year with your class or with an AP Comp study group that you have formed.

Tone and Attitude

We are guessing that these terms have confused you, as indeed, they have confused our own students in the past. Both terms refer to the author's perception and presentation of the material and the audience.

Tone, which often reinforces the mood of a piece, is easy to understand. Think of Edgar Allen Poe and the prevailing mood and tone of a short story such as "The Telltale Heart." There is no doubt that the single effect of this story is macabre horror, which clearly establishes the tone.

An author's attitude is not just the creation of a mood. It represents the stance or relationship the author has toward his or her subject. This type of analysis may require that you "read between the lines," which is the close reading of diction and syntax.

There are some basics for you to consider when determining tone and attitude.

The author can indicate several attitudes toward the reader:

- Talking down to the reader as an advisor
- Talking down to the reader as a satirist
- Talking eye-to-eye with the reader as an equal
- Talking up to the reader as a supplicant or subordinate

The attitude may also be formal or informal.

- Formal tends to use diction and syntax that are academic, serious, and authoritative.
- Informal is more conversational and engages the reader on an equal basis.

In "The Telltale Heart," it is fairly obvious that the diction and syntax help to create a macabre tone. At the same time, Poe's highly academic and mature diction and syntax create a formal attitude as he relates his tale to his reader as an equal.

Jonathan Swift in "A Modest Proposal" presents a satiric attitude as he speaks down to (instructs) his audience. Likewise, Charles Lamb in "A Dissertation on Roast Pig" engages his reader with an informal attitude in his satire.

If you want to see a subservient or subordinate attitude, see Chief Seattle's speech in our Practice Exam 1, essay question 2. Here, you will see how he employs diction and syntax to create a mocking humility that would serve his greater purpose.

The following is a list of adjectives often used to describe tone and attitude in a literary work. Feel free to add your own appropriate words.

bitter	objective	idyllic
sardonic	naïve	compassionate
sarcastic	joyous	reverent
ironic	spiritual	lugubrious
mocking	wistful	elegiac
scornful	nostalgic	gothic
satiric	humorous	macabre

vituperative	mock-serious	reflective
scathing	pedantic	maudlin
confidential	didactic	sentimental
factual	inspiring	patriotic
informal	remorseful	jingoistic
facetious	disdainful	detached
critical	laudatory	angry
resigned	mystified	sad
astonished		

> Be aware that tone and attitude are frequently described using a *pair* of words in the multiple-choice section of the AP English Language and Composition exam. For example: *bitter and disdainful*. Both adjectives must apply for the choice to be correct.

What follows is a set of activities that can provide practice in recognizing and analyzing tone and attitude. We suggest you try them as you progress through your AP Comp course. Consider the following passages:

Passage A

I am looking at a sunset. I am on the rim of the Grand Canyon. I have been on vacation for the past two weeks which I have been planning for over a year. I have always wanted to visit this geographic location. There are many people also looking at the same sight that I see. This is the first time I have witnessed this place and this event. There are many varied colors while this sunset is taking place. The sun disappears behind the Canyon walls, and darkness comes quickly after that.

Passage B

It was Monday morning. The sun was out, and I walked into the meeting. I was expecting to find some new people there. They were. I was introduced to them. The room was warm. Coffee was served. The meeting began, and the subject was our budget for the next year. There was discussion. I did not agree with many of the people there. A vote was taken after a period of time. The new budget was passed.

Passage C

I am looking at the new Wondercar. I am trying to decide whether or not to purchase or lease this car. It offers ABS, four-wheel drive, a V-8 engine, and the following extras: CD player, AC, power windows, door locks, etc., tinted glass, heated leather seats, a cellular phone, and luggage and ski racks. I would like the color forest green. The purchase price is $48,500. The monthly leasing payment after a $6,000 down payment would be $589.00 for three years.

Using your knowledge of tone, rewrite each of the above passages so that a specific tone is evident to your reader. Identify that tone/attitude. Once you have written the new passage, highlight those changes in diction and syntax which help you to create the tone and attitude you wanted.

Here is another activity that will allow you to practice your skills in analyzing tone and attitude:

Locate reviews of films, music, plays, cars, sports events, or teams—anything you can find that has been reviewed or criticized. These reviews can come from newspapers and/or periodicals you locate in an actual publication, or they can be from a *real* newspaper or periodical with articles posted on the Web. We suggest that you cut them out or print them out from the Internet.

Under each review:

- Cite the source and the date of the review
- State the *tone* the reviewer has
- Underline those words and/or phrases (*diction*) used in the review that support and/or develop this *tone*

As an extra practice, you might try this. Follow the directions above. Only this time, you will be collecting the reviews for only *one* film, sports event, and so forth. Let's see. You could try the *New York Times*, *USA Today*, the *Wall Street Journal*, *Time*, *Newsweek*, *People*, or *Entertainment Weekly*. Of course, you may know of others. Terrific; feel free to use them.

Again, try this with your class or study group. The more the merrier.

The following may serve as a final look at our review of style. We have been taking a rather concentrated look at some of the components of what the experts call "literary" style. As you know, two of the major components of style are: (1) the types of sentences an author chooses to use (*syntax*); and (2) word choice (*diction*). Below is a sample paragraph that provides some further practice with these two areas. *This is the first, bare-bones draft.*

> *Last night was chilly. I went into New York City. I went to see a reading of a play. It was a new play. It was a staged reading. It was read at the Roundabout Theater. The Roundabout Theater is on Broadway. It is on the corner of 45th Street. The play was written by Ruth Wolf. She writes about historical people. This play is about Mary Shelley. She was the wife of Percy Bysshe Shelley. Percy B. Shelley was a poet. He is a very famous Romantic poet. Mary Shelley wrote books. She wrote* Frankenstein. *Many people know this novel. Many people really like the story. There were more than 200 people there. The play was long. It had two acts. It takes place in France and Italy. It also takes place in heaven and hell. There are three main characters. One character is Mary Shelley. One character is Percy B. Shelley. One character plays the archangel and the devil. There is a lot of talking. There is little action. I liked the talking. I wished there was more action. It is called a comedy. Many of the scenes were not comical. The play could not make up its mind. I do not think it will be produced.*

1. Now, using your knowledge of syntax and diction, rewrite this paragraph using coordination, subordination, phrases, and so forth.
2. Once you have written a revised paragraph, work with someone and REWRITE it in a **new and different** way.

Here's an example of one way to revise the passage.

> *Last night, I went into chilly New York City to see a staged reading of a new play at the Roundabout Theater on the corner of 45th and Broadway. Ruth Wolf, who is known for her productions about historical figures, has written a play about Mary Shelley, the wife of the Romantic poet Percy Bysshe Shelley. Many people know Mary Shelley as the author of the popular novel* Frankenstein. *The play takes place in France, Italy, heaven, and hell with main characters Mary herself, Percy B. Shelley, and an archangel who doubles as the devil. The drama contains much dialogue and very*

little action, which I sorely missed. Billed as a comedy, this play seemed to be unable to make up its mind between being a comedy or a serious tragedy. Because of this problem, I don't believe this play has a real chance of being produced.

The "Connective Tissue" Issue

Throughout this book, we use the term *connective tissue*. For us, this "tissue issue" has four components. The most obvious refers to transitions between paragraphs or sections of a piece. The other three are not as readily recognizable as is transition, but you need to know that they play a major role in the coherence of a written work. The mature reader and writer will learn to recognize and employ these elements:

- Transition—indicates a logical connection between ideas
- Subject consistency—the subjects of the main clauses in a sequence of sentences are consistent (inconsistency is often the result of passive voice)
  Example: no: The <u>photography</u> was by Ansel Adams. <u>I</u> have always been a fan of this great photographer. The <u>temptation</u> to buy the photo due to the price was quite strong.
  yes: <u>I</u> have always been a fan of the great photographer Ansel Adams. Because of the price of one of his photographs, <u>I</u> was tempted to buy it.

- Tense consistency—the use of the same tense throughout the selection
  Example: no: When I have driven to work, I always used the same route.
  yes: I always use the same route when I drive to work.

- Voice consistency—use of the active voice and avoidance of the passive voice when possible
  Example: no: The bear was seen when Tim opened the door.
  yes: Tim opened the door and saw the bear.

Note: Another method of creating cohesion and topic adherence is the use of "echo words" or synonymous words or phrases throughout the selection.

Those authors you recognize as good writers are skilled at building connective tissue. You should be able to recognize it and to employ it in your own work.

<u>The following is a guide to transitional words and phrases.</u>

Most often used and most "natural" transitions in sentences or brief sequences of sentences:

- and
- but
- or
- nor
- for
- yet

Some other commonly used transitions between paragraphs or sections of longer works:

- Numerical: first, second, third, primarily, secondly, and so forth
- Sequential: then, finally, next
- Additional: furthermore, moreover, again, also, similarly
- Illustrative: for example, for instance, to illustrate
- Contrast, comparison, alternative: on the other hand, nevertheless, conversely, instead, however, still
- Cause and effect: therefore, consequently, as a result, accordingly
- Affirmation: of course, obviously, indeed

Here is an activity that will provide practice with transitions. Using one of your essays, highlight all of the transitions and complete the following:

The following are the *transition words/phrases* that I have used to connect each paragraph to the one before it.

1: _____

2: _____

3: _____

4: _____

5: _____

6: _____

7: _____

8: _____

9: _____

10: _____

If you find that you are missing a needed transition between paragraphs, indicate that on the appropriate line that corresponds to that paragraph. Then, write the needed transitional word or phrase.

> *Note:* This practice activity should be one which you do as often as possible. You may wish to do this type of editing with your class or study group. No matter how you do it, just DO IT.

Voice: Pen, Paper, Action!

Writing is a living process. Good writing moves the reader clearly from point to point. Voice and pacing play a major role in this process. Subjects are responsible for their actions. In the context of rhetorical analysis, the *first type of voice* is that "picture" of yourself as a writer that you consciously try to create for your reader. Just how do you want your reader to "see" and "hear" you: as confident, mature, knowledgeable, witty, reverent, friendly, caring, audacious . . . ? What? This first type of voice is the result of all of the elements that make up **style**.

And, one of those components is the *second type of voice*. This type of voice refers to *active* or *passive voice*, which simply is the relationship between the subject and its verb. Almost every instructor or writer who teaches says one thing—"Use ACTIVE voice."

Just What Is ACTIVE VOICE?

To answer this question, look at the following sentences:

> *The ball was thrown by Jessica.*

1. What is the subject? _____

2. What is the verb tense? _____

3. Is the verb simple or compound? _____

4. What is the prepositional phrase? _____

5. How many words are in the sentence? _____

Jessica threw the ball.

1. What is the subject? _____

2. What is the verb tense? _____

3. Is the verb simple or compound? _____

4. Is there a prepositional phrase? _____

5. How many words are in the sentence? _____

Which of the two sentences has the subject of the sentence doing the action? ____
Which one has the subject being acted upon? ____

> When the writing lets the reader know that the subject is *doing the acting*, you have ACTIVE VOICE. When the subject is acted upon or is the goal of the action, and, therefore, NOT responsible, you have PASSIVE VOICE.

With this information, now identify which of the two sentences above is active and which one is passive. Without doubt, we know you chose the second as active and the first as passive. Good for you.

Here's another example:

The treaty was signed last night.

Who signed the treaty? Whom do we blame if the treaty fails? We don't know, do we? Passive voice avoids responsibility. It is a primary tool of those who want to obfuscate or of those who lack confidence and decisiveness. Why not give the true picture and write:

Last night, the president of the United States and the president of Mexico signed a mutual defense treaty.

Here's a practice activity for you.

The huge red building was entered at the sound of the bell. Instructions were yelled at us by a mean-looking old lady. A crowd of six-year-olds was followed down a long hallway, up some steps, and down another corridor by me clutching my lunchbox. Mrs. Nearing's room was looked for. Our destination was reached when we were loudly greeted by a tall, black-haired woman. A tag was pressed to my chest after my name was asked and a tag was printed by her. Several big six-year-olds could be seen inside the room by me. The door was closed with a loud bang. The glass near the top of the door was kept from shattering by a network of wires. The wires were observed to be prison-like. So, back in school was I.

You should have noticed that every sentence is written in the passive voice. Awkward and tedious, isn't it? Now, it's your turn. Rewrite this passage by simply changing all of the passive constructions into active voice.

Compare Your Revision with Ours

At the sound of the bell, I entered the huge, red building with hundreds of other kids. Just inside the entrance, a mean-looking old lady yelled instructions at us. I clutched my lunchbox and followed a crowd of other six-year-olds down a long hallway, up some steps, and down another corridor as we looked for Mrs. Nearing's room. I knew we had reached our destination when a tall, black-haired woman loudly greeted us. She asked me my name, then she printed it on a sticky tag and pressed it to my chest. Once inside the room, I could see several other kids my age, some of them BIG. Finally, Mrs. Nearing closed the door with a loud bang. A network of wires kept the glass near the top of the door from shattering. These wires looked like the bars of a prison to me. I was back in school.

Have you noticed that many sentences written in passive voice contain a prepositional phrase beginning with *by*? That *by*-phrase immediately following the verb (usually compound) can be a clue that you have passive voice at work in the sentence. GET RID OF IT, if you can.

Note: There are times when you deliberately want to use passive voice, but it should be a very conscious choice on your part. Here are four questions to ask yourself.

- Do you want to avoid stating who/what is responsible for an action?
- Is there a specific goal or effect that you wish to emphasize?
- Do you want to create a "special effect"?
- Do you want to sound "academic" and avoid using the dreaded "first person" responsibility?
- If you can answer a loud "yes" to any or all of these questions, then you may decide to employ passive voice.

Let's hear your voice—loud and clear! Take responsibility for what you think, say, and write. This is your voice. It is the real you. Give it life. Don't suffocate it.

Pacing

Pacing is the "movement" of a literary piece from one point to another. The primary component of pacing is syntax: sentence length, sentence type, and punctuation. There are several ways to add variety and pacing to your writing by:

- using a mixture of sentence types, known as sentence variety;
- using the rhetorical question;
- using the imperative sentence;
- using the exclamatory sentence; and
- varying the beginnings of sentences.

For example, if you were to compose a brief paragraph about writing an AP English Language and Composition essay, you could write:

I like to write essays for AP Comp class. I like to think through an idea, and I like to try out different approaches to discussing an idea. My AP teacher gives us lots of time to prepare our essays. He gives us a topic. Then, he has us do an outline and then a first draft. We have our first draft read by a member of our peer group. I do my revision after this. I also read my essay aloud to someone. Then, I'm ready to hand it in to my instructor for grading.

Note that all the sentences begin with subject and verb. All the sentences, except for the second one, are simple. The second is no more than a compound sentence made up of two very simple main clauses. Do you feel the tediousness and immaturity of this paragraph? There is *nothing* grammatically wrong with any of the sentences. However, would you be happy with this paragraph if you had written it? Something is missing, and that something has to do with *pacing*.

Rewrite this paragraph so that there is a variety of sentences and sentence beginnings. How does your revision compare with ours?

> Because I like to think through ideas and try different approaches to presenting an idea, I really enjoy my AP Comp class. Another reason for my enjoying writing essays is my AP teacher's approach to composition. For him and, therefore, for us, writing is not a quick, hit-or-miss assignment. After we choose a topic, Mr. Damon allows plenty of time for preparation, which includes outlining, writing the first draft, and reading by our peer groups. It is only after completing these steps that I revise and write the final draft I will submit for grading. It's a good plan.

A Few Words About Coherence

Coherence is accepting your responsibility as a writer to "deliver the goods." Your reader has expectations you are obliged to meet.

- Basically, the reader looks for some kind of announcement as to what is to follow (the thesis, assertion, claim).
- Near the end of the introduction, the reader expects to find some hints about the major points that you will discuss in your piece of writing.
- The body of the presentation will develop the discussion of each major point.
- The reader will expect to be led logically from one major point to another via "connective tissue."
- The reader expects some sort of final comment or remark, not a summary. Among the many possibilities, this final "point" could be:
  — an interpretation of the significance of the points of your discussion;
  — a prediction;
  — an anecdote;
  — a question; or
  — a quote.

Make certain that your ending/conclusion is related to your discussion. Don't introduce new or irrelevant ideas or comments. Also, make sure that the final comment is consistent in tone and attitude with the rest of the paper.

Just as the reader has particular expectations of you as a writer, YOU have expectations when you read the writing of others and when you complete a rhetorical analysis of another's written work. Ask the very same questions that are asked of you.

An Essay Editing and Revision Template

We are going to provide you with a template for editing and revision that we recommend you use throughout the year for your own essays. The more you use this template for your own writing, the more comfortable you will be when it comes to analyzing the writing of others. It will become almost second nature to you.

Before you begin to write the revised draft of your essay, respond to each of the following *carefully*. If possible, ask for input from your peers. Read aloud to each other. *Listen* to what you have written.

"For me, having an audience who gives me feedback is really important and helps me to see what needs to be revised."
—Jessica K.,
    AP student

The title of my essay is _____.

I will organize my essay using (a rhetorical strategy) _____.

The thesis of my essay is in the _____ paragraph.

My intended tone/attitude is _____.

I have used the following rhetorical devices/elements to create this tone:

_____ in paragraph _____ _____ in paragraph _____

_____ in paragraph _____ _____ in paragraph _____

_____ in paragraph _____ _____ in paragraph _____

_____ in paragraph _____ _____ in paragraph _____

_____ in paragraph _____ _____ in paragraph _____

_____ in paragraph _____ _____ in paragraph _____

_____ in paragraph _____ _____ in paragraph _____

_____ in paragraph _____ _____ in paragraph _____

The following are the *transition words/phrases* I have used to connect each paragraph to the one before it.

1: _____

2: _____

3: _____

4: _____

5: _____

6: _____

7: _____

8: _____

9: _____

10: _____

I use the _____ tense as the predominant tense in my essay.

I have checked the verbs in each of my paragraphs. They are *all* in the predominant tense *except*:

1: _____ (tense) _____ Reason for using this tense is _____. (You must do this with each paragraph and with each verb.)

I have _____ sentences in my essay. _____ of them begin with the subject. _____ of them begin with a participle phrase. _____ of them begin with a relative clause. _____ of them begin with an adverbial clause. _____ of them begin with a prepositional phrase. _____ of them begin with an infinitive. _____ of them begin with a gerund.

I have _____ simple sentences in my essay; _____ compound sentences; _____ complex sentences; _____ compound-complex sentences.

I think I need to add more sentence variety to my presentation. _____ yes _____ no

I have made certain that there is a variety of sentence structures in my essay. _____ yes _____ no

My conclusion _____ *is* _____ *is not* a summary of what I have already said in my essay. If it is not a summary, identify the type of ending you have created. _____
_____

I have discussed this inventory of my first draft with _____. These are the suggested areas for improving my essay:

The *major* things I have to work on when I revise my essay are:

Rapid Review

- Analysis is the deconstruction of a passage into its components in order to examine how a writer develops a subject.
- The AP English Language exam requires the analysis of structure, purpose, style.
- Discourse is conversation between the text and the reader.
- Rhetoric is a term for all of the strategies, modes, and devices a writer employs.
- There are four major modes of discourse:
  — exposition
  — narration
  — description
  — argumentation
- Rhetorical strategies are used to develop the modes of discourse:
  — example
  — comparison and contrast
  — definition
  — cause and effect
  — process
  — analysis
  — classification
- Practice each of the rhetorical strategies.
- Style is the unique writing pattern of a writer.
- Style comprises:
  — subject matter
  — selection of detail
  — organization
  — point of view
  — diction
  — syntax

— language
— attitude
— tone
- Practice with stylistic devices.
- Review words that describe tone.
- Review "connective tissue":
  — transition
  — subject consistency
  — tense consistency
  — voice consistency
- Practice using active and passive voice.
- Practice recognizing pacing in professional writing and in your own essays by sentence variety:
  — construction
  — openings
  — types
- Utilize rubrics to gauge your essays.

CHAPTER 9

Comprehensive Review—Argument

IN THIS CHAPTER

Summary: Experience why everything is an argument. Examine the process for presenting a position that others will understand and accept.

Key Ideas
✪ Learn the format for the basic argumentative essay.
✪ Learn the difference between deduction and induction.
✪ Become familiar with logical fallacies.
✪ Practice reading and evaluating an argument.

Some Basics

What Is ARGUMENT?

In its broadest sense, all writing is argument. It is the presentation and defense or support of a specific thesis, assertion, or claim. This thesis can be a strongly held belief, a critical view of an issue, a presentation of an insight, a search for the truth, or even a description of that mountain view that moved you to tears that you hope others will share. To convince the reader to accept the position, the writer provides support using objective facts or logical evidence, and sometimes, even emotional appeals.

You can find argument almost anywhere: from ads in your favorite magazine or on television to academic journals, from "*Peanuts*" to political cartoons, from letters to the editor of *Sports Illustrated* to editorials in the *New York Times*, and from a plea to your parents to a president's speech to the nation. Possibly the only writing that is not an argument is a piece that offers no support for a claim.

What Is the Difference Between Argument and Persuasion?

The intended results of each of these strategies is where the difference lies. ALL persuasion is a type of argument. The goal of an argument is to have you accept the writer's thesis. However, with persuasion, after you've accepted the position of the writer, the goal is to have you get moving and *do something*. For example:

ARGUMENT: Walking is necessary for good health.

PERSUASION: I want you to walk every day for good health.

What Does the AP Expect Me to Be Able to Do with an Argumentative Essay?

Most frequently, the AP exam will present you with a prompt that could be:

- A brief excerpt
- A quotation
- A statement
- An anecdote

You will then be directed to take a position regarding:

- Author's position
- Statement's main idea
- Narrative's main point
- A collection of statements or quotations

Other types of argumentative prompts will ask you to:

- Write an essay indicating which idea among a given set is more valid
- Explore the validity of an assertion

No matter which type of argumentation prompt is given, the AP expects you to be able to:

- Take a position on the issue or situation
- Support your position using your own experience, reading, and/or observations

How Do You Argue a Point or Position?

Basically, support for your position on an issue should be rational and logical, not emotional. It should be objective rather than biased (one-sided). This support can be developed using any of the rhetorical strategies and devices we've reviewed for you in Chapter 8.

The classical formula for an argument is:

1. Present the issue/situation/problem.
2. State your (writer's) assertion/claim/thesis.
3. Support your claim.
4. Acknowledge and respond to real or possible opposing views.
5. Make your final comment or summary of the evidence.

The order of the presentation can be varied, and any of the rhetorical strategies can be employed. You must make certain that your support/evidence is appropriate and effective.

The Argument

Your argument can be:

- **Ethical**—an appeal to the reader's good sense, goodwill, and desire to "do the right thing"
- **Emotional**—an appeal to the reader's fear, patriotism, and so forth
- **Logical**—an appeal to inductive and deductive reasoning
    - *Induction*: forming a *generalization* from a set of specific examples. (Example: Margo has 17 stuffed teddy bears, 3 stuffed cows, 11 monkeys, 4 camels, and 6 stuffed elephants. Margo loves to collect stuffed animals.)
    - *Deduction*: reaching a probable *conclusion* based on given premises. A *premise* is a proposition that is proven or taken for granted. (Example: All high school seniors at this high school must write a research paper. Sean is a senior at this high school. Therefore, Sean must write a research paper.)

Be aware that conclusions can be drawn from implicit premises. These can include:

- Universal truths
- Possibilities that the reader will readily accept
- Familiar sayings
- Facts that everyone, including the reader, knows

Deduction uses the syllogism. A **syllogism** is the format of a formal argument that consists of a

Major premise:	*All A are C.*	*"All lions are cats."*
Minor premise:	*B is A.*	*"Leonard is a lion."*
Conclusion:	*Therefore, B is C.*	*"Leonard is a cat."*

You could also say, "Because Leonard is a lion, he is a cat." In this instance, you have suppressed one of the premises. However, you are confident that most people would agree that all lions are cats. Therefore, you would feel confident in leaving out that premise. But, you must be very careful, because you could end up with what we call a **logical fallacy**.

Logical fallacies are mistakes in reasoning and fall into several categories.

- *Non sequitur argument:* This Latin phrase means "does not follow." This is an argument with a conclusion that does not follow from the premise. (Example: Diane graduated from Vassar. She'll make a great lawyer.)
- *Begging the question:* Here is a mistake in which the writer assumes in his or her assertion/premise/thesis something that really remains to be proved. (Example: Taking geometry is a waste of time. High school students should not be required to take this course.)
- *Circular reasoning:* This mistake in logic restates the premise rather than giving a reason for holding that premise. (Example: I like to eat out because I enjoy different foods and restaurants.)
- *Straw-man argument:* Here is a technique we've all seen and heard used by politicians seeking election. The speaker/writer attributes false or exaggerated characteristics or behaviors to the opponent and attacks him on those falsehoods or exaggerations. (Example: You say you support allowing people under eighteen to drive alone. I'll never be able to understand why weak-willed drivers like you are willing to risk your life and the lives of all other drivers with these crazy teenagers on the road.)

- *Ad hominem argument:* This literally means to "argue against the man." This technique attacks the person rather than dealing with the issue under discussion. (Example: We all know Sam has several speeding tickets on his record. How can we trust him to vote for us on the issue of a trade agreement with Europe?)

- *Hasty generalization:* A person who makes a hasty generalization draws a conclusion about an entire group based on evidence that is too scant or insufficient. (Example: The veterinarian discovered a viral infection in five beagles. All beagles must be infected with it.)

- *Overgeneralization:* This is what we call stereotyping in most cases. Here, the writer/speaker draws a conclusion about a large number of people, ideas, things, etc. based on very limited evidence. (Example: All members of group A are not to be trusted.) Words such as *all, never, always,* and *every* are usually indicative of overgeneralization. It's best to use and to look for qualifiers (*some, seem, often, perhaps, frequently,* etc.) that indicate that the writer has an awareness of the complexities of the topic or group under discussion.

- *Post hoc argument:* This fallacy cites an unrelated event that occurred earlier as the cause of a current situation. (Example: I saw a black cat run across the street in front of my car five minutes before I was hit by a foul ball at the ball park. Therefore, the black cat is the cause of my bruised arm.)

- *Either/or argument:* With this fallacy, the writer asserts that there are only two possibilities, when, in reality, there are more. (Example: Tomorrow is April 15; therefore, I must mail in my tax return, or I will be arrested.)

There are several other categories of logical fallacies, but these are the most frequently encountered.

> During the year, carefully read editorials or ads in the print media. Check to see if you can locate any logical fallacies. It might be beneficial to do this with your class or study group.

The following activities provide you with some practice with induction, deduction, and analogy.

Induction: If induction is the process that moves from a given series of specifics to a generalization, these are the possible problems:

- The generalization covers many unobserved persons, objects, etc.
- If the conclusion begins with ALL, any exception would invalidate the generalization.
- Cited facts are incorrect.
- Assumed connections are incorrect.
- Assumption is a conclusion NOT supported by the evidence.

Practice:

A. Write a conclusion for the following:
   1. Television network USBC's drama series won this year's Emmy for Best Dramatic Series.
   2. USBC won the Emmy for Best Comedy Series.
   3. USBC won the Emmy for Best Talk Show.

4. *Therefore,* _____.

Are there any possible weaknesses in your conclusion?

B. Carefully read the following and briefly explain the possible error in the conclusion.
   1. The 43rd U.S. president is a Yale graduate.
   2. The 42nd U.S. president was a Yale Law School graduate.
   3. The 41st U.S. president was a Yale graduate.
   4. The last seven presidents were college graduates.
   5. *Therefore,* the president of the U.S. must have a college degree.

Deduction: If deduction is the process of moving from a general rule to a specific example (A = B; C = B; Therefore, C = A.), these are the possible problems:

- Not *all* of the given A falls into the given B category. There are exceptions.
- The given category B is incorrect.
- The second statement is *not* true or is incorrect. Therefore, the conclusion is invalid.
- The truth of the third statement is in question.

Practice:

A. Carefully read the following. Assume that statements 1 and 2 are true. Briefly state the possible error of the conclusion.
   1. Some Japanese cars are made in the United States.
   2. Toyota is a Japanese car.
   3. *Therefore,* all Toyotas are made in the United States.

B. Carefully read the following. Assume that statements 1 and 2 are true. Briefly state the possible error of the conclusion.
   1. No eagles are flamingos.
   2. All flamingos are birds.
   3. Therefore, no eagles are birds.

Analogy: If analogy is an argument based on similarities, these are the possible problems.

- Accepting the totality of the analogy by never questioning that there are differences between/among the items being compared that could invalidate the argument or conclusion.
- Exaggerating the similarities.

Practice:

A. Briefly identify the analogy in the following:

Both the doctor and the teacher must have special knowledge. People select their own doctors; therefore, people should be allowed to pick their own teachers.

B. Briefly explain the mistake in the following:

Both 2-year-olds and 10-year-olds have two legs, two eyes, two ears, and two arms. Ten-year-olds can read and write. Therefore, 2-year-olds should be able to read and write.

Reading the Argument

In the multiple-choice section of the AP English Language exam, you are asked to read several selections, many of which are argumentative. Remember two very important points. No matter how brief or how lengthy the text is:

1. There is a rhetorical context with a
   - writer
   - occasion or situation
   - audience

Any good argument will effectively utilize and address each of these elements.

2. Don't make the mistake of evaluating an argument based simply on who wrote it. Don't confuse the messenger with the message.

With this in mind, your task is to read the given text critically and to:

- Determine who the speaker is, what the situation is, and who the audience is.
- Identify the position of the speaker.
- Check off the points made in support of the assertion.

You can easily accomplish these three tasks by highlighting, underlining, checking, making marginal notes, or even outlining (if you have time). Once you have completed your initial reading, you need to ask yourself several questions. In the case of the actual AP English Language and Composition exam, your test makers will ask you the questions based on these points.

1. Are there any judgments in the presentation?
   — Evidence is needed to support judgments.

2. Recognize that fact is <u>not</u> the same as interpretation.
   — Fact: You know it with certainty and can verify it.
   — Interpretation: An explanation of the meaning and/or importance of a specific item.

   You must be able to distinguish between the two.

3. Distinguish between literal and ironic statements. Recognizing the difference between these two terms can save you from misreading the text.
   — Ironic: Saying the opposite from what you really mean, as in satire.
   — Clues to be aware of: diction, subject, selection of detail.
   — Literal: What you read is what is the reality.

4. Do not evaluate an argument based on its form. Look at the content. It's easy to be misled by "fabulous" writing.

Below is a checklist that functions as a rubric for the evaluation of any rhetorical argument.

— A clearly developed thesis is evident.
— Facts are distinguished from opinions.
— Opinions are supported and qualified.
— The speaker develops a logical argument and avoids fallacies in reasoning.

— Support for facts is tested, reliable, and authoritative.
— The speaker does not confuse appeals to logic and emotion.
— Opposing views are represented in a fair and undistorted way.
— The argument reflects a sense of audience.
— The argument reflects an identifiable voice and point of view.
— The piece reflects the image of a speaker with identifiable qualities (honesty, sincerity, authority, intelligence, etc.).

As practice, read the following editorial, which appeared in a recent teachers' newsletter.

> *Misters King and Prince could not have picked a more ironic day to have their anti-teacher tirade printed in* Today's News *than on Tuesday, January 13. Here were Matt King, executive director of the conservative magazine* The Right Position, *and Ray Prince, the chief economist for the conservative Small Business Conference, showing their poisonous fangs in their hissy-fit against the state's teachers' union and the state's education department.*
>
> *Here were two cobras from the antiteacher snake pit posturing about the need to end tenure and to create charter schools. These, said the two vipers, are among the steps "needed to revitalize education in our area and across the state." Later in their column, they continued with "declining student performance in recent years" is indicative of poor teaching quality.*
>
> *May I direct King and Prince to pages A5 and A28 of this very same* Today's News *edition. In this article were the names of 74 (4 of them from New High School) Intel competition semifinalists out of a total of 144 in our state. With about 50% of the state's semifinalists, this and our neighboring county had MORE winning contestants and MORE participants than any other region in the country. This is MORE than half the national total of 300 . . . [and] "more than six times as many as the second-ranked state, which had 21 semifinalists and the third-ranked state, which had 19."*
>
> *Hmmm . . . now, let me think. Which speaks more loudly about teacher quality and student motivation: the negative nagging of King and Prince or the positive professionalism and performance represented by the Intel story? I daresay—no contest. And, this type of professional proficiency and dedication is part and parcel of the standards and goals of ALL our state teachers.*
>
> *They would have to count the extraordinary number of national, state, and local awards our professionals and their pupils have earned. They would have to count the number of scholarships, volunteer hours, and AP courses our students have amassed. They would have to listen to a litany of academic awards, associations, and degrees with which our teachers are connected. They would have to read the hundreds of thank-you letters former students have written to their teachers.*
>
> *They would have to acknowledge that their scaly agenda needs to be shed.*
>
> *Rather than casting a "shadow over education" in this state, our teachers shine a bright light on the snake pits created by ignorance and negativity.*

Let's Use the Argument Checklist on This Editorial

1. The <u>thesis</u> is that Mr. King and Mr. Prince are incorrect about their position to end tenure and create charter schools. These two are wrong when they say "our area needs to revitalize education."

2. <u>Facts are distinguished from opinion</u>. Facts include the number of Intel scholarships in paragraph 3; the comparison of the writer's area with other school districts in paragraph 3, and the number of awards, etc. associated with the writer's school. Opinion is obvious in the analogy established between Mr. King and Mr. Prince and snakes.

3. Some <u>opinions are supported and others are not</u>. In some cases, numbers are cited, and in other cases, generalizations are used.

4. The editorial <u>avoids fallacies in most instances</u>. However, the emotional appeal and arguing from analogy is present.

5. The <u>editorial is developed using induction</u>. A possible fallacy here revolves around whether or not what is true about one school district may be true about all other school areas or for all teachers and students.

6. The <u>facts used come from current newspapers</u>. The writer cites statistics and gives the source. The comparison between New High School and other schools and school districts is based on statistics and facts.

7. The author uses <u>both logic and emotion</u>. The facts and statistics are given in separate paragraphs. Emotional and analogical aspects of the argument are in opinionated sections of the editorial.

8. The <u>opposing views</u> of King and Prince are presented to illustrate the position of the columnists factually.

9. The <u>audience</u> is obviously teachers and those involved in education.

10. The <u>point of view</u> of the writer is clearly negative toward King and Prince and positive toward the condition of education in the writer's school district and state.

11. The editorial reflects a writer who is sincere, angry, confident, and willing to find support for the assertion.

Note: Each of these statements about the given editorial could also be turned into a multiple-choice question. Keep in mind that the writers of the AP English Language and Composition exam are aware of all of the preceding information and will base their questions on the assumption that you are also familiar with it and can recognize the elements of argument when you read them.

Writing the Argument

While the multiple-choice section of the exam will present you with specific questions about specific texts, the argumentative essay in the second section of the test requires that you compose *your own argument* based on a given excerpt, quotation, statement, or anecdote.

You will have to plan and write your argument knowing that the AP reader will be evaluating your presentation based on the major points we have just reviewed.

How Should I Go About Writing My Argument?

We invite you to compose an argumentative essay based on the following prompt. We will take you through the prewriting process.

> *In a recent* USA Today *op-ed piece, titled "Poor Suffer from Lack of Internet Access," Julianne Malveaux stated, "While the Internet has hardly caused the gap between the [lower and higher rungs on the economic ladder], it is one of the many things that have made the gap greater."*
>
> —(Julianne Malveaux, *USA Today*, June 22, 2001)

In an effective, well-organized essay, defend, challenge, or qualify Ms. Malveaux's assertion.

The Planning/Prewriting Process

What follows is an example of the prewriting process that addresses the given prompt.

1. Reread the prompt and highlight important terms, ideas, etc.
2. *Take a position.* Defend "it is one of the many things that have made the gap greater."
3. *My topic is:* Internet is one cause of the widening gap between the haves and the have-nots.
4. *My thesis statement is:* I agree with Julianne Malveaux when she states that access to the Internet has widened the gap between the haves and the have-nots.
5. *I will develop my argument using:*
   —personal anecdote
   — specific examples of the gap (at least three)
   — statistics and facts that I can remember from the news, and other sources
6. The *specifics I will use to support my assertion are*:
   (Make certain examples are introduced, discussed, and linked to my thesis.)
7. I will use the *inductive* technique to develop my argument.
8. I will *end my argument* with the image of a single child with her nose against a window peering into a room filled with children using computers. The child outside is not alone. Behind her are many, many others, and they all look as if they are growing more and more anxious and angry at being left outside.

This planning took about 10 to 12 minutes to develop. Based on this planning, writing the essay is easy. As a class assignment or as personal practice, you would:

- Write your first draft
- Have the initial argument checklist completed by one of your peers
- Complete your second draft
- Complete the revision activity either by yourself or with a member of your peer reading group

If you have practiced this process throughout the year or semester, when the AP English Language exam rolls around, you will find this kind of writing second nature to you.

Rapid Review

- Argument can be ethical, emotional, or logical.
- Inductive reasoning forms generalizations.
- Deductive reasoning reaches conclusions based on given premises.
- A premise is a proven proposition or one that is taken for granted.

- A syllogism is the format of a formal argument:
  — All A is C.
  — B is A.
  — Therefore, B is C.
- Logical fallacies are intended or unintended errors in reasoning.
- Rhetorical fallacies are used to manipulate the audience.
- Read editorials and ads to try to locate any fallacies that may be present.
- Do practice exercises with induction and deduction and analogy.
- All argument has a rhetorical context: the writer, the occasion, and the audience.
- When reading arguments, locate judgments and find supporting evidence.
- Be certain to recognize and to separate fact from interpretation.
- Evaluate the argument according to the given rubrics.
- When writing an argument, make certain to:
  — address the prompt
  — take a position
  — state your thesis
  — develop your position with evidence

CHAPTER 10

Comprehensive Review—Synthesis

IN THIS CHAPTER

Summary: Examine the synthesis purpose and process, including the prompt.

Key Ideas

✪ Practice with reading and evaluating different types of texts from various mediums, including graphics.

✪ Work with summary, paraphrase, and inference.

✪ Learn different approaches to incorporating sources into the text of your essay.

Some Basics

What Is the Synthesis Essay?

Synthesis is the process in which you, as the writer, develop a thesis and, in the course of developing this thesis,

- you investigate a variety of sources, both print and visual;
- you choose which of these sources to include in your presentation;
- you respond to these sources and discuss how they relate to your position on the topic.

Note: A well-respected and experienced Advanced Placement English instructor, Jodi Rice, uses the following example to clarify the idea of *synthesis*: You're having a dinner party, and you consult two recipes you've been given and use bits of each to create your own, new dish. You let your dinner guests know that you invented the dish, but that you used and combined recipes from your grandmother and from the newspaper. You don't take credit for those two recipes, but you <u>do</u> take credit for what you did with them.

In the case of the AP Language exam, you only have time to write a first draft, and it must be clear, organized, logical, and thoughtful. In developing each of your major points, make certain to:

- Relate it to the thesis/claim
- Use specific examples (personal and otherwise)
- Use selected sources to support the major point
- Incorporate sources into the development of your point by using
  — Attribution and introduction of cited sources
  — Transitions
  — Mix of direct quotations, summary, and paraphrases

A Few Comments Before Beginning

Your AP Language class, as well as other courses across the curriculum, has taught you how to conduct, evaluate, and present research. You most likely have completed at least one research paper that required you to develop a thesis on a particular subject; to find, read, and annotate outside sources related to the topic; to determine which of the sources to use in support of your thesis; to incorporate these sources into your research paper; and to appropriately cite your sources.

If you've written this type of paper before, whether brief or lengthy, you're well on your way to being able to compose a successful synthesis essay.

The synthesis essay also requires you to be familiar with both **analysis** and **argument**. Because of this, we strongly urge you to review Chapters 5, 6, 8, and 9. Those skills needed to develop a successful essay of analysis or argument are requisites for composing a **synthesis** essay.

This chapter briefly reviews strategies and provides you with practice activities specifically related to writing the synthesis essay as it would most probably appear on the AP English Language exam.

Let's begin.

Note: We will use the synthesis prompt and sample essay from the Diagnostic Master exam (Chapter 3) as the basis for the following review segments.

Strategies

Strategy 1: Critical Reading of Texts

A word about the texts: The several texts you will be given for the synthesis prompt will be related to the topic, and you can be assured that each text has been evaluated and judged to be appropriate, of acceptable quality, and representing several points of view.

Critical reading of texts specifically for the synthesis essay demands that you determine the following:

- Purpose/thesis
- Intended audience
- Type of source (primary, secondary)
- Main points
- Historical context
- Authority of the author
- How the material is presented
- Type of evidence presented
- Source of the evidence
- Any bias or agenda
- How the text relates to the topic
- Support or opposition toward the thesis

Practice with Critical Reading

Our example: Here is a text provided in the Diagnostic Master exam's synthesis essay.

Source E

Broder, John M., "States Curbing Right to Seize Private Homes." *New York Times*, February 21, 2006.

The following passage is excerpted from an article published in the *New York Times*.

> "*Our opposition to eminent domain is not across the board,*" *he* [Scott G. Bullock of the Institute for Justice] *said. "It has an important but limited role in government planning and the building of roads, parks, and public buildings. What we oppose is eminent domain abuse for private development, and we are encouraging legislators to curtail it.*"
>
> *More neutral observers expressed concern that state officials, in their zeal to protect homeowners and small businesses, would handcuff local governments that are trying to revitalize dying cities and fill in blighted areas with projects that produce tax revenues and jobs.*
>
> "*It's fair to say that many states are on the verge of seriously overreacting to the* Kelo *decision,*" *said John D. Echeverria, executive director of the Georgetown Environmental Law and Policy Institute and an authority on land-use policy. "The danger is that some legislators are going to attempt to destroy what is a significant and sometimes painful but essential government power. The extremist position is a prescription for economic decline for many metropolitan areas around the county.*"

Our writer's critical reading of the passage provides the following information:

1. <u>Thesis</u>: ". . . What we oppose is eminent domain abuse for private development, and we are encouraging legislators to curtail it."
2. <u>Intended audience</u>: generally educated readers
3. <u>Main points</u>:
   A. qualified opposition to eminent domain
   B. opposed to eminent domain for private development
   C. acknowledges that there are those who see their position as handcuffing local officials
   D. Echeverria says, "The danger . . . " He fears legislation could destroy essential government power.

4. <u>Historical context</u>: 2006 in response to *Kelo* decision
5. <u>How material is presented:</u> Thesis + expert's direct quotation + acknowledgment of opposition + expert's direct quotation
6. <u>Type of evidence presented:</u> direct quotations of experts in the field
7. <u>Source of evidence:</u> expert opinions
8. <u>Any bias or agenda:</u> both sides of issue are presented
9. <u>How text relates to the topic:</u> specific statements for and against eminent domain
10. <u>Support or not for thesis:</u> one quotation supports a qualifying position: "I can empathize with the home owners affected by the recent 5:4 Supreme Court decision." The other quotation could be used to recognize those who would oppose it.

Note: This is a process that does not necessarily require that every point be written out. You could easily make mental notes of many of these items and jot down only those that you think you could use in your essay. You may prefer to annotate directly on the text itself.

Practice

Now, you complete a critical reading of another text from the Master exam on eminent domain.

Source C

Kelo v. New London. U.S. Supreme Court 125 S. Ct. 2655.
The following is a brief overview of a decision by the U.S. Supreme Court in 2005.

> Suzette Kelo, et al. v. <u>City of New London</u>, et al., *125 S. Ct. 2655 (2005)*, more commonly Kelo v. New London, *is a land-use law case argued before the <u>United States Supreme Court</u> on <u>February 22, 2005</u>. The case arose from a city's use of <u>eminent domain</u> to condemn privately owned real property so that it could be used as part of a comprehensive redevelopment plan.*
>
> The owners sued the city in Connecticut courts, arguing that the city had misused its eminent domain power. The power of eminent domain is limited by the <u>Fifth</u> and <u>Fourteenth Amendments to the United States Constitution</u>. The Fifth Amendment, which restricts the actions of the federal government, says, in part, that "private property [shall not] be taken for public use, without just compensation"; under Section 1 of the Fourteenth Amendment, this limitation is also imposed on the actions of U.S. state and local governments. Kelo and the other appellants argued that economic development, the stated purpose of the Development Corporation, did not qualify as public use.
>
> The Supreme Court's Ruling: This 5:4 decision holds that the governmental taking of property from one private owner to give to another in furtherance of economic development constitutes a permissible "public use" under the Fifth Amendment.

1. Purpose/thesis: _____

   _____

2. Intended audience: _____

3. Main points: _____

   _____

4. Historical context: _____

5. How material is presented: _____

6. Type of evidence presented: _____

_____

7. Source of evidence: _____

8. Any bias or agenda: _____

9. How text relates to topic: _____

_____

10. Support or opposition for my thesis: _____

What Types of Visual Texts Can I Expect on the AP Language Exam?

You can expect to encounter a variety of visual sources on the AP Language exam. They may include:

- Political cartoons
- Charts and graphs
- Posters
- Advertising
- Paintings
- Photographs

As with the steps involved in the critical reading of written material, visuals also require critical analysis. The following are steps you should consider when faced with a visual text:

- Identify the subject of the visual.
- Identify the major components, such as characters, visual details, and symbols.
- Identify verbal clues, such as titles, taglines, date, author, and dialogue.
- Notice position and size of details.
- Does the visual take a positive or negative position toward the issue?
- Identify the primary purpose of the visual.
- Determine how each detail illustrates and/or supports the primary purpose.
- Does the author indicate alternative viewpoints?

What Follows Is a Sample Critical Reading of a <u>Political Cartoon</u> Taken from the Master Exam

One type of text that could be used for the synthesis essay prompt on the AP English Language exam is the political cartoon. No, AP Language has not turned into a history or journalism course. But, it does recognize the variety of texts that can be created to advance or illustrate a particular thesis. The political cartoon does in a single- or multiple-frame presentation what would take hundreds of words in an essay, editorial, and so forth. It is a visual presentation of a specific point of view on an issue.

> *Note:* Even though the synthesis essay prompt may include political cartoons, or charts, or surveys, you are not required to use any of them. Your choice of texts depends on your purpose.

When dealing with a political cartoon, here are the specific steps to consider that are adapted from the critical reading of a visual.

- Identify the subject of the cartoon.
- Identify the major components, such as characters, visual details, and symbols.
- Identify verbal clues, such as titles, taglines, date, cartoonist, and dialogue.
- Notice position and size of details within the frame.
- Does the cartoon take a positive or negative position toward the issue?
- Identify the primary purpose of the cartoon.
- Determine how each detail illustrates and/or supports the primary purpose.
- Does the cartoonist indicate alternative viewpoints?

Notice that a political cartoon assumes the reader is aware of current events surrounding the specific issue. So, we recommend you begin to read a newspaper or news magazine regularly and/or watch a daily news program on TV. Even listening to a five-minute news summary on the radio as you drive to and from errands or school can give you a bit of background on what's happening in the world around you.

Example: Source D, political cartoon
The following political cartoon appeared in an Omaha, Nebraska, newspaper.

Jeff Koterba, *Omaha World Herald*, NE

1. <u>Subject of the cartoon:</u> eminent domain.
2. <u>Major components:</u> one chicken, one cow in a barnyard.
3. <u>Verbal clues:</u> Print size and form indicates the chicken is very excited, even panicked, while the cow is calm and unimpressed.
4. <u>Position and size of details:</u> The chicken and cow are drawn mostly to scale and perspectives with the chicken taking center stage.
5. <u>Position of the cartoonist:</u> Sees fears surrounding eminent domain as overexaggerated.

6. <u>Primary purpose of the cartoon:</u> Ridicule those who believe that all is lost if eminent domain remains in effect.

7. <u>How details illustrate the primary purpose:</u> Size and form of print indicates the chicken's state of mind. The sigh of the calmly chewing cow indicates its recognition of the chicken's silly warning. The chicken's last warning that says the cow is a threatening monster is just wrong and over the top.

8. <u>Indication of alternative viewpoints:</u> Yes, both sides are indicated.

As pointed out previously, each of these steps is important in understanding a political cartoon, but it is not necessary that you write out each of them every time you come across one in the newspaper, and so forth. Most of the analysis is done quickly in your mind, but when you are practicing techniques and strategies, it is most beneficial to write out, just as our writer did, each of the previous eight steps.

Practice critically reading political cartoons that you find in newspapers and news magazines. You might even try a few included in your history textbook.

Strategy 2: Selecting Sources

Once you've carefully read the prompt, critically read each of the given texts, and decided on your claim, you must choose which of the sources you will use in your essay. This choice is dependent on your answers to the following:

- What is your purpose?
- Is the text background information or pertinent information?
- Does the source give new information or information that other sources cover?
- Is this information that will add depth to the essay?
- Does this text reflect the viewpoints of any of the other texts?
- Does this text contradict the viewpoints of any of the other texts?
- Does the source support or oppose your claim?

Our writer has to make some important decisions about the seven texts provided in the Master synthesis essay prompt. As the writer answers each of the previous questions, he or she will decide which texts to use in the essay.

<u>My purpose:</u> to qualify the support and opposition to eminent domain
<u>Background information:</u> *Constitution* (Source A) *Kelo* decision (Source C)
<u>Pertinent information:</u> *60 Minutes* (Source B), Broder (Source E), Survey (Source G)

A helpful technique to answer the next several questions is to construct a quick chart that incorporates all of the sources at once. The following is a sample of such a chart.

SOURCE	TYPE OF INFO	ADDS DEPTH	REFLECTS VIEWS OF OTHER TEXTS	SUPPORT OF CLAIM
A	Primary and covered by Sources C and E	Yes	No	Yes and no
B	Covered by Sources C–G	Yes	Yes	Yes
C	Covered by Sources A, D, E	Yes	Yes, Sources D, G	Yes and no
D	Covered by Sources A, C	Not really	Yes, Sources A, C	Yes and no
E	Covered by Sources B, F, G	Yes	Yes, Sources B, F, G	Yes and no
F	Covered by Sources B, E, G	Not really	Yes, Sources B, E, G	Yes and no
G	Covered by Sources B–F	Yes	Yes, Sources B–F	Yes

There certainly is a great deal of information to gather and consider. The good news is that the more practice you have with this process, the more quickly you will be able to complete the task. Writing the answers to the previous questions for each of the given texts is a good practice technique for you. But, when it comes to a timed writing situation, you will be annotating the given texts as you read them and jotting down brief notes that reflect the type of thinking our writer performed previously. You will NOT have time to write answers to each question for each text. <u>But, you WILL be thinking about them as you read and as you plan.</u>

Practice responding to these questions using editorials, letters to the editor, and editorial cartoons that revolve around current events issues in which you have an interest. Don't ignore your school and local newspapers, and columnists in news magazines and newspapers. **Become an informed reader and citizen!**

After carefully considering each of the given texts, our reader has decided to eliminate both political cartoons because neither seems to add much depth. The other five sources can be used to develop a position.

Strategy 3: Choosing Which Parts of the Selected Texts to Use

Pay no attention to those texts you have eliminated. For those sources you have chosen to include in your essay, do the following:

- Review the notes/highlights on each of your chosen passages.
- Ignore those items you have not annotated.
- Determine if each excerpt contributes to the development of your thesis.
  — Identify the major point each will support.
  — Does it strengthen your position or not (if not, ignore it)?
  — How much of the excerpt will you use?
  — Why have it in your essay?
  — What comments can you make about it?

For example: You might construct a chart such as the following:

SOURCE:	A	B	C	F	G
	–Use all of excerpt	–City ¶ 1	–ID Kelo case ¶ 1	–Bullock "." 1st line in title	Survey ID
	–Use in Intro	–Background ¶ 1	–Summary in ¶3	–Echeverria"." Line 1, ¶3	–Major result lines 1 & 2
		–1st "." ¶ 2			
		–Mayor's position"." ¶7			
		–Blighted ¶8			

Our writer now has a clear idea of what part(s) of each text to use. The next task is to plan the essay. The following are some planning notes:

INTRO: *Background*
              Basic prompt info
              My room when grandmother visits
              My position—qualify

> POINT 1: Kelo *decision* + *Saleets (oppose current ruling)*
> *Saleets' mayor (supports ruling)*
> *My comments*
> POINT 2: *Broder* = *Bullock & Echeverria (both qualify and for ruling)*
> *Survey*

With this brief outline in mind, our writer knows where to place each of the chosen excerpts. If this were a class situation that allotted time for prewriting plans, more details would be possible when constructing the outline.

Note: Our writer chose to jot down a brief outline, but could have chosen to plan the essay in a number of different ways, such as:

- Mapping
- Charting

As we stated earlier in this chapter, for the AP English Language exam, you only have time to write a first draft, and it must be clear, organized, logical, and thoughtful. In developing each of your major points, make certain to:

- Relate it to the thesis/claim
- Use specific examples (personal and otherwise)
- Use selected sources to support the major point
- Incorporate sources into the development of your point
  — Attribution and introduction of cited sources
  — Transitions
  — Mix of direct quotations, summary, and paraphrases

A Note About Summary, Paraphrase, and Inference

No doubt you have been constructing summaries, paraphrases, and inferences as you learned the techniques of close reading and research. As a quick review, here are the definitions of these processes and an example of each. If you have any further questions, we strongly recommend you ask your instructor for clarification and further examples and/or practice.

Summary

If you want to summarize a text, you read closely and locate those key words and/or phrases that enable you to <u>reduce the piece into its essential point</u>(s).

Example: The previous *New York Times* article by Broder

Number of words in given text: 175

Number of key words underlined: 47

<u>Summary based on the key words and phrases:</u> *For many, the debate about eminent domain centers around opposing local governments using it to seize private property for private development or supporting eminent domain because cities face economic disaster without this necessary power.* (34 words)

Comments: The writer has whittled the original down by more than 73 percent to its essential point.

Practice this strategy on newspaper or magazine articles that you read regularly.

Note: Many online databases provide abstracts of longer articles when you perform a search. You might want to seek these out and read them to see how they are constructed to emphasize only the main points of the articles (Jodi Rice).

Paraphrase

To paraphrase a given text or part of a text, you transpose the original material into your own words. This will probably be close to the number of words in the original. In most cases, you need to cite the original.

Example: The first paragraph in the previous Source C

Paraphrase: Kelo v. New London *is an eminent domain case that was presented to the U.S. Supreme Court in February of 2005. The argument centered around New London using the power of eminent domain to seize private property so that it could be sold and used in the redevelopment of a section of this city (Source C).*

Comments: The original contains 67 words and two sentences, and the 54-word paraphrase is also two sentences long. Our writer has eliminated specific court numbers and the day of the month and combined several phrases into briefer and more direct ones. **Because this background on the *Kelo* case is NOT common knowledge and because our writer is NOT a recognized expert in this field, a citation is necessary.**

Practice this technique on sections of your own course textbooks and on newspaper or magazine articles you read regularly. You might also try to paraphrase the Master exam synthesis prompt itself, both the introduction and the assignment.

Inference

An inference is the process of drawing a conclusion based on specific material. By carefully considering the important information provided in the text, the reader reaches a conclusion or makes a judgment.

Example: Source B given in the synthesis essay prompt

Inference: *Considering the amount of time given to the Saleets as compared to the mayor of their town, one could conclude that 60 Minutes is more inclined to side with the homeowners over the local government in this eminent domain confrontation.*

Comments: Seven out of the ten paragraphs in this interview are positively related to the Saleets or their problem. The rhetorical question and answer given by the voiceover in paragraph five is indicative of the position of *60 Minutes*, and the diction used to describe both sides of the issue is more favorable toward the position of the Saleets.

Practice making inferences based on editorials or letters to the editor that you find in your local newspapers. Go a step further. Take a close look at ads you find in the magazines you read regularly and draw some conclusions about their purpose, their intended audience, and the specific way the ads are presented. Remember, you must be able to support each of your inferences from specifics found in the text itself.

Strategy 4: Incorporating Sources into the Text of Your Essay

Let's be realistic. The synthesis essay is not just a list of direct quotations from sources related to the topic. Once you have chosen your passages, you need to place them appropriately and interestingly within the actual text of your essay in the order that you've planned to best support your thesis/claim.

Just how do you do this? You could select from among the following techniques:

Direct quotation—full citation provided at beginning of the sentence

> *John Broder, in his February 21, 2006,* New York Times *article titled "States Curbing Right to Seize Private Homes," quotes Scott G. Bullock of the Institute for Justice: "Our opposition to eminent domain is not across the board . . . What we oppose is eminent domain abuse for private development, and we are encouraging legislators to curtail it."*

Direct quotation—citation placed outside the text

> *In a* 60 Minutes *interview presented on July 4, 2004, Jim Saleet, a homeowner being adversely affected by the current eminent domain policy, stated, "The bottom line is this is morally wrong . . . This is our home . . . We're not blighted. . . . This is a close-knit, beautiful neighborhood" (Source E).*

Paraphrase of and direct quotation from the third paragraph—citation placed outside of the text

> *John D. Echeverria, an authority on land-use policy, sees a danger arising from legislatures doing away with many of the powers of eminent domain. For the Director of the Georgetown Environmental Law and Policy Institute, if this policy change takes place across the country, there is a real danger that many urban areas will experience "economic decline" (Source E).*

Combination of direct quotation and paraphrase—citation provided outside of text; note the use of the ellipsis

> *In 2005, a 5–4 Supreme Court decision in the* Kelo v. New London *case ruled that ". . . the government taking of property from one private owner to give to another in furtherance of economic development constitutes a permissible 'public use' under the Fifth Amendment" (Source C).*

Notice that each of the examples integrates the source material into the text. The information is not just plopped down on the page. Take a close look at how our writer integrates the second example into the following paragraph in his essay.

> *Contrary to what the Court sees as "permissible public use" (Source C), I believe that a government taking a person's home or business away and allowing another private individual or company to take it over goes against the idea of our private property rights. A good example of this is the situation in Lakewood, Ohio, where the mayor wants to condemn a retired couple's home in order to make way for a privately owned, high-end condominium and shopping mall. As Jim Saleet said in his interview with* 60 Minutes *presented on July 4, 2004, "The bottom line is this is morally wrong . . . This is our home . . . We're not blighted. . . . This is a close-knit, beautiful neighborhood." The Saleets, who have paid off their mortgage, should be allowed to remain there as long as they want and pass it on to their children. Here, individual rights should prevail.*

Comments: Our writer uses the sources to establish negative feelings toward the current policy. The writer then refers to the *Kelo* decision in a summary and proceeds to introduce the context of the Saleet reference with the transition phrase, "A good example of this is . . . " Cohesiveness is achieved by referring to Source C, which was previously cited in the essay. The actual quotation is incorporated into the text with an introductory dependent clause. Two related sentences follow that reemphasize the writer's own position.

Practice: As you read, become aware of HOW professional writers incorporate sources into their writing. Use these as models to practice incorporating outside sources into your own sentences and/or essays.

Note: You might want to take a close look at reviews of movies and books. In many cases, you will find they include direct quotations from the dialogue of the film or passages from the book.

Strategy 5: Writing the Conclusion

Our writer has used each of the excerpts in the body of the essay, EXCEPT for the survey information. Although this number is quite important, it does not fit into the development of the body paragraphs. Therefore, the writer decides to incorporate this survey result into the conclusion. It will contribute to a strong final statement. Following are three different ways to use the survey.

Direct quotation—citation after sentence

> *68% of survey respondents said that they "favored legislative limits on the government's ability to take private property away from owners . . ." (Source G).*

Direct quotation—citation within sentence

> *According to a survey conducted by CNN on July 23, 2005, 66% of those responding said "never" to the question, "Should local governments be able to seize homes and businesses?"*

Paraphrase—citation outside sentence

> *In recent polls conducted by both the* Washington Times *and CNN, over 60% said no when asked if local governments should be able to take over private homes and businesses (Source G).*

Carefully consider how this sentence is incorporated into the concluding paragraph.

> *Ultimately, I have to agree with the large majority of people who responded to recent polls conducted by both the* Washington Times *and CNN. When asked if local governments should be able to take over private homes and businesses, over 60% said "no" (Source G). But, I will have to be open to the possibility that public use and the greater good may, in some cases, be the only viable solution to a complicated problem.*

Comments: The source material is sandwiched between two effective sentences. The first presents our writer's position and leads the reader to the cited excerpt employed to make the point. The last sentence begins with the word "But," which indicates that the writer is qualifying the cited sources in this paragraph and throughout the essay.

Final Comment

Remember, you MUST establish a position, and each source you choose to use MUST support and develop your position.

Rapid Review

- Establish a position on the issue.
- Critically read all given texts and any introductory material provided.
- Annotate your sources using the critical reading guidelines.
- Select appropriate sources to support your position and purpose.
- Choose appropriate excerpts from each of the selected sources that can help develop the thesis.
- Summarize, paraphrase, and draw inferences from selected material.
- Make certain you properly cite each source you incorporate into the essay.
- Construct a conclusion that clearly states a strong final point.
- Proofread.

STEP **5**

Build Your Test-Taking Confidence

Practice Exam 1

Practice Exam 2

PRACTICE EXAM 1

ANSWER SHEET FOR MULTIPLE-CHOICE QUESTIONS

1. _____   19. _____   37. _____

2. _____   20. _____   38. _____

3. _____   21. _____   39. _____

4. _____   22. _____   40. _____

5. _____   23. _____   41. _____

6. _____   24. _____   42. _____

7. _____   25. _____   43. _____

8. _____   26. _____   44. _____

9. _____   27. _____   45. _____

10. _____   28. _____   46. _____

11. _____   29. _____   47. _____

12. _____   30. _____   48. _____

13. _____   31. _____   49. _____

14. _____   32. _____   50. _____

15. _____   33. _____   51. _____

16. _____   34. _____   52. _____

17. _____   35. _____   53. _____

18. _____   36. _____   54. _____

I _____ did _____ did not complete this part of the test in the allotted 1 hour.

I had _____ correct answers. I had _____ incorrect answers. I left _____ blank.

I have carefully reviewed the explanations of the answers, and I think I need to work on the following types of questions:

PRACTICE EXAM I
ADVANCED PLACEMENT ENGLISH LANGUAGE

Section I

Total Time—1 hour

Carefully read the following passages and answer the questions that follow.

Questions 1–10 are based on the following passage excerpted from Charles Dickens's *Pictures from Italy*.

Magnificently stern and sombre are the streets of beautiful Florence; and the strong old piles of building make such heaps of shadow, on the ground and in the river, that there is another and different city of rich forms and fancies, always lying at our feet. Prodigious palaces, constructed for defence, with small distrustful windows heavily barred, and walls of great thickness formed of huge masses of rough stone, frown, in their old sulky state, on every street. In the midst of the city—in the Piazza of the Grand Duke, adorned with beautiful statues and the Fountain of Neptune—rises the Palazzo Vecchio, with its enormous overhanging battlements, and the Great Tower that watches over the whole town. In its court-yard—worthy of the Castle of Otranto in its ponderous gloom—is a massive staircase that the heaviest wagon and the stoutest team of horses might be driven up. Within it, is a Great Saloon, faded and tarnished in its stately decorations, and mouldering by grains, but recording yet, in pictures on its walls, the triumphs of the Medici and the wars of the old Florentine people. The prison is hard by, in an adjacent court-yard of the building—a foul and dismal place, where some men are shut up close, in small cells like ovens; and where others look through bars and beg; where some are playing draughts, and some are talking to their friends, who smoke, the while, to purify the air and some are buying wine and fruit of women-vendors; and all are squalid, dirty, and vile to look at. "They are merry enough, Signor," says the Jailer. "They are all blood-stained here," he adds, indicating, with his hand, three-fourths of the whole building. Before the hour is out, an old man, eighty years of age, quarrelling over a bargain with a young girl of seventeen, stabs her dead, in the market-place full of bright flowers; and is brought in prisoner, to swell the number.

Among the four old bridges that span the river, the Ponte Vecchio—that bridge which is covered with the shops of Jewellers and Goldsmiths—is a most enchanting feature in the scene. The space of one house, in the center, being left open, the view beyond is shown as in a frame; and that precious glimpse of sky, and water, and rich buildings, shining so quietly among the huddled roofs and gables on the bridge, is exquisite. Above it, the Gallery of the Grand Duke crosses the river. It was built to connect the two Great Palaces by a secret passage; and it takes its jealous course among streets and houses, with true despotism: going where it lists, and spurning every obstacle away, before it.

1. The purpose of the passage is to
   A. condemn the squalor of Florence
   B. entice visitors to Florence
   C. praise the Grand Duke
   D. present the dichotomy existing in Florence
   E. reveal the author's worldliness

2. The primary rhetorical strategy used by the author is
   A. narration
   B. description
   C. analysis
   D. process
   E. argument

3. In developing his purpose, the author uses all of the following rhetorical devices except:
   A. spatial organization
   B. metaphor and simile
   C. comparison and contrast
   D. imagery
   E. chronological order

4. Which of the following lines contains an example of paradox?
   A. line 17
   B. lines 18–19
   C. lines 4–5
   D. lines 26–27
   E. line 29

5. The most probable function of the selected detail which focuses on the murder of the young girl by the old man (20–22) is
   A. to emphasize the brutality of the citizens
   B. to establish a tone of pathos
   C. to criticize the city's government
   D. to warn visitors about the dangers of the city
   E. to emphasize the contrasts evident in the city

6. The abrupt shift caused by a lack of transition between paragraphs 1 and 2 serves to do all of the following except:
   A. reemphasize the unexpected nature of murder
   B. reinforce the idea that there is no connection between the two paragraphs
   C. reinforce the element of contrast
   D. reinforce the author's style
   E. immediately whisk the reader to a place of safety away from the murder scene

7. What can be inferred from the following details taken from the passage
   — "small distrustful windows" (4)
   — "walls of great thickness" (5)
   — "enormous overhanging battlements" (8)
   — "secret passage" (29)
   A. Florence was not architecturally sound.
   B. Florence was designed to protect its artwork.
   C. Florence had experienced both warfare and intrigue.
   D. Florence was unsuited for habitation.
   E. Florence was preparing for war.

8. Lines 11–22 contain examples of which of the following rhetorical device?
   A. antithetical images
   B. anecdotal evidence
   C. parallel structure
   D. denotation
   E. inversion

9. If one were building a house of horrors, which of the following would be best suitable as a model or inspiration?
   A. Piazza of the Grand Duke (6–7)
   B. Fountain of Neptune (7)
   C. Palazzo Vecchio (8)
   D. Ponte Vecchio (23)
   E. Gallery of the Grand Duke (28)

10. Which of the following terms has most probably undergone a shift in meaning from Dickens's time to its current usage?
    A. "stately" (12)
    B. "squalid" (18)
    C. "enchanting" (24)
    D. "jealous" (29)
    E. "obstacle" (30)

Questions 11–20 are based on the following passage from Margaret Atwood's "Origins of Stories."

Our first stories come to us through the air. We hear voices.   1

Children in oral societies grow up within a web of stories; but so do all children.   2
We listen before we can read. Some of our listening is more like listening in, to the
calamitous or seductive voices of the adult world, on the radio or the television or in our
daily lives. Often it's an overhearing of things we aren't supposed to hear, eavesdropping
on scandalous gossip or family secrets. From all these scraps of voices, from the
whispers and shouts that surround us, even from ominous silences, the unfilled gaps in
meaning, we patch together for ourselves an order of events, a plot or plots; these, then,
are the things that happen, these are the people they happen to, this is the forbidden
knowledge.

We have all been little pitchers with big ears, shooed out of the kitchen when the   3
unspoken is being spoken, and we have probably all been tale-bearers, blurters at the
dinner table, unwitting violators of adult rules of censorship. Perhaps this is what writers
are: those who never kicked the habit. We remained tale-bearers. We learned to keep
our eyes open, but not to keep our mouths shut.

If we're lucky, we may also be given stories meant for our ears, stories intended for   4
us. These may be children's Bible stories, tidied up and simplified and with the vicious
bits left out. They may be fairy tales, similarly sugared, although if we are very lucky
it will be left in. In any case, these tales will have deliberate, molded shapes, unlike
stories we have patched together for ourselves. They will contain mountains, deserts,
talking donkeys, dragons; and, unlike the kitchen stories, they will have definite
endings. We are likely to accept these stories being on the same level of reality as the
kitchen stories. It's only when we are older that we are taught to regard one kind of
story as real and the other kind as mere invention. This is about the same time we're
taught to believe that dentists are useful, and writers are not.

Traditionally, both the kitchen gossips and the readers-out-loud have been mothers   5
or grandmothers, native languages have been mother tongues, and the kinds of stories
that are told to children have been called nursery tales or old wives' tales. It struck me
as no great coincidence when I learned recently that, when a great number of prominent
writers were asked to write about the family member who had the greatest influence
on their literary careers, almost all of them, male as well as female, had picked their
mothers. Perhaps this reflects the extent to which North American children have been
deprived of the grandfathers, those other great repositories of story; perhaps it will come
to change if men come to share in early child care, and we will have old husbands' tales.
But as things are, language, including the language of our earliest-learned stories, is a
verbal matrix, not a verbal patrix . . .

11. One reason Atwood gives for the presence of
stories in children's lives is
A. scandalous gossip
B. family secrets
C. supernatural influences
D. listening
E. radio and television

12. The close association between the reader and
the author is immediately established by
A. a first person, plural point of view
B. placing the reader into a family situation
C. using accessible diction and syntax
D. being emotional
E. appealing to the child in the reader

13. The last sentence of paragraph 2, "From all these scraps . . ." to "forbidden knowledge," contains all of the following except:
    A. parallel structure
    B. a periodic sentence
    C. prepositional phrases
    D. a compound-complex sentence
    E. an ellipsis

14. The phrase "forbidden knowledge" in the last sentence of the second paragraph can best be categorized as
    A. a paradox
    B. a biblical allusion
    C. hyperbole
    D. antithesis
    E. understatement

15. According to the author, the writer is like a child because
    A. "We are likely to accept these stories being of the same level of reality as the kitchen stories" [paragraph 4]
    B. ". . . we are taught to regard one kind of story as real . . ." [paragraph 4, next to last line]
    C. "We remained tale-bearers" [paragraph 3]
    D. "We will have old husbands' tales" [paragraph 5]
    E. ". . . the kinds of stories that are told to children have been called nursery tales . . ." [paragraph 5]

16. A careful reading of the last two paragraphs of the excerpt can lead the reader to infer that
    A. society does not value the storyteller
    B. women should be the storytellers
    C. storytelling should be left to children
    D. men can never be storytellers
    E. the author is a mother herself

17. The predominant tone of the passage is best stated as
    A. scathingly bitter
    B. sweetly effusive
    C. reverently detailed
    D. wistfully observant
    E. aggressively judgmental

18. The author makes use of which of the following rhetorical strategies?
    A. narration and description
    B. exposition and persuasion
    C. process and analysis
    D. anecdote and argument
    E. cause and effect

19. A shift in the focus of the passage occurs with which of the following?
    A. "If we're lucky" [paragraph 4]
    B. "Perhaps this is what writers are . . ." [paragraph 3]
    C. "Traditionally, . . ." [paragraph 5]
    D. "Perhaps this reflects the extent to which North American children have been deprived of the grandfathers . . ." [paragraph 5]
    E. "But as things are, language, including the language of the earliest-learned stories . . ." [paragraph 5]

20. The primary purpose of the passage is to
    A. plead for men to tell more stories
    B. criticize censorship
    C. idealize children
    D. analyze storytelling
    E. look at the sources of storytelling

Questions 21-32 are based on the passage taken from an article by E. J. Graff titled "What Makes a Family?" that appears in *What is Marriage For?* published by Beacon Press, Boston, in 1999.

Most historians warn readers that to grasp "family" history, you must first abandon the idea that you already know what "family" means. "Family" seems to be a word invented by Humpty Dumpty, who told Alice that "a word means what I say it means, what I say it should mean, neither more nor less; the question is, which is to be master, that is all." Historians always remind us of the word's etymology. Our "family" is related to its root in the Roman "*familia*" just about as closely as a Chevy Suburban is related to an elephant and a camel-drawn caravan. Sure, both of them move, but who's inside and what are they doing there?

Inside the Roman *familia* was everyone in the household: legitimate children, adopted adults, secretaries, and other dependents, slaves of various ages. "The Romans rarely used it to mean family in the sense of kin," writes Roman family historian Suzanne Dixon.[1] What counted, rather, was ownership. The words for children, slaves, and servants were so often interchanged that historians can't always tell how many of which lived under one roof. And for good reason. The patriarch's rule was complete: he could educate, beat, sell, give, indenture, marry off, endow, or kill any one of them, almost at will.[2]

He could, of course, care for his *familia* as well. Romans lived with their slaves and servants so closely that it "in some ways resembled kinship, even if the slaves were always in the position of poor relations," explains Dixon.[3] [She] also cites one hard-fought custody battle between a freed slave and her former owners over who would keep the ex-slave's daughter, Patronia Iusta, a custody battle as vicious as that over Baby M.[4]

Romans didn't consider birth the only way to acquire offspring. Just as they felt free to expose (in other words, kill) any child they didn't need, they also felt free to adopt—adults, that is. Adoption's goal was not to nurture a child, but to install an heir to carry on the house, a goal better served by adults—and so nearly all adoptions were of grown men (yes, men). Adoptees were usually nephews or grandsons or cousins, sometimes adopted through a will. As one historian explains, "A citizen of Rome did not 'have' a child . . . The Romans made no fetish of natural kinship.[5] Choice, not biology, made a *familia*."

. . . the Roman's idea that "family" meant everyone under one roof, biologically related or not, lasted until the eighteenth century's end.[6]

Historians and anthropologists frankly throw up their hands and admit that they can't define "family" in a way that works universally. "Before the eighteenth century, no European language had a term for the mother-father-children group,"[7] one pair of historians writes, mainly because that grouping—although widespread—wasn't important enough to need its own word. A 1287 Bologna statute defined "family" to include a father, mother, brothers, sisters, daughters-in-law (sons brought home their wives), but Italy was an exception. For Northern and Western Europe, the extended family is a myth. New-marrieds almost always launched their own households—if their parents signed over the farm, the contract often included a clause insisting that the old folks must be built their own separate dwelling—socialized as much or more with neighbors and work partners, as well as with kin. Rather, the European family, like the Roman, included people we'd consider legal strangers: they were grouped together in that word "family," not by blood, but by whether they lived under one roof. "Most households included non-kin inmates, sojourners, boarders, or lodgers occupying rooms vacated by children or kin, as well as indentured apprentices and resident servants, employed either for domestic work about the house or as an additional resident labour force for the field or shop," writes historian Lawrence Stone of the British between 1500 and 1800. "This composite group was confusingly known as a 'family.'"[8] A baker might have a family of a dozen or fifteen, including four journeymen, two apprentices, two maidservants, and three or four bio-children, all of whom worked, lived, and ate under his roof, at his table, and by his rules. A baronet might have a family of thirty-seven, including seven daughters and twenty-eight servants. Or was that ten daughters and twenty-five servants? Historians grind their teeth as they try to figure out from church, census, and tax records which "menservants" and "maids" were children, stepchildren, or nephews, and which were hired labor. Children, apprentices, servants—all were under the master's rule. 50 55

In other words, until very recently, not love, not biology, but labor made a family.

---

[1] *"The Romans rarely used it to mean family"*: Dixon, 2. [All notes are the author's, except 4, 13, 14, 23–26, 33, and 35.]

[2] The Roman patriarch's legal authority to kill his family members was used mostly for newborns; there were social limits on his right to kill his family's adults, although the symbolic threat could be usefully wielded. Dixon, 36, and Susan Treggiari, personal communication.

[3] *"in some ways resembled kinship"*: Dixon, 114.

[4] *Baby M*: The child in a nationally publicized legal case in which a surrogate mother fought the biological father for legal custody.

[5] "A citizen of Rome did not 'have' a child": Veyne, "The Roman Empire," in Ariès and Duby, vol. 1, 9.

[6] For fuller discussions of the frustrating plasticity of "the family" (and, therefore, the impossibility of defining it and studying it as a single phenomenon), see, for instance, Dixon, Ch. 1; Gies and Gies, introduction; Burguière and Lebrun, "The One Hundred and One Families of Europe," in Burguière et al., vol. 2, 1–39; Cherlin, 85–87; Stone, FSM, 37–66; Laslett, Oosterveen, and Smith, introduction; and de La Roncière, "Tuscan Notables on the Eve of the Renaissance," in Ariès and Duby, vol. 2, 157–170.

[7] *"Before the eighteenth century no European language"*: Gies and Gies, 4.

[8] *"Most households included non-kin"*: Stone, FSM, 28. For illuminating glimpses of demographic and family historians straining to determine which "servants" were or were not biological children, see, for instance, Laslett, Osterveen, and Smith, and Rotberg and Rabb.

21. The thesis of the entire passage can be found in line(s)
A. 1–2
B. 9–10
C. 22
D. 27–29
E. 33–36

22. The purpose of the first paragraph is to
A. criticize historians
B. define *family*
C. prove the author's scholarly intent
D. ease the reader into a scholarly topic
E. establish the time frame of the passage

23. Footnote 4 is an example of a(n)
A. primary source
B. secondary source
C. assumption of the reader's background
D. author's aside
E. link to other sources

24. The opening sentence of the passage is an example of a(n)
A. cautionary tale
B. analogy
C. paradox
D. ad hoc argument
E. interrogative

25. The primary rhetorical technique employed by the author to develop this passage is
A. cause and effect
B. narration
C. description
D. process
E. definition

26. The tone of the passage can most accurately be described as
A. sarcastic and vituperative
B. conversational and scholarly
C. formal and pedantic
D. erudite and exhortative
E. humorous and detached

27. According to the passage, today's modern
family most resembles that found in
A. Rome in the time of the emperors
B. Bologna in the thirteenth century
C. Pre-eighteenth-century western Europe
D. Great Britain between the sixteenth and
nineteenth centuries
E. Pre-modern northern Europe

28. Lines 32–33 ("Historians . . . universally")
can be read as a reinforcement of a concept
expressed in lines
A. 2–5
B. 9–10
C. 22–24
D. 27–29
E. 41–44

29. Footnote 6 does all of the following, except:
A. provide primary sources for further
calculations and estimates
B. reinforce the concept of the amorphous
nature of the term *family*
C. demonstrate the breadth of the author's
research
D. point to references that the reader can
access for further study
E. disclaim any lapses or inadequacies in the
author's discussion of the subject

30. The author's anticipation of readers' questions
is demonstrated by her use of
A. diction
B. rhetorical questions
C. direct quotations
D. parentheticals
E. ellipsis

31. An ambiguous piece of information is found in
which of the following footnotes?
A. 2
B. 5
C. 6
D. 7
E. 8

32. Which of the following was not critical in the
evolution of the historical definition of family?
A. common living quarters
B. proprietary rights
C. inheritance
D. economic needs
E. sanguinity

Questions 33–43 are based on the following passage from Ralph Waldo Emerson's Oration before the Phi Beta Kappa society, at Cambridge University, August 31, 1837, entitled "The American Scholar."

It is remarkable, the character of the pleasure we derive from the best books. They impress us with the conviction that one nature wrote and the same reads. We read the verses of one of the great English poets, of Chaucer, of Marvell, of Dryden, with the most modern joy,—with a pleasure, I mean, which is in great part caused by the abstraction of all *time* from their verses. There is some awe mixed with the joy of our   5
surprise, when this poet, who lived in some past world, two or three hundred years ago, says that which lies close to my own soul, that which I also had well-nigh thought and said. But for the evidence thence afforded to the philosophical doctrine of the identity of all minds, we should suppose some pre-established harmony, some foresight of souls that were to be, and some preparation of stores for their future wants, like the fact   10
observed in insects, who lay up food before death for the young grub they should never see.

It would not be hurried by any love of system, by an exaggeration of instincts, to underrate the Book. We boil grass and the broth of shoes, so the human mind can be fed by any knowledge. And great and heroic men have existed who had almost no other   15
information than by the printed page. I only would say that it needs a strong head to bear that diet. One must be an inventor to read well. As the proverb says, "He that would bring home the wealth of the Indies, must carry out the wealth of the Indies." There is then creative reading as well as creative writing. When the mind is braced by labor and invention, the page of whatever book we read becomes luminous with   20
manifold allusion. Every sentence is doubly significant, and the sense of our author is as broad as the world. We then see, what is always true, that as the seer's hour of vision is short and rare among heavy days and months, so is its record, perchance, the least part of his volume. The discerning will read, in his Plato or Shakespeare, only the least part,—only the authentic utterances of the oracle;—all the rest he rejects, were it never   25
so many times Plato's and Shakespeare's.

Of course, there is a portion of reading quite indispensable to a wise man. History and exact science he must learn by laborious reading. Colleges, in like manner, have their indispensable office,—to teach elements. But they can only highly serve us when they aim not to drill, but to create; when they gather from far every ray of various   30
genius to their hospitable halls, and by the concentrated fires, set the hearts of their youth on flame. Thought and knowledge are natures in which apparatus and pretension avail nothing. Gowns and pecuniary foundations, though of towns of gold, can never countervail the least sentence or syllable of wit. Forget this, and our American colleges will recede in their public importance, whilst they grow richer every year.   35

33. In context, the word "oracle" in line 25 can best be interpreted to mean the
A. visionary writer
B. inventive writer
C. popular writer of a time
D. intuitive writer
E. writer as critic

34. In line 17, the word "diet" refers to
A. "broth of shoes" [paragraph 2, sentence 2]
B. "boil grass" [paragraph 2, sentence 2]
C. "any knowledge" [paragraph 2, sentence 2]
D. "any love" [paragraph 2, sentence 1]
E. "the printed page" [paragraph 2, sentence 3]

35. The speaker characterizes the great writers as being able to
   A. surprise the reader
   B. present universal truths
   C. create harmony in their writing
   D. be philosophical
   E. write about nature

36. The speaker's attitude toward great writers in the fourth sentence of paragraph 1 (lines 5–8) might best be described as
   A. skeptical
   B. confused
   C. accusative
   D. validated
   E. patronizing

37. The speaker's tone in the passage can best be described as
   A. pretentious
   B. analytical
   C. satirical
   D. ambiguous
   E. servile

38. All of the following lines use figurative language except:
   A. "It is remarkable, the character of the pleasure we derive from the best books. They impress us with the conviction that one nature wrote and the same reads."
   B. ". . . and some preparation of stores for their future wants, like the fact observed in insects . . ."
   C. "We boil grass and the broth of shoes, so the human mind can be fed by any knowledge."
   D. "I would only say that it needs a strong head to bear that diet. One must be an inventor to read well."
   E. "Gowns and pecuniary foundations, though of towns of gold, can never countervail the least sentence or syllable of wit."

39. After reading the passage, the reader can infer that the author desires to
   A. praise the work of current writers
   B. change the curriculum of the college
   C. change college administration
   D. warn against relying on academic appearances
   E. criticize the cost of college

40. The pronoun "this" in the last sentence of the passage refers to
   A. "But they can only highly serve us when they aim not to drill, but to create . . ."
   B. "History and exact science he must learn by laborious reading."
   C. "Thought and knowledge are natures in which apparatus and pretension avail nothing."
   D. "Forget this, and our American colleges will recede in their public importance . . ."
   E. "When the mind is braced by labor and invention, the page of whatever book we read becomes luminous with manifold allusion."

41. According to the speaker, the characteristics of the discerning reader include all of the following except:
   A. brings himself to the work
   B. makes connections with the past
   C. discards irrelevancies
   D. approaches difficult readings willingly
   E. aspires to be a writer

42. Paragraphs 1 and 2 develop their ideas using ALL of the following EXCEPT
   A. metaphor
   B. simile
   C. allusion
   D. paradox
   E. parallel structure

43. The purpose of the third paragraph is to
   A. defend the role of reading
   B. praise history and science
   C. delineate the qualities of an ideal college
   D. inspire student scholars
   E. honor college instructors

Questions 44–54 are based on the following excerpt from Joseph Conrad's *The Secret Sharer.*

On my right hand there were lines of fishing stakes resembling a mysterious system of half-submerged bamboo fences, incomprehensible in its division of the domain of tropical fishes, and crazy of aspect as if abandoned forever by some nomad tribe of fishermen now gone to the other end of the ocean; for there was no sign of human habitation as far as the eye could reach. To the left a group of barren islets, suggesting ruins of stone walls,   5
towers, and blockhouses, had its foundations set in a blue sea that itself looked solid, so still and stable did it lie below my feet; even the track of light from the westering sun shone smoothly, without that animated glitter which tells of an imperceptible ripple. And when I turned my head to take a parting glance at the tug which had just left us anchored outside the bar, I saw the straight line of the flat shore joined to the stable sea,   10
edge to edge, with a perfect and unmarked closeness, in one leveled floor half brown, half blue under the enormous dome of the sky. Corresponding in their insignificance to the islets of the sea, two small clumps of trees, one on each side of the only fault in the impeccable joint, marked the mouth of the river Meinam we had just left on the first preparatory stage of our homeward journey; and, far back on the inland level, a larger and   15
loftier mass, the grove surrounding the great Paknam pagoda, was the only thing on which the eye could rest from the vain task of exploring the monotonous sweep of the horizon. Here and there gleams as of a few scattered pieces of silver marked the windings of the great river; and on the nearest of them, just within the bar, the tug steaming right into the land became lost to my sight, hull and funnel and masts, as though the   20
impassive earth had swallowed her up without an effort, without a tremor. My eye followed the light cloud of her smoke, now here, now there, above the plain according to the devious curves of the stream, but always fainter and farther away, till I lost it at last behind the miter-shaped hill of the great pagoda. And then I was left alone with my ship, anchored at the head of the Gulf of Siam.   25

44. Within the passage, the long, sinuous sentences emphasize the
A. narrator's sense of anticipation
B. objectivity of nature
C. insecurity of the narrator
D. passive nature of the journey
E. fearful tone of the passage

45. In the next to last sentence of the passage (lines 21–24), "devious curves" most likely is used to reinforce
A. the unpredictability of the water
B. the hidden nature of the stream
C. the concept of the complexity of what lies beneath the surface of the story
D. the mystery of nature
E. all of the above

46. The passage as a whole can best described as
A. an interior monologue
B. a melodramatic episode
C. an evocation of place
D. a historical narrative
E. an allegory

47. The first sentence of the passage helps to establish tone by means of
A. structure that reflects the strangeness of the experience described
B. parallel structure that contrasts with the chaos of the situation
C. alliteration to heighten the imagery
D. irony to create a sense of satire
E. hyperbole that exaggerates the danger of the situation

48. Which of the following ideas can be supported based on the third sentence (lines 9–12) beginning with "And when I . . ."?
   A. The speaker enjoys watching boats sailing on the horizon.
   B. The speaker wants to revel in the beauty and grace of nature.
   C. The speaker responds to the symmetry and balance of nature.
   D. The speaker realizes how vulnerable man is in the universe.
   E. The speaker is fearful of the earth and sea.

49. All of the following contribute to the feeling of solitude except:
   A. ". . . the impassive earth had swallowed her up without an effort . . ."
   B. "a group of barren islets"
   C. "the grove surrounding the great Paknam pagoda"
   D. "the monotonous sweep of the horizon"
   E. "ruins of stone walls, towers, and blockhouses"

50. The passage is organized primarily by means of
   A. spatial description
   B. definition
   C. chronological order
   D. order of importance
   E. parallelism

51. In the third to last sentence of the passage (lines 18–21) beginning with "Here and there . . . ," the figure of speech used to describe "the windings of the great river" is
   A. personification
   B. simile
   C. apostrophe
   D. antithesis
   E. symbol

52. The writer emphasizes his solitude by using all of the following rhetorical techniques except:
   A. heavy descriptive emphasis placed on setting
   B. overt statement of the absence of other people
   C. tracking the departure of the tugboat
   D. diction that emphasizes desertion and neglect
   E. contrasting the present situation with previous times

53. A characteristic of the author's style is
   A. succession of allusions
   B. the use of emotional language
   C. terse sentence structure
   D. vividness of contrasting images
   E. shifts in points of view

54. The tone of the passage can best be described as
   A. cynical
   B. reflective
   C. sarcastic
   D. elegiac
   E. apathetic

END OF SECTION I

Section II

Total Time—2 hours

Question 1

Suggested Writing Time: 40 minutes

A new word has entered the American vocabulary: *affluenza*. A 1997 PBS documentary titled *Affluenza* introduced this new term and defined it: " n. 1. The bloated, sluggish, and unfulfilled feeling that results from efforts to keep up with the Joneses. 2. An epidemic of stress, overwork, waste, and indebtedness caused by dogged pursuit of the American Dream. 3. An unsustainable addiction to economic growth."

Since then, scholars, journalists, political leaders, artists, and even comedians have made America's ever-increasing consumption the subject of dire warnings, academic studies, social commentary, campaign promises, and late-night TV jokes.

Carefully read the following sources (including any introductory information). **Then, in an essay that synthesizes at least three of the sources, take a position that supports, opposes, or qualifies the claim that Americans are never satisfied. They are constantly wanting new things and are never content with what they have. There is a superabundance of "stuff," and Americans have lost their sense of meaning. As Sheryl Crow's 2002 lyrics state,** *"it's not having what you want. It's wanting what you've got."*

Make certain that you take a position and that the essay centers on your argument. Use the sources to support your reasoning; avoid simply summarizing the sources. You may refer to the sources by their letters (Source A, Source B, etc.) or by the identifiers in the parentheses below.

Source A (Aristotle's *Ethics*)
Source B (*The Declaration of Independence*)
Source C (John Stuart Mill's *Utilitarianism*)
Source D (Cartoon by Jim Sizemore)
Source E (Jessie H. O'Neill's *The Golden Ghetto: The Psychology of Affluence*)
Source F (Lewis Lapham's *Money and Class in America*)
Source G ("Wealth" by Andrew Carnegie)

Source A
Aristotle's *Nicomachean Ethics*

> *Certainly the future is obscure to us, while happiness, we claim, is an end and something in every way final. . . . If so, we shall call happy those among living men in whom these conditions are, and are to be fulfilled.*
>
> *Happiness is desirable in itself and never for the sake of something else. But honor, pleasure, reason, and every virtue we choose indeed for themselves, but we choose them also for the sake of happiness, judging that by means of them we shall be happy. Happiness, on the other hand, no one chooses for the sake of these, nor, in general, for anything other than itself. Happiness, then, is something final and self-sufficient.*
>
> *He is happy who lives in accordance with complete virtue and is sufficiently equipped with external goods, not for some chance period but throughout a complete life.*
>
> *To judge from the lives that men lead, most men seem to identify the good, or happiness, with pleasure: which is the reason why they love the life of enjoyment. The mass of mankind are evidently quite slavish in their tastes, preferring a life suitable to beasts.*

Practice Exam 1   ‹   191

With regard to what happiness is (men) differ, and the many do not give the same account as the wise. For the former think it is some plain and obvious thing, like pleasure, wealth, or honor. They differ, however, from one another—and often even the same man identifies it with different things, with health when he is ill, with wealth when he is poor.

Source B

The Declaration of Independence
From the opening paragraph of The Declaration of Independence.

We hold these Truths to be self-evident, that all Men are created equal, that they are endowed by their Creator with certain unalienable Rights: that among these are Life, Liberty, and the Pursuit of Happiness. That to secure these Rights, Governments are instituted among Men, deriving their just Powers from the Consent of the Governed . . .

Source C

Utilitarianism, written by John Stuart Mill, an eighteenth-century British philosopher, in 1863. Available at http://www.utilitarianism.com/mill2.htm.
The following is an excerpt from Chapter 2 entitled "What Utilitarianism Is."

. . . The creed which accepts as the foundation of morals, Utility, or the Greatest Happiness Principle, holds that actions are right in proportion as they tend to promote happiness, wrong as they tend to produce the reverse of happiness. By happiness is intended pleasure, and the absence of pain; by unhappiness, pain, and the privation of pleasure. . . .

. . . no intelligent human being would consent to be a fool, no instructed person would be an ignoramus, no person of feeling and conscience would be selfish and base, even though they should be persuaded that the fool, the dunce, or the rascal is better satisfied with his lot than they are with theirs. They would not resign what they possess more than he for the most complete satisfaction of all desires which they have in common with him. If they ever fancy they would, it is only in cases of unhappiness so extreme, that to escape from it they would exchange their lot for almost any other, however undesirable in their own eyes. A being of higher faculties [humans] requires more to make him happy, is capable probably of more acute suffering, and certainly accessible to it at more points, than one of the inferior type [animals]: but in spite of these liabilities, he can never really wish to sink into what he feels to be a lower grade of existence. . . . Whoever supposes that this preference takes place at a sacrifice of happiness—that the superior being, in anything like equal circumstances, is not happier than the inferior—confounds two very different ideas, of happiness and content. It is indisputable that the being whose capacities of enjoyment are low, has the greatest chance of having them fully satisfied; and a highly endowed being will always feel that any happiness which he can look for, as the world is constituted, is imperfect. But he can learn to bear its imperfections, but only because he feels not at all the good which those imperfections qualify. It is better to be a human being dissatisfied than a pig satisfied; better to be Socrates dissatisfied than the fool satisfied. And if the fool, or the pig, are of different opinion, it is because they only know their own side of the question. The other party to the comparison knows both sides.

Source D
Cartoon by Jim Sizemore
Available at http://www.cartoonstock.com/blowup.asp?imageref=jsi0087&artist=Sizemore,
   +Jim&topic=consumerism.
This cartoon appeared in a recent issue of *The New Yorker*.

"Something is missing."

Source E
O'Neill, Jesse H. *The Golden Ghetto: The Psychology of Affluence*, The Affluenza Project:
   Milwaukee, Wisconsin, 1997.
The following is adapted from passages in Jesse H. O'Neill's book and from the mission
statement of The Affluenza Project founded by O'Neill. http://www.affluenza.com.

> *The malaise that currently grips our country comes not from the fact that we don't have
> enough wealth, but from a terrifying knowledge that has begun to enter our conscious-
> ness that we have based our entire lives, our entire culture and way of being on the
> belief that "just a little bit more" will finally buy happiness.*
>
> *Although many people in our culture are beginning to question the assumptions of
> the American Dream, we still live in a time of compulsive and wasteful consumerism.*
>
> *Statistics to consider:*
> * *Per capita consumption in the United States has increased 45 percent in the
>   past twenty years.*
> * *During the same period, quality of life as measured by the index of social health
>   has decreased by roughly the same percentage.*
> * *The average working woman plays with her children forty minutes a week—
>   and shops six hours.*
> * *Ninety-three percent of teenage girls list shopping as their favorite pastime.*

Source F

Lapham, Lewis. *Money and Class in America: Notes and Observations on Our Civil Religion*, Grove Press: New York, 1988.

The following is a passage from Mr. Lapham's text.

I think it fair to say that the current ardor of the American faith in money easily surpasses the degrees of intensity achieved by other societies in other times and places. Money means so many things to us—spiritual as well as temporal—that we are at a loss to know how to hold its majesty at bay. . . .

Henry Adams in his autobiography remarks that although the Americans weren't much good as materialists they had been "so deflected by the pursuit of money" that they could turn "in no other direction." The natural distrust of the contemplative temperament arises less from the innate Philistinism than from a suspicion of anything that cannot be counted, stuffed, framed or mounted over the fireplace in the den. Men remain free to rise or fall in the world, and if they fail it must be because they willed it so. The visible signs of wealth testify to an inward state of grace, and without at least some of these talismans posted in one's house or on one's person an American loses all hope of demonstrating to himself the theorem of his happiness. Seeing is believing, and if an American success is to count for anything in the world it must be clothed in the raiment of property. As often as not it isn't the money itself that means anything; it is the use of money as the currency of the soul.

Against the faith in money, other men in other times and places have raised up countervailing faiths in family, honor, religion, intellect and social class. The merchant princes of medieval Europe would have looked upon the American devotion as sterile stupidity; the ancient Greek would have regarded it as a form of insanity. Even now, in the last decades of a century commonly defined as American, a good many societies both in Europe and Asia manage to balance the desire for wealth against the other claims of the human spirit. An Englishman of modest means can remain more or less content with the distinction of an aristocratic name or the consolation of a flourishing garden; the Germans show to obscure university professors the deference accorded by Americans only to celebrity; the Soviets honor the holding of political power; in France a rich man is a rich man, to whom everybody grants the substantial powers that his riches command but to whom nobody grants the respect due to a member of the National Academy. But in the United States a rich man is perceived as being necessarily both good and wise, which is an absurdity that would be seen as such not only by a Frenchman but also by a Russian. Not that the Americans are greedier than the French, or less intellectual than the Germans, or more venal than the Russians, but to what other tribunal can an anxious and supposedly egalitarian people submit their definitions of the good, the true and the beautiful if not to the judgment of the bottom line?

Source G

"Wealth" written by Andrew Carnegie,[1] published in *North American Review*, CCCXCI, June 1889. Available at http://facweb.furman.edu/~benson/docs/carnegie.htm.

The following is excerpted from the article by Andrew Carnegie.

The problem of our age is the proper administration of wealth, so that the ties of brotherhood may still bind together the rich and poor in harmonious relationship. The conditions of human life have not only been changed, but revolutionized, within the past few hundred years. In former days there was little difference between the dwelling, dress, food, and environment of the chief and those of his retainers.

The Indians are today where civilized man then was. When visiting the Sioux, I was led to the wigwam of the chief. It was just like the others in external appearance, and even within the difference was trifling between it and those of the poorest of his braves. The contrast between the palace of the millionaire and the cottage of the laborer with us today measures the change which has come with civilization.

This change, however, is not to be deplored, but welcomed as highly beneficial. It is well, nay, essential for the progress of the race, that the houses of some should be homes for all that is highest and best in literature and the arts, and for all the refinements of civilization, rather than that none should be so. Much better this great irregularity than universal squalor. Without wealth there can be no Maecenas.[2] The "good old times" were not good old times. Neither master nor servant was as well situated then as today. A relapse to old conditions would be disastrous to both—not the least so to him who serves—and would sweep away civilization with it. But whether the change be for good or ill, it is upon us, beyond our power to alter, and therefore to be accepted and made the best of. It is waste of time to criticize the inevitable.

[1]*Late nineteenth-century American capitalist and philanthropist*
[2]*Patron of the arts in ancient Rome*

Question 2

(Suggested time 40 minutes. This question counts as one-third of the total score for Section II.)

Carefully read Chief Seattle's oration to Governor Isaac I. Stevens, who had just returned from Washington, D.C., with orders to buy Indian lands and create reservations. In a well-written essay, identify Chief Seattle's purpose and analyze the rhetorical strategies he uses to convey his purpose. Consider such items as figurative language, organization, diction, and tone.

. . . Yonder sky that has wept tears of compassion upon my people for centuries untold, and which to us appears changeless and eternal, may change. Today is fair. Tomorrow it may be overcast with clouds. My words are like the stars that never change. Whatever Seattle says the great chief at Washington can rely upon with as much certainty as he can upon the return of the sun. The White Chief says that Big Chief at Washington sends us greetings of friendship and goodwill. This is kind of him for we know he has little need of our friendship in return. His people are many. They are like the grass that covers vast prairies. My people are few. They resemble the scattering trees of a storm-swept plain. The great, and I presume—good White Chief sends us word that he wishes to buy our lands but is willing to allow us enough to live comfortably. This indeed appears just, even generous, for the Red Man no longer has rights that he need respect, and the offer may be wise, as we are no longer in need of an extensive country. 1

There was a time when our people covered the land as the waves of a wind-ruffled sea cover its shell-paved floor, but that time long since passed away with the greatness of tribes that are now but a mournful memory. I will not dwell on, nor mourn over, our untimely decay, nor reproach my paleface brothers with hastening it as we too may have been somewhat to blame. 2

Youth is impulsive. When our young men grow angry at some real or imaginary wrong, and disfigure their faces with black paint, it denotes that their hearts are black, and our old men and old women are unable to restrain them. Thus it was when the white men first began to push our forefathers further westward. But let us hope that the hostilities between us may never return. We would have everything to lose and nothing to gain. 3

Our good father at Washington—for I presume he is now our father as well as yours—our great and good father, I say, sends us word that if we do as he desires he will protect us. But can that ever be? Your God is not our God! Your God loves your people and hates mine. He folds his strong protecting arms lovingly about the pale face—but he has forsaken his red children—if they really are his. Our God, the Great Spirit, seems also to have forsaken us. Our people are ebbing away like a rapidly receding tide that will never return. How then can we be brothers? We are two distinct races with separate origins and separate destinies. 4

To us the ashes of our ancestors are sacred and their resting place is hallowed ground. You wander far from the graves of your ancestors and seemingly without regret. Your dead cease to love you and the land of your nativity as soon as they pass the portals of the tomb and wander away beyond the stars. Our dead never forget the beautiful world that gave them being . . . and often return to visit, guide, console, and comfort the lonely hearted living. 5

It matters little where we pass the remnant of our days. They will not be many. The Indians' night promises to be dark. Not a single star of hope hovers above his horizon. Tribe follows tribe, and nation follows nation like the waves of the sea. It is the order of nature, and regret is useless. Your time of decay may be distant, but it will surely come, for even the white man whose God walked and talked with him as friend with friend, cannot be exempt from the common destiny. We may be brothers after all. We will see. 6

And when the Last Red Man shall have perished, these shores will swarm with the invisible dead of my tribe, and when your children's children think themselves alone, they will not be alone. At night when you think your cities are deserted, they will throng with the returning hosts that once filled them and still love this beautiful land. The White Man will never be alone. 7

Let him be just and deal kindly with my people, for the dead are not powerless. 8

Question 3

In his essay "The Wilderness Idea," Wallace Stegner states the following.

> *Without any remaining wilderness we are committed wholly, without chance for even momentary reflection and rest, to a headlong drive into our technological termite-life, the Brave New World of a completely man-controlled environment.*

Write a well-constructed essay that defends, challenges, or qualifies Stegner's statement using your own knowledge, experience, observation, or reading.

END OF SECTION II

ANSWER KEY

1. D	19. C	37. B
2. B	20. E	38. A
3. E	21. A	39. D
4. A	22. D	40. C
5. E	23. C	41. E
6. B	24. C	42. D
7. C	25. E	43. C
8. A	26. B	44. D
9. C	27. B	45. E
10. D	28. A	46. C
11. D	29. A	47. A
12. A	30. D	48. C
13. E	31. A	49. C
14. B	32. E	50. A
15. C	33. A	51. B
16. A	34. E	52. E
17. D	35. B	53. D
18. B	36. D	54. B

Explanations of Answers to the Multiple-Choice Section

The Dickens Passage

1. **D.** The very first sentence indicates the author's purpose. Here, the reader is told directly that Florence is both fanciful and somber, rich and stern.

2. **B.** This selection is based on a quite specific description of Florence and an area within the city. To correctly answer this question, the student needs to be familiar with the different types of rhetorical strategies.

3. **E.** The reader is brought from the general street scene to a specific prison and then to a specific scene outside the prison. Metaphors, similes, and imagery are found throughout the selection, such as "small cells like ovens," "distrustful windows." Contrast and comparison are provided with such phrases as "faded and tarnished Great Saloon" placed next to the "walls which record the triumphs of the Medici." The passage does *NOT* follow a specific timeline.

4. **A.** The test taker needs to know the definition of paradox and must be able to recognize it in a given text. Here, smoke is being used to purify the air even though it is in itself a pollutant.

5. **E.** Dickens is not warning people away from Florence, nor is he criticizing its government. What the text and its selection of details do is to reinforce the idea of Florence being a city of contrast (youth and age, life and death, bright flowers and squalid prisons).

6. **B.** There is no support from a close reading of the text that will allow you to defend choice B, which sees no connection between the two scenes described. Obviously both reveal aspects of Florence. Both are descriptive, with the second paragraph containing the selective contrast with the first paragraph.

7. **C.** Distrustful and secret are indicative of "intrigue," and building thick walls and huge battlements points to the need for protection from aggression. No other choice provides these same inferences.

8. **A.** A close look at each of the selected lines reveals opposites being placed side by side. This is the nature of antithesis.

9. **C.** The Palazzo Vecchio is described using such terms as "ponderous gloom," "faded" and "tarnished" and "mouldering." These are evocative of a place that is creepy and frightening. None of the other choices projects these qualities.

10. **D.** In Dickens's time, "jealous" was used to indicate the state of being watchful or closely guarded. If you look at the context of the line, you can see that "jealous" has nothing to do with our current use of the word.

The Atwood Passage

11. **D.** Although you might be inclined to accept A, B, or E as possible correct choices, you should be aware that these are specific things the child hears. Each of these would cancel the other out, because they would be equally valid. Choice C is nowhere to be found in the selection. Therefore, the appropriate choice is D, listening.

12. **A.** The very first word of the selection is "Our." This immediately links the writer and the reader. Both are vested with this choice of pronoun.

13. **E.** If you look carefully, you find examples of all of the choices except E. An ellipsis is punctuation comprising three periods. You find none in this sentence. Its function is to notify the reader that a piece of the text has been omitted.

14. **B.** The question makes reference to wanting or seeking something not permitted, such as Adam and Eve being warned not to eat of the forbidden fruit from the tree of knowledge. The other choices are simply not appropriate to the relationship between *forbidden* and *knowledge*.

15. **C.** This is a rather easy question. The entire third paragraph supports this idea.

16. **A.** The answer is clearly supported in the last sentence of paragraph 4. That which is immediately practical and helpful in a very tangible way is the more valuable.

17. **D.** Words, phrases used, and specific details given in this passage support the adjective "wistful" (paragraphs 3 and 4). She is observant throughout the passage as she provides details of the child acquiring her stories. The writer's wistfulness is reiterated in the last paragraph as she states her yearning for men to share in the language of storytelling.

18. **B.** The only choice that presents two strategies actually present in the text is B. The entire passage employs exposition to support the author's purpose. Even the final paragraph, which attempts to persuade, uses exposition to strengthen the appeal to have men welcomed into the language of storytelling. (If you are not crystal clear about the terminology used in the choices, this may be one of those questions you choose to skip, because it can be time consuming trying to determine the correct choice.)

19. **C.** The abruptness of "Traditionally," provides no real connection with the previous paragraph or the previous sentence. It is an obvious break that grabs the reader's attention and leads him or her to Atwood's point.

20. **E.** Throughout the passage, Atwood is taking a close look at the beginnings of storytelling. Although she does attempt to persuade us of the need to encourage men to tell their stories, this is not the primary purpose of the piece. It is important to also notice that the title is a clue to this answer.

The Family Passage

21. **A.** The entire passage is concerned with the concept of family in general, not just the Roman and pre-modern era family. The choices other than A all concern these.

22. **D.** Through humor, exaggeration, common allusions, and rhetorical questions, the author invites the reader to join <u>her</u> family as a prelude to a scholarly examination of the roots of the word *family*.

23. **C.** The footnote identifies a case that some readers may not be familiar with. No sources are cited or referenced. The footnote is strictly informative.

24. **C.** This is a vocabulary question that demands you know and can identify each of the terms. Knowing the definition of each can only lead you to choose C.

25. **E.** Each piece of information provided in the passage is given in terms of defining what a *family* is.

26. **B.** The first paragraph establishes the conversational tone with its lighthearted references. But, the author's use of footnotes, direct quotations from experts, and historical references all indicate a scholarly presentation.

27. **B.** If one closely reads the passage, the only location cited that has a family unit consisting of a mother, father, and children is Bologna in the thirteenth century.

28. **A.** The word *family* does NOT have a universal definition. Each culture and time period defined it according to its own circumstances.

29. **A.** This footnote contains NO specifics that were gathered via observation and experience. There is no data from census, and so forth.

30. **D.** Even though the reader can locate instances of choices C and E in both paragraphs, they are not responding to a probable reader-generated question. The parentheticals come immediately after a word or phrase that could raise questions from a reader.

31. **A.** The comment separated only by commas leaves the reader unclear as to whom the *personal communication* refers: Dixon, Treggiari, or the author.

32. **E.** Lines 24–25, 27–29, 43–44, and 56–57 support choices A, B, C, and D.

The Emerson Passage

33. **A.** If you go back to the next to last sentence of paragraph 2, you will see the phrase "the seer's hour of vision." Your knowledge of synonyms will lead you to choose A.

34. E. Using the process of substitution, it is not difficult to eliminate all choices other than "the printed page."

35. B. For Emerson, the universal crosses barriers between time and place. This idea is supported in the third sentence of paragraph 1.

36. D. Using the process of elimination while looking carefully at the given lines, you will discover that the only answer that correctly relates to Emerson's attitude is D. All the others are negative.

37. B. Vocabulary is a key factor in this question. In this passage, Emerson is "taking apart" the qualities of a great writer, book, and college. This is what an analytical essay does.

38. A. In the first two sentences of paragraph 1, Emerson is setting up the parameters of his argument. There is no figurative language here.

39. D. Carefully reading the last paragraph, especially the last three sentences, can only lead you to choose D. None of the other choices is logical within the context of the passage.

40. C. Antecedents come *before* the given pronoun, and as close as possible to that pronoun. With this in mind, the fifth sentence of paragraph 3 is the only choice that correctly and logically fits the criteria.

41. E. If you pay close attention to the second paragraph, you will find all the choices, except E.

42. D. Emerson alludes to "great English poets" in the first paragraph, and to a proverb and other writers in the second paragraph. Similes and metaphors can be found throughout both paragraphs, but no paradox is evident. Parallel structure/anaphora is used in lines 9–10 (". . . *suppose some pre-established . . . some foresight . . . some preparation . . .*")

43. C. Because this is an analytical passage, including the final paragraph, C is the only acceptable choice.

The Conrad Passage

44. D. The very nature of sentences that are long and flowing serves to create a corresponding mood of passivity, ease, and timelessness. This lack of tension in the structure is not indicated in any of the other choices.

45. E. Each of the choices deals with what is yet unknown to the narrator and the reader. The phrase "devious curves" foreshadows the complexity of the novella itself.

46. C. This exemplifies that choosing the correct answer can be dependent on the student's knowing definitions of terms and ability to recognize them in context. No other choice is acceptable in characterizing this passage.

47. A. This compound-complex sentence sets the task for the reader with its convoluted structure and imagery. This reflects the very essence the narrator is presenting to the reader of the strangeness of the experience.

48. C. The diction, which includes "joined," "edge to edge," and "half brown, half blue," supports the idea of balance and corresponding symmetry.

49. C. Choices A, B, D, and E all reinforce the feeling of abandonment and aloneness. Choice C does not contribute to this impression of isolation; it is rather just a descriptive detail.

50. A. By its very definition, spatial description will provide the reader an opportunity to sense the setting by means of directions, scale, dimension, and color.

51. B. Just find the word *as,* and you will easily locate the simile comparing the light to scattered pieces of silver.

52. E. A careful reading of the passage uncovers each of the given choices except E. Nowhere in the excerpt does the narrator indicate a contrast between the current situation and a previous one.

53. D. The passage contains no allusions, has no real emotional diction, and maintains a constant first person point of view. And, most obviously, it does not rely on short, direct sentences. Therefore, the only choice is D.

54. B. The entire passage involves the reader in the narrator's thoughtful and reflective observations about his or her surroundings.

KEY IDEA

Rubric for the Affluenza Synthesis Essay

A **9** essay has all the qualities of an 8 essay, and the <u>writing style</u> is especially <u>impressive</u>, as is the analysis and integration of the specifics related to affluenza and the given sources.

An **8** essay <u>effectively</u> and <u>cohesively</u> addresses the prompt. It clearly takes a position on affluenza and supports the argument using carefully integrated and appropriate evidence, including at least three of the given sources. The essay also shows the writer's <u>ability to control language</u>.

A **7** essay has all the properties of a 6 essay, only with a <u>more complete</u>, well-developed, and integrated argument, or a more mature writing style.

A **6** essay <u>adequately</u> addresses the prompt. The argument centers on affluenza and integrates, as well as makes use of, appropriate evidence, including at least three references from the given sources. These elements are less fully integrated and/or developed than scores in the 7, 8, or 9 range. The writer's ideas are expressed with clarity, but the writing may have a few errors in syntax and/or diction.

A **5** essay demonstrates that the writer <u>understands the prompt</u>. The argument/claim/position about affluenza is generally understandable, but the development and/or integration of appropriate evidence, and at least three of the given sources are limited or uneven. The writer's ideas are expressed clearly with a few errors in syntax or diction.

A **4** essay is <u>not an adequate response</u> to the prompt. The writer's argument indicates a misunderstanding, an oversimplification, or a misrepresentation of the assigned task. The writer may use evidence that is not appropriate or not sufficient to support the argument, or may use fewer than three of the given sources. The writing presents the writer's ideas, but it may indicate immaturity of style and control.

A **3** essay is a lower 4 because it is <u>even less effective</u> in addressing the question. It is also less mature in its syntax and organization.

A **2** essay indicates <u>little success in speaking to the prompt</u>. The writer may misread the question, only summarize the given sources, fail to develop the required argument, or simply ignore the prompt and write about another topic. The writing may also lack organization and control of language and syntax. (***Note:*** **No matter how well written, a summary will never rate more than a 2.**)

A **1** essay is a lower 2 because it is even <u>more simplistic</u>, <u>disorganized</u>, and <u>lacking in control of language</u>.

Student A

Affluenza. This new word created only nine years ago aptly describes the pervasive illness in American society and culture that involves our obsession with wealth and possessions. Symptoms include stress, a hollow feeling of still not having enough to be happy, credit and debt, and depression-ridden withdrawals when the dream becomes a nightmare.

The justification for our gluttony is, as some would say in its defense, written into our Declaration of Independence. "We hold these Truths to be self-evident . . . the unalienable right to life, liberty, and the pursuit of happiness" they shout. "We have the unalienable rights of freedom to buy everything to make ourselves happy, and we'll live with it!" The Enlightenment ideals of the 18th century have been tweaked to fit those of Bergdorf-Goodman and eBay.

1

2

In a country where we have no national religion, we did find something that tied us 3
together. Money quickly became our national religion, with the wealthy as its priests.
Rockefeller and Carnegie were our first high priests. Social Darwinists to the core, they
lived and preached the power of copper, gold, oil, commerce, and wealth from their
glittering towers, and the plebian masses ate the crumbs left over, hoping to become
a member of the clergy some day. "This change, however, is . . . welcomed as highly
beneficial," cries the high priest Carnegie. "Much better this great irregularity than
universal squalor" (Source G).

But, is it much better? As pictured in a recent *New Yorker* cartoon, when a rich man 4
and woman lie in bed surrounded by paintings, lamps, sculptures, and other luxurious
odds and ends, and say to each other, "Something is missing," it is indicative of the fact
that they and we don't begin to realize how deep a truth this is (Source D). What they
are missing is a meaning, an intimacy, a happiness in their lives. That can't be found in a
four-poster bed with lavish objet d'art encroaching from all sides.

Perhaps the worst thing about affluenza is the way it is taught to the children of 5
today. According to statistics provided by Jesse H. O'Neill's *The Golden Ghetto: The
Psychology of Affluence*, most working mothers play with their children forty minutes a
week. They SHOP six hours a week (Source E). The family is replaced by shopping bags
strewn across the bed. No wonder ninety-three percent of teenage girls list shopping as
their favorite hobby. They can't go to the beach without designer bikinis. They can't
listen to music without an iPod, and it <u>must</u> be accessorized!

We hold these truths to be self-evident: money buys <u>things</u>, no more, no less. It 6
can't replace people, or love, or nature, or travel to places where they just don't worship
<u>things</u> as much as we do. It's time for America to wake up and stop smelling the designer
perfume and ink on the greenbacks. There's no cure for affluenza but ourselves.

Student B

In a world in which material possessions are looked upon as treasures to be collected 1
and guarded, the thought of being content with what one has is considered a prehistoric
myth. America, the main culprit, has been infected by what PBS calls "affluenza." This
"disease" has crept into American homes causing "an epidemic of stress, overwork, waste,
and indebtedness." [introduction to prompt] The claim that Americans are never satisfied
holds much validity and gains more validity as the economy continues to flourish.

As the economy continues to grow and produce objects in which Americans can 2
become infatuated, one can only see America's affluenza infection worsening. A recent
cartoon in which a husband and wife peer over their bed sheets into a vast room ridden
with trinkets and stuffed with mere junk, one can only agree with the claim that
Americans value "stuff" too much (Source D). The cartoon described ends with a witty
comment, "Something is missing." This cartoon is a clear satirical look at what America
has become. Although the room is already stuffed with belongings, the couple feels that
something is missing, showing that Americans are never happy with what they have.

To be happy is one thing, but to buy happiness is something completely different.   3
Yet, Americans have fallen into the trap of widespread consumerism. O'Neill states
that "we have based . . . our entire culture . . . on the belief that 'just a little bit more'
will finally buy happiness" (Source E). He, then, continues on to provide statistics
showing that "93% of teenage girls list shopping as their favorite pastime." It is a sad
reality that what we have is never good enough; that, hopefully, a new pair of shoes
will bring happiness for at least a day or two. America's future, its youth, are the ones
with the most serious infection of affluenza, and as time ticks on that infection only
continues to grow.

Happiness has been a goal of America since its creation, *The Declaration of*   4
Independence states that Americans have the "unalienable" rights: life, liberty, and the
pursuit of happiness (Source B). Although we continue to pursue happiness, American's
idea of happiness has taken a drastic turn. Our idea of happiness in today's standards is
to be rich, and have anything and everything we want. Our days are consumed with the
prospect of reaching happiness. Money is what drives us to work extra hours, but what
will that money buy us? Not happiness, but simply objects—objects that may bring us
happiness for a day or so, but will never satisfy us in the long run.

America's affluenza infection has become a widespread epidemic. Society has become   5
infatuated with purchases and gifts in hopes of finding happiness. Americans are truly
never satisfied with what they have. As America continues to buy, the affluenza only
roots itself deeper into our society and into our future.

Rating the Student Essays: Affluenza

Student A
This is a high-range essay for the following reasons:

- The essay opens dramatically, immediately catching the reader's attention. It creatively defines the term and implies the argument to follow.
- The writer establishes a tone and voice through diction and allusion: *shout, tweaked, Bergdorf,* and *eBay.*
- The writer illustrates the argument by presenting an extended analogy.
- Following a rhetorical question that serves as a transitional device, the writer adeptly incorporates and comments on one of the sources.
- Personal examples and strong details and images continue to support and develop the writer's position.
- The writer employs proper citation guidelines.
- The conclusion is especially effective because it enforces the opening, leaves the reader with the essence of the argument, and presents the writer's thesis as a parting comment.

Student B
This is a mid-range essay for the following reasons:

- The writer states a position on Americans being afflicted with affluenza: "The claim that Americans are never satisfied holds much validity and gains more validity as the economy continues to flourish."
- The writer recognizes and addresses the demands of the prompt.

- The writer properly integrates transitions.
- Varied sentence structure is evident in the analysis.
- The development is organized into an orderly presentation.
- The essay presents a clear thesis in the next-to-last paragraph: "Money is what drives us to work extra hours, but what will that money buy us? Not happiness, but simply objects—objects that may bring us happiness for a day or so, but will never satisfy us in the long run."
- The analysis of the writer's sources is brief, leaving the reader looking for more development.

Sample Student Essays

Rubrics for Seattle Passage

High-Range Essay

- Clearly identifies Seattle's purpose and attitude
- Successfully and effectively analyzes the rhetorical strategies used to accomplish the author's purpose
- Effectively cites specifics from the text to illustrate rhetorical devices and their meanings and effects on the oration
- Indicates a facility with organization
- Effectively manipulates language
- Few, if any, syntactical errors

Mid-Range Essay

- Correctly identifies Seattle's purpose and attitude
- Understands the demands of the prompt
- Cites specific examples of rhetorical devices found in the text and effects on the oration
- Ideas clearly stated
- Less well-developed than the high-range essays
- A few lapses in diction or syntax

Low-Range Essay

- Inadequate response to the prompt
- Misunderstands, oversimplifies, or misrepresents Seattle's purpose and attitude
- Insufficient or inappropriate use of examples to develop the demands of the prompt
- Lack of mature control of elements of essay writing

Students apparently found the question quite accessible. Most recognized the figurative language used in the passage and were able to incorporate examples into their essays. They were able to recognize the purpose and emotional appeal of Seattle's oration. The more perceptive writers recognized the subtleties of Seattle's manipulation of the situation—his implied sarcasm and his subtle threatening predictions.

Chief Seattle Passage—Student Sample A

In his oration to Governor Isaac I. Stevens, Chief Seattle attempts to convince the whites that they should deal fairly with the Native Americans despite their inferior status. Through the use of rhetorical strategies and devices like figurative language, organization, diction, and tone, he appeals both to the pride and the reason of the Governor, reminding him that, though weak, the Natives are not powerless.

Chief Seattle begins his oration in a friendly manner, appealing to the Governor and the white's pride while recognizing their superior status. He refers to the Governor as "the great" and "the good White Chief" throughout the piece, hoping the governor will look favorably on his subordinance despite the mocking that is hidden in his words. Seattle takes responsibility for the plight of the Natives, another strategy that undoubtedly makes him more respectable and admirable to the Governor, although he does not necessarily believe his people are truly at fault. In yet another attempt to get or remain on the Governor's "good side," Seattle says that the young Indian warriors' "hearts are black," blaming them and not the whites for the warfare and distrust that characterizes the Native American–American relationship. To increase his own credibility, Seattle uses the simile "my words are like the stars that never change," once more emphasizing his steadfastness and ability to work with the Americans. By presenting himself as inferior, apologetic, responsible and respectful, Seattle attempts to win Stevens' favor.

In addition to promoting his own respectability, Seattle emphasizes differences between his people and the Americans. Appreciating the Americans' "generosity" and "friendship and goodwill," Seattle points out the differences between the two peoples in a respectful manner. He calls the whites his "paleface brothers," but is certain to point out that they believe in different supreme beings, have different customs, are "two distinct races with separate origins and separate destinies." With rhetorical questions like "How then can we be brothers?" Seattle suggests that the two peoples cannot intermingle through no fault of their own. Instead of blaming the Americans, he implies that they are just and kind and that the peoples' lack of friendship is just the way it's supposed to be.

Despite his calm, almost compromising attitude throughout his oration, Chief Seattle does, at certain points, warn Governor Stevens of the power of his people. Short of belligerent, these comments are often made in a manner that implies rather than openly affirms Native American strength and lack of fear. With the emotional statement "Indians' night promises to be dark," Seattle almost suggests that his people have nothing to lose if the relationship with the Americans goes sour. They have already lost so much that they will fight to the end. Seattle warns that "these shores will swarm with the invisible dead of my tribe . . . the White Man will never be alone." Thus, he reminds Stevens that, even though his people are but "the scattering trees of a storm-swept plain," they are strong—a force to be reckoned with. In a respectful manner, he manages to threaten Stevens and clearly deliver his message that the tribe will not so easily be destroyed.

In addition to warning the Governor, acting respectfully and emphasizing the inherent differences between the two peoples, Chief Seattle gives a sense of the unfair treatment his tribe has suffered. In his oration so deeply saturated with figurative language, balanced sentences, carefully chosen diction, and hidden implications, the Chief conveys his message loud and clear. Though weak in number, his people are strong in heart; though inferior in legal status, his tribe is superior in customs and values. The governor may buy their land, but, Seattle reminds him, he may never buy their pride or their silence.

Chief Seattle Passage—Student Sample B

Chief Seattle, one of great speakers for the Native Americans, spoke out against Governor Stevens in an attempt to discourage the buying of more Indian land. His style which includes similes, rhetorical questions, and emotional diction, not only gets his point across, but warns and denounces the whites as well.

Right in the beginning, Seattle starts emotionally with "wept tears of compassion" to try to gain a sympathy for his people. Later on in the passage, he exclaims, "Your God is not our God!" and blatantly announces "Your God loves your people and hates mine." These harsh words obviously convey Chief Seattle's anger and disapproval.

To further increase the emotional appeal, Seattle employs rhetorical questions in an attempt to make the reader wonder and empathize. He states ". . . he will protect us. But can that ever be?" and "How then can we be brothers? We are two distinct races." Since this was addressed to Governor Isaac, what this did was it made the Governor question himself whether the buying of more Indian land and pushing the Indians west are right and moral. In addition, the rhetorical questions allow Chief Seattle to express his anger better.

The use of similes in this piece not only add a poetic touch, but also effectively describe the decrease in Native Americans and the increase in whites. He compares the invasive whites as "grass that covers vast prairies" while describing the disappearing Indians as "scattering trees of a storm-swept plain." The storm that swept through clearly also represents the whites that pushed the Native Americans westward or bought their land. By comparing the whites to grass that grows anywhere they want and as a storm, Chief Seattle subtly establishes the idea that whites are land-hungry and greedy.

In addition, the Chief denounces certain cultural aspects of whites through a series of antitheses. As he uses "To us the ashes of our ancestors are sacred . . . You wander . . . from the graves . . . without regret" and "your dead cease to love you . . . Our dead never forget the beautiful world," there seems to be a criticism of whites as loveless people who don't respect the dead. And, as a final warning, Chief Seattle says, "Your time of decay may be distant, but it will surely come . . ." As he tried to tell the whites that what they have done will eventually cause their demise.

In all, Chief Seattle's speech to Governor Isaac not only achieves his purpose of discouraging the actions of the whites, but warns and denounces the culture of the whites as well.

Rating Student Sample A

This is a high-range essay for the following reasons:

- An immediate and clear indication of Seattle's purpose and attitude
- Understanding and discussion of Seattle's attitude and purpose (paragraph 2)
- Demonstration of a mature voice
- Thorough and effective connection between texts and insights (last two sentences of paragraph 2)
- Superior use of connective tissue—transitions and echo words ("in addition," "despite his calm," "acting respectfully," "winning favor")
- Refers to a variety of rhetorical strategies and devices to support the writer's assertion (paragraph 3: rhetorical questions), (paragraph 3: cause and effect), (paragraph 4: details), (paragraph 4: figurative language)
- Mature perceptions and insights (paragraph 2, sentence 2), (paragraph 4, sentence 2), (paragraph 5, next to last sentence)
- Mature writing style (last sentence)

   This high-range essay indicates the clear voice of a mature writer and reader. Once the writer has committed to Seattle's purpose and attitude, the writer develops in each successive paragraph a supporting aspect of the stated purpose and/or attitude.

Rating Student Sample B

This is a mid-range essay for the following reasons:

- Concise, on-target development of prompt
- Indicates an understanding of the oration
- Makes intelligent points, but does not always develop them or defend them (paragraph 3, last sentence)
- Each paragraph deals with a different strategy (paragraph 2: emotional details), (paragraph 3: rhetorical questions), (paragraph 4: simile), (paragraph 5: antithesis)
- Good connective tissue
- A few lapses in syntax and diction (paragraph 3, next to last sentence)

   This essay is indicative of a writer who understands both the passage and the prompt. There is an adequate analysis of the rhetorical strategies and devices present in the text, and the student reaches for unique insights (paragraph 4, last sentence). The lack of development of a couple of the cited points places this essay squarely in the mid-range.

Rubrics for the Stegner Essay

High-Range Essay

- Correctly identifies Stegner's position and attitude regarding the environment *and* wilderness
- Effectively presents a position about Stegner's position *and* attitude
- Clear writer's voice
- Successfully defends his or her position
- Presents carefully reasoned arguments making reference to specific examples from personal experience, knowledge, reading
- Effectively manipulates language
- Few, if any, syntactical errors

Mid-Range Essay

- Correctly identifies Stegner's position and attitude about the environment *and* wilderness
- Understands the demands of the prompt
- Clearly states the position of the writer
- Presents a generally adequate argument that makes use of appropriate examples
- Less well-developed than the high-range essay
- Ideas clearly stated
- A few lapses in diction or syntax

Low-Range Essay

- Inadequate response to the prompt
- Misunderstands, oversimplifies, or misrepresents Stegner's position and attitude
- Insufficient or inappropriate use of examples to develop the writer's position
- Lack of mature control of elements of essay writing

This prompt posed some difficulties for students. Many had a tendency to address only one aspect of it: the loss of wilderness. Often, they did not adequately connect this to the Brave New World concept of a human-controlled environment. The stronger writers included references to and discussions of the "reflection and rest" in their essays. Many student writers opposed Stegner's position by expanding on the concept of wilderness. Those who agreed with Stegner cited pertinent illustrations ranging from the rain forest to gasoline princes to overpopulation and the ozone layer. Contradictory and qualifying essays relied heavily on humankind's "frontier spirit" and artistic endeavors.

Stegner Passage—Student Sample A

Wallace Stegner writes in an essay, "Without any remaining wilderness we are   1
committed wholly, without chance for even momentary reflection and rest, to a headlong
drive into our technological termite-life, the Brave New World of a completely man-
controlled environment." This excerpt attempts to convey that humankind is on a direct
path to a highly mechanical and technological world; one that is ideal in man's quest
for scientific and technological dominance over nature. According to Stegner, man has
neglected to stop and smell the proverbial patch of roses. The idea that humankind
aims at ultimately dominating the earth with its technological advances can be tenable.
However, Stegner's argument is fallacious because people DO pause to observe and
introspect.

Humans have been in constant search of enlightenment in the world since time   2
immemorial. Like all other organisms, man tends to innovate in order to better
adapt to his natural surroundings. As time progresses, man develops more and better
ways to survive. From the days of the Enlightenment, to the Scientific Revolution, to
the Industrial Revolution, and to the computerized world of today, humankind has
persistently been pursuing ways to analyze and control his environment. During the

Enlightenment, natural philosopher Francis Bacon developed the scientific method as a set process which experiments ought to follow. His methodology has been adhered to since then in experimentation throughout the world. Using this method, Benjamin Franklin experimented with a kite in a storm and discovered electricity. Other thinkers utilized Franklin's findings and developed ways to use new energy sources. One concept has led to another and another, eventually arriving at our highly evolved world today.

These advances serve to benefit man's survival, which is why Stegner sees humans as heading for a man-controlled environment. To relieve nature-related hardships, man seeks ways to make things more comfortable for himself. For instance, air-conditioning was invented to control temperature. Another example of man controlling his environment can be found in the area of transportation: automobiles, trains, airplanes, ships, etc. Man is naturally slow, and to adapt himself to the large world, he creates machines to do the transporting. All of the inventions in the world today demonstrate attempts mankind has made in order to survive and to make life more "livable," and in these efforts, man controls nature.

3

Though Stegner's case that humanity's focus on dominating their environment can be defended, his idea that people ignore the need to rest for reflection is erroneous. While scientific and technological advancement is a commanding aspect of humankind, it is not as if history, art and culture do not exist. These facets of human society contribute to introspection. We create art to express modes of self-examination. Musicians, painters, sculptors, poets, and other artists concentrate on reflecting about man and his world. We study history as a method of introspection, and, in so doing, we essentially examine our past and reflect on it. There exist in this world goals other than the desire to control nature with technology. Humans are not "committed wholly, without chance for even momentary reflection and rest," to dominate the globe.

4

While Stegner's concept of humanity's desire to attain dominance over nature contains truth, his notion that people do not focus on anything else is false. Yes, humans do possess the tendency to explore and conquer. However, humans do not exclude all else in life. We are not always in pursuit of scientific and technological accomplishment. We are also seekers of cultural, artistic and philosophical achievement.

5

Stegner Passage—Student Sample B

Wallace Stegner wrote that, "Without any remaining wilderness we are committed wholly, without chance for even momentary reflection and rest, to a headlong drive into our technological termite-life, the Brave New World of a completely man-controlled environment." It seems that in writing this, Stegner expresses his concern for the receding forests and other wilderness areas, along with the extinction of the species that populate them. His concern is quite justified, for as we use our natural resources, we destroy those species that we now share this planet with.

It has long been known that unlike the other species of the Earth, the one known as Homo Sapiens does not adapt well to its environment. Instead, this species adapts the environment to it, and the Devil take anything that stands in its way. Homo Sapiens cannot bear the fierce winters of New England or the hot summers of the Caribbean, so it chops down trees to build houses. It does this without the slightest concern for the other species that call the forest home. Many terrible injuries have been dealt to the eco-system of this planet because of the lack of concern Homo Sapiens has shown. Holes in the ozone layer, which let terrible amounts of ultra-violet radiation bombard the earth. The constant growth of the Sahara Desert, and the destruction of the rainforests are painful examples of Homo Sapiens' ignorance, painful not just to other species, but to Homo Sapiens itself. It seems as though Homo Sapiens does not realize that when all the trees are gone, there will be no oxygen left for anyone. Hopefully before that atrocity is carried out, for it is almost sure that it will be, Homo Sapiens will figure out how to adapt very quickly.

When Stegner wrote of a "completely man-controlled environment," he is talking of a world where our species has destroyed the wilderness or at least bent it totally to our will. He writes of a world with cities, inhabited "termite-like" by reflective Homo Sapiens, the size of which no one has ever seen, most likely with rampant air pollution. Let us hope that we are not one day forced, as in "Lost in Space," to seek out other planets to live on because ours is taking its last breath. This is one possibility; Stegner is warning us to change our ignorant ways before it is too late, and he certainly has the right idea. For, if we don't, we will have truly become exactly like our hated enemy, the virus.

Rating Student Sample A

This is a high-range essay for the following reasons:

- Effectively covers the points made by Stegner in his statement
- Clearly takes a position regarding Stegner's statement
- Thoroughly develops the argument with specific examples and historical references (paragraphs 2 and 3)
- Indicates and discusses the fallacy of Stegner's statement (paragraphs 4 and 5)
- Good topic adherence
- Thorough development of the points of the writer's argument
- Mature voice, diction, and syntax

This high-range essay was written by a student who is both confident and well-versed and one who has balanced the presentation with scientific and introspective illustrations in support of the argument.

Rating Student Sample B

This is a mid-range essay for the following reasons:

- Clearly understands Stegner's statement and the demands of the prompt
- Creative voice is present
- An interesting objectification of humanity (paragraph 2—"Homo Sapiens")
- Strong conclusion
- Linkage between man's destruction of the wilderness and its consequences needs further development
- Development of the argument needs further support
- A few syntactical errors
- Lacks needed transitions

This student writer has a definite opinion to which he or she gives a strong voice. Although there is a strong, clear opening and conclusion, the body paragraphs containing the argument need further development.

PRACTICE EXAM 2

ANSWER SHEET FOR MULTIPLE-CHOICE QUESTIONS

1. _____	19. _____	37. _____
2. _____	20. _____	38. _____
3. _____	21. _____	39. _____
4. _____	22. _____	40. _____
5. _____	23. _____	41. _____
6. _____	24. _____	42. _____
7. _____	25. _____	43. _____
8. _____	26. _____	44. _____
9. _____	27. _____	45. _____
10. _____	28. _____	46. _____
11. _____	29. _____	47. _____
12. _____	30. _____	48. _____
13. _____	31. _____	49. _____
14. _____	32. _____	50. _____
15. _____	33. _____	51. _____
16. _____	34. _____	52. _____
17. _____	35. _____	53. _____
18. _____	36. _____	54. _____

I _____ did _____ did not complete this part of the test in the allotted 1 hour.

I had _____ correct answers. I had _____ incorrect answers. I left _____ blank.

I have carefully reviewed the explanations of the answers, and I think I need to work on the following types of questions:

PRACTICE EXAM 2
ADVANCED PLACEMENT ENGLISH LANGUAGE

Section I

Total Time—1 hour

Carefully read the following passages and answer the questions that follow.

Questions 1–10 are based on the following passage from Annie Dillard, *What an Essay Can Do*.

In some ways the essay can deal in both events and ideas better than the short story can, because the essayist—unlike the poet—may introduce the plain, unadorned thought without the contrived entrances of long-winded characters who mouth discourses. This sort of awful evidence killed "the novel of idea." (But eschewing it served to limit fiction's materials a little further, and likely contributed to our being left with the short story of scant idea.) The essayist may reason; he may treat of historical, cultural, or natural events, as well as personal events, for their interest and meaning alone, without resort to fabricated dramatic occasions. So the essay's materials are larger than the story's.

The essay may deal in metaphor better than the poem can, in some ways, because prose may expand what the lyric poem must compress. Instead of confining a metaphor to half a line, the essayist can devote to it a narrative, descriptive, or reflective couple of pages, and bring forth vividly its meanings. Prose welcomes all sorts of figurative language, of course, as well as alliteration, and even rhyme. The range of rhythms in prose is larger and grander than that of poetry. And it can handle discursive idea, and plain fact, as well as character and story.

The essay can do everything a poem can do, and everything a short story can do—everything but fake it. The elements in any nonfiction should be true not only artistically—the connections must hold at base and must be veracious, for that is the convention and the covenant between the nonfiction writer and his reader. Veracity isn't much of a drawback to the writer; there's a lot of truth out there to work with. And veracity isn't much of a drawback to the reader. The real world arguably exerts a greater fascination on people than any fictional one; many people at least spend their whole lives there, apparently by choice. The essayist does what we do with our lives; the essayist thinks about actual things. He can make sense of them analytically or artistically. In either case he renders the real world coherent and meaningful; even if only bits of it, and even if that coherence and meaning reside only inside small texts.

1. Which rhetorical technique does the author employ to focus the reader's attention on the specific topic of the passage?
   A. use of parallel structure
   B. identifying herself with her audience
   C. beginning each paragraph with the same subject
   D. use of passive voice
   E. use of anecdote

2. Based on a careful reading of the first paragraph, the reader can conclude that the author blames the death of the "novel of idea" on
   A. real life and situations
   B. simplicity
   C. appeal to philosophy
   D. reliance on historical data
   E. artificiality

3. The primary rhetorical strategy the author uses to develop the first paragraph is
   A. process
   B. narration
   C. description
   D. cause and effect
   E. definition

4. Near the end of the third paragraph, Dillard states, "The essayist does what we do with our lives; the essayist thinks about actual things. He can make sense of them analytically or artistically." The most probable reason for the author choosing to write two separate sentences rather than constructing a single, longer sentence using a listing, is
   A. to reinforce cause and effect
   B. both subjects are of equal importance, although separate processes
   C. to create a parallel situation
   D. to contrast the two ideas
   E. to highlight the criticism of fictional writing

5. In paragraph 3, in the sentence beginning with "The real world . . .," the word "there" refers to
   A. the fictional world
   B. novels
   C. poetry
   D. "the real world"
   E. short stories

6. The primary rhetorical strategy the author uses to develop the second paragraph is
   A. contrast and comparison
   B. narration
   C. argument
   D. description
   E. analogy

7. In terms of her position on her subject, the author can best be categorized as
   A. an adversary
   B. a critic
   C. an advocate
   D. an innovator
   E. an artist

8. An example of parallel structure is found in which of the following lines taken from the passage?
   A. "But eschewing it served to limit fiction's materials a little further, and likely contributed to our being left with the short story of scant idea."
   B. "The essay may deal in metaphor better than the poem can, in some ways, because prose may expand what the lyric poem must compress."
   C. "The elements in any nonfiction should be true not only artistically—the connections must hold at base . . ."
   D. ". . . that is the convention and the covenant between the nonfiction writer and his reader."
   E. "In either case he renders the real world coherent and meaningful; even if only bits of it, and even if that coherence and meaning reside only inside small texts."

9. The contrast between the short story writer and the essayist is based on which of the following?
   A. reflection
   B. presentation
   C. fundamental reality
   D. content
   E. clarity of purpose

10. The tone of the passage can best be described as
    A. impartial and critical
    B. condescending and formal
    C. candid and colloquial
    D. clinical and moralistic
    E. confident and informative

Questions 11–21 are based on the following passage in which Henry James responds to a literary critic's ideas about the state of the English novel.

There is one point at which the moral sense and the artistic sense lie very near together; that is in the light of the very obvious truth that the deepest quality of a work of art will always be the quality of the mind of the producer. In proportion as that intelligence is fine will the novel, the picture, the statue partake of the substance of beauty and truth. To be constituted of such elements is, to my vision, to have purpose enough. No good novel will ever proceed from a superficial mind; that seems to me an axiom which for the artist in fiction, will cover all needful moral ground: if the youthful aspirant take it to heart it will illuminate for him many of the mysteries of "purpose." There are many other useful things that might be said to him, but I have come to the end of my article, and can only touch them as I pass. The critic in the Pall Mall Gazette, whom I have already quoted, draws attention to the danger, in speaking of the art of fiction, of generalizing. The danger that he has in mind is rather, I imagine, that of particularizing. I should remind the ingenuous student first of the magnificence of the form that is open to him, which offers to sight so few restrictions and such innumerable opportunities. The other arts, in comparison, appear confined and hampered; the various conditions under which they are exercised are so rigid and definite. But the only condition that I can think of attaching to the composition of the novel is, as I have already said, that it be sincere. This freedom is a splendid privilege, and the first lesson of the young novelist is to learn to be worthy of it. "Enjoy it as it deserves," I should say to him; "take possession of it, explore it to its utmost extent, publish it, rejoice in it. All life belongs to you, and do not listen either to those who would shut you up into corners of it and tell you that it is only here and there that art inhabits, or to those who would persuade you that this heavenly messenger wings her way outside of life altogether, breathing superfine air, and turning away her head from the truth of things. There is no impression of life, no manner of seeing it and feeling it, to which the plan of the novelist may not offer a place; you have only to remember that talents so dissimilar as those of Alexander Dumas and Jane Austen, Charles Dickens and Gustave Flaubert have worked in this field with equal glory. Do not think too much about optimism and pessimism; try and catch the color of life itself. If you must indulge in conclusions, let them have the taste of a wide knowledge. Remember that your first duty is to be as complete as possible—to make as perfect a work. Be generous and delicate and pursue the prize. (1884)

11. James draws a distinction between the purpose of the novel and
    A. the moral theme
    B. the artistic sense
    C. the mind of the producer
    D. obvious truth
    E. the substance of beauty

12. From the opening of the passage, it is clear that the author's attitude toward the creation of a work of art is
    A. democratic
    B. indifferent
    C. superficial
    D. reverent
    E. elitist

13. According to James, beauty and truth are directly related to
    A. the novel
    B. intelligence
    C. a picture
    D. a statue
    E. vision

14. According to the fourth sentence, the word "axiom" can best be defined as
A. a mystery
B. an anecdote
C. a paradox
D. a rule of thumb
E. a proverb

15. In the fifth sentence, "There are many other useful things that might be said to him, but I have come to the end of my article, and can only touch them as I pass," the pronoun "him" refers to
A. "youthful aspirant"
B. "the critic"
C. "the producer"
D. the artist in fiction
E. the author

16. In the seventh sentence, "The danger that he has in mind is rather, I imagine, that of particularizing." The word "rather" establishes
A. a paradox
B. an analogy
C. an ambiguity
D. a syllogism
E. an antithesis

17. According to Henry James, the freest form of art is
A. sculpting
B. painting
C. speaking
D. writing
E. photography

18. In the middle of the passage, the sentence "'Enjoy it as it deserves,' I should say to him; 'take possession of it, explore it to its utmost extent, publish it, rejoice in it,'" includes an example of
A. a complex sentence
B. parallel structure
C. an analogy
D. inversion
E. passive voice

19. In the second half of the passage, if the student follows the logic and advice of James in the set of sentences beginning with "This freedom is a splendid . . ." and ending with "the truth of things," that student would have to
A. imitate the great writers
B. pray for inspiration
C. recognize that only after death can a writer be assessed properly
D. ignore James's advice
E. turn away from writing

20. Also in the middle of the passage is a sentence beginning with "All life belongs . . ." and ending with "the truth of things." The metaphor, "this heavenly messenger," contained in this sentence refers to
A. freedom
B. the teacher
C. sincerity
D. art
E. the critic

21. The overall tone of the passage can best be described as
A. informal and sarcastic
B. condescending and sardonic
C. didactic and exhortative
D. reverential and laudatory
E. indignant and contemptuous

Questions 22–35 are based on the following passage from Herman Melville's "Moby-Dick."

Nantucket! Take out your map and look at it. See what a real corner of the world   1
it occupies; how it stands there, away off shore, more lonely than the Eddystone
lighthouse. Look at it—a mere hillock, and elbow of sand; all beach, without a background. There is more sand there than you would use in twenty years as a substitute
for blotting paper. Some gamesome wights* will tell you that they have to plant weeds
there, they don't grow naturally; they import Canada thistles; they have to send beyond
seas for a spile† to stop a leak in an oil cask; that pieces of wood in Nantucket are
carried about like bits of the true cross in Rome; that people there plant toadstools
before their houses, to get under the shade in summer time; that one blade of grass
makes an oasis, three blades a day's walk in a prairie; that they wear quicksand shoes,
something like Laplander snowshoes; that they are so shut up, belted about, every way
inclosed, surrounded, and made an utter island of by the ocean, that to their very chairs
and tables small clams will sometimes be found adhering, as to the backs of sea turtles.
But these extravaganzas only show that Nantucket is no Illinois.

Look now at the wondrous traditional story of how this island was settled by the   2
red-men. Thus goes the legend. In olden times an eagle swooped down upon the
New England coast, and carried off an infant Indian in his talons. With loud lament
the parents saw their child borne out of sight over the wide waters. They resolved to
follow in the same direction. Setting out in their canoes, after a perilous passage they
discovered the island, and there they found an empty ivory casket,—the poor little
Indian's skeleton.

What wonder, then, that these Nantucketers, born on a beach, should take to the   3
sea for a livelihood! They first caught crabs and quahogs in the sand; grown bolder,
they waded out with nets for mackerel; more experienced, they pushed off in boats
and captured cod; and at last, launching a navy of great ships on the sea, explored
this watery world; put an incessant belt of circumnavigations round it; peeped in
at Behring's Straits; and in all seasons and all oceans declared everlasting war with
the mightiest animated mass that has survived the flood; most monstrous and most
mountainous! That Himmalehan, salt-sea Mastodon, clothed with such portentousness
of unconscious power, that his very panics are more to be dreaded than his most fearless
and malicious assaults!

And thus have these naked Nantucketers, these sea hermits, issuing from their   4
ant-hill in the sea, overrun and conquered the watery world like so many Alexanders;
parceling out among them the Atlantic, Pacific, and Indian oceans, as the three pirate
powers did Poland. Let America add Mexico to Texas, and pile Cuba upon Canada; let
the English overswarm all India, and hang out their blazing banner from the sun; two
thirds of this terraqueous globe are the Nantucketer's. For the sea is his; he owns it, as
Emperors own empires; other seamen having but a right of way through it. Merchant
ships are but extension bridges; armed ones but floating forts; even pirates and
privateers, though following the sea as highwaymen the road, they but plunder other
ships, other fragments of the land like themselves, without seeking to draw their living
from the bottomless deep itself. The Nantucketer, he alone resides and riots on the sea;
he alone, in Bible language, goes down to it in ships; to and fro ploughing it as his own

---

* wights: human beings
† spile: a small plug

special plantation. *There* is his home; *there* lies his business, which a Noah's flood would not interrupt, though it overwhelmed all the millions in China. He lives on the sea, as prairie dogs in the prairie; he hides among the waves, he climbs them as mountain goats climb the Alps. For years he knows not the land; so that when he comes to it at last, it smells like another world, more strangely than the moon would to an Earthsman. With the landless gull, that at sunset folds her wings and is rocked to sleep between billows; so at nightfall, the Nantucketer, out of sight of land, furls his sail, and lays him to his rest, while under his very pillow rush herds of walruses and whales.

22. The controlling analogy of the passage is
   A. Nantucket to Illinois
   B. sea to land
   C. Noah to Nantucket
   D. moon to Earthsman
   E. legends to reality

23. Melville describes Nantucketers as all of the following <u>except</u>:
   A. conquerors
   B. natives of the sea
   C. farmers of the sea
   D. strangers to the land
   E. exploiters of the Native American claims

24. The tone of the passage can best be described as
   A. self-congratulatory and confident
   B. formal and pompous
   C. admiring and hyperbolic
   D. informal and cynical
   E. pedantic and objective

25. The most probable reason for repeating and italicizing "*There*" in the middle of paragraph 4 at the beginning of two main clauses in the same sentence is to
   A. force the reader to look for an antecedent
   B. sound poetic
   C. provide a break in a long, complicated sentence
   D. emphasize the sense of place
   E. indicate sympathy for the plight of the Nantucketer

26. The shift in the focus of the piece occurs in which line?
   A. The first sentence of paragraph 2
   B. The first sentence of paragraph 3
   C. The first sentence of paragraph 4
   D. The third sentence in paragraph 4
   E. The last sentence

27. The first paragraph contains an extended example of
   A. parallel structure
   B. anecdote
   C. periodic sentence
   D. generalization
   E. argument

28. Melville retells the Native American legend of how the island was settled in order to
   A. have his audience identify with the Native American population
   B. make the passage seem like a parable
   C. contrast with the reality of the Nantucketers
   D. bring a mythic quality to the subject
   E. highlight the plight of the Nantucketers

29. The development of paragraph 3 is structured around
   A. spatial description
   B. selection of incremental details
   C. central analogy
   D. parallel structure
   E. paradox

30. This passage can best be classified as an example of an argument based on
   A. definition
   B. cause and effect
   C. analysis
   D. process
   E. analogy

31. One may conclude from the information contained in paragraph 3 that "Himmalehan, salt-sea Mastedon" refers to
   A. the ocean
   B. the whale
   C. the power of nature
   D. Biblical vengeance
   E. emperors

32. The purpose of the passage is most probably to
A. encourage people to settle on Nantucket
B. use Nantucket as a model of ecological conservation
C. honor the indomitable spirit of the Nantucketers
D. plead for the return of Nantucket to the Native Americans
E. present a nostalgic reminiscence of the writer's birthplace

33. Melville uses *thus* twice in this passage: once in the second paragraph to begin the Native American legend about the island being settled. All of the following are reasons for using *thus* in the first sentence of paragraph 4 except
A. to begin a comparative legend with the Nantucketers settling the sea
B. to balance the first part of the passage with the second part
C. to indicate a kind of cause and effect relationship
D. to reinforce the formality of his presentation
E. to further connect the inhabitants to the island and its legends

34. The subtle humor of the first paragraph is dependent upon
A. paradox
B. hyperbole
C. juxtaposition
D. irony
E. ad hominem argument

35. The last sentence of the passage continues the analogy between
A. reality and illusion
B. night and day
C. man and animal
D. gull and walrus
E. sea and land

Questions 36–44 are based on the following passage from Lucy Stone, "A Disappointed Woman," a speech she gave to the national women's rights convention in Cincinnati, Ohio, in October, 1855.

The last speaker alluded to this movement as being that of a few disappointed   1
women. From the first years to which my memory stretches, I have been a disappointed
woman. When, with my brothers, I reached forth after the sources of knowledge, I
was reproved with "It isn't fit for you; it doesn't belong to women." Then there was but
one college in the world where women were admitted, and that was in Brazil. I would
have found my way there, but by the time I was prepared to go, one was opened in the
state of Ohio—the first in the United States where women and Negroes could enjoy
opportunities with white men. I was disappointed when I came to seek a profession
worthy an immortal being—every employment was closed to me, except those of a
teacher, the seamstress, and the housekeeper. In education, in marriage, in religion, in
everything, disappointment is the lot of woman. It shall be the business of my life to
deepen this disappointment in every woman's heart until she bows down to it no longer.
I wish that women, instead of being walking show-cases, instead of begging of their
fathers and brothers the latest and finest new bonnet, would ask of them their rights.

The question of Woman's Rights is a practical one. The notion has prevailed that   2
it was only an ephemeral idea; that it was but women claiming their right to smoke
cigars in the streets, and to frequent bar-rooms. Others have supposed it a question of
comparative intellect; others still, of sphere. Too much has already been said and written
about women's sphere. Trace all the doctrines to their source and they will be found to
have no basis except in the usages and prejudices of the age. This is seen in the fact that
what is tolerated in woman in one country is not tolerated in another. In this country
women may hold prayer-meetings, etc., but in other countries it is written upon their
houses of worship, "Women and dogs, and other impure animals, are not permitted
to enter." Wendell Phillips says, "The best and greatest thing one is capable of doing,
that is his sphere." I have confidence in the Father to believe that when He gives us the
capacity to do anything, He does not make a blunder. Leave women, then, to find their
sphere. And do not tell us before we are born even, that our province is to cook dinners,
darn stockings, and sew on buttons. . . ."

36. The tone of the passage can best be described as
  A. pedantic and cynical
  B. flippant and irreverent
  C. reverent and somber
  D. indignant and argumentative
  E. ambivalent and resigned

37. A major hypothesis presented by the speaker is that
  A. religion is the cause of women's position in the United States
  B. women are not as intelligent as men
  C. education is the only way to cure the evils of society
  D. the question of Women's Rights is a philosophical issue
  E. women and African Americans are on the same level

38. What can the reader infer based upon the sentence found in the middle of paragraph 1 that begins with "I was disappointed . . ." and ending with "and the housekeeper"?
  A. Lucy Stone is not a religious person.
  B. Teaching was not considered a worthy profession.
  C. The speaker is an adventurer.
  D. Stone values the opinions of others.
  E. She is married with children.

39. The thesis of the passage is best expressed in
  A. paragraph 1, sentence 3 ("When, with my brothers . . .")
  B. paragraph 1, sentence 7 ("In education . . .")

C. paragraph 2, sentence 1
("The question . . .")

D. paragraph 2, sentence 6
("This is seen . . .")

E. paragraph 3, sentence 9
("Wendell Phillips says . . .")

40. Stone develops her speech using all of the following except:
A. an ad hominem argument
B. an anecdote
C. direct quotations
D. facts
E. an ethical appeal

41. In light of the passage, how can the following sentence near the end of the first paragraph best be characterized? "It shall be the business of my life to deepen this disappointment in every woman's heart until she bows down to it no longer."
A. ironic and paradoxical
B. analytical and pedantic
C. formal and detached
D. informal and anecdotal
E. allegorical and ambivalent

42. Based on a careful reading of the passage, one can assume that the speaker
A. believes that women are superior to men
B. believes that religion is the salvation of women
C. believes in fate and destiny
D. believes that foreign countries are more enlightened about women's rights than the United States
E. is disappointed with her female contemporaries

43. In the sentence beginning with "Wendell Phillips says . . ." in the middle of paragraph 2, Lucy Stone develops her point using
A. an analogy
B. a straw-man argument
C. a syllogism
D. an ad hominem argument
E. sarcasm

44. The speaker's purpose is most probably to
A. explain
B. exhort
C. amuse
D. describe
E. narrate

Questions 45-54 are based on the following excerpt from a review and discussion by Christopher Jencks of *American Dream: Three Women, Ten Kids, and a Nation's Drive to End Welfare*, written by Jason DeParle and published by Viking/Penguin in 2005. The review appeared in the December 15, 2005, edition of *The New York Review of Books*.

[According to the US Census Bureau] The poverty rate for single mothers [who headed their own households and had children under eighteen] was only 36 percent in 2003, compared to 44 percent in 1994, when unemployment was about what it had been in 1996.[4]

The official poverty rate has serious flaws. It omits food stamps, free medical care,   5
housing subsidies, and taxes. So it is important to see whether direct measures of material hardship tell the same story. The Agriculture Department's Food Security Survey (FSS) is a good place to begin. It asks mothers whether money problems forced them to skip meals or cut the size of their meals at any point during the previous twelve months. Between April 1995 and April 2001, as the welfare rolls were being cut in half,   10
the fraction of single mothers who said they had to limit what they ate fell from 17.7 to 12.5 percent.[5] By 2003, with unemployment slightly above its 1995 level, the percentage of mothers who reported cutting back what they ate had risen, but only to 13.8 percent.

The FSS also asked mothers whether there was a time when their children were not getting enough to eat. The proportion who said this was the case fell from 10.6 percent   15
in 1995 to 7.8 percent in 2001 and had only risen to 8.0 percent in 2003.[6] Both of these measures are consistent with the official poverty rate in suggesting that even when unemployment was 6 percent, single mothers did better after welfare reform than before.

The proportion of unmarried mothers living in someone else's home is another   20
indicator of financial stress. Some mothers live in someone else's home by choice, but most get their own place when their income rises. Twenty-two percent of unmarried mothers lived in someone else's home in both 1989 and 2000.[7] When welfare reform passed, its critics also predicted a surge in the number of families living in public shelters. The United States does not collect national data on trends in homelessness,   25
but in Milwaukee, which cut about ten thousand families from its welfare rolls, [Jason] DeParle reports that the number of families in shelters on an average night rose by only forty-one. On December 12, 2004, Boston counted 1,157 homeless children in the city, down from 1,274 a decade earlier.[8] Nationally, the proportion of children not living with either their mother or their father was the same in 2004 as in 1994.   30

These measures of material well-being can be summarized in two ways. Defenders of welfare reform stress the fact that the proportion of single mothers who cannot afford to rent their own housing is no higher today than in 1996, and that the proportion who report not having enough to eat has fallen significantly. Critics of welfare reform stress

4 US Census Bureau, *Historical Poverty Tables*, www.census.gov/hhes/www/poverty/histpov/hstpov4.html.

5 Scott Winship and Christopher Jencks, "How Did the Social Policy Changes of the 1990s Affect Maternal Hardship Among Single Mothers? Evidence from the CPS Food Security Supplement," Kennedy School of Government, Working Paper RWP04-027, June 2004 (ksgnotes1.harvard.edu/Research/wpaper.nsf/rwp/RWP04027/$File/rwp04 -027-Winship-Jencks.pdf). The comparisons between 1995 and 2001 use the common screen.

6 Tabulations by Scott Winship.

7 I am indebted to Joseph Swingle of Wellesley College for all the estimates derived from the Census Bureau's Annual Demographic Survey.

8 Friends of Boston's Homeless, "2004 City of Boston Homeless Census: Homeless Families Increase Dramatically," available at www.fobh.org/census.htm, accessed August 26, 2004. The title of this report refers to an increase between 2003 and 2004.

the fact that millions of single-parent families still have trouble putting food on the
table and that even larger numbers cannot afford an apartment of their own. Welfare   35
reform is clearly a success relative to the dismal situation that prevailed in the United
States before 1996. But the country is still a long way from achieving the goals that
more compassionate societies set for themselves.

45. The argument presented in this passage is
based on
A. Constitutional rights
B. government interventions
C. personal experience
D. anecdotes
E. statistical data

46. The organizational pattern of the passage is
A. general to specific
B. specific to general
C. familiar to unfamiliar
D. most important to least important
E. cause and effect

47. The reader may infer from lines 35–38 that the
writer
A. believes welfare is clearly a success
B. believes welfare is failing to meet dismal
situations
C. admires the welfare programs of countries
other than those of the United States
D. maintains that there has been little need for
welfare reform since 1996
E. believes that the goals of the United States
are the proper ones

48. The tone of the passage can best be described as
A. factual
B. sarcastic
C. laudatory
D. ironic
E. sentimental

49. Which of the given footnotes is a primary
source?
A. 4
B. 5
C. 6
D. 7
E. 8

50. A critical reader of this passage should ask all
of the following questions about footnote 7
<u>except</u>:

A. What is the relationship between Swingle
and the author of this review?
B. How many estimates were actually
constructed?
C. To what does the word *all* refer?
D. What are Swingle's qualifications as a
reliable source?
E. Can I locate an annotated citation about
Swingle in another section of this review?

51. Another effective means of presenting the
statistical material found in this passage would
most probably be a(n)
A. personal anecdote
B. short story
C. one-act play
D. chart or graph
E. interview with a homeless mother

52. The footnote that most likely reflects a specific
bias is found in
A. 4
B. 5
C. 6
D. 7
E. 8

53. In lines 35–38, the author's bias/agenda is most
clearly evidenced through
A. statistical information and interpretation
B. definition
C. description
D. diction and syntax
E. summarization

54. Based on a careful reading of footnote 5, the
reader can correctly assume that Winship and
Jencks are
A. recognized authorities in this field
B. social workers
C. students
D. welfare reformers
E. employees of the federal government

END OF SECTION I

Section II

Question 1

Suggested Writing Time: 40 minutes

Based on the Constitutional First Amendment guarantee of the right to freedom of speech, some citizens and citizen groups have used public burning of the American flag as a means of political expression. A proposed amendment to the *U.S. Constitution* states: "The Congress shall have the power to prohibit the physical desecration of the flag of the United States." Is desecrating the flag a legitimate form of expression guaranteed by the Constitution? Should the Constitution be amended to protect the flag?

   Carefully read the following sources (including any introductory information). **Then, in an essay that synthesizes at least three of the sources for support, take a position that defends, challenges, or qualifies the claim that the flag should be protected under a constitutional amendment.**

   Make certain that you take a position and that the essay centers on your argument. Use the sources to support your reasoning; avoid simply summarizing the sources. You may refer to the sources by their letters (Source A, Source B, etc.) or by the identifiers in the parentheses below.

Source A (First Amendment to the *U.S. Constitution*)
Source B (The Proposed Amendment)
Source C (*USA Today* Survey)
Source D (Two Supreme Court Decisions)
Source E (Rehnquist's Dissenting Opinion)
Source F (Editorial in the *Los Angeles Times*)
Source G (Congressional Votes)
Source H (Political Cartoon by Clay Bennett)
Source I (Editorial by Todd Lindberg)

Source A
From "The Bill of Rights," *The U.S. Constitution.*

> #### *Amendment I*
>
> *Congress shall make no law respecting an establishment of religion, or prohibiting the free exercise thereof; or abridging the freedom of speech, or of the press; or the right of the people peaceably to assemble, and to petition the government for a redress of grievances.*

Source B
The Proposed Amendment to the *U.S. Constitution* taken from *The Congressional Record.* Available at https://www.congress.gov/congressional-report/108thcongress/senate-report/334/1.

> #### *The full text of the amendment:*
>
> *The Congress shall have power to prohibit the physical desecration of the flag of the United States.*

Source C

Results of a survey conducted by *USA Today*, June 23–25, 2006, http://www.usatoday .com/news/washington/2006-06-26-poll-results_x.htm.

Some people feel that the U.S. Constitution should be amended to make it illegal to burn or desecrate the American flag as a form of political dissent. Others say that the U.S. Constitution should not be amended to specifically prohibit flag burning or desecration. Do you think the U.S. Constitution should or should not be amended to prohibit burning or desecrating the American flag?

Results based on 516 national adults in Form B:

Date asked	Yes, amended	No, not	No opinion
June 23–25, 2006	45%	54%	2%

Source D

Two Supreme Court Decisions related to the desecration of the flag. Available at http://www.firstamendmentcenter.org/speech/flagburning/overview.aspx?topic= flag-burning_overview.

Texas v. Johnson, 491 U.S. 397 (1989), was a decision by the Supreme Court of the United States. The question the Supreme Court had to answer was: "Is the desecration of an American flag, by burning or otherwise, a form of speech that is protected under the First Amendment?" Justice William Brennan wrote the 5–4 majority decision in holding that the defendant's act of flag burning was protected speech under the First Amendment to the United States Constitution.

The court held that the First Amendment prevented Texas from punishing the defendant for burning the flag under the specified circumstances. The court first found that burning of the flag was expressive conduct protected by the First Amendment. The court concluded that Texas could not criminally sanction flag desecration in order to preserve the flag as a symbol of national unity. It also held that the statute did not meet the state's goal of preventing breaches of the peace, since it was not drawn narrowly enough to encompass only those flag burnings that would likely result in a serious disturbance, and since the flag burning in this case did not threaten such a reaction.

Subsequently, Congress passed a statute, the 1989 Flag Protection Act, making it a federal crime to desecrate the flag. In the case of United States v. Eichman, 496 U.S. 310 (1990), that law was struck down by the same five-person majority of justices as in Texas v. Johnson, 491 U.S. 397 (1989).

Source E

Chief Justice William Rehnquist's dissenting opinion in the *Texas v. Johnson* (1989) case. Available at http://www.bc.edu/bc_org/avp/cas/comm/free_speech/texas.html.

In his dissenting opinion in Texas v. Johnson (1989), regarding Texas law against flag burning, the late Chief Justice William H. Rehnquist wrote,

> *The American flag, then, throughout more than 200 years of our history, has come to be the visible symbol embodying our Nation. It does not represent the views of any particular political party, and it does not represent any particular political philosophy. The flag is not simply another "idea" or "point of view" competing for recognition in the marketplace of ideas. Millions and millions of Americans regard it with an almost mystical reverence regardless of what sort of social, political, or philosophical beliefs they may have. I cannot agree that the First Amendment invalidates the Act of Congress, and the laws of 48 of the 50 States, which make criminal the public burning of the flag.*

Rehnquist also argued that flag burning is "no essential part of any exposition of ideas" but, rather "the equivalent of an inarticulate grunt or roar that, it seems fair to say, is most likely to be indulged in not to express any particular idea, but to antagonize others."

Source F

"The case for flag-burning: An amendment banning it would make America less free." An editorial that appeared in the *Los Angeles Times*, June 27, 2006.

> *THERE ARE MANY ARGUMENTS AGAINST a proposed constitutional amendment to outlaw "the physical desecration of the flag of the United States." Let us count the ways in which the amendment, which is disturbingly close to the 67 votes required for Senate approval, is unworthy of that body's support:*
>
> - *It's a "solution" to a problem that doesn't exist. There has been no epidemic of flag-burning since the Supreme Court ruled in 1989 that destruction of Old Glory as a protest was symbolic speech protected by the 1st Amendment.*
> - *As Sen. Mitch McConnell (R-Ky.) pointed out, "The First Amendment has served us well for over 200 years. I don't think it needs to be altered." Placing a no-flag-burning asterisk next to the amendment's sweeping guarantee of free speech is a mischievous idea, and it could invite amendments to ban other sorts of speech Americans find offensive.*
>
> *But the best argument against the flag amendment is the one some opponents are reluctant to make for fear of political fallout: It would make America less free.*
>
> *Rare as flag-burning may be, a nation that allows citizens to denounce even its most sacred symbols is being true to what the Supreme Court in 1964 called the "profound national commitment to the principle that debate on public issues should be uninhibited, robust and wide-open, and that it may well include vehement, caustic, and sometimes unpleasantly sharp attacks on government and public officials."*
>
> *In that decision, and in 1989, the court interpreted the free-speech protections of the First Amendment generously but correctly. The Senate, including Feinstein and fellow Democrat and Californian Barbara Boxer (who has opposed a flag-burning amendment in the past), should let those decisions be.*

Source G

Congressional votes regarding proposed constitutional amendment regarding desecration of the flag. Available at http://en.wikipedia.org/wiki/Flag_Burning_Amendment#Congressional_votes.

The chronology of the House of Representatives' action upon the flag-desecration amendment running over a period of more than ten years:

Congress	Resolution(s)	Vote date	Yeas	Nays
104th Congress	House Joint Resolution 79	June 28, 1995	312	120
	Senate Joint Resolution 31	December 12, 1995	63	36
105th Congress	House Joint Resolution 54	June 12, 1997	310	114
106th Congress	House Joint Resolution 33	June 24, 1999	305	124
	Senate Joint Resolution 14	March 29, 2000	63	37
107th Congress	House Joint Resolution 36	July 17, 2001	298	125
108th Congress	House Joint Resolution 4	June 3, 2003	300	125
109th Congress	House Joint Resolution 10	June 22, 2005	286	130
	Senate Joint Resolution 12	June 27, 2006	66	34

Source H

Political Cartoon by Clay Bennett, the *Christian Science Monitor*, Boston, July 4, 2006. Available at http://www.cagle.com/news/FlagBurning2/2.asp.

Clay Bennett, *Christian Science Monitor*, Boston 7/4/06

Source I

An excerpt from "The Star-Spangled Banner," an editorial by Todd Lindberg that appeared in the *Washington Times*, July 4, 2006. Available at http://washingtontimes.com/op-ed/20060703-102601-1107r.htm.

. . . the last thing that a constitutional amendment banning flag-burning strikes me as is a slippery slope toward broader restriction on freedom of expression. There are two reasons for this.

First, the flag is the flag; the only reason to accord it special status (if that's what you decide) is that it is, in fact, the singular national symbol. We are not even talking about a ban on burning red, white, and blue things, such as bunting, nor of suppressing the debate over whether banning the burning of the flag is a good thing. It's not hypocrisy but rather a pretty good philosophical point to say that the flag, as the symbol of the freedom to burn, baby, burn, is the one thing you shouldn't burn. For if you burn the freedom to burn, you have no freedom. For more on the danger that lies in this direction, see the collapse of the Weimar Republic in Germany.

On the other hand, the flag is not the freedom itself but its symbol. The freedom continues even if a particular flag is consumed in fire. To burn the flag is not to burn the only flag. There is no "the" flag, only flags; or if there is "the" flag, it is an idea of the flag and therefore beyond the reach of the flames.

Except that a perfectly acceptable way to dispose of a worn-out flag, according to the old Boy Scout manual Dad gave me, is by burning. The ceremony is to be at all times respectful and somber. Here, one reveres "the" flag by seeing to it that "a" flag gets decommissioned properly. So the symbolic content is always present. When someone burns a flag in protest, it's just not about the fire and the piece of cloth. The flag is indeed a symbol of a political community, and I'm not sure that political communities can get by without symbols.

The second reason I'm not worried about a slippery slope constricting expression once you ban flag-burning is that in the current environment, socially enforced restraints on expression are far broader and more important than legal restraints. In the case of flag-burning, if you do it now, most Americans will think you are an ingrate jerk, as noted above. But even if a constitutional amendment passes, no one is proposing the death penalty for flag-burning, nor life in prison. If you get busted, you can probably look forward to a few days in the clink, plus adulatory editorials in the New York Times.

So while I am not a great supporter of an amendment banning flag-burning, neither do I think that such an amendment would do harm if passed. If I were a member of the Senate, I would have voted for it. That's because as an elected officeholder, I would feel more solicitous of the national symbol, as perhaps befits someone who has chosen to hold office in accordance with the principles and procedures of the political community in question.

Question 2

Carefully read the following two passages on London fog. In a well-structured essay, compare the two selections with regard to purpose and style. Consider such elements as diction, figurative language, organization, syntax, and manipulation of language.

London was the first great city in history to be fuelled by coal. The combination of ever greater quantities of coal being burned by an expanding population, and London's naturally misty situation in a marshy river valley, meant London was plagued by regular fogs from Stuart times on. The worst lasted from November 1879 to March 1880 without a break.   1

In 1936–7, 322 tons of solid matter per square mile was deposited on Archbishop's Park, Lambeth, which meant nearly 30,000 tons of matter a year   2 *was deposited on London from smoky atmosphere. At the same time central London received 18 per cent less sunshine than the inner suburbs. In 1934 there was fog from 10 November to 1 December, and deaths from respiratory diseases tripled. The fog of 1952 was estimated to have caused 4000 deaths. The Clean Air Act was passed in 1956, and the last great London fog was in 1962.*

(Tim Goodwin, 1997)

Fog everywhere. Fog up the river, where it flows among green aits and meadows; 1
fog down the river, where it rolls defiled among tiers of shipping and waterside pollutions of a great (and dirty) city. Fog on the Essex marshes, fog on the heights, fog creeping into the cabooses of [coal barges]. Fog lying out on the yards, and hovering in the rigging of great ships; fog drooping on the gunwales of barges and small boats. Fog in the eyes and throats of ancient Greenwich pensioners, wheezing by the firesides of their wards; fog in the stem and bowl of the afternoon pipe of the wrathful skipper, down in his close cabin; fog cruelly pinching the toes and fingers of his shivering little 'prentice boy on deck. Chance people on the bridges peeping over the parapets into a nether sky of fog, with fog all round them, as if they were up in a balloon, and hanging in the misty clouds.

(Charles Dickens, *Bleak House*, 1852–53)

Question 3

In one section of *Walden*, Henry David Thoreau ponders the advice offered by elders in a society. Carefully read the following passage from this American classic. Then, in a well-constructed essay argue how your position on advice from elders relates to that of Thoreau. Use appropriate evidence from your own experiences, readings, and observations to explain and support your argument.

What everybody echoes or in silence passes by as true today may turn out to be falsehood tomorrow, mere smoke of opinion, which some had trusted for a cloud that would sprinkle fertilizing rain on their fields. What old people say you cannot do, you try and find that you can. Old deeds for old people, and new deeds for new. Old people did not know enough once, perchance, to fetch fresh fuel to keep the fire a-going; new people put a little dry wood under a pot, and are whirled around the globe with the speed of birds, in a way to kill old people, as the phrase is. Age is no better, hardly so well, qualified for an instructor as youth, for it has not profited so much as it has lost. One may almost doubt if the wisest man has learned anything of absolute value by living. Practically, the old have no very important advice to give the young, their own experience has been so partial, and their lives have been such miserable failures, for private reasons, as they must believe; and it may be that they have some faith left which belies that experience, and they are only less young than they were. I have lived some thirty years on this planet, and I have yet to hear the first syllable of valuable or even earnest advice from my seniors. They have told me nothing, and probably cannot tell me anything to the purpose. Here is life, an experiment to a great extent untried by me; but it does not avail me that they have tried it. If I have any experience which I think valuable, I am sure to reflect that this my Mentors said nothing about . . .

END OF SECTION II

ANSWER KEY

1. C	19. D	37. E
2. E	20. D	38. B
3. D	21. C	39. B
4. B	22. B	40. A
5. D	23. E	41. A
6. A	24. C	42. E
7. C	25. D	43. C
8. E	26. B	44. B
9. C	27. A	45. E
10. E	28. D	46. B
11. C	29. B	47. C
12. E	30. E	48. A
13. B	31. B	49. A
14. D	32. C	50. B
15. A	33. D	51. D
16. E	34. B	52. E
17. D	35. E	53. D
18. B	36. D	54. C

Explanations of Answers to the Multiple-Choice Section

The Annie Dillard Passage

1. **C.** Each paragraph opens with the words "the essay." With this repetition, Dillard guarantees that the reader's focus does not waver. It also provides the organizational framework of the passage. There is no passive voice present. (By the way, the previous sentence is an example of passive voice.) The author relates no personal narrative and does not identify herself with her audience.

2. **E.** In the first two sentences, the author blames "contrived entrances" for killing "the novel of idea." She supports this in the next to the last sentence in paragraph 1 by criticizing "fabricated dramatic occasions." Both of these examples point to the artificial construct of fiction.

3. **D.** The first paragraph contains two major cause-and-effect situations. The first is found in sentences 1–3, and the second is found in the last two sentences.

4. **B.** The first of the two sentences states what the essayist does: he thinks. The second sentence tells the reader *how* he thinks and writes. By writing two separate sentences, Dillard reinforces the equal importance of each of these points.

5. **D.** A careful reading of the sentence and a knowledge of how to locate antecedents can only lead the reader to choose "the real world." Any other choice negates the correct meaning of antecedent/referent.

6. **A.** The second paragraph clearly develops its point through a contrast and comparison between prose and poetry. None of the other strategies is present in the paragraph.

7. **C.** Dillard's subject is the essay. Her position is one of unswerving allegiance to its form and function. Nowhere does she criticize the essay or the essayist, and nowhere does she discuss innovations or the changing of its form. Dillard **is** an artist. This classification, however, does not reveal her stance on the essay form.

8. **E.** Knowing the definition of parallel structure and being able to recognize it makes the choice of E an easy one. ("Even if . . . even if . . .")

9. **C.** Look carefully at sentences 1–3 of paragraph 3 and notice the author's use of the words "connections," "covenant," "veracity," and "truth." With this specific diction, the only appropriate choice is C.

10. **E.** The only choice that contains two adjectives that are *BOTH* applicable to the author's tone in this passage is E. The purpose of the essay is to inform/explain the function of the essay and the essayist. This, in itself, is the support for choosing E. The confidence is apparent in the writer's discussion of the other forms of literature.

The Henry James Passage

11. **C.** This is located in the first sentence. Here James tells his audience that the quality of the mind of the producer is the key factor in creating high-quality art. The moral and artistic grow out of this quality. "Obvious truth" refers to his premise, and beauty is a by-product of the process.

12. **E.** James's diction is indicative of an elitist attitude. Note phrases such as "No good novel will ever proceed from a superficial mind . . ." He closes out any other possibility for a creative endeavor of quality.

13. **B.** The question demands your close attention to the structure of the sentence. In this instance, beauty as truth is directly proportionate to intelligence. "This" applies to the novel, picture, statue. And, it is James's vision.

14. **D.** A rule of thumb is a generally accepted truth as to how to proceed. In this context, James presents a ground rule for the young writer.

15. **A.** This is a straight question about antecedents. To find the referent, look back at the sentence preceding this one.

16. **E.** One needs to know and recognize examples of the terms used in this question. Here, "rather" opposes "generalizing" with "particularizing."

17. **D.** The sentence in the middle of the passage beginning with "The other arts . . ." will indicate to the careful reader that James is

making a point to the student that art forms other than the novel are "confined and hampered." No other choice is appropriate in this context.

18. **B.** It is easy to see the parallel structure in this sentence. Notice "enjoy it"; "explore it"; "publish it"; "rejoice in it." The other choices are not present.

19. **D.** This question may seem daunting at first, but careful examination of the structure of the lines reveals that James is telling the student not to allow himself to be cornered into following advice that limits his horizons. Ironically, James has already limited the scope of art and the artist.

20. **D.** The pronoun "this" in the middle of the sentence beginning with "All life belongs to you . . ." is your best clue to the answer "This" is referring to the word "art." Therefore, the only appropriate choice is D.

21. **C.** Through both the process of elimination and recognizing that both parts of your answer must be correct, the only appropriate choice is didactic, because the author is attempting to instruct the young novelist and exhortative in his urging the young writer to "catch the color of life itself."

The Herman Melville Passage

22. **B.** Throughout the passage, Melville builds his description on the comparison between items connected to the sea and those related to the land. Choices A and C are examples of this controlling analogy. D is another specific detail provided, and E is an example used by Melville to reinforce his description of the Nantucketer.

23. **E.** Paragraph 4 supports choices A, B, C, and D. The only choice not supported in the text is E.

24. **C.** The diction and selection of detail all support the tone of admiration. The hyperbole can easily be seen in paragraph 1 and the end of paragraph 3.

25. **D.** Italics are used for very definite reasons. The purpose here is for emphasis. Melville wants to draw the reader back to the only other italicized word in the piece— *Nantucket*—the very first word of the passage.

26. **B.** Here, pronouns are very important. In paragraph 2, *this* refers the reader to paragraph 1, which is about the island. *These* in paragraph 4 refers to the previous paragraph, which is about the inhabitants of Nantucket. The last sentence of the passage, while quite moving, indicates, again, a reference to Nantucketers. However, *these* in the first sentence of paragraph 3 is a definite shift in focus from the island to its inhabitants.

27. **A.** The only choice appearing in the first paragraph is parallel structure, which is used throughout the listing of "extravaganzas" that Melville bestows on Nantucket. Many of the items in the listing begin with the word *that*.

28. **D.** Keeping in mind the central focus of the passage, Melville's retelling of the Native American legend is not to highlight or focus on Native Americans, but to reinforce his attitude toward the Nantucketers, whom he perceives in mythic proportions. He compares them to Noah, to Alexander the Great, and to Emperors.

29. **B.** The question requires the reader to be aware of the consecutive details that build in size and importance: from the clam to the whale.

30. **E.** The entire passage develops Melville's opinion about both Nantucket and its inhabitants using analogies. For example, in paragraph 1, pieces of wood are "carried about like bits of the true cross." The entire second paragraph is a portrait built on a Native American legend. The last sentence of paragraph 3 employs an analogy comparing a "the mightiest animated mass" with "salt-sea Mastodon." Paragraph 4 compares Nantucketers to "Emperors," to "sea hermits," "so many Alexanders," etc. Any instance of the other choices is constructed using analogies.

31. **B.** The whale is a "mightiest animated mass." This can only refer to the largest creature in the sea. "Himmalehan" and "Mastadon" reinforce the power and size of the creature.

32. **C.** The tone, diction, syntax, and selection of detail all point to Melville's admiration of the fortitude, perseverance, and uniqueness of the Nantucketer.

33. **D.** In this question, the repetition balances the dual focus: the island and its inhabitants. The diction and syntax of this selection are not formal, but rather a grand folk myth of epic proportions.

34. **B.** Beginning with "There is more sand" and continuing to the end of the paragraph, Melville presents examples dependent upon extreme exaggeration.

35. **E.** The paragraph develops an extended analogy that compares the world of the sea to that of the land, such as sea to prairie, sailor to prairie dog. None of the other choices are valid in this context.

The Lucy Stone Passage

36. **D.** If you chose E, you're out of our class for the day. Seriously, it is obvious that the speaker both is outraged about the treatment of women and demands the right of women to be recognized. No other choice is correct in both descriptions.

37. **E.** The fifth sentence in paragraph 1 provides the answer to this question. In these two lines, the student should see that Stone makes a case that both women and blacks are not being educated and are by implication being treated in the same way.

38. **B.** If the student carefully looks at the sixth sentence in paragraph 1, he or she will see that it is valid to conclude that the speaker does not hold teaching in high esteem.

39. **B.** Each of these lines plays an important role in the speech. However, only one plays the role of controlling the entire thought process. The other choices are subtopics.

40. **A.** Anecdotal support is found in the first six sentences of paragraph 1. A direct quotation is located in the second half of paragraph 2. Facts are used in the fourth and fifth sentences of paragraph 1, and the appeal to emotion is presented in the seventh sentence of paragraph 2. There is no ad hominem argument in the speech.

41. **A.** Stone wants women to rise up and stop the oppression of their gender. But, according to this statement, she must actually see to it that women are oppressed until they can no longer bear it. It is only then that Stone sees their being willing to demand their rights.

42. **E.** If you look carefully at the section of the speech beginning with "I wish that women . . ." and ending with "frequent bar-rooms," you will note that Stone says she is disappointed that women concern themselves only with the superficial. Her remarks about religion, foreign countries, fate, and men are in opposition to the actual choices. Notice the use of the word *ephemeral*.

43. **C.** The speaker aims for a logical conclusion when she points to Phillips' definition of sphere. She creates an implied syllogism that if God cannot make a mistake, if God created each of us to do our best, this must apply to all—men and women alike.

44. **B.** To exhort: to urge, to warn earnestly. In her speech, Lucy Stone is urging her audience to begin to stand up for their rights as women. She wants them to understand what is oppressing them and, as a result, to "no longer bow down to it." A careful reading of the passage will indicate that the basis for the speech is *NOT* telling a story, nor is there an attempt to amuse or describe. The last sentence provides the final impetus for her exhortation.

The Poverty Excerpt

45. **E.** The writer desires to remain as objective as possible. This is accomplished by avoiding any personal narratives, any debates about the right to entitlements, or any specific stories about those living in poverty. The author provides in paragraph after paragraph a compilation of specific statistics gathered from the U.S. Census Bureau.

46. **B.** Each paragraph provides specific statistics to support the claim that welfare reform is not a complete success. This thesis is presented at the end of the passage, *NOT* at the beginning.

47. **C.** There is an indictment of the United States for failing to enact the policies and meet the goals that other countries have already put into practice.

48. **A.** A cursory look at the inclusion and preponderance of statistics and other data with little personal commentary support this choice.

49. **A.** All other footnotes cite sources, depend on other sources, or are personal commentary.

50. **B.** It doesn't matter how many estimates there are. What is important is the authority and reliability of Swingle.

51. D. The presentation of so many statistics from various years demands a visual representation for clarity and ease of understanding. The other choices would only address a subjective aspect of the topic.

52. E. This source comes from an organization whose very name states its potential bias and agenda.

53. D. The words *dismal* and *but*, plus the phrases *still a long way from* and *more compassionate* all point to the author's disapproval of the current policies of the United States.

54. C. Within the footnote, *Working Paper* and the Internet address point to a recent research project submitted to an academic institution.

Sample Student Essays

Rubrics for Flag Amendment Synthesis Essay

A **9** essay has all the qualities of an 8 essay, and the <u>writing style</u> is especially <u>impressive</u>, as is the analysis and integration of the specifics related to the proposed flag desecration amendment and the given sources.

An **8** essay <u>effectively</u> and <u>cohesively</u> addresses the prompt. It clearly takes a position on the proposed flag desecration amendment and supports the argument using carefully integrated and appropriate evidence, including at least three of the given sources. The essay will also show the writer's <u>ability to control language</u>.

A **7** essay has all the properties of a 6, only with a <u>more complete</u>, well-developed, and integrated argument or a more mature writing style.

A **6** essay <u>adequately</u> addresses the prompt. The argument is on the proposed flag desecration amendment and integrates, as well as makes use of, appropriate evidence, including at least three references from the given sources. These elements are less fully integrated and/or developed than scores in the 7, 8, 9 range. The writer's ideas are expressed with clarity, but the writing may have a few errors in syntax and/or diction.

A **5** essay demonstrates that the writer <u>understands the prompt</u>. The argument/claim/position about the proposed flag desecration amendment is generally understandable, but the development and/or integration of appropriate evidence and at least three of the given sources is limited or uneven. The writer's ideas are expressed clearly with a few errors in syntax or diction.

A **4** essay is <u>not an adequate response</u> to the prompt. The writer's argument indicates a misunderstanding, an oversimplification, or a misrepresentation of the assigned task. The writer may use evidence that is not appropriate or not sufficient to support the argument, or may use fewer than three of the given sources. The writing presents the writer's ideas, but may indicate immaturity of style and control.

A **3** essay is a lower 4 because it is <u>even less effective</u> in addressing the question. It is also less mature in its syntax and organization.

A **2** essay indicates <u>little success in speaking to the prompt</u>. The writer may misread the question, only summarize the given sources, fail to develop the required argument, or simply ignore the prompt and write about another topic. The writing may also lack organization and control of language and syntax. (***Note:*** **No matter how well written, a summary will never rate more than a 2.**)

A **1** essay is a lower 2 because it is even <u>more simplistic</u>, <u>disorganized</u>, and <u>lacking in control of language</u>.

Student A

Some were shocked. Others were indifferent. Still others were proud. What event   1
could cause such an array of emotions in so many different people? The burning of the
American flag. However, what seems to lead to even more controversy than the actual
burning of the flag is the legal ramifications of flag-burning—specifically, whether
or not it should be banned by the Constitution. Politicians in favor of such a law are
proposing a one-sentence amendment to the First Amendment to target the "desecration"
of the flag. But such an amendment is just not necessary.

Supreme Court Chief Justice William Rehnquist vehemently protested the burning   2
of the flag, stating, "Millions and millions of Americans regard it with an almost
mystical reverence." Indeed, quite true is that declaration, which matches the regard—in
the forms of laws which criminalize public flag-burning—of 48 states to such a symbol
(Source E). And, of course, the ultimate reflection of this point of view exists in the
very amendment causing such ruckus, which states, "The Congress shall have power to
prohibit the physical desecration of the flag of the United States" (Source B).

However, if Americans are in such cohesive opinion of flag-burning, or so it would   3
seem, why are some still setting fire to the beloved stars and stripes? Once again, we
return to the respected Chief Justice Rehnquist, who also states that "[The flag] does not
represent any particular political philosophy" (Source F). In a sense, this makes the flag
mutable enough to represent all things politically American, such as government officials
or even government policy. Such is the reasoning that the *Los Angeles Times* justified the
burning of the flag—as "attacks on government and public officials" (Source F). But,
other than a crowd's "distaste" at the politicians of America, another, more practical
explanation rights the burning of the flag: disposing it. According to Todd Lindberg,
the Boy Scout manual delineates a "ceremony" for getting the flag "decommissioned
properly. So the symbolic content is always present" (Source I). Such a respectful gesture
to a flag that has served its days seems almost shameful to ban.

Then, of course, arises the issue of freedom of speech. An opinion of Senator   4
McConnell of Kentucky finds that, "Placing a no-flag-burning asterisk next to the
amendment's sweeping guarantee of free speech . . . could invite amendments to ban
other sorts of speech" (Source F). Such a thought seems a little flawed in the snowball-
down-a-hill way, but the adage "power corrupts," no matter how trite, might still give
the idea enough fuel to scorch. However, Mr. Lindberg of the *Washington Times* proved
the hypocrisy of such an amendment best. A ban on "the symbol of the freedom to
burn, baby, burn," leaves a paradoxical taste in anyone's mouth. Limiting the freedom to
destroy freedom means, to Mr. Lindberg and many others, "you have no freedom."

But "burn, baby, burn" doesn't exactly sound like a right "of the people peaceably   5
to assemble," as stated in the First Amendment of the Constitution (Source A). Fire is
hardly a symbol of peace, and one could almost make the argument that burning the
flag is equivalent to yelling "fire!" in a crowded theater (almost, but not in the landmark

case of *Texas v. Johnson*). The justices of the Supreme Court ruled that the burning of the flag caused neither "breaches of the peace" nor "a serious disturbance" (Source D). Furthermore, United States v. Eichman voices the same opinion, thus, effectively eliminating the Flag Protection Act of 1989 (Source D). And, finally, to sooth the naysayers voicing opinions of a free-for-all burn, a 2006 *Los Angeles Times* editorial reports that "no epidemic of flag-burning" has occurred since such rulings. Indeed, flag-burning, as a freedom, fulfills all legal qualifications as an act of peaceful expression. No harm, no foul.

Ultimately, the voice of the people clearly decrees that an amendment to rid flag-burning is superfluous. The Supreme Court has already sanctioned flag-burning as a right in the penumbra of the First Amendment, and that Amendment, throughout its decade of existence, hasn't achieved the needed majority of Congress (Source G). But the sovereign of this state, the people, says it all. The 2006 poll in *USA Today* shows a minor, but significant 54 percent majority of the American public believing an amendment against flag-burning is unnecessary (Source C). Mr. Lindberg really did say it best in his own editorial: ". . . most Americans will think you are an ingrate jerk . . . But even if a constitutional amendment passes, no one is proposing the death penalty for flag-burning." Flag-burning is unpatriotic at best, but Americans have enough common sense not to use flag-burning as a favorite pastime without a law on their backs.

6

Student B

Over the course of American history, political freedoms and inalienable rights have been the ultimate treasure of the American people. As a nation, we pride ourselves on our right to express our opinions without threat of punishment. From the Supreme Court ruling against the Alien and Sedition Acts to the current flag burning issue, free speech has been upheld.

1

In the cases of *Texas v. Johnson* and the *U.S. v. Eichman*, the Supreme Court has said that the act of desecrating the American flag is not illegal (Source D). This reliable source states that flag burning does not directly threaten anyone; in fact, a reference to the flag is amorphous. The flag is a symbol that takes billions of forms across the entire country. As stated in Source I, "There is no 'the' flag . . . it is an idea of the flag and therefore beyond the reach of the flames." An anti-flag burning amendment would be nebulous and would be incapable of addressing a specific act of flag desecration.

2

A survey taken by *USA Today* indicated that more than half of those Americans tallied do not want such an amendment added (Source C). The Constitution is a document for the people, by the people, and of the people; therefore, if an opinion is to matter, it should be the viewpoint of the people. They are the ones who need to abide by the laws and should have some say in their construction.

3

However, when Congress voted a series of six times, every single time there were more representatives for the amendment than were against it (Source G). There is a serious discrepancy between the people and their representatives. The author of Source F

4

expresses his opinion on this matter, maintaining that if these representatives passed the amendment, it would severely restrict the freedoms that we as Americans have come to love.

The first amendment to the Constitution has clauses that are contradictory to the 5 proposed anti-flag burning amendment (Source A). The proposed amendment would restrict the provided freedoms and would "prohibit the physical desecration of the flag of the United States." Source F claims that the destruction of Old Glory as a protest was symbolic speech protected by the First Amendment. Though the editorial may be biased, the author makes a provocative argument. This country has been content with the First Amendment. Why change it now? It may even create more of a problem. Telling someone to do something often provokes him to do the opposite. When a child is told to refrain from an action, the typical response is for the child to test the parent. Clay Bennet's ironic political cartoon (Source H) reinforces this idea. It shows an American flag marked with the quote, "do not desecrate." The cartoon mocks the idea of forbidding the desecration of the flag and demonstrates that the amendment may not be taken seriously and may possibly have the opposite effect from what it is trying to enforce.

It is apparent that the government and the people are currently undecided on the 6 issue. When it resurfaces, and it will, the representatives will be faced with a conundrum: "yea" or "nay." Hopefully, the representatives will see the contradictions and turn down the amendment for the good of the American people and their freedom.

Rating the Student Essays: Flag Amendment

Student A

This high-range paper:

- Effectively introduces the argument and indicates the opposition in paragraph 1
- Opens with an interesting example of parallelism
- Clearly establishes the writer's position against the amendment
- Exhibits strong control of language: diction, syntax, transitions, rhetorical questions
- Builds a cohesive and convincing argument against the amendment by effectively introducing, combining, and commenting on appropriate sources
- Employs transition to further the development of the points in the argument: *however*, *then*, *but*, *ultimately*
- Creates mature concluding sentences in each paragraph that drive home the writer's position
- Smoothly integrates and cites sources material
- Presents a coherent, strong voice and tone

Student B

This mid-range essay:

- Opens convincingly by including outside information to indicate the writer's position against the amendment
- Incorporates and properly cites at least three sources to support the argument
- Adequately comments on the synthesized material and includes some relevant outside information to reinforce the sources used
- Indicates an understanding of the process of writing a synthesis essay

- Demonstrates control of language through diction and syntax
- Recognizes the bias in source material
- Adds to the argument by creating an analogous situation: the child testing the parents
- Understands tone and intent

Rubrics for "Fog" Essays

High-Range Essay

- Successfully identifies the purpose of each passage
- Effectively compares the style of each passage
- Refers to appropriate examples from each passage
- Effectively analyzes devices such as diction, organization, syntax, and manipulation of language in a clear voice
- Good connective tissue
- Focused organization and development
- Few, if any, flaws

Mid-Range Essay

- Correctly identifies the purpose of each passage
- Adequately compares the style of each passage
- Uses specifics from each passage to analyze rhetorical devices
- Adequately links examples to the analysis of the style and purpose of each passage
- Less well-developed than the high-range essays
- A few lapses in diction or syntax

Low-Range Essay

- Inadequate response to the prompt
- Misunderstands, oversimplifies, summarizes, or misrepresents the purpose and style of each passage
- Insufficient or inappropriate use of examples to develop the demands of the prompt
- Lack of adequate control of elements of essay writing

"Fog" Passages—Student Sample A

A concept defined in the literal sense can be quite different from that same idea defined in the figurative sense. When comparing the Goodwin and Dickens passages, it becomes evident that different approaches in describing the famous London fogs result in two images at radically opposite ends of the "fog spectrum." Differences in stylistic elements, particularly diction and tone, are critical in creating two distinct and opposing descriptions.

1

The Goodwin passage could easily be categorized as nothing more than a newspaper or textbook article. Expository in nature, the piece highlights the facts pertaining to the London fogs. He includes such facts as the tons of solid matter per square mile in a section of London in 1937, and how much less sunshine was in London as compared to the inner suburbs. The didactic tone of the passage lends itself to explanation of factual details. Moreover, the diction is marked by technical jargon, such as "solid matter per square mile." This combination of tone and diction is instrumental in presenting a fact-based description of London fog. Because the piece is founded on facts only, it seems that the purpose would be to educate/inform the audience about this unique phenomenon. It also seems the author wants to underline the harmful consequences of the fogs, such as the indicated respiratory disease and excessive pollution.

2

On the other hand, Dickens implements a style, which personifies the fog. The diction in the piece is critical in giving the fog animate qualities. Figurative language like "creeping" and "lying out on the yards," give London fogs a life-like quality. The fog is also "hovering," "drooping" and "wheezing." These characteristics give the reader the eerie feeling that the fog is human and is going to take over. Moreover, the diction in this passage uses simple, everyday words, and not the technical vocabulary employed in the Goodwin paragraph. The tone of the Dickens description is concerned with the emotional impression that fog gives to the bystander. Because the tone and diction are more figurative in nature, Dickens' purpose appears to be to relate the London fogs emotional qualities to the reader so that the reader feels as if surrounded by this fog. Dickens style leads to a totally opposite impression of the fog, and it also achieves a different purpose.

3

These two passages employ differing stylistic elements to meet different ends. Goodwin is successful in presenting a factual analysis. Dickens, on the other hand, uses rhetorical devices to create an almost living-breathing image of the fog, one that is all-enveloping.

4

"Fog" Passages—Student Sample B

These two passages describe fog in England in two completely opposite ways. The first passage, written by Tim Goodwin, gives an objective view of the fog, stating its qualities in a list-like manner. The author of the second passage uses parallel structure and figurative language to give a more impressionistic view of London fog.

1

The first passage is something one would find in an encyclopedia. It first gives an explanation of why there is so much fog in London. It then goes on to give exact dates and amounts of fog in London. Goodwin gives the reader details and statistics to illustrate the continuing problems related to fog. He connects the effects from 1879 to 1962. For example, in 1936 nearly 30,000 tons of matter were deposited on London. Towards the end of the passage Goodwin uses chronological organization to discuss the last of the great London fogs. This is a detached conclusion to a purely objective piece of writing.

2

The second passage is extremely different from the first passage. Charles Dickens gives an impressionistic description of the London fog. His repetition of the word "fog" makes an imprint on the reader's mind. Dickens also uses parallel structure, beginning almost every sentence or clause with "fog." This constantly reminds the reader that Dickens is describing fog, which is everywhere. Dickens also personifies the fog, writing that it is "cruelly pinching the toes and fingers of his shivering little 'prentice boy." Dickens makes it seem more menacing and powerful. He also uses an analogy towards the end of the passage, saying that the people feel "as if they were up in a balloon, and hanging in the misty clouds." Because the fog is everywhere, there is no distinction between earth and sky. This gives the reader a lasting impression on how the fog is omnipresent.

3

Selection One and Selection Two are two very different passages with two very different purposes. Each passage is well suited for its purpose; the first is straightforward and explanatory, while the second evokes emotions and feelings.

4

Rating Student Sample A

This is a high-ranking essay for the following reasons:

- Effectively presents and discusses the purpose and intent of each passage (end of paragraph 2), (end of paragraph 3)
- Thoroughly addresses the stylistic differences between the two pieces (paragraph 2), (paragraph 3)
- Strongly supports his or her position with appropriate details from the passage (paragraphs 2 and 3)
- Well-focused throughout
- Mature voice and clear style

This high-ranked essay that is both informative and direct is so well-focused that the reader can almost see the writer's mind at work. And, as a result, the audience comes away with a clear understanding of the differences between the style and purpose of the two excerpts.

Rating Student Sample B

This is a mid-range essay for the following reasons:

- Clearly indicates an understanding and an application of the prompt (paragraph 1)
- Good control of sentence structure

- Provides specifics from each text to support the analysis (paragraph 1), (paragraph 3)
- Clear transitions
- Clear topic adherence
- Obvious development lacking connections to insights resulting from a close reading of the texts
- A few syntax and diction errors

This mid-range essay is a concise, "bare-bones" presentation. Its strength lies in its clear focus and appropriateness of support. However, these citations are more like listings rather than serving as the foundation for discussions of their implications.

Rubrics for the Thoreau Passage

High-Range Essay

- Correctly identifies Thoreau's attitude about the value of advice given by elders
- Effectively presents a position about Thoreau's attitude
- Clear writer's voice
- Successfully defends his or her position
- Presents carefully reasoned arguments making reference to specific examples from personal experience, knowledge, reading
- Effectively manipulates language
- Few, if any, syntactical errors

Mid-Range Essay

- Correctly identifies Thoreau's attitude about the value of advice given by elders
- Understands the demands of the prompt
- Clearly states the position of the writer
- Presents a generally adequate argument which makes use of appropriate examples
- Less well-developed than the high-range essay
- Ideas clearly stated
- A few lapses in diction or syntax

Low-Range Essay

- Inadequate response to the prompt
- Misunderstands, oversimplifies or misrepresents Thoreau's attitude
- Insufficient or inappropriate use of examples to develop the writer's position
- Lack of mature control of elements of essay writing

This prompt presented students with the opportunity to sound off about their place in the pecking order. Interestingly enough, the majority of the student writers disagreed with Thoreau or, at least, qualified his remarks. Relatively few chose to speak about parental advice, but they were willing to admit the influence of teachers, scientists/explorers, and grandparents. Often the anecdotal material rambled and needed to be connected back to the ideas of Thoreau. However, even with these shortcomings, the majority of the students obviously found this excerpt and prompt to be easily accessible.

Thoreau Passage—Student Sample A

In this passage, Henry David Thoreau clearly states that progress is made from 1
generation to generation. However, Thoreau discredits his elders, writing "They have
told me nothing, and probably cannot tell me anything." Instead, I would like to argue
that the knowledge of those who are older and wiser is of great value. To illustrate this
thesis, three examples will be used, first, a doctoral student, second, the protagonist of
Mary Shelley's Frankenstein, and third, the twentieth-century poet, T. S. Eliot.

The doctoral student in question is studying physics, the science of motion. In order 2
to reach graduate school, the student must first graduate from elementary, middle and high
school. During those years, the student learns to read, an ancient art taught him by a
teacher—one who is older than he is and can impart knowledge to him. The numerous
teachers he will have impart laws of mathematics, science, and nature. He must learn
these rules established by scientists like Descartes, Einstein, and Aristotle. Eventually,
he will reach college, where professors will continue to introduce the student to fields
like calculus and quantum mechanics. Knowledge of all these fields is necessary for the
student to pursue his doctoral work; he must obtain information of the past in order to
formulate his own ideas in the future.

From another perspective, Victor Frankenstein, the title character in Mary Shelley's 3
chef d'oeuvre spends his childhood reading metaphysical scientists of the Middle Ages. He
later attends university, where his professor instructs him in the natural sciences. Victor
then spends years assembling the theories of his elders into a new form, one that will let
him re-create life. Bringing the monster to life is a collaborative effort of his creativity and
the genius of those who live before him.

Finally, T. S. Eliot firmly believed that one must first study literature before 4
creating it. Evidence of this theory is most clearly demonstrated in the opening lines
of The Wasteland, which reference the beginning of Chaucer's Canterbury Tales.
Other allusions to Shakespeare, Greek tragedy, and far Eastern religions are scattered
throughout the text. By recognizing the significant contributions of his elders, Eliot
derived his own place in history. These allusions demonstrate that Eliot felt learning
from others was crucial to forming his opinion.

In conclusion, all three examples refute Thoreau's statement that "Age is no better, 5
hardly so well-qualified for an instructor of youth." The doctoral student, Victor
Frankenstein, and T. S. Eliot all illustrate the importance of learning from the past as a
means of promoting the present.

Thoreau Passage—Student Sample B

Do old people offer valuable advice? Why of course they do! Life has not changed 1
so much that old people cannot relate to teenage life today. Experience is key to giving
advice. The ability to empathize and understand is very important for an older person to
give advice to a younger person. Henry David Thoreau's point of view in "Walden" is
that old people are not capable of offering decent advice. He is incorrect in holding this

creed because he does not realize that older people once played through childhood, once matured through puberty, and once became adults. If advice is needed, older people are the best source.

It is common for teenagers to find interest in members of the opposite sex. Occasionally, these young couples have trouble getting along. The relationship takes a turn for the worst. Ready to console her teary-eyed granddaughter sits grandma. At age 70, she has been happily married for nearly 45 years. Presenting her shoulder to her granddaughter to cry on, the grandmother talks of her many high school and college relationships. For a moment granddaughter pauses her crying to giggle at grandma's silly stories, but in reality, she is still faced with her own broken heart to deal with. After hours of bonding, the two hug and smile. Grandma's advice on men came from her own experiences. She'd never thought that so many heartaches would ever do her any good. Pleased with life, a husband, children, and grandchildren, this older woman would never worry about those past flings again. But, when her devastated little grandbaby was hurt by a young man, she reached back for those early love stories. She used her bad experiences to her granddaughter's advantage. She showed another woman that there will be plenty of men before "the one." Thoreau, on the other hand, would ask anyone rather than an elder for advice. His past experiences led him to believe that he will never "hear the first syllable of valuable or even earnest advice from [his] seniors."

Everything happens for a reason. When people say things, there is a reason behind them. No matter what life tosses at someone, it's had to happen to someone before. If someone has lived life for seventy years, they've got to have plenty of stories to share about experiences life has shared with them. Henry David Thoreau is an unlucky man for not seeing the beauty in the elderly. They are the most respectable people and give superior advice because they have experienced it all. Older people are the buttress of life today. Their actions shaped the way and set precedents for future generations. Older people have lots to say, whether it be on teenage relationships or any topic. You name it, they've lived it!

Rating Student Sample A

This is a high-range essay for the following reasons:

- Clearly establishes a position regarding Thoreau's assertion
- Thoroughly develops the argument with hypothetical and literary references
- Good topic adherence
- Excellent connective tissue
- Thorough development of the argument that reveals a well-read writer
- Mature voice, diction, and syntax
- Indicative of a willingness to stretch with regard to manipulation of language (paragraph 3, sentence 1) and support for the writer's position (paragraph 4)

This high-range essay is clear, coherent, cohesive, and compact. It reveals a confident, smooth writing style. There is nothing extraneous contained in this concise, well-organized presentation.

Rating Student Sample B

This is a mid-range essay for the following reasons:

- Establishes a clear voice (paragraph 2)
- Indicates an understanding of the text and the prompt
- Addresses the prompt
- Presents a reasonable argument in support of the writer's assertion
- Demonstrates topic adherence
- Interesting use of parallel structure (paragraph 1)
- Needs transitions (paragraphs 2 and 3)
- Paragraphing errors (paragraphs 2, 3)
- Several syntactical errors

The writer of this mid-range essay chose to develop his or her argument with an extended example. The conversational tone, although simple and straightforward, clearly supports the writer's position.

5 Minutes to a 5

180 Activities and Questions in

5 Minutes a Day

Check off each activity as it is completed.

1. ❏	46. ❏	91. ❏	136. ❏
2. ❏	47. ❏	92. ❏	137. ❏
3. ❏	48. ❏	93. ❏	138. ❏
4. ❏	49. ❏	94. ❏	139. ❏
5. ❏	50. ❏	95. ❏	140. ❏
6. ❏	51. ❏	96. ❏	141. ❏
7. ❏	52. ❏	97. ❏	142. ❏
8. ❏	53. ❏	98. ❏	143. ❏
9. ❏	54. ❏	99. ❏	144. ❏
10. ❏	55. ❏	100. ❏	145. ❏
11. ❏	56. ❏	101. ❏	146. ❏
12. ❏	57. ❏	102. ❏	147. ❏
13. ❏	58. ❏	103. ❏	148. ❏
14. ❏	59. ❏	104. ❏	149. ❏
15. ❏	60. ❏	105. ❏	150. ❏
16. ❏	61. ❏	106. ❏	151. ❏
17. ❏	62. ❏	107. ❏	152. ❏
18. ❏	63. ❏	108. ❏	153. ❏
19. ❏	64. ❏	109. ❏	154. ❏
20. ❏	65. ❏	110. ❏	155. ❏
21. ❏	66. ❏	111. ❏	156. ❏
22. ❏	67. ❏	112. ❏	157. ❏
23. ❏	68. ❏	113. ❏	158. ❏
24. ❏	69. ❏	114. ❏	159. ❏
25. ❏	70. ❏	115. ❏	160. ❏
26. ❏	71. ❏	116. ❏	161. ❏
27. ❏	72. ❏	117. ❏	162. ❏
28. ❏	73. ❏	118. ❏	163. ❏
29. ❏	74. ❏	119. ❏	164. ❏
30. ❏	75. ❏	120. ❏	165. ❏
31. ❏	76. ❏	121. ❏	166. ❏
32. ❏	77. ❏	122. ❏	167. ❏
33. ❏	78. ❏	123. ❏	168. ❏
34. ❏	79. ❏	124. ❏	169. ❏
35. ❏	80. ❏	125. ❏	170. ❏
36. ❏	81. ❏	126. ❏	171. ❏
37. ❏	82. ❏	127. ❏	172. ❏
38. ❏	83. ❏	128. ❏	173. ❏
39. ❏	84. ❏	129. ❏	174. ❏
40. ❏	85. ❏	130. ❏	175. ❏
41. ❏	86. ❏	131. ❏	176. ❏
42. ❏	87. ❏	132. ❏	177. ❏
43. ❏	88. ❏	133. ❏	178. ❏
44. ❏	89. ❏	134. ❏	179. ❏
45. ❏	90. ❏	135. ❏	180. ❏

AN INTRODUCTION

Before You Begin...

The following 180 questions and activities are based on the material presented in the formal text of *5 Steps to a 5: AP English Language and Composition*. These questions and activities are created as supplementary material to both the text and your own AP English Language course. There are four sections presented in the order of the original contents: Multiple Choice, Analysis, Argument, and Synthesis. The material progresses from basic to complex in each section. Some activities stand alone, while others have two or more connected activities. We recommend that you work your way through each section in the given order. However, you can certainly peruse the activities and pick and choose as you desire. Whatever works best for you.

You will find answers with explanations at the end of the activities. If you need further clarification of a question or explanation, you should review the related material in the appropriate chapter in the *5 Steps to a 5* text.

Introduction to 5 Steps English Language

Before doing anything else, acquaint yourself with *5 Steps to a 5: AP English Language*. Then, complete this first 5-minute activity to quickly review what you found after scanning the text.

	YES	NO
1. I've looked over the table of contents.	✓	
2. I've found out the date of the AP Language exam.		✓

3. I've carefully reviewed the three approaches to preparing for the exam located on pages 8–11.

4. I've made a decision about which approach would be best for me, or I've decided to develop my own study plan.

5. I've completed the walk through of the Diagnostic/Master exam in Chapter 3.

Day 2

Multiple Choice

1. Match each of the following MC stems with its appropriate category.

A Factual   **B** Technical   **C** Analytical   **D** Inferential

_____ 1. The antecedent of ___ can be found in line ___ …

_____ 2. The speaker's purpose when using parallel structure in lines ___ …

_____ 3. What is the effect of ___?

_____ 4. What is the dominant technique used in lines ___?

_____ 5. What is the author's attitude toward the subject?

_____ 6. The primary rhetorical function of lines ___ is to …

_____ 7. Which of the following rhetorical devices is used in line ___?

_____ 8. The word ___ in context (line ___) is best interpreted to mean …

Types of Multiple Choice Questions: Factual

Carefully read the following. Then complete the activity that follows.

John Adams—excerpts from *A Dissertation of the Canon and Feudal Law* (1765)

Liberty cannot be preserved without a general knowledge among
the people, who have a right, from the frame of their nature, to
knowledge, as their Great Creator, who does nothing in vain, has
given them understandings, and a right, an indisputable, unalienable,
indefeasible,[1] divine right to that most dreaded and envied kind of   5
knowledge; I mean, of the characters and conduct of their rulers.
Rulers are no more than attorneys, agents, and trustees, for the people;
and if the cause, the interest and trust, is insidiously betrayed, or
wantonly trifled away, the people have a right to revoke the authority
that they themselves have deputed, and to constitute able and better   10
agents, attorneys, and trustees. And the preservation of the means
of knowledge among the lowest ranks is of more importance to the
public than all the property of all the rich men in the country. It is
even of more consequence to the rich themselves, and to their
posterity. The only question is whether there it is a public   15
emolument;[2] and if it is, the rich ought undoubtedly to contribute,
in the same proportion as to other public burdens – that is,
in proportion to their wealth, which is secured by public expenses.
But none of the means of information are more sacred
or have been cherished with more tenderness and care by the settlers   20
of America, than the press. Care has been taken that the art of printing
should be encouraged, and that it should be easy and cheap and safe
for any person to communicate his thoughts …

Let us dare to read, think, speak, and write. Let every order and degree among the people rouse their attention and animate their resolution. ... Let us examine into the nature of that power, and the cruelty of that oppression, which drove our forefathers from their homes. ... Let us recollect it was liberty, the hope of liberty for themselves and us and ours, which conquered all the discouragements, dangers, and trials. ...

In a word, let every sluice[3] of knowledge be opened and set a-flowing.

25

30

---

[1]not able to be overturned
[2]salary or fee
[3]a gate for controlling the flow of water

1. In line 13, the antecedent of *it* is

   A. "the property of all the rich men" (13)
   B. "a right to revoke authority" (9)
   C. "a general knowledge among the people" (1–2)
   D. "the preservation of the means of knowledge" (11–12)
   E. "the characters and conduct of their rulers" (6)

2. In line 26, *that power* refers to
   A. rulers
   B. oppression
   C. the "Great Creator"
   D. liberty
   E. knowledge

Types of Multiple Choice Questions: Technical

Carefully read the following. Then complete the activity that follows.

John Adams – excerpts from *A Dissertation of the Canon and Feudal Law* (1765)

Liberty cannot be preserved without a general knowledge among
the people, who have a right, from the frame of their nature, to
knowledge, as their Great Creator, who does nothing in vain, has
given them understandings, and a right, an indisputable, unalienable,
indefeasible,[1] divine right to that most dreaded and envied kind of   5
knowledge; I mean, of the characters and conduct of their rulers.
Rulers are no more than attorneys, agents, and trustees, for the people;
and if the cause, the interest and trust, is insidiously betrayed, or
wantonly trifled away, the people have a right to revoke the authority
that they themselves have deputed, and to constitute able and better   10
agents, attorneys, and trustees. And the preservation of the means
of knowledge among the lowest ranks is of more importance to the
public than all the property of all the rich men in the country. It is
even of more consequence to the rich themselves, and to their posterity.
The only question is whether there it is a public emolument;[2] and if   15
it is, the rich ought undoubtedly to contribute, in the same proportion
as to other public burdens – that is, in proportion to their wealth,
which is secured by public expenses. But none of the means of
information are more sacred or have been cherished with more
tenderness and care by the settlers of America, than the press.   20
Care has been taken that the art of printing should be encouraged,
and that it should be easy and cheap and safe for any person to
communicate his thoughts …

Let us dare to read, think, speak, and write. Let every order and degree among the people rouse their attention and animate their resolution. … Let us examine into the nature of that power, and the cruelty of that oppression, which drove our forefathers from their homes. … Let us recollect it was liberty, the hope of liberty for themselves and us and ours, which conquered all the discouragements, dangers, and trials. …

In a word, let every sluice[3] of knowledge be opened and set a-flowing.

———————

[1] not able to be overturned
[2] salary or fee
[3] a gate for controlling the flow of water

1. Lines 18–31 contain all of the following rhetorical devices except

A. repetition
B. appeal to pathos (emotion)
C. simile
D. metaphor
E. appeal to authority (ethos)

2. Which of the following devices is dominant in lines 24–30?

A. euphemism
B. colloquial language
C. analogy
D. anaphora
E. rhetorical question

Types of Multiple Choice Questions: Analytical

Carefully read the following. Then complete the activity that follows.

John Adams – excerpts from *A Dissertation of the Canon and Feudal Law* (1765)

Liberty cannot be preserved without a general knowledge among the people, who have a right, from the frame of their nature, to knowledge, as their Great Creator, who does nothing in vain, has given them understandings, and a right, an indisputable, unalienable, indefeasible,[1] divine right to that most dreaded and envied kind of knowledge; I mean, of the characters and conduct of their rulers. Rulers are no more than attorneys, agents, and trustees, for the people; and if the cause, the interest and trust, is insidiously betrayed, or wantonly trifled away, the people have a right to revoke the authority that they themselves have deputed, and to constitute able and better agents, attorneys, and trustees. And the preservation of the means of knowledge among the lowest ranks is of more importance to the public than all the property of all the rich men in the country. It is even of more consequence to the rich themselves, and to their posterity. The only question is whether there it is a public emolument;[2] and if it is, the rich ought undoubtedly to contribute, in the same proportion as to other public burdens – that is, in proportion to their wealth, which is secured by public expenses. But none of the means of information are more sacred or have been cherished with more tenderness and care by the settlers of America, than the press. Care has been taken that the art of printing should be encouraged, and that it should be easy and cheap and safe for any person to communicate his thoughts …

5

10

15

20

Let us dare to read, think, speak, and write. Let every order and degree among the people rouse their attention and animate their resolution. ... Let us examine into the nature of that power, and the cruelty of that oppression, which drove our forefathers from their homes. ... Let us recollect it was liberty, the hope of liberty for themselves and us and ours, which conquered all the discouragements, dangers, and trials. ...

In a word, let every sluice[3] of knowledge be opened and set a-flowing.   30

---

[1]not able to be overturned
[2]salary or fee
[3]a gate for controlling the flow of water

1. The point-of-view in this passage is primarily that of a ...

   A. patriot who is exhorting Americans to uphold freedom of the press
   B. scholar who is reiterating significant ideas from the Declaration of Independence
   C. lawyer who is concerned with restraints on American freedom
   D. teacher who is advocating the values of education
   E. president who is serving the American people

2. The purpose of mentioning the "forefathers" in line 26 is most probably to

   A. remind the people of their previous struggles for freedom
   B. establish a parallel between present and past responses to oppression
   C. re-focus the audience's attention from emotion to action
   D. create a sense of anger in the audience
   E. contrast the power of the king to the power of liberty

Types of Multiple Choice Questions: Inferential

Carefully read the following. Then complete the activity that follows.

John Adams – excerpts from *A Dissertation of the Canon and Feudal Law* (1765)

Liberty cannot be preserved without a general knowledge among
the people, who have a right, from the frame of their nature, to
knowledge, as their Great Creator, who does nothing in vain, has
given them understandings, and a right, an indisputable, unalienable,
indefeasible,[1] divine right to that most dreaded and envied kind of   5
knowledge; I mean, of the characters and conduct of their rulers.
Rulers are no more than attorneys, agents, and trustees, for the
people; and if the cause, the interest and trust, is insidiously betrayed,
or wantonly trifled away, the people have a right to revoke the authority
that they themselves have deputed, and to constitute able and better   10
agents, attorneys, and trustees. And the preservation of the means
of knowledge among the lowest ranks is of more importance to the
public than all the property of all the rich men in the country. It is even
of more consequence to the rich themselves, and to their posterity.
The only question is whether there it is a public emolument;[2] and if it is,   15
the rich ought undoubtedly to contribute, in the same proportion as
to other public burdens – that is, in proportion to their wealth, which
is secured by public expenses. But none of the means of information
are more sacred or have been cherished with more tenderness and care by
the settlers of America, than the press. Care has been taken that the   20
art of printing should be encouraged, and that it should be easy and
cheap and safe for any person to communicate his thoughts …

Let us dare to read, think, speak, and write. Let every order and
degree among the people rouse their attention and animate their

resolution. … Let us examine into the nature of that power, and the 25
cruelty of that oppression, which drove our forefathers from their homes.
… Let us recollect it was liberty, the hope of liberty for themselves
and us and ours, which conquered all the discouragements, dangers,
and trials. …

    In a word, let every sluice[3] of knowledge be opened and set a-flowing. 30

---

[1]not able to be overturned
[2]salary or fee
[3]a gate for controlling the flow of water

1. It can be inferred by line 30, "In a word, let every sluice of knowledge be opened and set a-flowing," that Adams

  A. possessed an inherent tendency to empathize with the rich
  B. supported the education of individuals from all social classes
  C. feared reprisals from the king of England over water rights
  D. explored nature with same zeal he brought to educational reform
  E. highlighted the significance of the natural world in order to establish an environmental movement

Working with Multiple Choice

Excerpt from *The Journey Home* by Edward Abbey (1977)

Anyway—why go into the desert? Really, why do it? That sun, roaring
at you all day long. The fetid, tepid, vapid little water holes slowly
evaporating under a scum of grease, full of cannibal beetles, spotted toads,
horsehair worms, liver flukes, and down at the bottom, inevitably, the pale
cadaver of a ten-inch centipede. Those pink rattlesnakes down in   5
The Canyon, those diamondback monsters thick as a truck driver's
wrist that lurk in shady places along the trail, those unpleasant solpugids[1]
and unnecessary Jerusalem crickets that scurry on dirty claws across your
face at night. Why? The rain that comes down like lead shot and wrecks
the trail, those sudden rockfalls of obscure origin that crash like thunder   10
ten feet behind you in the heart of a dead-still afternoon. The ubiquitous
buzzard, so patient – but only so patient.

———————
[1]also known as sun spiders

This passage contains ALL of the following rhetorical devices EXCEPT

1. personification

2. metaphor

3. rhetorical question

4. simile

5. parallel structure

Working with Multiple Choice

> Excerpt from *The Journey Home* by Edward Abbey (1977)
>
> Anyway – why go into the desert? Really, why do it? That sun, roaring
> at you all day long. The fetid, tepid, vapid little water holes slowly
> evaporating under a scum of grease, full of cannibal beetles, spotted
> toads, horsehair worms, liver flukes, and down at the bottom, inevitably,
> the pale cadaver of a ten-inch centipede. Those pink rattlesnakes down   5
> in The Canyon, those diamondback monsters thick as a truck driver's
> wrist that lurk in shady places along the trail, those unpleasant solpugids[1]
> and unnecessary Jerusalem crickets that scurry on dirty claws across your
> face at night. Why? The rain that comes down like lead shot and wrecks
> the trail, those sudden rockfalls of obscure origin that crash like thunder   10
> ten feet behind you in the heart of a dead-still afternoon. The ubiquitous
> buzzard, so patient—but only so patient.
>
> _____
>
> [1] also known as sun spiders
>
> The intended effect of this passage is most probably
>
> 1. exhaustion and apprehension
>
> 2. curiosity and adversity
>
> 3. anger and activism
>
> 4. fear and loathing
>
> 5. adventure and entrepreneurship

5 Minutes to a 5

Working with Multiple Choice

Carefully read the following passage from John Steinbeck's *Cannery Row*, then answer the question that follows.

> Cannery Row in Monterey in California is a poem, a stink, a grating
> noise, a quality of light, a tone, a habit, a nostalgia, a dream. Cannery
> Row is the gathered and scattered, tin and iron and rust and splintered
> wood, chipped pavement and weedy lots and junk heaps, sardine
> canneries of corrugated iron, honky tonks, restaurants and whore   5
> houses, and little crowded groceries, and laboratories and flophouses. Its
> inhabitant are, as the man once said, "whores, pimps, gamblers and sons
> of bitches," by which he meant Everybody. Had the man looked through
> another peephole he might have said, "Saints and angels and martyrs and
> holymen" and he would have meant the same thing.   10

The major rhetorical strategy used in this passage to define Cannery Row is

1. process

2. argument

3. cause/effect

4. comparison/contrast

5. narration

Day 9

5 Minutes to a 5

Working with Multiple Choice

Excerpt from: "Thoughts on the Present State of American Affairs," *Common Sense* by Thomas Paine, 1776

O ye that love mankind! Ye that dare oppose, not only the tyranny, but the tyrant, stand forth! Every spot of the old world is overrun with oppression. Freedom hath been hunted round the globe. Asia, and Africa, have long expelled her. — Europe regards her like a stranger, and England hath given her warning to depart. O! Receive the fugitive, and prepare in time an asylum for mankind.   5

1. This paragraph contains examples of all of the following except

   A. metaphor
   B. parallelism
   C. simile
   D. exhortation
   E. hyperbole

2. The tone of this paragraph can best be described as

   A. assertive and irreverent
   B. pedantic and reserved
   C. indignant and arrogant
   D. apologetic and effusive
   E. zealous and passionate

5 Minutes to a 5

Working with Multiple Choice

"I know what all these NPR-listening, Starbucks-guzzling parents want. They want their Ambers and their Alexanders to grow up in a cozy womb of noncompetition, where everybody shares tofu and Little Red Riding Hood and the big, bad wolf set up a commune."   —Rick Reilly

1. In the context of the passage, the phrase *Starbucks-guzzling* can be best interpreted to mean

   A. uncoordinated
   B. sentimental
   C. pretentious
   D. educated
   E. overprotective

2. The tone of this passage can best be described as

   A. pleasant and supportive
   B. critical and sarcastic
   C. harsh and degrading
   D. ironic and capricious
   E. warm and humorous

3. The passage contains examples of each of the following rhetorical techniques except

   A. hyperbole
   B. analogy
   C. sarcasm
   D. parody
   E. satire

Working with Multiple Choice

Excerpt from "The Art of Controversy" by Ambrose Bierce (1906)

The kind of "argument" here illustrated by horrible example …
characterizes men's reasoning in general. It is the rule everywhere – in
oral discussion, in books, in newspapers. Assertions that mean nothing,
testimony that is not evidence, facts having no relation to the matter
in hand, and (everywhere and always) the sickening non sequitur: the   5
conclusion that has nothing to with the premises. I know not if there is
another life, but if there is I do hope that to obtain it all will have to pass
a rigid examination in logic and the art of not being a fool.

    In an unfriendly controversy it is important to remember that the
public, in most cases, neither cares for the outcome of the fray, nor will   10
remember its incidents. The controversialist should therefore confine
his efforts and powers to accomplishment of two main purposes: (1)
entertainment of the reader; (2) personal gratification. For the first
of these objects no rules can be given; the good writer will entertain
and the bad one will not, no matter what is the subject. The second   15
is accomplishable (a) by guarding your self-respect; (b) by destroying
your adversary's self-respect; (c) by making him respect you, against his
will, as much as you respect yourself; (d) by provoking him into the
blunder of permitting you to despise him. It follows that any falsification,
prevarication, dodging, misrepresentation or other cheating on the part of   20
one antagonist is a distinct advantage to the other, and by him devoutly
to be wished. The public cares nothing for it, and if deceived will forget
the deception; but *he* never forgets. I would no more willingly let my
opponent find a flaw in my truth, honesty and frankness than in fencing I
would let him beat down my guard. Of that part of victory which consists   25
in respecting yourself and making your adversary respect you, you can
be always sure if you are worthy of respect; of that part which consists
in despising him and making him despise himself you are not sure; that

depends on his skill. He may be a very despicable person yet so cunning
of fence – that is to say, so frank and honest in writing – that you will
not find out his unworth. Remember that what you want is not so much
to disclose his meanness to the reader (who cares nothing about it) as to
make him disclose it to your private discernment. That is the whole gospel
of controversial strategy.

1. In line 23, *he* refers to

A. the public
B. the author
C. an antagonist
D. a writer
E. the reader

2. This passage can best be described as

A. informative and judicial
B. descriptive and dramatic
C. journalistic and educational
D. argumentative and satirical
E. accusatory and political

Working with Multiple Choice, Meaning in Context

Based on your careful reading of the following brief excerpt from Annie Dillard's *Pilgrim at Tinker Creek*, what is the meaning of *skein* in line 4?

> Out of the dimming sky a speck appeared, then another, and another. It was the starlings going to roost. They gathered deep in the distance, flock sifting into flock, and strayed towards me, transparent and whirling, like smoke. They seemed to unravel as they flew, lengthening in curves, like a loosened skein.

In context, *skein* (line 5) means

A. a banner or flag
B. whirling smoke
C. a length of yarn wound in a long, loose coil
D. a flock of starlings
E. a tightly bound ball of yarn

Working with Multiple Choice, Meaning in Context

Carefully read the following passage.

"… and feeling an inclination to count the flocks that might pass within the reach of my eye in one hour, I dismounted, seated myself on an eminence, and began to mark with my pencil, making a dot for every flock that passed."
—James Audubon, *Ornithological Biographies*, 1831–1839

Based on the context, what would be an appropriate synonym for *eminence* in line 3?

A. blind
B. mound
C. ground
D. bench
E. blanket

Working with Multiple Choice, Meaning in Context

Carefully read the following two sentences from "US Could Be Headed for a Constitutional Crisis, Regardless of Election Day Outcome" by Andy Kiersz for *Business Insider*, November 8, 2016.

> [There is]… immense power that comes with the office of President – this person becomes Commander in Chief of the most powerful military in the history of the world while also holding the reins of the wealthiest economy in the history of the world – and the rush to the head that such puissance entails.
>
> Presidentialism is ineluctably problematic because it operates according to the rule of "winner-take-all" – an arrangement that tends to make democratic politics a zero-sum game, with all the potential for conflict such games portend….

5

1. In context, *puissance* in line 5 most probably means

A. wealth
B. presidency
C. military
D. administration
E. power

2. In context, *ineluctably* in line 6 most probably means

A. constitutionally
B. unavoidably
C. legislatively
D. legally
E. administratively

Multiple Choice, Metonymy, Frederick Douglass

Chapter 15, "Covey, The Negro Breaker," *My Bondage and My Freedom,* by Frederick Douglass

Our house stood within a few rods of the Chesapeake bay, whose broad bosom was ever <u>white with sails</u> from every quarter of the habitable globe. Those beautiful vessels, robed in purest white, so delightful to the eye of freemen, were to me so many shrouded ghosts, to terrify and torment me with thoughts of my wretched condition. I have often, in   5
the deep stillness of a summer's Sabbath, stood all alone upon the banks of that noble bay, and traced, with saddened heart and tearful eye, the <u>countless number of sails moving off to the mighty ocean</u>. The sight of these always affected me powerfully. My thoughts would compel utterance; and there, with no audience but the Almighty, I would pour   10
out my soul's complaint in my rude way, with an apostrophe to the moving multitude of ships.

1. The underlined words/phrases in lines 2 and 8 are examples of
   A. simile
   B. hyperbole
   C. antithesis
   D. denotation
   E. metonymy

2. In the context of the last sentence in lines 9–12, *apostrophe* means

    A. a shout out
    B. a silent prayer
    C. a hopeful wish
    D. a call for help
    E. a hateful curse

Multiple Choice: Purpose of Footnotes

After carefully reading the passage below and its accompanying footnote, answer the question that follows.

This passage is excerpted from: "The Drone Presidency" by David Cole, which appeared in the August 18, 2016, issue of *The New York Review of Books*.

… A recent study focused on the targeted Pakistani border regions found that residents living there are in fact less opposed to drones than the Pakistani population as a whole.[4]

5

---

[4]Aqil Shah, "Drone Blowback in Pakistan Is a Myth. Here's Why," *The Washington Post*, May 17, 2016.

The primary purpose of Footnote 4 is to

    A. provide added support in favor of your viewpoint

    B. explain why you used a piece of information

    C. acknowledge the source of the information

    D. provide further information or sources that can provide added information on the specific topic

    E. acknowledge an opposing position or idea

5 Minutes to a 5

Day 18

Multiple Choice: Purpose of Footnotes

After carefully reading the passage below and its accompanying footnote, answer the question that follows.

> Excerpted from: "The Revolution: Treason and Rescue" by Susan Dunn, a review of *The Quartet: Orchestrating the Second American Revolution, 1783-1789* by Joseph J. Ellis, that appeared in the August 18, 2016, issue of *The New York Review of Books*.

> "…Opposing [Alexander] Hamilton's financial plan and embracing a states' rights interpretation of the Constitution, the "former champion of the ultranationalist vision," in Ellis's words, would found, with [Thomas] Jefferson, the opposition Republican Party.[2]

---

[2]The party founded by Jefferson and Madison was the Republican Party and not, as it is sometimes called, the Democratic-Republican Party.

Footnote 2 is an example of a(n)
- A. primary source
- B. secondary source
- C. assumption of the reader's background
- D. author's aside comment
- E. link to other sources

Multiple Choice: Purpose of Footnotes

After carefully reading the passage below and its accompanying footnote, answer the question that follows.

Excerpted from: "The Sorcerer of Jazz" by Adam Shatz, a review of *Bitches Brew* by George Grella Jr. that appeared in the September 29, 2016, issue of *The New York Review of Books*.

…His [Miles Davis] voice was especially beautiful on ballads, which he would sometimes perform with a stemless Harmon mute that lent his playing a beseeching, breath-like timbre, and a restrained yet smoldering eroticism.[1]

_____

[1]In the early 1970s, Davis stopped playing ballads. As he explained to the pianist Keith Jarrett, he liked playing them so much.

The primary purpose of Footnote 1 is to

    A. provide added support in favor of the author's viewpoint
    B. explain why the author used a piece of information
    C. acknowledge the source of the information
    D. provide added information on the specific topic
    E. acknowledge an opposing position or idea

Multiple Choice:
Purpose of Footnotes

After carefully reading the passage below and its accompanying footnote, answer the question that follows.

> Excerpted from: "Razing the Bar: Developmental Students Shattering Expectations in a First-Year Learning Community" by Cheryl Hogue Smith and Maya Jimenez that appeared in the September 2014, issue of *TETYC*.

> We recognize that our small study brings to mind questions that need further explanation. For example, how can the quadripolar model help students get past their fear of failure?[8]

---

[8]See Smith, Cheryl Hogue. "Interrogating Texts: From Deferent to Efferent and Aesthetic Reading Practices," *Journal of Basic Writing* 31.1 (2012): 59-77.   (21)

Footnote 8 is an example of a(n)

   A primary source
   B secondary source
   C assumption of the reader's background
   D author's aside comment
   E link to other sources

5 Minutes to a 5

Multiple Choice: Purpose of Footnotes

After carefully reading the passage below and its accompanying footnote, answer the question that follows.

Excerpts from Thoreau's *Cape Cod* (1849–1857), as presented in *The Thoreau Reader* (2009), published by the Thoreau Society, Chapter 5, "The Wellfleet Oysterman"

In the course of the evening I began to feel the potency of the clam which I had eaten, and I was obliged to confess to our host that I was no tougher than the cat he told of; but he answered, that he was a plain-spoken man, and he could tell me that it was all imagination. At any rate, it proved an <u>emetic</u> in my case, and I was made quite sick   5
by it for a short time, while he laughed at my expense. I was pleased to read afterward, in *Mourt's Relation*[15] of the landing of the Pilgrims in Provincetown Harbor, these words: "We found great muscles (the old editor says that they were undoubtedly sea-clams) and very fat and full of sea-pearl; but we could not eat them, for they made us all sick   10
that did eat, as well sailors as passengers, ... but they were soon well again." It brought me nearer to the Pilgrims to be thus reminded by a similar experience that I was so like them. Moreover, it was a valuable confirmation of their story, and I am prepared now to believe every word of *Mourt's Relation*. I was also pleased to find that man and the   15
clam lay still at the same angle to one another. But I did not notice sea-pearl. Like Cleopatra, I must have swallowed it.[16] I have since dug these clams on a flat in the Bay and observed them. They could squirt full ten feet before the wind, as appeared by the marks of the drops on the sand.

[15] *Mourt's Relation*: written 1620–21, describes landing of the Pilgrims at Cape Cod, settlement at Plymouth, relations with Indians, the First Thanksgiving and the arrival of the ship *Fortune*; published in London in 1622

[16] In Pliny the Elder's *History of the World*, Cleopatra, at a banquet with Marc Antony, crushed a very large pearl, dissolved it in wine or vinegar, and drank it.

1. The primary purpose of Footnote 15 is to

   A. provide added support in favor of the author's viewpoint

   B. explain why the author used a piece of information

   C. acknowledge the source of the information

   D. provide further information on the specific topic

   E. acknowledge an opposing position or idea

2. The primary purpose of Footnote 16 is to

   A. provide added support in favor of the Thoreau's viewpoint

   B. explain why Thoreau used a piece of information

   C. acknowledge the source of the information

   D. provide further information on the specific topic

   E. acknowledge an opposing position or idea

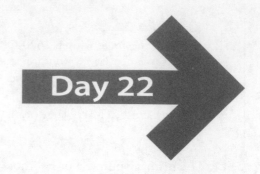
Multiple Choice: Purpose of Footnotes

After carefully reading the passage below and its accompanying footnote, answer the question that follows.

> Excerpts from Thoreau's *Cape Cod* (1849–1857), as presented in *The Thoreau Reader* (2009), published by the Thoreau Society, Chapter 5, "The Wellfleet Oysterman"
>
> Finally, filling our pockets with doughnuts, which he [oysterman] was pleased to find that we called by the same name that he did, and paying for our entertainment, we took our departure; but he followed us out of doors, and made us tell him the names of the vegetables which he had raised from seeds that came out of the *Franklin*. They   5
> were cabbage, broccoli,[19] and parsley. As I had asked him the names of so many things, he tried me in turn with all the plants which grew in his garden, both wild and cultivated. It was about half an acre, which he cultivated wholly himself. Besides the common garden vegetables, there were Yellow-Dock, Lemon Balm, Hyssop, Gill-go-over-the-   10
> ground, Mouse-ear, Chick-weed, Roman Wormwood, Elecampane, and other plants. As we stood there, I saw a fish-hawk stoop to pick a fish out of his pond.

---

[19] Said to be the first printed mention of broccoli cultivation in America, although it was grown by Thomas Jefferson in 1767

The primary purpose of Footnote 19 is to
   A. provide added support in favor of the author's viewpoint
   B. explain why the author used a piece of information
   C. acknowledge the source of the information
   D. provide further information on the specific topic
   E. acknowledge an opposing position or idea.

Multiple Choice: Meaning in Context

Carefully read lines 1–11 of the Thoreau passage from "The Wellfleet Oysterman" and answer the question that follows.

> In the course of the evening I began to feel the potency of the clam
> which I had eaten, and I was obliged to confess to our host that I was
> no tougher than the cat he told of; but he answered, that he was a plain-
> spoken man, and he could tell me that it was all imagination. At any rate,
> it proved an *emetic* in my case, and I was made quite sick by it for a short   5
> time, while he laughed at my expense. I was pleased to read afterward,
> in *Mourt's Relation*[15] of the landing of the Pilgrims in Provincetown
> Harbor, these words: "We found great muscles (the old editor says that
> they were undoubtedly sea-clams) and very fat and full of sea-pearl; but
> we could not eat them, for they made us all sick that did eat, as well   10
> sailors as passengers, ... but they were soon well again."

Based on the context of the first five lines, *emetic* (line 5) most probably means

    A. causing toughness
    B. causing potency
    C. causing nightmares
    D. causing suspicions
    E. causing vomiting

Day 24

Modes of Discourse

When dealing with rhetoric and rhetorical analysis, the most general of categories is the "Modes of Discourse." These four modes are listed below. Match each of the following definitions with its correct term. No item is used more than once.

A Exposition   **B** Narration   **C** Description   **D** Argument

____ 1. writing that appeals to one or more of the five senses

____ 2. writing that explains or informs, widely used in non-fiction

____ 3. writing that presents a claim/position/assertion for acceptance by an audience

____ 4. writing that tells a story or retells a series of events

Modes of Discourse

Match each of the following passages with its correct Mode of Discourse. No term is used more than once.

A Exposition **B** Narration **C** Description **D** Argument

___ **1.** It was a bright cold day in April, and the clocks were striking thirteen. Winston Smith, his chin nuzzled into his breast in an effort to escape the vile wind, slipped quickly through the glass doors of Victory Mansions, though not quickly enough to prevent a swirl of gritty dust from entering along with him. **George Orwell, *1984*, 1949**

___ **2.** We hold these truths to be self-evident, that all men are created equal, that they are endowed by their Creator with certain unalienable Rights, that among these are Life, Liberty and the pursuit of Happiness. (**Declaration of Independence, 1776**)

___ **3.** The idiosyncrasy of this town is smoke. It rolls sullenly in slow folds from the great chimneys of the iron-foundries, and settles down in black, slimy pools on the muddy streets. Smoke on the wharves, smoke on the dingy boats, on the yellow river – clinging in a coating of greasy soot to the house-front, the two faded poplars, the faces of the passers-by. (**Rebecca Harding Davis, "Life in the Iron Mills," 1861**)

___ **4.** How far a man could slide was gauged by observing our back-road neighbors – the out-of-work miners who had dragged their families to our corner of Ohio from the desolate hollows of Appalachia, the tightfisted farmers, the surly mechanics, the balked and broken men. (**Scott Russell Sanders, "Under the Influence," 1989**)

Terminology Connected to Rhetorical Analysis

Match each of the following terms with its best definition.

_____Diction   A. mental pictures produced by using specific words/phrases

_____Connotation   B. literal, dictionary type of definition

_____Syntax   C. word choice

_____Imagery   D. arrangement of words, word order, and punctuation in a written text

_____Denotation   E. meaning associated with a word/phrase that is not really from a dictionary

Close Reading of Rhetorical Analysis Prompts

Read the Prompt!

Carefully read the following excerpt from Ralph Waldo Emerson's *Self-Reliance* (1841). Then, in a well-written essay analyze the rhetorical strategies Emerson uses to achieve his purpose.

1. What are the two items you are required to address in your essay?

2. Even though it's not specifically mentioned in the prompt, what must you make certain to do as you develop your essay?

Close Reading of Rhetorical Analysis Prompts

Read the Prompt!

Carefully read Rick Reilly's column titled "The Weak Shall Inherit the Gym" that appeared in the May 14, 2001, issue of *Sports Illustrated*. Then, in a well-written essay identify the author's tone toward his subject and analyze how he rhetorically achieves this tone. Make certain to cite specific references to the text.

1. What are the two items you, as the writer, must address in your essay?

2. Is this prompt asking you to take a position on Reilly's subject?

3. Does this prompt expect generalities about what Reilly has to say?

4. Having closely read and annotated the prompt, what specific items will you be looking for and underlining as you read through the text?

↓ 5 Minutes to a 5

Close Reading Rhetorical Analysis Prompts

In the early 1800s, Tecumseh helped organize a confederation of Native Americans. In the following speech to American leaders, Tecumseh addresses the desire of white settlers to claim more and more Indian land. Read the speech carefully. Then in a well-written essay analyze the rhetorical strategies he uses to achieve his purpose.

1. Does this prompt identify Tecumseh's reaction to "the desire of white settlers to claim more and more Indian land"?

2. According to the prompt, must you state *your* position on this subject?

3. Is the prompt expecting you to include personal experience or reading?

4. This is a two-pronged prompt. What are the two items that must be addressed in the essay?

Day 30

The Thesis

Carefully read the following excerpt from "Education," an essay by Ralph Waldo Emerson, 1883.

… The whole theory of the school is on the nurse's or mother's knee. The child is as hot to learn as the mother is to impart. There is mutual delight. The joy of our childhood in hearing beautiful stories from some skillful aunt who loves to tell them, must be repeated in youth. The boy wishes to learn to skate; to coast, to catch a fish in the brook, to hit a mark with a snowball or a stone; and a boy a little older is just as well pleased to teach him these sciences. Not less delightful is the mutual pleasure of teaching and learning the secret of algebra, or of chemistry, or of good reading and good recitation of poetry or of prose, or of chosen facts in history or in biography.

Nature provided for the communication of thought by planting with it in the receiving mind a fury to impart it. 'Tis so in every art, in every science. One burns to tell the new fact, the other burns to hear it. See how far a young doctor will ride or walk to witness a new surgical operation. I have seen a carriage maker's shop emptied of all its workmen into the street, to scrutinize a new pattern from New York. So in literature, the young man who has taste for poetry, for fine images, for noble thoughts, is insatiable for this nourishment, and forgets all the world for the more learned friend – who finds equal joy in dealing out his treasures.

1. Underline the thesis statement.

2. The purpose of the passage is to ___inform ___persuade/argue ___entertain.

3. The organization is ___chronological ___spatial ___least to most important ___ most to least important.

Steps in Writing a Thesis Statement

You are about to take a close look at the development of a valid thesis statement. This is a skill that is required of you as an AP English Language student. The AP English Language exam assumes you have developed this skill, can recognize it in given texts, and can use it to structure your own essay.

Go to YouTube and carefully watch the following video:

> https://www.youtube.com/watch?v=vgZLPGT5llg   (3:30)

Summarize this video in one sentence.

Steps in Writing a Thesis Statement

Carefully watch the following video:

    https://www.youtube.com/watch?v=vgZLPGT5llg   (3:30)

Complete a SOAPS "analysis" of this video.

    The **S**ubject is

    The **O**ccasion is

    The **A**udience is

    The **P**urpose is

    The **S**peaker is

Steps in Writing a Thesis Statement

Make certain you have watched the following video:

   https://www.youtube.com/watch?v=vgZLPGT5llg   (3:30)

Assume this video is going to be the basis for an explanatory essay. Write the first draft of the thesis statement for that essay.

Steps in Writing a Thesis Statement

Make certain you have watched the following video:

https://www.youtube.com/watch?v=vgZLPGT5llg   (3:30)

Assume this video is going to be the basis for an **argument essay**. Write the first draft of the thesis statement for that essay.

5 Minutes to a 5

Diction

Using your knowledge of diction, classify the diction used in each of the following statements. Choose from the list below. You may use more than one adjective to describe the diction.

romantic	pretentious	metaphorical	colloquial
emotional	moralistic	informal	formal
detached	pedantic	esoteric	refined
scholarly	patriotic	slang	aggressive

1. When I pass a flowering zucchini plant in a garden, my heart skips a beat. —Gwyneth Paltrow

2. I should be a postage stamp. That's the only way I'll get licked. —Mohammed Ali

3. Let us not seek the Republican answer or the Democratic answer, but the right answer. Let us not seek to fix the blame for the past. Let us accept our own responsibility for the future. —John F. Kennedy

4. My life, my choices, my mistakes, my lessons, not your business. —Kid Cudi

5. A leader is best when people barely know he exists, when his work is done, his aim fulfilled, they will say: we did it ourselves. —Lao Tzu

6. Stop lookin' at what you ain't got, and start being thankful for what you do got. —T.I.

Syntax, Sentence Types

Carefully read each of the following sentences and determine to what category each belongs:

C Cumulative   **P** Periodic   **I** Inverted

____1. To believe your own thought, to believe that what is true for you in your private heart is true for all men, that is genius.
   —Ralph Waldo Emerson, "Self-Reliance"

____2. To save man from the morass of propaganda, in my opinion, must be one of the chief aims of education.
   —Martin Luther King, Jr., "On Education"

____3. Like the waters of the river, like the motorists on the highway, and like the yellow trains streaking down the Santa Fe tracks, drama, in the shape of exceptional happenings, had never stopped there.
   —Truman Capote, *In Cold Blood*

____4. It's easy to explain how Lorraine Adams knows so much about the illegal Algerian community in America, about credit card fraud, about terrorism and FBI investigations.
   —Neil Gordon, "Under Surveillance"

____5. Life he claimed was a ceaseless battle for survival.

____6. Unprovided with original learning, uninformed in the habits of thinking, unskilled in the arts of composition, I resolved – to write a book.
   —Edward Gibbon *Memoirs of My Life*

5 Minutes to a 5

⟨ **293**

___7. He described what he ate, what he saw and what he heard, conjuring the delicate fragrance of a mango grove, the slap of a pitchy tar on the cedar planks of a hull and a peculiar black-and-white striped wild ass – the first description of a zebra.

—Sara Wheeler, "The Highbrow Hijacker"

___8. What an excellent essay she wrote yesterday in class.

___9. For example, after a year in jail, I'd awaken in a tremble, reliving all the terror, seeing it all again with ten-fold intensity, remembering for days afterward.

—Neil Cassady, *Collected Letters, 1944-1967*

___10. Around her gathered the elders of the tribe.

Syntax, Sentence Structure

Read the following excerpt from Congresswoman Barbara Jordan's Keynote Address to the Democratic National Convention in 1992. Identify the syntactical device of the underlined items. You are to choose from:

Cumulative sentence   Rhetorical question   Parallel structure   Inversion

> At this time; at this place; at this event sixteen years ago—I presented a keynote address. I thank you for the return engagement and with modesty would remind you that we won the presidency in November, 1976. Why not 1992?
>
> It is possible to win. It is possible but you must believe we can and will do it…
>
> …Some things need to change.
>
> We can change the direction of America's economic engine and become proud and competitive again. The American Dream is not dead. True, it is gasping for breath but it is not dead. However, there is no time to waste because the American Dream is slipping away from too many. It is slipping away from too many black and brown mothers and their children; from the homeless of every color and sex; from immigrants living in communities without water and sewer systems. The American Dream is slipping away….

The underlined portions of this text are examples of _____
_____.

Syntax, Sentence Structure

Carefully read the following passage. Then identify the obvious syntactical structure(s) used by the author. You may choose from the list below. You may also choose more than one item.

Cumulative sentence   Periodic sentence   Inverted sentence
Rhetorical question   Parallelism

An excerpt from *Campus Racism 101* by Nikki Giovanni

Is it difficult to attend a predominantly white college? Compared with what? Being passed over for promotion because you lack credentials? Being turned down for jobs because you are not college educated? Joining the armed forces or going to jail because you cannot find an alternative to the streets? Let's have a little perspective here. Where can you go and what can you do that frees you from interacting with the white American mentality? You're going to interact; the only question is, will you be in some control of yourself and your actions, or will you be controlled by others? I'm going to recommend self-control.

Syntax, Sentence Structure

Carefully read the following passage. Then identify the syntactical structure(s) used by the author. You may choose from the list below. You may also choose more than one item.

Cumulative sentence   Periodic sentence   Inverted sentence
Rhetorical question   Parallelism

An excerpt from Thoreau's *Walden*

I wanted to live deep and suck out the marrow of life, to live so sturdily and Spartan-like as to put to rout all that was not life, to cut a broad swath and shave close, to drive life into a corner, and reduce it to its lowest terms.

Syntax, Sentence Structure

Carefully read the following passage. Then identify the syntactical structure(s) used by the author. You may choose from the list below. You may also choose more than one item.

Cumulative sentence   Periodic sentence   Inverted sentence
Rhetorical question   Parallelism

An excerpt from "Speech after Being Convicted of Voting in the 1872 Presidential Election" by Susan B. Anthony

To them ["women and their female posterity"] this government has no just powers derived from the consent of the governed. To them this government is not a democracy. It is not a republic. It is an odious aristocracy; a hateful oligarchy of sex; the most hateful aristocracy ever established on the face of the globe; an oligarchy of wealth, where the rich govern the poor. An oligarchy of learning, where the educated govern the ignorant, or even an oligarchy of race, where Saxon rules the African, might be endured; but this oligarchy of sex, which makes father, brothers, husband, sons, the oligarchs over mother and sisters, the wife and daughters, of every household – which ordains all men sovereigns, all women subjects, carries dissention, discord and rebellion into every home of the nation.

5

10

Syntax, Sentence Structure

Carefully read the following:

"On a Sharecropper's Overalls" by James Agee from *Let Us Now Praise Famous Men*

The structures sag ... The edges of the thigh pockets become stretched and lie open, fluted, like the gills of a fish. The bright seams lose their whiteness and are lines and ridges. The whole fabric is shrunken to size, which was bought large. The whole shape, texture, color, finally substance, all are changed. The shape, particularly along the urgent   5
frontage of the thighs, so that the whole structure of the knee and musculature of the thigh is sculpted there.... The texture and the color change in union, by sweat, sun, laundering, between the steady pressures of its use and age: both, at length, into realms of fine softness and marvel of draping and velvet plays of light which chamois and silk can only   10
suggest, not touch; and into a region and scales of blues, subtle, delicious and deft beyond what I have ever seen elsewhere approached except in rare skies, the smoky light some days are filled with, and some of the blues of Cezanne.

Let's look at this descriptive paragraph ONLY in terms of its sentence structure. Consider the sentences in light of three types:

- cumulative
- periodic
- inverted

1. Sentences 1, 2, 3, and 4 are examples of _____ sentences.

2. Sentences 5 and 6 are examples of _____ sentences.

3. Sentence 7 is an example of a _____ sentence.

Practice Writing a Cumulative Sentence

Using the several brief sentences given below construct a single, cumulative/loose sentence.

Jessica always begins her writing sessions the same way.

She turns on her radio.

She sets her radio to Sirius XM.

She sets Sirius XM to the classical channel.

She puts her phone on mute.

She opens her laptop.

She cracks her knuckles.

She says "alrighty then."

Practice Writing a Periodic Sentence

Using the same brief sentences given for the construction of the cumulative sentence, construct a single, periodic sentence.

Jessica always begins her writing sessions the same way.

She turns on her radio.

She sets her radio to Sirius XM.

She sets Sirius XM to the classical channel.

She puts her phone on mute.

She opens her laptop.

She cracks her knuckles.

She says "alrighty then."

Practice Writing an Inverted Sentence

Convert each of the following into an inverted sentence.

1. All of the instructor's comments were delivered in her email.

2. A very famous writer lives in the house next door.

Playing with Diction #1

The following is the first sentence of Lincoln's "The Gettysburg Address." Using your knowledge about the effects diction can have on a text, rewrite this excerpt using informal/casual/relaxed diction.

Four score and seven years ago our fathers brought forth on this continent, a new nation, conceived in Liberty, and dedicated to the proposition that all men are created equal.

Locating the Thesis Statement

Below is the first paragraph of Arthur Schlesinger, Jr.'s essay "The Crisis of American Masculinity." (*Esquire*, 1958)

What has happened to the American male? For a long time, he seemed utterly confident in his manhood, sure of his masculine role in society, easy and definite in his sense of sexual identity. The frontiersmen of James Fennimore Cooper, for example, never had any concern about masculinity; they were men, and it did not occur to them to think twice about it. Even well into the twentieth century, the heroes of Dreiser, of Fitzgerald, of Hemingway remain men. But one begins to detect a new theme emerging in some of these authors, especially in Hemingway: the theme of the male hero increasingly preoccupied with proving his virility to himself. And by mid-century, the male role had plainly lost its rugged clarity of outline. Today men are more and more conscious of maleness not as a fact but as a problem. The ways by which American men affirm their masculinity are uncertain and obscure. There are multiplying signs, indeed, that something has gone badly wrong with the American male's conception of himself. (172)

Underline the thesis statement.

Locating the Thesis Statement

Here are the first two paragraphs of George Orwell's classic essay, "Politics and the English Language." (1946)

Most people who bother with the matter at all would admit that the English language is in a bad way, but it is generally assumed that we cannot by conscious action do anything about it. Our civilization is decadent, and our language – so the argument runs – must inevitably share in the general collapse. It follows that any struggle against the abuse of language is a sentimental archaism, like preferring candles to electric light or hansom cabs to aeroplanes. Underneath this lies the half-conscious belief that language is a natural growth and not an instrument which we shape for our own purposes.

          5

Now, it is clear that the decline of a language must ultimately have political and economic causes: it is not due simply to the bad influence of this or that individual writer. But an effect can become a cause, reinforcing the original cause and producing the same effect in an intensified form, and so on indefinitely. A man may take to drink because he feels himself to be a failure, and then fail all the more completely because he drinks. It is rather the same thing that is happening to the English language. It becomes ugly and inaccurate because our thoughts are foolish, but the slovenliness of our language makes it easier for us to have foolish thoughts. The point is that the process is reversible. Modern English, especially written English, is full of bad habits which spread by imitation and which can be avoided if one is willing to take the necessary trouble. If one gets rid of these habits one can think more clearly, and to think clearly is a necessary first step towards political regeneration: so that the fight against bad

          10

          15

          20

English is not frivolous and is not the exclusive concern of professional writers. I will come back to this presently, and I hope that by that time the meaning of what I have said here will have become clearer. Meanwhile, here are five specimens of the English language as it is now habitually written.

Underline the thesis statement.

Choosing the Best Thesis Statement

Based on a prompt that asks for an essay that discusses the merits of *Huckleberry Finn*, rank each of the following possible thesis statements from strongest to weakest.

A Strongest   **B** Strong   **C** Weak   **D** Weakest

___ My Dad thinks that *Huckleberry Finn* is Mark Twain's best novel.

___ *Huckleberry Finn* is Mark Twain's best novel.

___ Although some would argue that *The Adventures of Tom Sawyer* is Mark Twain's ultimate achievement, *Huckleberry Finn* has to be rated as his best because of its use of satire, imagery, and characterization.

___ *Huckleberry Finn* was written by Mark Twain in 1885.

Basic Rhetorical Analysis

Carefully read the following passage excerpted from Willa Cather's 1920 essay titled "The Art of Fiction."

Any first rate novel or story must have in it the strength of a
dozen fairly good stories that have been sacrificed to it. A good
workman can't be a cheap workman; he can't be stingy about wasting
material, and he cannot compromise. Writing ought either to be the
manufacture of stories for which there is a market demand – a business   5
as safe and commendable as making soap or breakfast foods – or it
should be an art, which is always a search for something for which
there is no market demand, something new and untried, where the
values are intrinsic and have nothing to do with standardized values.
The courage to go on without compromise does not come to a writer   10
all at once – nor, for that matter, does the ability. Both are phases
of natural development. In the beginning the artist, like his public,
is wedded to old forms, old ideals, and his vision is blurred by the
memory of old delights he would like to recapture.

1. The primary rhetorical strategy used to develop this paragraph is

   A. argument
   B. example
   C. description
   D. cause & effect
   E. process

2. The sentence beginning in line 4 with "Writing ought either to …" and ending in line 9 with "standardized values." is an example of a

___ periodic sentence   ___cumulative sentence   ___inverted sentence

3. According to Cather, a good novelist
   A. is cheap with money
   B. is wedded to old forms
   C. follows standardized values
   D. does not compromise
   E. avoids using old stories

Rhetorical Analysis, Twain, #1

Below is a single paragraph from "Two Ways of Seeing a River" by Mark Twain, from his autobiographical *Life on the Mississippi* (1883). You are going to engage with this passage in several different ways. Carefully read the passage.

Now when I had mastered the language of this water and had come to
know every trifling feature that bordered the great river as familiarly as I
knew the letters of the alphabet, I had made a valuable acquisition. But
I had lost something, too. I had lost something which could never be
restored to me while I lived. All the grace, the beauty, the poetry had gone   5
out of the majestic river! I still keep in mind a certain wonderful sunset
which I witnessed when steamboating was new to me. A broad expanse
of the river was turned to blood; in the middle distance the red hue
brightened into gold, through which a solitary log came floating, black
and conspicuous; in one place a long, slanting mark lay sparkling upon   10
the water; in another the surface was broken by boiling, tumbling rings,
that were as many-tinted as an opal; where the ruddy flush was faintest,
was a smooth spot that was covered with graceful circles and radiating
lines, ever so delicately traced; the shore on our left was densely wooded,
and the sombre shadow that fell from this forest was broken in one place   15
by a long, ruffled trail that shone like silver; and high above the forest wall
a clean-stemmed dead tree waved a single leafy bough that glowed like a
flame in the unobstructed splendor that was flowing from the sun. There
were graceful curves, reflected images, woody heights, soft distances; and
over the whole scene, far and near, the dissolving lights drifted steadily,   20
enriching it, every passing moment, with new marvels of coloring.

Locate the thesis/topic sentence and underline it.

Rhetorical Analysis, Twain, #2

Below is a single paragraph from "Two Ways of Seeing a River" by Mark Twain, from his autobiographical *Life on the Mississippi* (1883).

Now when I had mastered the language of this water and had come to
know every trifling feature that bordered the great river as familiarly as I
knew the letters of the alphabet, I had made a valuable acquisition. But
I had lost something, too. I had lost something which could never be
restored to me while I lived. All the grace, the beauty, the poetry had gone   5
out of the majestic river! I still keep in mind a certain wonderful sunset
which I witnessed when steamboating was new to me. A broad expanse
of the river was turned to blood; in the middle distance the red hue
brightened into gold, through which a solitary log came floating, black
and conspicuous; in one place a long, slanting mark lay sparkling upon   10
the water; in another the surface was broken by boiling, tumbling rings,
that were as many-tinted as an opal; where the ruddy flush was faintest,
was a smooth spot that was covered with graceful circles and radiating
lines, ever so delicately traced; the shore on our left was densely wooded,
and the sombre shadow that fell from this forest was broken in one place   15
by a long, ruffled trail that shone like silver; and high above the forest wall
a clean-stemmed dead tree waved a single leafy bough that glowed like a
flame in the unobstructed splendor that was flowing from the sun. There
were graceful curves, reflected images, woody heights, soft distances; and
over the whole scene, far and near, the dissolving lights drifted steadily,   20
enriching it, every passing moment, with new marvels of coloring.

"Something" is used twice in line 4. To what is it referring? Underline the word
or phrase.

Rhetorical Analysis, Twain, #3

Below is a single paragraph from "Two Ways of Seeing a River" by Mark Twain, from his autobiographical *Life on the Mississippi* (1883).

Now when I had mastered the language of this water and had come to
know every trifling feature that bordered the great river as familiarly as I
knew the letters of the alphabet, I had made a valuable acquisition. But
I had lost something, too. I had lost something which could never be
restored to me while I lived. All the grace, the beauty, the poetry had gone   5
out of the majestic river! I still keep in mind a certain wonderful sunset
which I witnessed when steamboating was new to me. A broad expanse
of the river was turned to blood; in the middle distance the red hue
brightened into gold, through which a solitary log came floating, black
and conspicuous; in one place a long, slanting mark lay sparkling upon the   10
water; in another the surface was broken by boiling, tumbling rings, that
were as many-tinted as an opal; where the ruddy flush was faintest, was
a smooth spot that was covered with graceful circles and radiating lines,
ever so delicately traced; the shore on our left was densely wooded, and
the sombre shadow that fell from this forest was broken in one place by   15
a long, ruffled trail that shone like silver; and high above the forest wall
a clean-stemmed dead tree waved a single leafy bough that glowed like a
flame in the unobstructed splendor that was flowing from the sun. There
were graceful curves, reflected images, woody heights, soft distances; and
over the whole scene, far and near, the dissolving lights drifted steadily,   20
enriching it, every passing moment, with new marvels of coloring.

1. The purpose of the passage is to ___inform ___persuade/argue ___entertain.

2. The primary rhetorical strategy employed in this paragraph is ___cause/effect ___definition ___description ___classification ___narration

3. The organization is ___chronological ___spatial ___least to most important ___ most to least important.

Rhetorical Analysis, Twain, #4

Below is a single paragraph from "Two Ways of Seeing a River" by Mark Twain, from his autobiographical *Life on the Mississippi* (1883).

Now when I had mastered the language of this water and had come to know every trifling feature that bordered the great river as familiarly as I knew the letters of the alphabet, I had made a valuable acquisition. But I had lost something, too. I had lost something which could never be restored to me while I lived. All the grace, the beauty, the poetry had gone   5
out of the majestic river! I still keep in mind a certain wonderful sunset which I witnessed when steamboating was new to me. A broad expanse of the river was turned to blood; in the middle distance the red hue brightened into gold, through which a solitary log came floating, black and conspicuous; in one place a long, slanting mark lay sparkling upon   10
the water; in another the surface was broken by boiling, tumbling rings, that were as many-tinted as an opal; where the ruddy flush was faintest, was a smooth spot that was covered with graceful circles and radiating lines, ever so delicately traced; the shore on our left was densely wooded, and the sombre shadow that fell from this forest was broken in one place   15
by a long, ruffled trail that shone like silver; and high above the forest wall a clean-stemmed dead tree waved a single leafy bough that glowed like a flame in the unobstructed splendor that was flowing from the sun. There were graceful curves, reflected images, woody heights, soft distances; and over the whole scene, far and near, the dissolving lights drifted steadily,   20
enriching it, every passing moment, with new marvels of coloring.

The sentence beginning with "A broad expanse of the river…" (line 7) and ending with "flowing from the sun." (line 18) is 143 words long. What is the purpose of a sentence of this length in the middle of this paragraph? Clue: This passage is about the Mississippi River. Write your response in only one sentence.

5 Minutes to a 5

Rhetorical Analysis, *Walden*, #1

Carefully read the following excerpt from Thoreau's *Walden,* Chapter 4, "Sounds."

When I meet the engine with its train of cars moving off with planetary
motion – or, rather, like a comet, for the beholder knows not if with that
velocity and with that direction it will ever revisit this system, since its
orbit does not look like a returning curve – with its steam cloud like a
banner streaming behind in golden and silver wreaths, like many a downy   5
cloud which I have seen, high in the heavens, unfolding its masses to the
light – as if this traveling demigod, this cloud-compeller, would ere long
take the sunset sky for the livery of his train; when I hear the iron horse
make the hills echo with his snort like thunder, shaking the earth with his
feet, and breathing fire and smoke from his nostrils (what kind of winged   10
horse or fiery dragon they will put into the new Mythology I don't know),
it seems as if the earth had got a race now worthy to inhabit it. If all were
as it seems, and men made the elements their servants for noble ends! If
the cloud that hangs over the engine were the perspiration of heroic deeds,
or as beneficent as that which floats over the farmer's fields then the   15
elements and Nature herself would cheerfully accompany men on their
errands and be their escort.

Using an argument of analogy, Thoreau's claim/assertion/thesis is _____

_____.

Rhetorical Analysis, *Walden*, #2

Carefully read the following passage from "Economy," Chapter 1 of Thoreau's *Walden* (1854):

> When I meet the engine with its train of cars moving off with planetary motion – or, rather, like a comet, for the beholder knows not if with that velocity and with that direction it will ever revisit this system, since its orbit does not look like a returning curve – with its steam cloud like a banner streaming behind in golden and silver wreaths, like many a downy   5 cloud which I have seen, high in the heavens, unfolding its masses to the light – as if this traveling demigod, this cloud-compeller, would ere long take the sunset sky for the livery of his train; when I hear the iron horse make the hills echo with his snort like thunder, shaking the earth with his feet, and breathing fire and smoke from his nostrils (what kind of winged   10 horse or fiery dragon they will put into the new Mythology I don't know), it seems as if the earth had got a race now worthy to inhabit it. If all were as it seems, and men made the elements their servants for noble ends! If the cloud that hangs over the engine were the perspiration of heroic deeds, or as beneficent as that which floats over the farmer's fields, then the   15 elements and Nature herself would cheerfully accompany men on their errands and be their escort.

1. The primary analogy developed in lines 1–3 compares a train to a _____.

2. The primary analogy developed in lines 8–11 compares the locomotive to a _____.

3. The primary literary device Thoreau employs in the construction of this description of an engine and its train is _____simile or _____metaphor.

5 Minutes to a 5

Rhetorical Analysis, *Walden*, #3

Carefully read the following passage from "Economy," Chapter 1 of Thoreau's *Walden* (1854):

> As with our colleges, so with a hundred "modern improvements": there is an illusion about them; there is not always a positive advance…. Our inventions are wont to be pretty toys, which distract our attention from serious things. They are but improved means to an unimproved end, an end which it was already but too easy to arrive at; as railroads lead   5
> to Boston or New York. We are in great haste to construct a magnetic telegraph from Maine to Texas, but Maine and Texas, it may be, have nothing important to communicate. Either is in such a predicament as the man who was earnest to be introduced to a distinguished deaf woman, but when he was presented, and one end of her ear trumpet was   10
> put into his hand, had nothing to say. As if the main object were to talk fast and not to talk sensibly. We are eager to tunnel under the Atlantic and bring the Old World some weeks nearer to the new, but perchance the first news that will leak through into the broad, flapping American ear will be that the Princess Adelaide has the whooping cough. After all,   15
> the man whose horse trots a mile in a minute does not carry the most important messages.

1. Underline the thesis statement.

2. Based on this paragraph, the reader can assume that the primary purpose of the complete essay is to ___inform ___argue ___narrate ___describe

Playing with Diction

Diction and Tone

The following is one of Mark Twain's famous quotations. Using your knowledge about the effects diction can have on a text, rewrite this metaphorical, folksy quotation using bombastic/pompous diction.

> It's not the size of the dog in the fight; it's the size of the fight in the dog
> —Mark Twain

Working the Rhetorical Analysis Prompt

Carefully read the following prompt:

> In "Message to President Franklin Pierce" (1854), Chief Seattle (chief of the Suquamish and Duwamish tribes of the Pacific Northwest, also important to the "white man" as Seattle was named after him) criticizes and cautions the attitudes and behaviors of the white man. After critically reading the speech, compose an essay analyzing the rhetorical devices used by Chief Seattle to convey his message.

1. Underline the essential elements of the prompt.

2. From a careful reading of the prompt, you can determine the basic information about this text to be (based on the College Board's **SOAPS** technique for rhetorical analysis):

   The **S**ubject is

   The **O**ccasion is

   The **A**udience is

   The **P**urpose is

   The **S**peaker is

5 Minutes to a 5

Working the Rhetorical Analysis Prompt

Carefully read the following prompt:

> Carefully read Judy Brady's essay "I Want a Wife," originally published in *Ms.* magazine in 1972 and reprinted as "Why I [Still] Want a Wife" in the same magazine in 1990. Then compose a well-written essay in which you analyze Brady's use of rhetorical strategies to reveal what she believes to be society's attitude toward the role of husbands and wives in the United States.

1. Underline the essential elements of the prompt.

2. From a careful reading of the prompt, you can determine the basic information about this text to be (based on the College Board's **SOAPS** technique for rhetorical analysis):

The **S**ubject is

The **O**ccasion is

The **A**udience is

The **P**urpose is

The **S**peaker is

Active and Passive Voice #1

Read the following carefully. Underline each instance of passive voice.

During the hot summer of 1776, the Declaration of Independence was written by Thomas Jefferson, and the bondage was broken between Britain and the American colonies. The Yankees were at last separated from the dictatorial monarchy and its supporters. The War of Independence was fought by the joined colonies, and the stars and stripes were very soon unfurled.

Active and Passive Voice #2

Revise this sentence using ACTIVE voice.

Even though a great deal of money is spent by people, hip-hop music is often hated.

Active and Passive Voice #3

Try rewriting this passage using ONLY ACTIVE VOICE.

During the hot summer of 1776, the Declaration of Independence was written by Thomas Jefferson, and the bondage was broken between Britain and the American colonies. The Yankees were at last separated from the dictatorial monarchy and its supporters. The War of Independence was fought by the joined colonies, and the stars and stripes were very soon unfurled.

→ 5 Minutes to a 5

Summarizing Texts using an excerpt from Chapter 1, "The Prison Door," of *The Scarlet Letter* by Nathaniel Hawthorne (1850)

Carefully read the following passage.

A throng of bearded men, in sad-colored garments and gray, steeple-crowned hats, intermixed with women, some wearing hoods, and others bareheaded, was assembled in front of a wooden edifice, the door of which was heavily timbered with oak and studded with iron spikes.

The founders of a new colony, whatever Utopia of human virtue   5
and happiness they might originally project, have invariably recognized
it among their earliest practical necessities to allot a portion of the virgin
soil as a cemetery, and another portion as the site of a prison.... Certain it
is that, some fifteen or twenty years after the settlement of the town, the
wooden jail was already marked with weather-stains and other indications   10
of age which gave a yet darker aspect to its beetle-browed and gloomy
front. The rust on the ponderous iron-work of its oaken door looked
more antique than anything else in the New World. Like all that pertains
to crime, it seemed never to have known a youthful era. Before this ugly
edifice, and between it and the wheel-track of the street, was a grass plot,   15
much overgrown with burdock, pigweed, apple-peru,[1] and such unsightly
vegetation, which evidently found something congenial in the soil that
had so early borne the black flower of civilized society, a prison. But
on one side of the portal, and rooted almost at the threshold, was a wild
rosebush, covered, in this month of June, with its delicate gems, which   20
might be imagined to offer their fragrance and fragile beauty to the

prisoner as he went in, and to the condemned criminal as he came forth to his doom, in token that the deep heart of Nature could pity and be kind to him.

This rosebush, by a strange chance, has been kept alive in history; but whether it had merely survived out of the stern old wilderness, so long after the fall of the gigantic pines and oaks that originally overshadowed it – or whether as there is fair authority for believing, it had sprung up under the footsteps of the sainted Ann Hutchison,[2] as she entered the prison door – we shall not take upon us to determine. Finding it so directly on the threshold of our narrative, which is now about to issue from that inauspicious portal, we could hardly do otherwise than pluck one of its flowers, and present it to the reader. It may serve, let us hope, to symbolize some sweet moral blossom that may be found along the track, or relieve the darkening close of a tale of human frailty and sorrow.

25

30

35

---

[1] a throne apple, a coarse weed

[2] Branded as a heretic for advocating women's equality and their right to pray in public, she was exiled from the Massachusetts Bay Colony.

Summarize the first sentence.

Determining Tone using an excerpt from Chapter 1, "The Prison Door," of *The Scarlet Letter* by Nathaniel Hawthorne (1850)

Carefully read the following passage.

A throng of bearded men, in sad-colored garments and gray, steeple-crowned hats, intermixed with women, some wearing hoods, and others bareheaded, was assembled in front of a wooden edifice, the door of which was heavily timbered with oak and studded with iron spikes.

The founders of a new colony, whatever Utopia of human virtue   5
and happiness they might originally project, have invariably recognized it among their earliest practical necessities to allot a portion of the virgin soil as a cemetery, and another portion as the site of a prison.... Certain it is that, some fifteen or twenty years after the settlement of the town, the wooden jail was already marked with weather-stains and other indications   10
of age which gave a yet darker aspect to its beetle-browed and gloomy front. The rust on the ponderous iron-work of its oaken door looked more antique than anything else in the New World. Like all that pertains to crime, it seemed never to have known a youthful era. Before this ugly edifice, and between it and the wheel-track of the street, was a grass   15
plot, much overgrown with burdock, pigweed, apple-peru,[1] and such unsightly vegetation, which evidently found something congenial in the soil that had so early borne the black flower of civilized society, a prison. But on one side of the portal, and rooted almost at the threshold, was a wild rosebush, covered, in this month of June, with its delicate gems,   20
which might be imagined to offer their fragrance and fragile beauty to the

5 Minutes to a 5

prisoner as he went in, and to the condemned criminal as he came forth
to his doom, in token that the deep heart of Nature could pity and be
kind to him.

     This rosebush, by a strange chance, has been kept alive in history;   **25**
but whether it had merely survived out of the stern old wilderness,
so long after the fall of the gigantic pines and oaks that originally
overshadowed it – or whether as there is fair authority for believing, it
had sprung up under the footsteps of the sainted Ann Hutchison,[2] as
she entered the prison door – we shall not take upon us to determine.   **30**
Finding it so directly on the threshold of our narrative, which is now
about to issue from that inauspicious portal, we could hardly do
otherwise than pluck one of its flowers, and present it to the reader. It
may serve, let us hope, to symbolize some sweet moral blossom that
may be found along the track, or relieve the darkening close of a tale of   **35**
human frailty and sorrow.

---

[1] a throne apple, a coarse weed

[2] Branded as a heretic for advocating women's equality and their right to pray in public,
she was exiled from the Massachusetts Bay Colony.

1. What is the overall tone of this chapter?

2. Underline or highlight the words/phrases that support your description of tone.

Composing the Thesis Statement using an excerpt from Chapter 1, "The Prison Door," of *The Scarlet Letter* by Nathaniel Hawthorne (1850)

Having carefully read and responded to the two previous activities, you should be prepared to deal with a prompt related to "The Prison-Door" in Hawthorne's *The Scarlet Letter*. Compose the first draft of a thesis statement that addresses the following prompt:

"The Prison-Door," the first chapter of Hawthorne's *The Scarlet Letter*, presents the reader with a characterization of a town and its inhabitants. Write a well-written essay that analyzes how Hawthorne creates this portrait. Make certain to make direct references to the text.

Thesis statement:

5 Minutes to a 5

Working with Tone

After carefully reading the following movie review,

- state the TONE the reviewer has toward the movie/book/music/play;
- underline those words and/or phrases (Diction) used in the review which support/develop this tone.

"*Ben-Hur* Review: A Remake Disaster of Biblical Proportions"

By Peter Travers, August 19, 2016, <http://www.rollingstone.com/movies/reviews/ben-hur-movie-review-w435330>

The last of the summer's movie epics is a digitalized eyesore hobbled in every department by staggering incompetence. I'm talking about *Ben-Hur*, a remake of William Wyler's 1959 milestone (there was also a 1925 silent version) that won Charlton Heston an Oscar in the title role and put the climactic chariot race in the action-movie canon. No time capsule inclusion or little gold men for this poor reboot, however. Executive producers Mark Burnett and his wife Roma Downey have been pushing projects … aimed squarely at those moviegoers interested in religious themes…. No harm in that, except the artistic kind. The new *Ben-Hur*, directed [by] Timur Bekmanbetov (*Wanted*), stars Jack Huston (so dazzling on *Boardwalk Empire,* so dreary here)…

The actors rarely rise above the level of monotonous, and that includes Morgan Freeman as an African sheik who sells horses for chariot races. To be fair, you can see a glint of mischief in Freeman's eyes. But the movie soon blots out any hint of fun, ferocity or imagination. *Ben-Hur* wants to preach, brother, preach, but it lacks the essential quality to do that effectively: soul.

1. The tone is _____.
2. Underline the words/phrases that are used to construct this tone.

Day 67

Rhetorical Analysis, Dickens, #1

Carefully read the following excerpt from the essay "Our English Watering Place" by Charles Dickens (1851)

Half-awake and half-asleep, this idle morning in our sunny window on the edge of a chalk cliff in the old-fashioned watering place to which we are a faithful resorter[1], we feel a lazy inclination to sketch its picture.

Sky, sea, beach, and village lie as still before us as if they were sitting for the picture. It is dead low-water. A ripple plays among the ripening corn upon the cliff as if it were faintly trying from recollection to imitate the sea, and the world of butterflies hovering over the crop of radish seed are as restless in their little way as the gulls are in their larger manner when the wind blows. But the ocean lies winking in the sunlight like a drowsy lion – its glassy waters scarcely curve upon the shore – the fishing boats in the tiny harbor are all stranded in the mud – our two colliers (our watering place has a maritime trade employing that amount of shipping) have not an inch of water within a quarter of a mile of them, and they turn, exhausted, on their sides, like faint fish of an antediluvian species. Rusty cables and chains, ropes and rings, under-most parts of posts and piles and confused timber defenses against the waves lie strewn about in a brown litter of tangled seaweed and fallen cliff which looks as if a family of giants had been making tea here for ages and had observed an untidy custom of throwing their tea leaves on the shore.

5

10

15

20

---

[1]a frequenter of resorts

1. Underline each example of simile and metaphor that Dickens uses to describe the seascape above.

2. _____ What is the over-all effect of the imagery presented in the passage?

   A. anger and agitation

   B. curiosity and suspicion

   C. stillness and serenity

   D. fear and loathing

   E. excitement and anticipation

Practice with Rhetorical Techniques

Carefully read each of the following statements.

A policeman shoots himself in his leg as he returns his gun to his holster.

The Titanic was advertised as 100% unsinkable; but it sank on its very first voyage in 1912.

In Shakespeare's *Romeo and Juliet*, Romeo finds Juliet in a drugged sleep. Believing she is dead, he kills himself. And, when Juliet awakens and finds Romeo dead at her feet, she, too, kills herself.

Although different in situation and subject matter, each of the statements is an example of

A. hyperbole
B. understatement
C. antithesis
D. sarcasm
E. irony

Rhetorical Analysis, "On the Tragedies of Shakspeare," Charles Lamb (1822), #1

The following set of questions is based on a careful reading of Charles Lamb's essay "On the Tragedies of Shakspeare."

Note: *Charles Lamb (1775-1834)—English essayist and critic*

Charles Lamb: On the Tragedies of Shakspeare [sic]

The truth is, the characters of Shakspeare [sic] are so much the objects of meditation rather than of interest or curiosity as to their actions, that while we are reading any of his great criminal characters – Macbeth, Richard, even Iago – we think not so much of the crimes which they commit, as of the ambition, the aspiring spirit, the intellectual activity, 5
which prompts them to overleap these moral fences. Barnwell[1] is a wretched murderer; there is a certain fitness between his neck and the rope; he is the legitimate heir to the gallows; nobody who thinks at all can think of any alleviating circumstances in his case to make him a fit object of mercy. Or to take an instance from the higher tragedy, what else but 10
a mere assassin is Glenalvon?[2] Do we think of anything but of the crime which he commits, and the rack which he deserves? That is all which we really think about him.

Whereas in corresponding characters in Shakspeare [sic], so little do the actions comparatively affect us, that while the impulses, the inner 15
mind in all its perverted greatness, solely seems real and is exclusively attended to, the crime is comparatively nothing. But when we see these things represented, the acts which they do are comparatively everything,

their impulses nothing. The state of sublime emotion into which we are
elevated by those images of night and horror which Macbeth is made
to utter, that solemn prelude with which he entertains the time till the
bell shall strike which is to call him to murder Duncan – when we no
longer read it in a book, when we have given up that vantage ground
of abstraction which reading possesses over seeing, and come to see a
man in his bodily shape before our eyes actually preparing to commit
a murder, if the acting be true and impressive, as I have witnessed it in
Mr. K.'s performance of that part, the painful anxiety about the act, the
natural longing to prevent it while it yet seems unperpetrated, the too
close pressing semblance of reality, give a pain and an uneasiness which
totally destroy all the delight which the words in the book convey, where
the deed doing never presses upon us with the painful sense of presence: it
rather seems to belong to history – to something past and inevitable, if it
has anything to do with time at all. The sublime images, the poetry alone,
is that which is present to our minds in the reading.

20

25

30

---

[1]George Barnwell robbed and killed his uncle to fund his relationship with
a prostitute. His story was made into an English drama in 1731.

[2]A character in a 1770 English drama who murders to gain wealth and power

1. The thesis is found in lines ___1–6 ___9–10 ___11–13

2. The purpose of this essay is to ___inform ___argue ___entertain.

Rhetorical Analysis, "On the Tragedies of Shakspeare," Charles Lamb (1822), #2

The following set of questions is based on a careful reading of Charles Lamb's essay "On the Tragedies of Shakspeare."

Charles Lamb: On the Tragedies of Shakspeare [sic]

The truth is, the characters of Shakspeare [sic] are so much the objects of meditation rather than of interest or curiosity as to their actions, that while we are reading any of his great criminal characters – Macbeth, Richard, even Iago – we think not so much of the crimes which they commit, as of the ambition, the aspiring spirit, the intellectual activity, which prompts them to overleap these moral fences. Barnwell[1] is a wretched murderer; there is a certain fitness between his neck and the rope; he is the legitimate heir to the gallows; nobody who thinks at all can think of any alleviating circumstances in his case to make him a fit object of mercy. Or to take an instance from the higher tragedy, what else but a mere assassin is Glenalvon?[2] Do we think of anything but of the crime which he commits, and the rack which he deserves? That is all which we really think about him.

Whereas in corresponding characters in Shakspeare [sic], so little do the actions comparatively affect us, that while the impulses, the inner mind in all its perverted greatness, solely seems real and is exclusively attended to, the crime is comparatively nothing. But when we see these things represented, the acts which they do are comparatively everything, their impulses nothing. The state of sublime emotion into which we are elevated by those images of night and horror which Macbeth is made

5

10

15

20

to utter, that solemn prelude with which he entertains the time till the
bell shall strike which is to call him to murder Duncan – when we no
longer read it in a book, when we have given up that vantage ground
of abstraction which reading possesses over seeing, and come to see a
man in his bodily shape before our eyes actually preparing to commit   25
a murder, if the acting be true and impressive, as I have witnessed it in
Mr. K.'s performance of that part, the painful anxiety about the act, the
natural longing to prevent it while it yet seems unperpetrated, the too
close pressing semblance of reality, give a pain and an uneasiness which
totally destroy all the delight which the words in the book convey, where   30
the deed doing never presses upon us with the painful sense of presence: it
rather seems to belong to history – to something past and inevitable, if it
has anything to do with time at all. The sublime images, the poetry alone,
is that which is present to our minds in the reading.

---

[1]George Barnwell robbed and killed his uncle to fund his relationship with a prostitute.
His story was made into an English drama in 1731.

[2]A character in a 1770 English drama who murders to gain wealth and power

1. Lamb's primary strategy to organize his presentation is
   A. exposition
   B. cause and effect
   C. description
   D. comparison and contrast
   E. definition

2. Lamb develops his primary organizational strategy using
   A. examples
   B. narration
   C. description
   D. process
   E. classification

Day 71

Rhetorical Analysis, "On the Tragedies of Shakspeare," Charles Lamb (1822), #3

The following set of questions is based on a careful reading of Charles Lamb's essay "On the Tragedies of Shakspeare."

Charles Lamb: On the Tragedies of Shakspeare [sic]

The truth is, the characters of Shakspeare [sic] are so much the objects of meditation rather than of interest or curiosity as to their actions, that while we are reading any of his great criminal characters – Macbeth, Richard, even Iago – we think not so much of the crimes which they commit, as of the ambition, the aspiring spirit, the intellectual activity, which prompts them to overleap these moral fences. Barnwell[1] is a wretched murderer; there is a certain fitness between his neck and the rope; he is the legitimate heir to the gallows; nobody who thinks at all can think of any alleviating circumstances in his case to make him a fit object of mercy. Or to take an instance from the higher tragedy, what else but a mere assassin is Glenalvon?[2] Do we think of anything but of the crime which he commits, and the rack which he deserves? That is all which we really think about him.

Whereas in corresponding characters in Shakspeare [sic], so little do the actions comparatively affect us, that while the impulses, the inner mind in all its perverted greatness, solely seems real and is exclusively attended to, the crime is comparatively nothing. But when we see these things represented, the acts which they do are comparatively everything, their impulses nothing. The state of sublime emotion into which we are elevated by those images of night and horror which Macbeth is made

5

10

15

20

5 Minutes to a 5

to utter, that solemn prelude with which he entertains the time till the bell shall strike which is to call him to murder Duncan – when we no longer read it in a book, when we have given up that vantage ground of abstraction which reading possesses over seeing, and come to see a man in his bodily shape before our eyes actually preparing to commit a murder, if the acting be true and impressive, as I have witnessed it in Mr. K.'s performance of that part, the painful anxiety about the act, the natural longing to prevent it while it yet seems unperpetrated, the too close pressing semblance of reality, give a pain and an uneasiness which totally destroy all the delight which the words in the book convey, where the deed doing never presses upon us with the painful sense of presence: it rather seems to belong to history – to something past and inevitable, if it has anything to do with time at all. The sublime images, the poetry alone, is that which is present to our minds in the reading.

25

30

---

[1]George Barnwell robbed and killed his uncle to fund his relationship with a prostitute. His story was made into an English drama in 1731.

[2]A character in a 1770 English drama who murders to gain wealth and power

1. According to the second paragraph, what perspective does reading have that seeing does not?

2. According to Lamb, what is the major difference between the effect of reading a Shakespearean play and seeing a Shakespearean play?

3. According to Lamb, what is the difference between action and impulse when we see a play performed as opposed to just reading it?

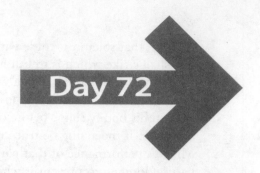

Rhetorical Analysis, "On the Tragedies of Shakspeare," Charles Lamb (1822), #4

The following set of questions is based on a careful reading of Charles Lamb's essay "On the Tragedies of Shakspeare."

Charles Lamb: On the Tragedies of Shakspeare [sic]

…Whereas in corresponding characters in Shakspeare [sic], so little do the actions comparatively affect us, that while the impulses, the inner mind in all its perverted greatness, solely seems real and is exclusively attended to, the crime is comparatively nothing. But when we see these things represented, the acts which they do are comparatively   5
everything, their impulses nothing. The state of sublime emotion into which we are elevated by those images of night and horror which Macbeth is made to utter, that solemn prelude with which he entertains the time till the bell shall strike which is to call him to murder Duncan – when we no longer read it in a book, when we have   10
given up that vantage ground of abstraction which reading possesses over seeing, and come to see a man in his bodily shape before our eyes actually preparing to commit a murder, if the acting be true and impressive, as I have witnessed it in Mr. K.'s performance of that part, the painful anxiety about the act, the natural longing to prevent it   15
while it yet seems unperpetrated, the too close pressing semblance of reality, give a pain and an uneasiness which totally destroy all the delight which the words in the book convey, where the deed doing never presses upon us with the painful sense of presence: it rather seems to belong to history – to something past and inevitable, if it has   20

anything to do with time at all. The sublime images, the poetry alone,
is that which is present to our minds in the reading.

---

[1]George Barnwell robbed and killed his uncle to fund his relationship with a prostitute.
His story was made into an English drama in 1731.

[2]A character in a 1770 English drama who murders to gain wealth and power

The highlighted sentence above has 188 words. That's probably one of the longest
sentences you've ever come across; plus it's not written in modern idiom using
modern syntax. If you were asked to summarize this sentence, it would be quite a
task. So, to save you agony, choose the best of the summary statements from among
those given below.

1. Reading a Shakespearean play is an intellectual activity, but seeing it performed by
   a good actor is physical. (18 words)

2. When we read the scene, where Macbeth ponders the terrors of killing Duncan,
   we become intellectually lifted and emotionally involved; however, when we see it
   performed by a good actor we are physically affected by the reality of the action.
   (40 words)

3. As readers of a scene from a Shakespearean play like Macbeth, we are put into an
   elevated mental state of emotion, but we physically react to a good actor performing
   the same scene. (34 words)

Day 73

Diction

From Ronald Reagan's First Inaugural Address.

The following is a brief excerpt from Ronald Reagan's First "Inaugural Address." Using your knowledge of diction, rewrite this excerpt using objective/detached diction.

This is the first time in history that this ceremony has been held, as you have been told, on this West Front of the Capitol. Standing here, one faces a magnificent vista, opening up on this city's special beauty and history. At the end of this open mall are those shrines to the giants on whose shoulders we stand.

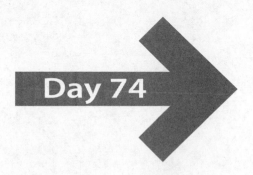

Purpose: Says/Does

Carefully read the following passage.

"On a Sharecropper's Overalls" by James Agee from *Let Us Now Praise Famous Men*

The structures sag….The edges of the thigh pockets become stretched and
lie open, fluted, like the gills of a fish. The bright seams lose their whiteness
and are lines and ridges. The whole fabric is shrunken to size, which was
bought large. The whole shape, texture, color, finally substance, all are
changed. The shape, particularly along the urgent frontage of the thighs,   5
so that the whole structure of the knee and musculature of the thigh is
sculpted there…. The texture and the color change in union, by sweat, sun,
laundering, between the steady pressures of its use and age: both, at length,
into realms of fine softness and marvel of draping and velvet plays of light
which chamois and silk can only suggest, not touch; and into a region and   10
scales of blues, subtle, delicious and deft beyond what I have ever seen
elsewhere approached except in rare skies, the smoky light some days are
filled with, and some of the blues of Cezanne.

Not only must you be able to identify, you *must* also be able to discuss *what purpose*
using a certain rhetorical strategy, device, or technique serves. With this in mind, let's
examine the Agee paragraph from the standpoint of SAY/DOES.

If the subject of sentence 7 (lines 7–13) is the changing texture and color of the sharecropper's overalls, what is the purpose of following that with a long string of phrases
and clauses, together with the use of a colon and a semicolon? Take a risk. Try to
answer this question in terms of says/does. Think about the beginning which says that
BOTH the texture AND the color of the overalls change. WHY would Agee choose
to write this description the way he does? What is he trying to do?

Just try to write one to three sentences. No more.

Satire – Review Some Basics

The following is an excerpt from a Mississippi State University satirical journalistic essay titled: "Major Technological Breakthrough: BIO-Optic Organized Knowledge Device (BOOK)." Carefully read the passage, then answer the questions that follow.

> The Mississippi State University English Department announces its employment of a radically innovative technological device, the BOOK.
>
> BOOK is a revolutionary breakthrough in technology: no wires, no electric circuits, no batteries, nothing to be connected or switched on. It is so easy to use, even a child can operate it.
>
> Compact and portable, it can be used anywhere – even when sitting in an armchair by the fire, yet powerful enough to hold as much information as a [flash drive].
>
> Here is how it works: BOOK is constructed of sequentially numbered sheets of paper (recyclable), each capable of holding thousands of bits of information. The pages are locked together with a custom-fit device called a binding, which keeps the sheets in their correct sequence.

Satire is the use of sarcasm, irony, and/or wit to ridicule or mock. With this in mind, check those items listed below that apply to the passage you just read.

1. This is an example of ____direct (obviously stated) or ____indirect (communicated via characters in a situation) satirical style.

2. The passage can be classified as ____Horatian (light-hearted, fun) or ____Juvenalian (bitter, angry, attacking).

3. Underline at least three examples of *verbal irony* (an inversion of meaning) in this excerpt.

Working with Satire

Each of the following headlines can be classified as satire. Read each carefully, then answer the questions that follow.

Man Claims Local Bagel Shop Is a "Basic Human Right"

Amsterdam High School Relocates to Save Historic Coffee Shop

A Modest Proposal to Convert Shopping Malls into Prisons

Man Injures Shoppers Fighting for "Almost Handicapped" Parking Spot

These headlines share all of the following characteristics except

A. related to contemporary issues
B. dependent on literary background
C. uses irony
D. uses exaggeration
E. uses humor

Satire Analysis

Carefully read the following excerpt from "'Sexing Up' the Statue of Liberty," by Peter Fenton (*The Satirist*, September 17, 2016)

> I suggest a fashion makeover of Lady Liberty [The Statue of Liberty]. Why not a snappy little black suit, with knee-length skirt and fitted jacket showing her ample curves? (Admit it America: she's plus-sized.) Or, maybe a cool pair of colorful leggings over a knee-length tunic? And instead of that crown-of-spikes thing on her head, a cute newsboy cap or a cool straw boater? In one hand, she could be holding a leather clutch, in the other an iPhone7 instead of that silly torch....

Let's do this, fashionistas! Free Lady Liberty from Fashion Hell!

1. What aspect of society is the writer satirizing?

2. What is the purpose of this satire?

Satire Analysis

Carefully read the following excerpt from "'Sexing Up' the Statue of Liberty," by Peter Fenton (*The Satirist*, September 17, 2016)

> I suggest a fashion makeover of Lady Liberty [The Statue of Liberty]. Why not a snappy little black suit, with knee-length skirt and fitted jacket showing her ample curves? (Admit it America: she's plus-sized.) Or, maybe a cool pair of colorful leggings over a knee-length tunic? And instead of that crown-of-spikes thing on her head, a cute newsboy cap or a cool straw boater? In one hand, she could be holding a leather clutch; in the other an iPhone7 instead of that silly torch….

Let's do this, fashionistas! Free Lady Liberty from Fashion Hell!

1. This is an example of ___direct ___indirect satirical style.

2. The passage can be classified as ___Horatian ___Juvenalian.

3. In constructing the satire, the writer primarily uses

    A. understatement
    B. allusion
    C. hyperbole
    D. irony
    E. parody

Satire Analysis

During the mid-19th century, Tammany Hall, a political machine led by Boss Tweed, swindled an estimated 75 to 200 million dollars from New York City. Carefully consider the following political cartoon drawn by Thomas Nast for *The New York Times* from that time period.

– **Thomas Nast**

1. This 19th century political cartoon can be classified as ___Horatian ___Juvenalian.

2. Cite three items from the cartoon that led you to this conclusion.

Satire Analysis

Not even The Declaration of Independence is immune to satire. Watch the satirical video at https://www.youtube.com/watch?v=uMIyh2rpjkg. Then respond to the following questions.

1. This YouTube video, which satirizes The Declaration of Independence, can be classified as ____ Horatian ____ Juvenalian.

2. This satirical video relies primarily on
   A. allusion
   B. parody
   C. irony
   D. hyperbole
   E. understatement

Rhetorical Analysis: FDR's Inaugural Address, #1

The following set of questions is based on a careful reading of Franklin Delano Roosevelt's First Inaugural Address delivered on March 4, 1933, in the midst of America's Great Depression. The transcript of the speech is printed below. You can also listen to an audio of FDR actually giving the address at

http://www.history.com/speeches/franklin-d-roosevelts-first-inaugural-address

Franklin Delano Roosevelt's First Inaugural Address

I am certain that my fellow Americans expect that on my induction into the Presidency I will address them with a candor and a decision which the present situation of our Nation impels. This is preeminently the time to speak the truth, the whole truth, frankly and boldly. Nor need we shrink from honestly facing conditions in our country today. This great Nation will endure as it has endured, will revive and will prosper. So, first of all, let me assert my firm belief that the only thing we have to fear is fear itself – nameless, unreasoning, unjustified terror which paralyzes needed efforts to convert retreat into advance. In every dark hour of our national life a leadership of frankness and vigor has met with that understanding and support of the people themselves which is essential to victory. I am convinced that you will again give that support to leadership in these critical days.

In such a spirit on my part and on yours we face our common difficulties. They concern, thank God, only material things. Values have shrunken to fantastic levels; taxes have risen; our ability to pay has fallen; government of all kinds is faced by serious curtailment of income; the means of exchange are frozen in the currents of trade; the withered leaves of industrial enterprise lie on every side; farmers find no markets for their produce; the savings of many years in thousands of families are gone.

More important, a host of unemployed citizens face the grim problem of existence, and an equally great number toil with little return. Only a foolish optimist can deny the dark realities of the moment.

Yet our distress comes from no failure of substance. We are stricken by no plague of locusts. Compared with the perils which our forefathers conquered because they believed and were not afraid, we have still much to be thankful for. Nature still offers her bounty and human efforts have multiplied it. Plenty is at our doorstep, but a generous use of it languishes in the very sight of the supply. Primarily this is because the rulers of the exchange of mankind's goods have failed, through their own stubbornness and their own incompetence, have admitted their failure, and abdicated. Practices of the unscrupulous money changers stand indicted in the court of public opinion, rejected by the hearts and minds of men.

True they have tried, but their efforts have been cast in the pattern of an outworn tradition. Faced by failure of credit they have proposed only the lending of more money. Stripped of the lure of profit by which to induce our people to follow their false leadership, they have resorted to exhortations, pleading tearfully for restored confidence. They know only the rules of a generation of self-seekers. They have no vision, and when there is no vision the people perish.

The money changers have fled from their high seats in the temple of our civilization. We may now restore that temple to the ancient truths. The measure of the restoration lies in the extent to which we apply social values more noble than mere monetary profit.

Happiness lies not in the mere possession of money; it lies in the joy of achievement, in the thrill of creative effort. The joy and moral stimulation of work no longer must be forgotten in the mad chase of evanescent profits. These dark days will be worth all they cost us if they teach us that our true destiny is not to be ministered unto but to minister to ourselves and to our fellow men.

Recognition of the falsity of material wealth as the standard of success goes hand in hand with the abandonment of the false belief that public office and high political position are to be valued only by the standards of pride of place and personal profit; and there must be an end to a conduct in banking and in business which too often has given to a sacred trust the likeness of callous and selfish wrongdoing. Small wonder that confidence languishes, for it thrives only on honesty, on honor, on the sacredness of obligations, on faithful protection, on unselfish performance; without them it cannot live.

Restoration calls, however, not for changes in ethics alone. This Nation asks for action, and action now.

Our greatest primary task is to put people to work. This is no unsolvable problem if we face it wisely and courageously. It can be accomplished in part by direct recruiting by the Government itself, treating the task as we would treat the emergency of a war, but at the same time, through this employment, accomplishing greatly needed projects to stimulate and reorganize the use of our natural resources.

Hand in hand with this we must frankly recognize the overbalance of population in our industrial centers and, by engaging on a national scale in a redistribution, endeavor to provide a better use of the land for those best fitted for the land. The task can be helped by definite efforts to raise the values of agricultural products and with this the power to purchase the output of our cities. It can be helped by preventing realistically the tragedy of the growing loss through foreclosure of our small homes and our farms. It can be helped by insistence that the Federal, State, and local governments act forthwith on the demand that their cost be drastically reduced. It can be helped by the unifying of relief activities which today are often scattered, uneconomical, and unequal. It can be helped by national planning for and supervision of all forms of transportation and of communications and other utilities which have a definitely public character. There are many ways in which it can be helped, but it can never be helped merely by talking about it. We must act and act quickly.

Finally, in our progress toward a resumption of work we require two safeguards against a return of the evils of the old order; there must be a strict supervision of all banking and credits and investments; there must be an end to speculation with other people's money, and there must be provision for an adequate but sound currency.

These are the lines of attack. I shall presently urge upon a new Congress in special session detailed measures for their fulfillment, and I shall seek the immediate assistance of the several States.

Through this program of action we address ourselves to putting our own national house in order and making income balance outgo. Our international trade relations, though vastly important, are in point of time and necessity secondary to the establishment of a sound national economy. I favor as a practical policy the putting of first things first. I shall spare no effort to restore world trade by international economic readjustment, but the emergency at home cannot wait on that accomplishment.

The basic thought that guides these specific means of national recovery is not narrowly nationalistic. It is the insistence, as a first consideration, upon the interdependence of the various elements in all parts of the United States – a recognition of the old and permanently important manifestation of the American spirit of the pioneer. It is the way to recovery. It is the immediate way. It is the strongest assurance that the recovery will endure.

In the field of world policy I would dedicate this Nation to the policy of the good neighbor—the neighbor who resolutely respects himself and, because he does so, respects the rights of others—the neighbor who respects his obligations and respects the sanctity of his agreements in and with a world of neighbors.

If I read the temper of our people correctly, we now realize as we have never realized before our interdependence on each other; that we can not merely take but we must give as well; that if we are to go forward, we must move as a trained and loyal army willing to sacrifice for the good of a common discipline, because without such discipline no progress is made, no leadership becomes effective. We are, I know, ready and willing to submit our lives and property to such discipline, because it makes possible a leadership which aims at a larger good. This I propose to offer, pledging that the larger purposes will bind upon us all as a sacred obligation with a unity of duty hitherto evoked only in time of armed strife.

With this pledge taken, I assume unhesitatingly the leadership of this great army of our people dedicated to a disciplined attack upon our common problems.

Action in this image and to this end is feasible under the form of government which we have inherited from our ancestors. Our Constitution is so simple and practical that it is possible always to meet extraordinary needs by changes in emphasis and arrangement without loss of essential form. That is why our constitutional system has proved itself the most superbly enduring political mechanism the modern world has produced. It has met every stress of vast expansion of territory, of foreign wars, of bitter internal strife, of world relations.

It is to be hoped that the normal balance of executive and legislative authority may be wholly adequate to meet the unprecedented task before us. But it may be that an unprecedented demand and need for undelayed action may call for temporary departure from that normal balance of public procedure.

I am prepared under my constitutional duty to recommend the measures that a stricken nation in the midst of a stricken world may require. These measures, or such other measures as the Congress may build out of its experience and wisdom, I shall seek, within my constitutional authority, to bring to speedy adoption.

But in the event that the Congress shall fail to take one of these two courses, and in the event that the national emergency is still critical, I shall not evade the clear course of duty that will then confront me. I shall ask the Congress for the one remaining instrument to meet the crisis – broad Executive power to wage a war against the emergency, as great as the power that would be given to me if we were in fact invaded by a foreign foe.

For the trust reposed in me I will return the courage and the devotion that befit the time. I can do no less.

We face the arduous days that lie before us in the warm courage of the national unity; with the clear consciousness of seeking old and precious moral values; with the clean satisfaction that comes from the stern performance of duty by old and young alike. We aim at the assurance of a rounded and permanent national life.

We do not distrust the future of essential democracy. The people of the United States have not failed. In their need they have registered a mandate that they want direct, vigorous action. They have asked for discipline and direction under leadership. They have made me the present instrument of their wishes. In the spirit of the gift I take it.

In this dedication of a Nation we humbly ask the blessing of God. May He protect each and every one of us. May He guide me in the days to come.

Rhetorical Analysis: FDR's Inaugural Address, #2

Carefully read the first three paragraphs of FDR's speech and address each of the questions that follow.

Franklin Delano Roosevelt's First Inaugural Address

I am certain that my fellow Americans expect that on my induction into
the Presidency I will address them with a candor and a decision which the
present situation of our Nation impels. This is preeminently the time to
speak the truth, the whole truth, frankly and boldly. Nor need we shrink
from honestly facing conditions in our country today. This great Nation   5
will endure as it has endured, will revive and will prosper. So, first of all,
let me assert my firm belief that the only thing we have to fear is fear
itself — nameless, unreasoning, unjustified terror which paralyzes needed
efforts to convert retreat into advance. In every dark hour of our national
life a leadership of frankness and vigor has met with that understanding   10
and support of the people themselves which is essential to victory. I am
convinced that you will again give that support to leadership in these
critical days.

In such a spirit on my part and on yours we face our common
difficulties. They concern, thank God, only material things. Values   15
have shrunken to fantastic levels; taxes have risen; our ability to pay
has fallen; government of all kinds is faced by serious curtailment of
income; the means of exchange are frozen in the currents of trade; the
withered leaves of industrial enterprise lie on every side; farmers find
no markets for their produce; the savings of many years in thousands of   20
families are gone.

More important, a host of unemployed citizens face the grim problem of existence, and an equally great number toil with little return. Only a foolish optimist can deny the dark realities of the moment.

1. Begin your analysis of the speech with

S _____

O _____

A _____

P _____

S _____

TONE _____

2. Underline the thesis.

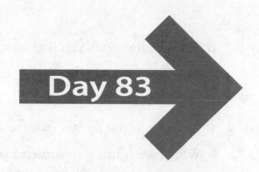
Rhetorical Analysis:
FDR's Inaugural Address, #3

Carefully read the first two paragraphs of FDR's speech and address each of the questions that follow.

Franklin Delano Roosevelt's First Inaugural Address

I am certain that my fellow Americans expect that on my induction into the Presidency I will address them with a candor and a decision which the present situation of our Nation impels. This is preeminently the time to speak the truth, the whole truth, frankly and boldly. Nor need we shrink from honestly facing conditions in our country today. This great Nation   5
will endure as it has endured, will revive and will prosper. So, first of all, let me assert my firm belief that the only thing we have to fear is fear itself — nameless, unreasoning, unjustified terror which paralyzes needed efforts to convert retreat into advance. In every dark hour of our national life a leadership of frankness and vigor has met with that understanding   10
and support of the people themselves which is essential to victory. I am convinced that you will again give that support to leadership in these critical days.

      In such a spirit on my part and on yours we face our common difficulties. They concern, thank God, only material things. Values   15
have shrunken to fantastic levels; taxes have risen; our ability to pay has fallen; government of all kinds is faced by serious curtailment of income; the means of exchange are frozen in the currents of trade; the withered leaves of industrial enterprise lie on every side; farmers find no markets for their produce; the savings of many years in thousands of   20
families are gone.

1. In which line(s) do you find an appeal to logos?

2. In which line(s) do you find an appeal to ethos?

3. In which line(s) do you find an appeal to pathos?

4. In which line(s) do you find metaphor(s)?

5. What tone is being constructed using the metaphor(s)?

Rhetorical Analysis: FDR's Inaugural Address, #4

Carefully read paragraphs four and five of FDR's speech and address each of the questions that follow.

[Note: The last line of the preceding paragraph reads: "Only a foolish optimist can deny the dark realities of the moment."]

Yet our distress comes from no failure of substance. We are stricken by no plague of locusts. Compared with the perils which our forefathers conquered because they believed and were not afraid, we have still much to be thankful for. Nature still offers her bounty and human efforts have multiplied it. Plenty is at our doorstep, but a generous use of it languishes   5
in the very sight of the supply. Primarily this is because the rulers of the exchange of mankind's goods have failed, through their own stubbornness and their own incompetence, have admitted their failure, and abdicated. Practices of the unscrupulous money changers stand indicted in the court of public opinion, rejected by the hearts and minds of men.   10

       True they have tried, but their efforts have been cast in the pattern of an outworn tradition. Faced by failure of credit they have proposed only the lending of more money. Stripped of the lure of profit by which to induce our people to follow their false leadership, they have resorted to exhortations, pleading tearfully for restored confidence. They know only the   15
rules of a generation of self-seekers. They have no vision, and when there is no vision the people perish.

1. What is the function of *Yet* at the beginning of paragraph four?

2. In the first two sentences of the excerpt, what is the purpose of the use of anastrophe?

3. *this* in line 6 refers to what?

4. Throughout the second paragraph, *they* refers to whom?

5. What is the primary purpose of these two paragraphs?

Rhetorical Analysis: FDR's Inaugural Address, #5

Carefully read paragraphs 6, 7, and 8 of FDR's speech and address each of the questions that follow.

The money changers have fled from their high seats in the temple of our civilization. We may now restore that temple to the ancient truths. The measure of the restoration lies in the extent to which we apply social values more noble than mere monetary profit.

Happiness lies not in the mere possession of money; it lies in the joy of achievement, in the thrill of creative effort. The joy and moral stimulation of work no longer must be forgotten in the mad chase of evanescent profits. These dark days will be worth all they cost us if they teach us that our true destiny is not to be ministered unto but to minister to ourselves and to our fellow men.

Recognition of the falsity of material wealth as the standard of success goes hand in hand with the abandonment of the false belief that public office and high political position are to be valued only by the standards of pride of place and personal profit; and there must be an end to a conduct in banking and in business which too often has given to a sacred trust the likeness of callous and selfish wrongdoing. Small wonder that confidence languishes, for it thrives only on honesty, on honor, on the sacredness of obligations, on faithful protection, on unselfish performance; without them it cannot live.

1. Biblical allusion is found in which two lines of this passage?

2. What is the primary rhetorical appeal used in paragraphs 6, 7, and 8?

3. Locate each of these rhetorical devices used to construct this primary rhetorical appeal:
   - Anastrophe in line ___
   - Metaphor in lines ___ and ___.
   - Personification in lines ___ and ___.
   - Parallelism/Anaphora in line ___ and ___.

Rhetorical Analysis: FDR's Inaugural Address, #6

Carefully read paragraphs 6, 7, and 8 of FDR's speech and address each of the questions that follow.

The money changers have fled from their high seats in the temple of our civilization. We may now restore that temple to the ancient truths. The measure of the restoration lies in the extent to which we apply social values more noble than mere monetary profit.

Happiness lies not in the mere possession of money; it lies in the joy of achievement, in the thrill of creative effort. The joy and moral stimulation of work no longer must be forgotten in the mad chase of evanescent profits. These dark days will be worth all they cost us if they teach us that our true destiny is not to be ministered unto but to minister to ourselves and to our fellow men.   10

Recognition of the falsity of material wealth as the standard of success goes hand in hand with the abandonment of the false belief that public office and high political position are to be valued only by the standards of pride of place and personal profit; and there must be an end to a conduct in banking and in business which too often has given to a sacred trust the   15
likeness of callous and selfish wrongdoing. Small wonder that confidence languishes, for it thrives only on honesty, on honor, on the sacredness of obligations, on faithful protection, on unselfish performance; without them it cannot live.

In one sentence state the main thought of these three paragraphs.

Rhetorical Analysis: FDR's Inaugural Address, #7

Carefully read paragraphs 9, 10, and 11 of FDR's speech and address each of the questions that follow.

Restoration calls, however, not for changes in ethics alone. This Nation asks for action, and action now.

Our greatest primary task is to put people to work. This is no unsolvable problem if we face it wisely and courageously. It can be accomplished in part by direct recruiting by the Government itself, treating the task as we would treat the emergency of a war, but at the same time, through this employment, accomplishing greatly needed projects to stimulate and reorganize the use of our natural resources.

Hand in hand with this we must frankly recognize the overbalance of population in our industrial centers and, by engaging on a national scale in a redistribution, endeavor to provide a better use of the land for those best fitted for the land. The task can be helped by definite efforts to raise the values of agricultural products and with this the power to purchase the output of our cities. It can be helped by preventing realistically the tragedy of the growing loss through foreclosure of our small homes and our farms. It can be helped by insistence that the Federal, State, and local governments act forthwith on the demand that their cost be drastically reduced. It can be helped by the unifying of relief activities which today are often scattered, uneconomical, and unequal. It can be helped by national planning for and supervision of all forms of transportation and of communications and other utilities which have a definitely public character. There are many ways in which it can be helped, but it can never be helped merely by talking about it. We must act and act quickly.

1. What is the purpose of the first paragraph in this passage?

2. To what does "this" in line 9 refer?

3. What syntactical technique is the basis of the sentences in lines 16–22?

4. What are the two major tasks cited by FDR?

Rhetorical Analysis: FDR's Inaugural Address, #8

Carefully read paragraphs 12, 13, 14, and 15 of FDR's speech and address each of the questions that follow.

Finally, in our progress toward a resumption of work we require two safeguards against a return of the evils of the old order; there must be a strict supervision of all banking and credits and investments; there must be an end to speculation with other people's money, and there must be provision for an adequate but sound currency.   5

These are the lines of attack. I shall presently urge upon a new Congress in special session detailed measures for their fulfillment, and I shall seek the immediate assistance of the several States.

Through this program of action we address ourselves to putting our own national house in order and making income balance outgo.   10
Our international trade relations, though vastly important, are in point of time and necessity secondary to the establishment of a sound national economy. I favor as a practical policy the putting of first things first. I shall spare no effort to restore world trade by international economic readjustment, but the emergency at home cannot wait on that   15
accomplishment.

The basic thought that guides these specific means of national recovery is not narrowly nationalistic. It is the insistence, as a first consideration, upon the interdependence of the various elements in all parts of the United States – a recognition of the old and permanently   20
important manifestation of the American spirit of the pioneer. It is the way to recovery. It is the immediate way. It is the strongest assurance that the recovery will endure.

1. *these* in lines 6 and 17 refers to what?

2. *this* in line 9 refers to what?

3. Parallelism is the predominant syntactical technique in which of these paragraphs?

4. What is the purpose of parallel structure in this context?

Rhetorical Analysis: FDR's Inaugural Address, #9

Carefully read paragraphs 17, 18, and 19 of FDR's speech and address each of the questions that follow.

If I read the temper of our people correctly, we now realize as we have never realized before our interdependence on each other; that we can not merely take but we must give as well; that if we are to go forward, we must move as a trained and loyal army willing to sacrifice for the good of a common discipline, because without such discipline no   5
progress is made, no leadership becomes effective. We are, I know, ready and willing to submit our lives and property to such discipline, because it makes possible a leadership which aims at a larger good. This I propose to offer, pledging that the larger purposes will bind upon us all as a sacred obligation with a unity of duty hitherto evoked only in time   10
of armed strife.

With this pledge taken, I assume unhesitatingly the leadership of this great army of our people dedicated to a disciplined attack upon our common problems.

Action in this image and to this end is feasible under the form   15
of government which we have inherited from our ancestors. Our Constitution is so simple and practical that it is possible always to meet extraordinary needs by changes in emphasis and arrangement without loss of essential form. That is why our constitutional system has proved itself the most superbly enduring political mechanism the modern world   20
has produced. It has met every stress of vast expansion of territory, of foreign wars, of bitter internal strife, of world relations.

5 Minutes to a 5

1. To what does "this pledge" in line 12 refer?

2. In line 15, to what does "Action in this image" refer? "to this end"?

3. According to paragraph 18, to what position does FDR appoint himself?

4. The argument presented in this passage is dependent upon what type of argument?

Rhetorical Analysis: FDR's Inaugural Address, #10

Carefully read paragraphs 23 and 24 of FDR's speech and address each of the questions that follow.

> But in the event that the Congress shall fail to take one of these two courses, and in the event that the national emergency is still critical, I shall not evade the clear course of duty that will then confront me. I shall ask the Congress for the one remaining instrument to meet the crisis – broad Executive power to wage a war against the emergency, as great as the power that would be given to me if we were in fact invaded by a foreign foe.
>
> For the trust reposed in me I will return the courage and the devotion that befit the time. I can do no less.

5

1. What is the purpose of beginning paragraph 23 with *But in the event that the Congress shall fail to take one of these two courses* rather than with (1) If the Congress shall fail…; or (2) In the event that the Congress fails to take one…?

2. Lines 5–7 continue to develop which extended analogy?

Rhetorical Analysis: FDR's Inaugural Address, #11

Carefully read the last four paragraphs of FDR's speech and address each of the questions that follow.

> For the trust reposed in me I will return the courage and the
> devotion that befit the time. I can do no less.
>   We face the arduous days that lie before us in the warm courage
> of the national unity; with the clear consciousness of seeking old and
> precious moral values; with the *clean satisfaction* that comes from the   5
> stern performance of duty by old and young alike. We aim at the
> assurance of a rounded and permanent national life.
>   We do not distrust the future of essential democracy. The
> people of the United States have not failed. In their need they have
> registered a mandate that they want direct, vigorous action. They   10
> have asked for discipline and direction under leadership. They have
> made me the present instrument of their wishes. In the spirit of the
> gift I take it.
>   In this dedication of a Nation we humbly ask the blessing of
> God. May He protect each and every one of us. May He guide me   15
> in the days to come.

1. Underline those words/phrases that help to build the appeal to pathos.

2. According to this last passage, on what is FDR basing his authority (ethos)?

Rhetorical Analysis: FDR's Inaugural Address, #12

1. Based on your careful reading and analysis of FDR's first inaugural address, which of the following would be the best choice of a title for an essay based on this speech.

   A. FDR's impact on the Great Depression
   B. It's War!
   C. A Time for Necessary Change
   D. All we have to fear is fear itself
   E. I Am Your New General

2. On what did you base your choice?

Practice Writing a Thesis Statement in Response to an Analysis Prompt

Based on your careful reading of Franklin Delano Roosevelt's First Inaugural Address, compose a thesis statement that could be used as the basic for a rhetorical analysis essay that addresses the following prompt:

> Franklin Delano Roosevelt's delivered his First Inaugural Address on March 4, 1933, to a nation deep in the midst of the Great Depression. Compose a well-written essay that identifies FDR's purpose and analyzes the rhetorical strategies he uses to achieve his purpose.

Day 94

Close Reading of Argument Prompts, #1

Read the Prompt!

In her chapter "Serving in Florida," in *Nickel and Dimed*, Barbara Ehrenreich goes undercover to investigate the world of minimum wage jobs, in this case waiting tables at a restaurant in Florida. Ehrenreich learned that one of the dishwashers at the restaurant, a poor Czech immigrant named George, would be fired for taking a small amount of food. Ehrenreich states:

> "In real life I am moderately brave, but plenty of brave people shed their courage in POW camps, and maybe something similar goes on in the infinitely more congenial milieu of the low-wage American workplace. Maybe, in a month or two more at Jerry's, I might have regained my crusading spirit. Then again, in a month or two I might have turned into a different person altogether – say the kind of person who would have turned George in."

Reflect on Ehrenheich's statement. Then, in a well-written essay, take a position on the author's assertion about the possibility of the environment affecting people's personalities and moral compass. Support your argument with appropriate evidence from your reading, observation, and/or experience.

1. Underline the essential elements of the prompt.

Close Reading of Argument Prompts, #2

Thoreau states, "Unjust laws exist; shall we be content to obey them, or shall we endeavor to amend them, and obey them until we have succeeded, or shall we transgress them at once?... If [the law] is of such a nature that it requires you to be the agent of injustice to another, then, I say, break the law."

In a well-written essay, take a position on Thoreau's position regarding breaking an unjust law in order to bring about societal change. Support your argument with appropriate evidence from your reading, observation, and/or experience.

1. What is Thoreau's position about breaking an unjust law?

2. Does Thoreau qualify his position? Underline that part of the quotation that supports your answer.

Reading the Argument Prompt, #3

The use of non-violence as a tactic for demanding social justice has long been a topic of debate. Consider the statements made by two leaders of the Civil Rights Movement.

"The end of violence or the aftermath of violence is bitterness. The aftermath of nonviolence is reconciliation and the creation of a beloved community." —Martin Luther King, Jr.

"And you can't stop it [violence] with love, not love of those things down there, no. So, we only mean vigorous action in self-defense, and that vigorous action we feel we're justified in initiating by any means necessary." —Malcolm X

In a well-developed essay, take a position on non-violent resistance as a method for social change. Support your argument with appropriate evidence from your reading, experiences, or observations to support your assertion.

1. Does this prompt require you to use/refer to either one or both of the quotations given above?

2. Could you use a novel or movie as material to support your claim?

3. Should you be afraid to take a position that you feel would be unpopular with your audience?

Argument Terms, #1

Below are examples of some frequently used terms when referring to argument. Match each term with its correct example. Each term is used only once.

1. begging the question

2. red herring

3. bandwagon

4. either/or

5. straw man

____ You know, if this is the official car of the winners of the World Series, it's the one I'll buy.

____ People who support allowing 16-year-olds the right to drive just want to give teenagers the right to drive any way they want without having to face any consequences.

____ Do you want to get a college education or be poor all your life?

____ We didn't publish Carrie's photograph because we don't think it was deserving of publication.

____ That novel is obviously not worth reading because I don't recognize the author.

Argument Terms, #2

Below are examples of some frequently used terms when referring to argument. Match each term with its correct example. Each term is used only once.

1. rhetorical question

2. ethos

3. pathos

4. logos

5. faulty analogy

____ A student writer cites experts in the field that's the subject of her research paper.

____ Is that his brother? He's got to be a really good basketball player.

____ An argument uses facts, statistics, and the opinions of experts to support a claim that a pitcher player deserves to be inducted into the Baseball Hall of Fame.

____ During a speech, the speaker says to the audience, "Don't you all just love this weather?"

____ A commercial for the Animal Rescue League shows videos and still photos of dogs and cats in poor physical condition.

Argument Terms, #3

Below are examples of some frequently used terms when referring to argument. Match each term with its correct example. Each term is used only once.

1. ad hominem

2. post hoc

3. non-sequitor

4. circular reasoning

5. hasty generalization

____ You can't believe him because he always lies.

____ Judge Carter's brother owns a supermarket; therefore, he's not able to impartially judge this case against Whole Foods.

____ Since I bought my new computer, I've been getting much better grades. It's got to be the new laptop.

____ Obviously Tim's a really poor driver because he failed his first driver's test.

____ Carrie will do very well at Yale because her mother graduated from there.

Argument – Rhetorical Appeals

Below is a checklist which functions as a rubric for the evaluation of any rhetorical argument. Characterize each item as an appeal to **logos** or **ethos** or **pathos**

_____ 1. A clearly developed thesis is evident

_____ 2. Facts are distinguished from opinions.

_____ 3. Opinions are supported and qualified.

_____ 4. The speaker develops a logical argument and avoids fallacies in reasoning.

_____ 5. Support for facts is tested, reliable, and authoritative.

_____ 6. The speaker does not confuse appeals to logic and emotion.

_____ 7. Opposing views are represented in a fair and undistorted way.

_____ 8. The argument reflects a sense of audience.

_____ 9. The argument reflects an identifiable voice and point-of-view.

_____ 10. The piece reflects the image of a speaker with identifiable qualities – (honesty, sincerity, authority, intelligence, etc.).

Techniques of Argument

The Revolutionary War patriot Patrick Henry ended his famous speech with "Give me liberty or give me death." This statement is related to all of the following except:

A. pathos

B. antithesis

C. false dilemma

D. hyperbole

E. logos

Assumptions vs. Inferences, #1

Arguments rely on assumptions and inferences. An **assumption** is something we take for granted that the author does not feel the need to prove. Usually, assumptions are not stated. An **inference** is a conclusion that something is true because we believe something else seems to be true. The inference is based on the assumption.

In the following activity, you will be given a situation. (1) What can you likely infer in this situation? (2) On what assumption is your inference based?

1. Situation: A police car follows your car for several blocks.

Inference:

Assumption:

2. Situation: Your cell phone rings in the middle of the night.

Inference:

Assumption:

5 Minutes to a 5

Assumptions vs. Inferences, #2

Arguments rely on assumptions and inferences. An **assumption** is something we take for granted that the author does not feel the need to prove. Usually, assumptions are not stated. An **inference** is a conclusion that something is true because we believe something else to be true. The inference is based on the assumption.

Carefully read the text given below. Then complete the activity that follows.

An excerpt from the essay "Why I Want a Wife" by Judy Brady

I belong to that classification of people known as wives. I am a wife. And, not altogether incidentally, I am a mother.

    Not too long ago a male friend of mine appeared on the scene fresh from a recent divorce. He had one child, who is, of course, with his ex-wife. He is looking for another wife. As I thought about him while I was ironing one evening, it suddenly occurred to me that I, too, would like to have a wife.

1. What is the inference the author will support in her essay?

2. On what assumption(s) does the author base this inference?

Arguments and Political Ads

Some of the most obvious examples of argument can be found in political ads. You will be working with one of the most famous and successful TV ads of past presidential campaigns.

Carefully watch this political ad available on YouTube. Then, complete the activity that follows.

Signs of Hope & Change (2008)
https://www.youtube.com/watch?v=EcRA2AZsR2Q

1. What are the three words/phrases emphasized in this campaign video?

2. What is the best description of the tone of this campaign video?
   A. objective and formal
   B. positive and hopeful
   C. positive and instructive
   D. informal and religious
   E. subjective and defensive

Argument – Reading a Visual (Ad)

Go to the following website and carefully "read" the given ad:

   https://malaysiabrl.files.wordpress.com/2015/02/5300b6d67ccf9.jpeg

Based on your careful reading of the ad

1. What argument does this ad present?

2. This ad uses ___deductive ___inductive reasoning.

3. This ad is based on an appeal to ___logic ___emotions.

4. This ad argues from ___authority ___analogy ___facts/statistics.

Arguments and Political Ads

Some of the most obvious examples of argument can be found in political ads. You will be working with one of the most famous and successful TV ads of past presidential campaigns.

Carefully watch this political ad available on YouTube. Then, complete the activity that follows.

"*Daisy*" Ad from the 1964 LBJ Presidential Campaign
https://www.youtube.com/watch?v=dDTBnsqxZ3k

1. In ONE sentence, summarize this campaign video.

2. This campaign video appeals primarily to ___ethos ___logos ___pathos.

Reading a Political Cartoon

Carefully read the following political cartoon.

Given the title of the political carton and the size and placement of the items pictured in it, what can you conclude is the cartoonist's primary purpose?

Summary of an Argument

Carefully read the following passage from an essay by Montaigne. Then complete the activity that follows. Take your time. Remember, with practice, you will become comfortable dealing with the idiom and syntax of various time periods.

"The Profit of One Man is the Loss of Another" Montaigne (1580)

DEMADES the Athenian condemned one of his city, whose trade it was to sell the necessaries for funeral ceremonies, upon pretence that he demanded unreasonable profit, and that that profit could not accrue to him, but by the death of a great number of people. A judgment that appears to be ill grounded, forasmuch as no profit whatever can possibly   5
be made but at the expense of another, and that by the same rule he should condemn all gain of what kind soever. The merchant only thrives by the debauchery of youth, the husbandman by the dearness of grain, the architect by the ruin of buildings, lawyers and officers of justice by the suits and contentions of men: nay, even the honor and office of divines   10
are derived from our death and vices. A physician takes no pleasure in the health even of his friends, says the ancient Greek comic writer, nor a soldier in the peace of his country, and so of the rest. And, which is yet worse, let every one but dive into his own bosom, and he will find his private wishes spring and his secret hopes grow up at another's expense.   15
Upon which consideration it comes into my head, that nature does not in this swerve from her general polity; for physicians hold, that the birth, nourishment and increase of every thing is the dissolution and corruption of another.

Summarize this argument paragraph in no more than 2–3 sentences.

Reading a Chart or Graph

Carefully "read" the following graph.

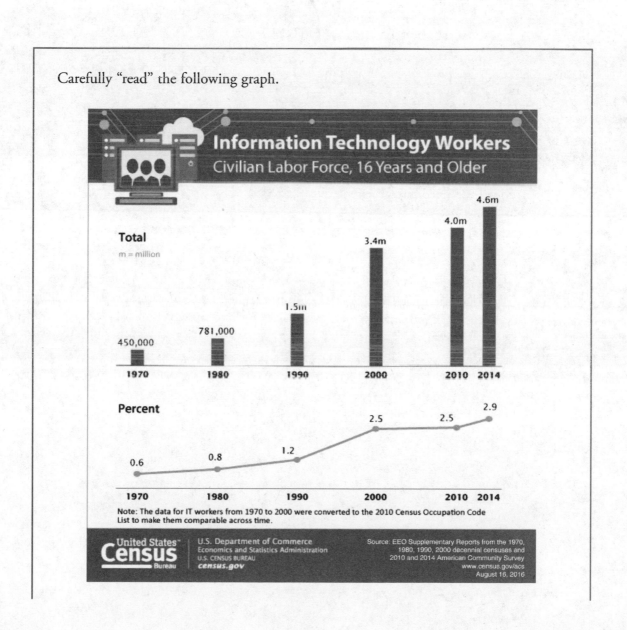

1. What is the topic?

2. What's being measured?

3. What are the patterns and trends?

4. When did the U.S. Census Bureau publish this chart?

5. What is the source for the chart?

6. What is one inference that can be supported with this chart?

Drawing Inferences

Carefully read the following bar graph.

Hours of TV (Including Internet Streaming) watched in 1 week by students in four 11th grade English classes in a Suburban High School in St. Louis, Missouri, in May, 2016

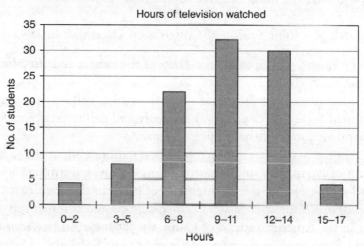

1. List two inferences that you can draw from this bar graph.

2. Based on your two inferences, write a preliminary thesis statement for an argument essay.

5 Minutes to a 5

Analyzing an Argument, FDR Speech, #1

Carefully read the following speech by FDR the day after the bombing of Pearl Harbor in 1941. Then answer the questions that follow.

FDR's Speech to a Joint Session of Congress on December 8, 1941

Mr. Vice President, Mr. Speaker, members of the Senate and the House of Representatives:

Yesterday, December 7th, 1941 — a date which will live in infamy — the United States of America was suddenly and deliberately attacked by naval and air forces of the Empire of Japan.   5

The United States was at peace with that nation, and, at the solicitation of Japan, was still in conversation with its government and its Emperor looking toward the maintenance of peace in the Pacific.

Indeed, one hour after Japanese air squadrons had commenced bombing in the American island of Oahu, the Japanese Ambassador to   10
the United States and his colleague delivered to our Secretary of State a formal reply to a recent American message. And, while this reply stated that it seemed useless to continue the existing diplomatic negotiations, it contained no threat or hint of war or of armed attack.

It will be recorded that the distance of Hawaii from Japan makes   15
it obvious that the attack was deliberately planned many days or even weeks ago. During the intervening time the Japanese Government has deliberately sought to deceive the United States by false statements and expressions of hope for continued peace.

The attack yesterday on the Hawaiian Islands has caused severe   20
damage to American naval and military forces. I regret to tell you that very many American lives have been lost. In addition, American ships

have been reported torpedoed on the high seas between San Francisco and Honolulu.

Yesterday the Japanese Government also launched an attack against Malaya. 25

Last night Japanese forces attacked Hong Kong.

Last night Japanese forces attacked Guam.

Last night Japanese forces attacked the Philippine Islands.

Last night the Japanese attacked Wake Island. 30

And this morning the Japanese attacked Midway Island.

Japan has therefore undertaken a surprise offensive extending throughout the Pacific area. The facts of yesterday and today speak for themselves. The people of the United States have already formed their opinions and well understand the implications to the very life and safety 35 of our nation.

As Commander-in-Chief of the Army and Navy I have directed that all measures be taken for our defense, that always will our whole nation remember the character of the onslaught against us.

No matter how long it may take us to overcome this premeditated 40 invasion, the American people, in their righteous might, will win through to absolute victory.

I believe that I interpret the will of the Congress and of the people when I assert that we will not only defend ourselves to the uttermost but will make it very certain that this form of treachery shall never again 45 endanger us.

Hostilities exist. There is no blinking at the fact that our people, our territory and our interests are in grave danger.

With confidence in our armed forces, with the unbounding determination of our people, we will gain the inevitable triumph. 50 So help us God.

I ask that the Congress declare that since the unprovoked and dastardly attack by Japan on Sunday, December 7th, 1941, a state of war has existed between the United States and the Japanese Empire.

President Franklin D. Roosevelt – December 8, 1941 55

Perform a quick analysis of FDR's speech using the popular strategy called **SOAPS**:

The **Subject** of the speech is

The **Occasion** is

The **Audience** is

The **Purpose** is

The **Speaker** is

Analyzing an Argument,
FDR Speech, #2

> FDR's Speech to a Joint Session of Congress on December 8, 1941
>
> What is the purpose of using a chronological organization in FDR's speech?

Analyzing an Argument, FDR Speech, #3

FDR's Speech to a Joint Session of Congress on December 8, 1941

What is the purpose of using parallel structure in lines 27–31?

Analyzing an Argument, FDR Speech, #4

FDR's Speech to a Joint Session of Congress on December 8, 1941

What is the purpose of using *us* in line 39 and *we* in line 44 in FDR's speech?

Developing the Argument

Carefully read the following passage from Thoreau's *Walden*, "Economy," Chapter 1 (1854)

> One says to me, "I wonder that you do not lay up money; you love to travel; you might take the cars[1] and go to Fitchburg today and see the country." But I am wiser than that. I have learned that the swiftest traveller is he that goes afoot. I say to my friend, Suppose we try who will get there first. The distance is thirty miles; the fare ninety cents. That is   5
> almost a day's wages. I remember when wages were sixty cents a day for laborers on this very road. Well, I start now on foot, and get there before night; I have travelled at that rate by the week together. You will in the meanwhile have earned your fare, and arrive there some time tomorrow, or possibly this evening, if you are lucky enough to get a job in season.   10
> Instead of going to Fitchburg, you will be working here the greater part of the day. And so, if the railroad reached round the world, I think that I should keep ahead of you; and as for seeing the country and getting experience of that kind, I should have to cut your acquaintance altogether.

_____

[1]train(s)

1. Underline the topic sentence/thesis.

2. What is the primary strategy Thoreau uses to develop and support his argument?

5 Minutes to a 5

Deduction, Induction

Identify each of the following as either (**A**) Deductive or (**B**) Inductive reasoning.

_____1. Joe has acute appendicitis; obviously he is quite ill.

_____2. After seeing her three shelves of albums devoted to classical music, I was certain Jessica would appreciate my offering her tickets to the latest Bach concert in the park.

_____3. The latest polls indicate over 75% of the Plaid Party favor Ms. Starke. Phil is a member of the Plaid Party. Therefore, he will vote for Ms. Starke.

_____4. It's dangerous to drive on icy roads. I just heard the traffic report describing icy conditions on the local streets, so I'm not going to drive this morning.

_____5. Our pet toy poodle eats a full can of dog food a day and only gets one 15-minute walk per day; no wonder she's overweight.

Developing an Argument

Carefully read the following passage from a pre-election opinion column. Then, complete the activity that follows.

> An excerpt from "Voting Isn't the Only Way to Contribute" by Jason Brennan, associate professor of strategy, economics, ethics, and public policy at the McDonough School of Business at Georgetown University, *Newsday*, October 14, 2016
>
> …[Most] arguments…fail to show voting is anything special. Voting is just one of many ways to discharge the duties [of a citizen]. It might not be an especially good way. There are thousands of ways other than voting to exercise civic virtue, to avoid complicity with injustice, to avoid free-riding, to repay a debt or to help others. You can hold a productive job that adds to the social surplus. You could make art or work in a hospital. You could organize, write letters to the editor, protest, volunteer, or donate to charities or political organizations. The average auto mechanic does more good for society by fixing cars than by voting.

By the very fact that this essay appears in the editorial/opinion section of the newspaper, we know that this is an argument. Let's take a closer look at this excerpt.

1. Does the author make any appeal to ethos? ___Yes ___No If yes, underline your evidence.

2. Bracket the claim/assertion/position stated in this passage.

3. The last sentence of this paragraph is an example of
   A. straw-man argument
   B. circular reasoning
   C. post-hoc argument
   D. hasty generalization
   E. either/or argument

Arguments and Political Ads

Some of the most obvious examples of argument can be found in political ads. You will be working with one of the most famous and successful TV ads of past presidential campaigns.

Carefully watch this political ad available on YouTube. Then, complete the activity that follows.

> Ronald Reagan's "Morning In America" (1984) https://www.youtube.com/watch?v=EU-IBF8nwSY

1. In ONE sentence state the thesis of this campaign video.

2. The main point of this campaign video is primarily developed using

___induction   ___deduction.

Analyzing an Argument, "Ain't I a Woman?" #1

Carefully read the following speech delivered by Sojourner Truth (1797–1883) on May 29, 1851, at the Women's Convention, Akron, Ohio.

Ain't I a Woman?

Well, children, where there is so much racket there must be something out of kilter. I think that 'twixt the negroes of the South and the women at the North, all talking about rights, the white men will be in a fix pretty soon. But what's all this here talking about?

That man over there says that women need to be helped into   5
carriages, and lifted over ditches, and to have the best place everywhere. Nobody ever helps me into carriages, or over mud puddles, or gives me any best place! And ain't I a woman? Look at me! Look at my arm! I have ploughed and planted, and gathered into barns, and no man could head me! And ain't I a woman? I could work as much and eat as much as a man   10
– when I could get it – and bear the lash as well! And ain't I a woman? I have borne thirteen children, and seen most all sold off to slavery, and when I cried out with my mother's grief, none but Jesus heard me! And ain't I a woman?

Then they talk about this thing in the head; what's this they call it?   15
[member of audience whispers, "intellect"] That's it, honey. What's that got to do with women's rights or negroes' rights? If my cup won't hold but a pint, and yours holds a quart, wouldn't you be mean not to let me have my little half measure full?

Then that little man in black there, he says women can't have as   20
much rights as men, 'cause Christ wasn't a woman! Where did your Christ come from? Where did your Christ come from? From God and a woman! Man had nothing to do with Him.

If the first woman God ever made was strong enough to turn the world upside down all alone, these women together ought to be able to turn it back, and get it right side up again! And now they is asking to do it, the men better let them.

Obliged to you for hearing me, and now old Sojourner ain't got nothing more to say.

In which paragraphs can you locate each of the following appeals?
A. logos
B. ethos
C. pathos

Analyzing an Argument, "Ain't I a Woman?" #2

Carefully read the following speech delivered by Sojourner Truth (1797–1883) on May 29, 1851, at the Women's Convention, Akron, Ohio.

Ain't I a Woman?

Well, children, where there is so much racket there must be something out of kilter. I think that 'twixt the negroes of the South and the women at the North, all talking about rights, the white men will be in a fix pretty soon. But what's all this here talking about?

That man over there says that women need to be helped into carriages, 5
and lifted over ditches, and to have the best place everywhere. Nobody ever helps me into carriages, or over mud puddles, or gives me any best place! And ain't I a woman? Look at me! Look at my arm! I have ploughed and planted, and gathered into barns, and no man could head me! And ain't I a woman? I could work as much and eat as much as a man – when I could 10
get it – and bear the lash as well! And ain't I a woman? I have borne thirteen children, and seen most all sold off to slavery, and when I cried out with my mother's grief, none but Jesus heard me! And ain't I a woman?

Then they talk about this thing in the head; what's this they call it? [member of audience whispers, "intellect"] That's it, honey. What's that got 15
to do with women's rights or negroes' rights? If my cup won't hold but a pint, and yours holds a quart, wouldn't you be mean not to let me have my little half measure full?

Then that little man in black there, he says women can't have as much rights as men, 'cause Christ wasn't a woman! Where did your Christ come 20
from? Where did your Christ come from? From God and a woman! Man had nothing to do with Him.

If the first woman God ever made was strong enough to turn the world upside down all alone, these women together ought to be able to turn it back, and get it right side up again! And now they is asking to do it, the men better let them. 25

Obliged to you for hearing me, and now old Sojourner ain't got nothing more to say.

What is the purpose of the repetition of "Ain't I a woman"?

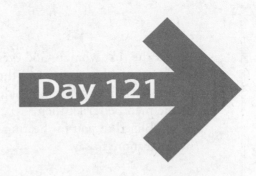

Analyzing an Argument, "Ain't I a Woman?" #3

Carefully read the following speech delivered by Sojourner Truth (1797–1883) on May 29, 1851, at the Women's Convention, Akron, Ohio.

Ain't I a Woman?

Well, children, where there is so much racket there must be something out of kilter. I think that 'twixt the negroes of the South and the women at the North, all talking about rights, the white men will be in a fix pretty soon. But what's all this here talking about?

That man over there says that women need to be helped into carriages, 5
and lifted over ditches, and to have the best place everywhere. Nobody ever helps me into carriages, or over mud- puddles, or gives me any best place! And ain't I a woman? Look at me! Look at my arm! I have ploughed and planted, and gathered into barns, and no man could head me! And ain't
I a woman? I could work as much and eat as much as a man – when I 10
could get it – and bear the lash as well! And ain't I a woman? I have borne thirteen children, and seen most all sold off to slavery, and when
I cried out with my mother's grief, none but Jesus heard me! And ain't
I a woman?

Then they talk about this thing in the head; what's this they call it? 15
[member of audience whispers, "intellect"] That's it, honey. What's that got to do with women's rights or negroes' rights? If my cup won't hold but a pint, and yours holds a quart, wouldn't you be mean not to let me have my little half measure full?

Then that little man in black there, he says women can't have as 20
much rights as men, 'cause Christ wasn't a woman! Where did your Christ come from? Where did your Christ come from? From God and a woman! Man had nothing to do with Him.

If the first woman God ever made was strong enough to turn the world upside down all alone, these women together ought to be able to turn it back, and get it right side up again! And now they is asking to do it, the men better let them.

  Obliged to you for hearing me, and now old Sojourner ain't got nothing more to say.

1. How can the diction of this speech be best described?

2. What is the overall effect of the passage?

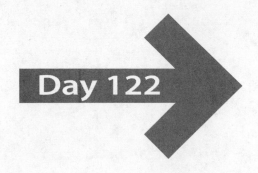

Argument – A Letter to the Editor

Carefully read the following letter-to-the-editor written in response to an editorial column that appeared in October 26, 2016, issue of *The New York Times*.

To the Editor:

[In his column titled "The Meaning of Bob Dylan's Silence"], Adam Kirsch applauds Bob Dylan's nonresponsiveness to the Nobel committee as an assertion of his artistic freedom, in particular suggesting that Mr. Dylan is refusing to be defined as an artist by the Nobel committee's expression of approval.

Yet isn't Mr. Dylan compromising that very artistic integrity by doing IBM TV commercials, where, in return for money, he is essentially permitting IBM to publicly proclaim its endorsement of his artwork?

ERIC BERNSTEIN

New York

1. Which of the three rhetorical appeals does this writer use? ___ethos ___logos ___pathos

2. Is the writer's assertion/claim directly stated or implied/inferred? If directly stated, underline it. If implied/inferred, state the assertion in your own words.

Commercials

Go to YouTube and view the commercial found at:

> https://www.youtube.com/watch?v=zJBcbnSqGz8

1. The tone of the commercial is

2. I'm basing my conclusion about tone on

(Check those that apply and cite specifics from the commercial for each checked item.)

___ diction

___ action

___ characters

___ setting

Commercials

Go to YouTube and view the commercial found at:

https://www.youtube.com/watch?v=zJBcbnSqGz8

1. This commercial uses ___deductive ___inductive reasoning.

2. This commercial is based on an appeal to ___self-interest ___emotions.

3. This commercial argues from ___authority ___analogy ___facts/statistics

4. The producers of this commercial hope you will buy this product because you are taken in by a ___hasty/over generalization ___either/or argument.

"What to the Slave Is the Fourth of July?" #1

The next several questions are based on your careful reading of the excerpts from Frederick Douglass's "What to the Slave Is the Fourth of July?" This speech was delivered to a northern, white audience in Rochester, New York, on July 5, 1852, at the invitation of the Rochester Ladies Anti-Slavery Society. The following is the opening paragraph from Douglass's speech.

> Fellow citizens, pardon me, and allow me to ask, why am I called upon to speak here today? What have I or those I represent to do with your national independence? Are the great principles of political freedom and of natural justice, embodied in that Declaration of Independence, extended to us? And am I, therefore, called upon to bring our humble offering to the national altar, and to confess the benefits, and express devout gratitude for the blessings resulting from your independence to us?

1. The entire paragraph is made up of what specific rhetorical device?

2. What purpose does the use of this rhetorical device serve?

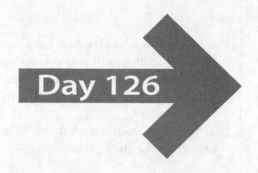

"What to the Slave Is the Fourth of July?" #2

Carefully read the following passage from Frederick Douglass's "What to the Slave Is the Fourth of July?"

Fellow-citizens; above your national, tumultuous joy, I hear the mournful wail of millions! whose chains, heavy and grievous yesterday, are, to-day, rendered more intolerable by the jubilee shouts that reach them. If I do forget, if I do not faithfully remember those bleeding children of sorrow this day, "may my right hand forget her cunning, and may my tongue cleave to the roof of my mouth!" To forget them, to pass lightly over their wrongs, and to chime in with the popular theme, would be treason most scandalous and shocking, and would make me a reproach before God and the world. My subject, then fellow-citizens, is AMERICAN SLAVERY. I shall see, this day, and its popular characteristics, from the slave's point of view. Standing, there, identified with the American bondman, making his wrongs mine, I do not hesitate to declare, with all my soul, that the character and conduct of this nation never looked blacker to me than on this 4th of July! Whether we turn to the declarations of the past, or to the professions of the present, the conduct of the nation seems equally hideous and revolting. America is false to the past, false to the present, and solemnly binds herself to be false to the future. Standing with God and the crushed and bleeding slave on this occasion, I will, in the name of humanity which is outraged, in the name of liberty which is fettered, in the name of the constitution and the Bible, which are disregarded and trampled upon, dare to call in question and to denounce, with all the emphasis I can command, everything that serves to perpetuate slavery – the great sin and shame of America!

5

10

15

20

"I will not equivocate; I will not excuse;" I will use the severest language I can command; and yet not one word shall escape me that any man, whose judgment is not blinded by prejudice, or who is not at heart a slaveholder, shall not confess to be right and just....

Taking into consideration the title of the speech from which this excerpt is taken, underline the thesis statement.

"What to the Slave Is the Fourth of July?" #3

Carefully read the following passage from Frederick Douglass's "What to the Slave Is the Fourth of July?"

> For the present it is enough to affirm the equal manhood of the Negro
> race. Is it not astonishing that, while we are plowing, planting, and
> reaping, using all kinds of mechanical tools, erecting houses, constructing
> bridges, building ships, working in metals of brass, iron, copper, silver, and
> gold; that while we are reading, writing, and ciphering, acting as clerks,   5
> merchants, and secretaries, having among us lawyers, doctors, ministers,
> poets, authors, editors, orators, and teachers; that we are engaged in all the
> enterprises common to other men – digging gold in California, capturing
> the whale in the Pacific, feeding sheep and cattle on the hillside, living,
> moving, acting, thinking, planning, living in families as husbands, wives,   10
> and children, and above all, confessing and worshipping the Christian
> God, and looking hopefully for life and immortality beyond the grave –
> we are called upon to prove that we are men?

Douglass's use of listing in this paragraph is most likely intended to show all of the
following except:
  A. The idea that slaves engage in the same activities as free men
  B. The idea that slaves worship the same God as free men
  C. The idea that slaves contribute greatly to the advancement of the American
     nation
  D. The ability for slaves to embrace the potential for economic empowerment
  E. The acknowledgement that slaves have the ability to attain the same professional
     and artistic merit as free men

5 Minutes to a 5

"What to the Slave Is the Fourth of July?" #4

Carefully read the following passage from Frederick Douglass's "What to the Slave Is the Fourth of July?"

At a time like this, scorching irony, not convincing argument, is needed. Oh! had I the ability, and could I reach the nation's ear, I would today pour out a fiery stream of biting ridicule, blasting reproach, withering sarcasm, and stern rebuke. For it is not light that is needed, but fire; it is not the gentle shower, but thunder. We need the storm, the whirlwind, 5 and the earthquake. The feeling of the nation must be quickened; the conscience of the nation must be roused; the propriety of the nation must be startled; the hypocrisy of the nation must be exposed; and its crimes against God and man must be denounced.

1. The author uses *storm*, *whirlwind*, and *earthquake* to

A. illustrate his disgust toward the hypocrisy of the nation
B. create a metaphor for the Fourth of July
C. convey that America needs to be roused, exposed, and punished for its brutality and hypocrisy
D. shift his tone from factual to scathing
E. attempt to incite rebellion

2. In context, the word *quickened* in line 6 is best interpreted to mean

A. to congeal
B. to stimulate
C. to appeal
D. to reinvent
E. to harden

3. What is most probably the intended effect of the imagery used in this paragraph?

   A. Forgiveness after condemnation of America's hypocrisy

   B. Disappointment and illustrating the political climate of the nation

   C. Ridicule and exposing disastrous nature of immorality

   D. Enlightenment and reviving the spiritual nature of the audience

   E. Overdue awakening with a strong impetus for change

"What to the Slave Is the Fourth of July?" #5 Evaluation Checklist

Now that you have completed the four previous activities related to Douglass's speech "What to the Slave Is the Fourth of July?," complete the following checklist evaluation of Douglass's rhetorical argument.

1. A clearly developed thesis is evident. ___yes ___no ___not applicable

2. Facts are distinguished from opinions. ___yes ___no ___not applicable

3. Opinions are supported and qualified. ___yes ___no ___not applicable

4. The speaker develops a logical argument and avoids fallacies in reasoning.
   ___yes ___no ___not applicable

5. Support for facts is tested, reliable, and authoritative.
   ___yes ___no ___not applicable

6. The speaker does not confuse appeals to logic and emotion.
   ___yes ___no ___not applicable

7. Opposing views are represented in a fair and undistorted way.
   ___yes ___no ___not applicable

8. The argument reflects a sense of audience. ___yes ___no ___not applicable

9. The argument reflects an identifiable voice and point-of-view.
   ___yes ___no ___not applicable

10. The piece reflects the image of a speaker with identifiable qualities
    (honesty, sincerity, authority, intelligence, etc.). ___yes ___no ___not applicable

Reading Visual Arguments

Go to the following ad on the net and carefully "read" it.

http://graphicdesignjunction.com/wp-content/uploads/2012/09/
print+advertising+21.jpg

In ONE sentence, what argument is being made?

Analysis of an Argument

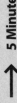

Carefully read the following letter to the editor from the opinion pages of a newspaper. Then, complete the activity that follows.

Now Is the Time to Raise the Gas Tax

Re "A Needed Infrastructure Plan" (editorial, November 27):

By Caroline Fleischer, transportation consultant

The Sea Cliff Bugle, December 6, 2016

There is a simple way to solve the problem of public funding of both highways and public transportation.

In 1993 the federal government raised the national gasoline tax to 18.4 cents to support the National Highway Trust Fund. The tax has not been raised since. No one seemed to be thinking ahead when only a few cents   5
every few years would have provided a strong National Highway Trust Fund today.

Currently gas prices are low, so why not raise both federal and state gas taxes? This could fully fund the National Highway Trust Fund and its Mass Transit Account.   10

No one can deny that we all benefit from good roads, bridges and public transportation. Even with legislative gridlock and partisan bickering in Washington, increasing funding for the Highway Trust Fund and its Mass Transit Account should be a critical issue on which both the president and Congress can agree.   15

Let's take a closer look at this excerpt.

1. The writer primarily appeals to ___ethos ___logos ___pathos

2. Bracket the claim/assertion/position stated in this passage.

3. The assertion made in lines 8–10 can best be characterized as
   A. red herring argument
   B. hasty generalization
   C. post-hoc argument
   D. either/or argument
   E. ad hominem argument

Analysis of Arguments in Commercials

Go to YouTube and view the commercial found at:

https://www.youtube.com/watch?v=k4q6muVH6FE

1. This commercial uses ___deductive ___inductive reasoning.

2. This commercial is primarily based on an appeal to ___logos ___pathos.

3. This commercial primarily argues from ___authority ___analogy ___facts/statistics

4. The producers of this commercial hope you will buy this product because you are taken in by a ___bandwagon appeal ___straw-man argument ___either/or argument

Analysis of an Argument

Carefully read the following letter to the editor from a recent issue of *The New York Times*. Then, complete the activity that follows.

To the Editor: [The] suggestion that the United States should adopt ranked-choice voting (*Note: Voters have the option to rank the candidates from first to last, and any candidate with a majority of first choices wins.*), just as in any other election. It is long overdue. Australia, whose electoral system I have studied extensively, has used ranked choice for almost a hundred years.

Beyond giving voters the ability to take a chance on a third party, ranked choice would immediately defuse the toxic polarization of our national political scene by psychologically reframing how we see the choices we face. Replacing our red-versus-blue Armageddon with something more nuanced would make us a less angry country almost overnight.

Ranked choice would also make voting more complicated; this could overwhelm some voters and depress turnout. Australia deals with this problem effectively by combining mandatory voting with some ingenious procedures that simplify the decision process while preserving an enviable level of freedom of choice. We would do well to learn from Australia's example.

M.G.N., Livingston, N.J., professor of economics at CUNY

Letters to the editor are miniature arguments. With that in mind, complete the abbreviated checklist that follows for this particular letter to the editor. Place a check beside each item that is evident in the given text.

____A clearly thesis is evident. (If so, underline it.)

____Facts are distinguished from opinions.

___Support for facts is tested, reliable, and authoritative.

___Opinions are supported and qualified.

___The writer presents a logical argument and avoids fallacies in reasoning.

___The writer does not confuse appeals to logic and emotion.

___The writer is aware of his audience.

___Opposing views are represented in a fair and undistorted way.

___The argument presents an identifiable voice and point-of-view.

___The piece reflects the image of a writer with identifiable qualities (honesty, sincerity, authority, intelligence, etc.)

Arguments and Political Ads

Some of the most obvious examples of argument can be found in political ads. You will be working with one of the most famous and successful TV ads of past presidential campaigns.

Carefully watch this political ad available on YouTube. Then, complete the activity that follows.

George H.W. Bush's "Revolving Door" (1988)
https://www.youtube.com/watch?v=PmwhdDv8VrM

1. The tone of the commercial is _____.

2. List at least three specifics from the video that support your conclusion about tone.

Argument, Montaigne, #1

Carefully read this excerpt from an essay by Michel de Montaigne, the founder of the essay. Don't panic with the date. Take your time. Remember you must become comfortable dealing with the idiom and syntax of various time periods.

"The Profit of One Man is the Loss of Another" Montaigne (1580)

DEMADES the Athenian condemned one of his city, whose trade it was to sell the necessaries for funeral ceremonies, upon pretence that he demanded unreasonable profit, and that that profit could not accrue to him, but by the death of a great number of people. A judgment that appears to be ill grounded, forasmuch as no profit whatever can possibly   5
be made but at the expense of another, and that by the same rule he should condemn all gain of what kind soever. The merchant only thrives by the debauchery of youth, the husbandman by the dearness of grain, the architect by the ruin of buildings, lawyers and officers of justice by the suits and contentions of men: nay, even the honor and office of divines   10
are derived from our death and vices. A physician takes no pleasure in the health even of his friends, says the ancient Greek comic writer, nor a soldier in the peace of his country, and so of the rest. And, which is yet worse, let every one but dive into his own bosom, and he will find his private wishes spring and his secret hopes grow up at another's expense.   15
Upon which consideration it comes into my head, that nature does not in this swerve from her general polity; for physicians hold, that the birth, nourishment and increase of every thing is the dissolution and corruption of another.

Underline the thesis statement.

5 Minutes to a 5

Argument, Montaigne, #2

Take another careful look at the following essay by Montaigne. Then complete the activity that follows. Take your time. Remember, with practice, you will become comfortable dealing with the idiom and syntax of various time periods.

"The Profit of One Man is the Loss of Another" Montaigne (1580)

DEMADES the Athenian condemned one of his city, whose trade it was to sell the necessaries for funeral ceremonies, upon pretence that he demanded unreasonable profit, and that that profit could not accrue to him, but by the death of a great number of people. A judgment that appears to be ill grounded, forasmuch as no profit whatever can possibly be made but at   5
the expense of another, and that by the same rule he should condemn all gain of what kind soever. The merchant only thrives by the debauchery of youth, the husbandman by the dearness of grain, the architect by the ruin of buildings, lawyers and officers of justice by the suits and contentions of men: nay, even the honor and office of divines are derived from our death   10
and vices. A physician takes no pleasure in the health even of his friends, says the ancient Greek comic writer, nor a soldier in the peace of his country, and so of the rest. And, which is yet worse, let every one but dive into his own bosom, and he will find his private wishes spring and his secret hopes grow up at another's expense. Upon which consideration it comes   15
into my head, that nature does not in this swerve from her general polity; for physicians hold, that the birth, nourishment and increase of every thing is the dissolution and corruption of another.

1. This is a brief argument primarily uses the appeal to ___ethos ___logos ___pathos.
2. The primary method of development is
   A. definition
   B. contrast/comparison
   C. classification
   D. example
   E. extended analogy

Practice Writing a Thesis Statement in Response to an Argument Prompt, #1

In "Me Talk Pretty One Day" (2000) a selection from an essay collection of the same name, David Sedaris and his peers do not defend themselves against a belittling and vindictive French teacher out of fear. However, in spite of this fear, Sedaris' and his classmates' fluency in French drastically improves.

In a well-written essay take a position on the use of fear as an effective source of motivation. Support your argument with appropriate evidence from your reading, observation, and/or experience.

Visual Argument – Build a Poster, #1

Here's your chance to be a budding commercial artist. Assume you have been given an assignment to create a poster on leadership. All you are given is the blank poster board with the word LEADERSHIP printed on the bottom of the poster. Your job is to create a dynamite poster that says leadership to anyone who sees it.

Leadership

No need to actually draw. All you need to do is list the following:

- What assertion about leadership will this poster be presenting?
- What is your main object/center of attention?
- Is your main object a photo or a drawing/painting?
- How much of the available space will your object take up?
- Last, but certainly not least, who is your audience?

Visual Argument – Build a Poster, #2

You have completed the preliminary overview of your poster on leadership. Let's continue with Part 2.

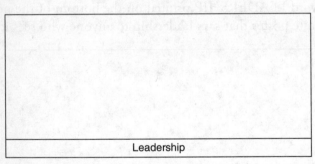

Leadership

No need to actually draw. All you need to do is list the following:

- In addition to your main object, are there any other objects in the poster?
- What are they?
- Where are they positioned in relation to the main object?
- Any words/phrase/sentence?
- If so, what are they? Where are they? What size are they in relation to the main object?
- Any predominant color? What is it? Where will it be used?

Visual Argument – Build a Poster, #3

You have completed the general overview of your poster on leadership. Let's go on to #3.

Leadership

Now that you've completed a general overview of your leadership poster, answer the following questions:

1. What is your assertion/claim about leadership?

2. To which of the appeals does your visual argument primarily rely on?

___ethos ___logos ___pathos.

3. What is your primary rhetorical strategy in constructing this assertion?

4. What is the tone of your poster? (Check all that apply.)

___positive ___negative ___formal ___informal ___serious ___humorous

___inspirational ___accusatory ___satirical ___pompous ___laudatory

___preachy ___tense ___sad ___happy ___busy ___serene ___hopeful

Visual Argument – Build a Poster, #4

Now that you've completed parts 1, 2, and 3 of this poster project, here is your final activity.

Leadership

Using no more than 3–5 sentences, compose a paragraph that presents to your audience what this poster is and what its assertion is.

Organizing an Argument Essay, #1

You have been assigned an argument essay that addresses *your* position on a topic introduced by your English and American History instructors who are team teaching a unit on responsibilities of young adults. One of the topics that came under discussion was requiring all 18-year-olds to register for one year of national service. This service could be in the military, working with a conservation group, working with people with disabilities, mentoring children in grades 1–5, or in any number of service areas.

Among the given quotations were:

> JFK's "Ask not what your country can do for you. Ask what you can do for your country." (1961)

> "An enlightened regard for themselves constantly prompts Americans to assist one another and inclines them willingly to sacrifice a portion of their time and property to the welfare of the state." —Alexis de Tocqueville (1835)

> "[Mandatory national service and conscription] rests on the assumption that your kids belong to the state. If we buy that assumption then it is for the state – not for parents, the community, the religious institutions or teachers – to decide who shall have what values and who shall do what work, when, where and how in our society." —Ronald Reagan (1979)

> 13th Amendment: "Neither slavery nor involuntary servitude, except as a punishment for crime whereof the party shall have been duly convicted, shall exist within the United States, nor any place subject to their jurisdiction."

In a well-written essay present your position on this topic and support your assertion using your knowledge and personal experience.

Briefly, state your position on mandatory national service for all 18-year-olds.

Organizing an Argument Essay, #2

You have written your brief statement of your position on one-year mandatory national service for all 18-year-olds.

Your next step is to decide on your major reason(s) for your position. Briefly list them.

Organizing an Argument Essay, #3

You have written your brief statement of your position on one-year mandatory national service for all 18-year-olds and listed your reasons for holding this point-of-view.

Look over your list and check off your most important reasons.

Day 145

Organizing an Argument Essay, #4

You now know your **S**ubject; you are the **S**peaker, and you know your **P**urpose. To complete this SOAPStone analysis and prep going, answer each of the following questions:

What is the **O**ccasion (the situation in which your essay will be presented)?

Who is your **A**udience?

What **TONE** are you planning to use?

Organizing an Argument Essay, #5

You've completed the first four steps in organizing your argument essay on the topic of one year mandatory national service for 18-year-olds. With this information in mind:

Compose the first draft of the introductory paragraph to your argument essay. Make certain to include both your thesis statement and one of the four quotations given in the prompt.

⟶ **5 Minutes to a 5**

Day 147

Reading Sample Synthesis Prompts, #1

Read the Prompt!

The media have given much attention to the demonstrations revolving around police and their tactics. Different representations, points of view, and agendas have led people to question what they think about the laws and controversy surrounding police activity, and what action, if any, needs to be taken. Some argue that there should be stricter laws surrounding law enforcement protocols, including the regulation that all officers should be required to wear body cameras. Others, however, argue that police officers have been wrongly accused and that all officers involved need to be acquitted.

Carefully read the following sources, including the introductory information for each source. Then synthesize information from at least three of these sources and incorporate it into a coherent, well-developed essay that evaluates what action needs to be taken, if any, to solve the controversial issue of police brutality.

Source A:

University of Baltimore. "Baltimore 68: Riots and Rebirth."
Website: http://archives.ubalt.edu/bsr/index.html

Source B:

Irby, Nathan C., Jr. "Recalling Baltimore's 1968 Riots." *Baltimore Sun*. April 3, 1998. Online. http://articles.baltimoresun.com/1998-04-03/news/1998093147_1_baltimore-riot-gay-street-east-baltimore

Source C:

Botelho, Greg, et al. "Baltimore protests: Crowds, police stand off after curfew." CNN. April 29, 2015. Online. http://www.cnn.com/2015/04/28/us/baltimore-riots/

Source D:

Picket, Kerry. "Nation of Islam and Gangs To Embattled Cities: We're in Control." *The Daily Caller*. April 27, 2015. Online. http://dailycaller.com/2015/04/27/nation-of-islam-and-gangs-to-embattled-cities-were-in-control/

Source E:

Political cartoon: http://www.cagle.com/patrick-chappatte/2016/07/divisiveness

Source F:

Charts/Graphs: http://mappingpoliceviolence.org/

Source G:

FBI National Press Office: https://www.fbi.gov/news/pressrel/press-releases/fbi-releases-2015-preliminary-statistics-for-law-enforcement-officers-killed-in-the-line-of-duty – Thanks to Lena Stypeck

1. What type of synthesis prompt is this?
   A. contrast and comparison
   B. cause and effect
   C. analysis
   D. argument
   E. overview

2. Underline the assignment given in the prompt.

3. Before beginning to write your essay, which of the following steps should you complete? (Check all that apply.)
   ___Carefully read and annotate the prompt.
   ___ Make a preliminary decision as to where you stand in relationship to the topic.
   ___ Read and quickly annotate each of the sources.
   ___ Decide which of the sources you will use.
   ___Quickly jot down main points you wish to make and where the sources will be placed.

Reading Sample Synthesis Prompts, #2

The question of what makes a good leader is very much a part of the conversation in today's political, business, and cultural worlds. In a 2010 article "What Shakespeare's 'Henry V' Tells Us about Leadership, Motivation, Wooing and Hanging," that appeared in the *Knowledge @ Wharton*, Michael Useem, co-director of "The Leadership Journey" and director of the Wharton Center for Leadership and Change Management stated, "By watching how historical figures behave in settings far before our time – in this case, looking at the characters Shakespeare brought to life in *Henry V* – we often get very good insights into what is vital in our own leadership or managerial moments" Adding emphasis to this point-of-view could be George Santayana's famous statement: "Those who cannot remember the past are condemned to repeat it."

Carefully read the following sources, including the introductory information. Then, in a well-written essay that synthesizes at least three of these sources, evaluate the qualities of effective leadership.

Make certain that your essay centers on your argument. Use the sources to support your position; avoid merely summarizing. You may refer to the sources by their letters (Source A, Source B, etc.) or by the identifiers in the parentheses beside each source.

Source A (Useem)

http://knowledge.wharton.upenn.edu/article/what-shakespeares-henry-v-tells-us-about-leadership-motivation-wooing-and-hanging/

Source B (Shakespeare)

William Shakespeare's *Henry V*, ACT IV Scene 2

Source C (Miller)

https://www.army.mil/article/156778/Veterans_reflect_on_Battle_of_Mogadishu

Source D (Kennedy)

Inaugural Address of President John F. Kennedy Washington, D.C., January 20, 1961

Source E (MacArthur)

Speech delivered at MacArthur's retirement from West Point http://www.artofmanliness.com/2008/08/01/the-35-greatest-speeches-in-history/

Source F (Queen Elizabeth I)

Speech to the Soldiers Assembled to Repel the Spanish Armada, 1588

Source G (Bowden)

The difficulty of recognizing excellence in its own time http://www.theatlantic.com/magazine/archive/2013/06/abraham-lincoln-is-an-idiot/309304/

1. According to the prompt, underline the *subject* of this synthesis essay.

2. According to the prompt, if you used Source G (Bowden) twice in your essay, could you count that as TWO sources?

3. According to the prompt, do you have to refer to George Santayana's statement in your essay? Michael Useem's quotation?

Synthesis: Choosing and Using Sources, Headlights, #1

Even though headlight glare doesn't pose a problem for you, you've heard your parents and grandparents complain about it. You've even been in the car when your grandfather was driving and swerved the car because he said he could not see with all the headlight glare. You figure that for your own safety and the safety of others, something should be done to address this problem. Coincidently, you see and read an article about this very situation, and that sets you to thinking about what should or could be done to remedy the situation. So, you decide to write a column about this for your local newspaper.

As a result of your preliminary research, you've located five sources. Listed below is bibliographic information you've jotted down for each of them.

A. Too bright headlights? New technology causing concerns for some drivers http://articles.orlandosentinel.com/2011-01-15/business/os-auto-scscolumn-011611-20110115_1_xenon-lights-mainstream-vehicles-nissan-leaf/2

B. Drivers' Perceptions of Headlight Glare from Oncoming and Following Vehicles http://www-nrd.nhtsa.dot.gov/Pubs/809-669.PDF

Technical Report Published By: National Center for Statistics and Analysis Advanced Research and Analysis

October 2013

C. Countermeasures for Reducing the Effects of Headlight Glare

Prepared by:

Douglas Mace The Last Resource Bellefonte, PA 16823

Philip Garvey The Pennsylvania Transportation Institute University Park, PA 16802

Richard J. Porter Richard Schwab

Werner Adrian University of Waterloo Ontario, Canada

Prepared for:

The AAA Foundation for Traffic Safety 1440 New York Avenue, N.W. Washington, D.C. 20005 202-638-5944 www.aaafoundation.org

December 2001

D. Fight Headlight Glare

Ronald Porep, Republished from SafetyIssues Issue 6 http://www.safetyissues.com/magazine/2015/5/HeadLightGlare/HeadLightGlare.htm

E. Don't be a victim of headlight glare! New petition set up by Lightmare reinstates need to install SolarLite Solar Powered Road Studs

Katy Young Marketing Co-ordinator

ClearView Traffic Group 10/01/2014

www.clearviewtraffic.com

Which of the sources would appear to offer the BEST overview of the problem?

A. A and D
B. B only
C. C only
D. D and E
E. B and C

Synthesis: Choosing and Using Sources, #2

Let's assume that when driving at night, you find that the glare from on-coming headlights interferes with your clear vision of the road and traffic around you. You buy a pair of yellow anti-glare glasses for night driving, but this doesn't really help. Coincidently, you see and read an article about this very situation, and that sets you to thinking about what should or could be done to remedy the situation. So, you decide to write a column about this for your local newspaper.

As a result of your preliminary research, you've located five sources. Listed below is bibliographic information you've jotted down for each of them.

A. Too-bright headlights? New technology causing concerns for some drivers http://articles.orlandosentinel.com/2011-01-15/business/os-auto-scscolumn-011611-20110115_1_xenon-lights-mainstream-vehicles-nissan-leaf/2

B. Drivers' Perceptions of Headlight Glare from Oncoming and Following Vehicles http://www-nrd.nhtsa.dot.gov/Pubs/809-669.PDF

    Technical Report Published By: National Center for Statistics and Analysis Advanced Research and Analysis

    October 2013

C. Countermeasures for Reducing the Effects of Headlight Glare

    Prepared by:

    Douglas Mace The Last Resource Bellefonte, PA 16823

    Philip Garvey The Pennsylvania Transportation Institute

    Richard J. Porter Richard Schwab

    Werner Adrian University of Waterloo

Prepared for:

The AAA Foundation for Traffic Safety 1440 New York Avenue, N.W. Washington, D.C. 20005 202-638-5944 www.aaafoundation.org

December 2001

D. Fight Headlight Glare

Ronald Porep, Republished from SafetyIssues Issue 6 http://www.safetyissues .com/magazine/2015/5/HeadLightGlare/HeadLightGlare.htm

E. Don't be a victim of headlight glare! New petition set up by Lightmare reinstates need to install SolarLite Solar Powered Road Studs

Katy Young Marketing Co-ordinator

ClearView Traffic Group 10/01/2014

www.clearviewtraffic.com

What is the item in the bibliographic information that should make you question the validity of sources A and C?

Practice with Summary

Carefully read the following brief excerpt from Thomas Paine's *Common Sense*.

> To talk of friendship with those in whom our reason forbids us to have faith, and our affections wounded through a thousand pores instruct us to detest, is madness and folly. Every day wears out the little remains of kindred between us and them, and can there be any reason to hope, that as the relationship expires, the affection will increase, or that we shall agree better, when we have ten times more and greater concerns to quarrel over than ever? (81 words)

Compose a one sentence summary of this passage.

Practice with Direct Quotation, Paraphrase, and Summary, #1

Let's assume you are interested in writing a synthesis essay that deals with the eating for good health. One of the sources you decide to investigate is an article titled "The Amalfi Diet and Its Benefits" that appears in the June, 2014, issue of *Hospital Dietician's Newsletter*. Below is a passage from it, written by Dorothy Craig, which you believe to be important.

> …The Amalfi diet is one of the best diets for weight loss, weight maintenance, and cardiovascular health. Unlike many diets, the Amalfi diet is a lifestyle diet that imposes only a few restrictions. Followers should limit the consumption of refined sugars and should eat red meat only once or twice a month. Other integral parts of the diet include eating smaller portions and exercising daily to mirror the Amalfi Coast lifestyle. Research studies demonstrate the benefits of the diet: reduced cholesterol levels, decreased chances of falling prey to a variety of diseases, such as Alzheimer's, diabetes, and even depression….

Which sentence is most probably the thesis statement? Why?

Practice with Direct Quotation, Paraphrase, and Summary, #2

Let's assume you are interested in writing a synthesis essay that deals with the eating for good health. One of the sources you decide to investigate is an article titled "The Amalfi Diet and Its Benefits" that appears in the June, 2014, issue of *Hospital Dietician's Newsletter*. Below is a passage from it, written by Dorothy Craig, which you believe to be important.

> …The Amalfi diet is one of the best diets for weight loss, weight maintenance, and cardiovascular health. Unlike many diets, the Amalfi diet is a lifestyle diet that imposes only a few restrictions. Followers should limit the consumption of refined sugars and should eat red meat only once or twice a month. Other integral parts of the diet include eating smaller portions and exercising daily to mirror the Amalfi Coast lifestyle. Research studies demonstrate the benefits of the diet: reduced cholesterol levels, decreased chances of falling prey to a variety of diseases, such as Alzheimer's, diabetes, and even depression….

Which sentence lends itself to being directly quoted? Incorporate it into a text that follows this sentence:

The high rating given the Amalfi diet is not just friendly, neighborly advice. **YOUR SENTENCE.**

Practice with Direct Quotation, Paraphrase, and Summary, #3

Let's assume you are interested in writing a synthesis essay that deals with the eating for good health. One of the sources you decide to investigate is an article titled "The Amalfi Diet and Its Benefits" that appears in the June, 2014, issue of *Hospital Dietician's Newsletter*. Below is a passage from it, written by Dorothy Craig, which you believe to be important.

> …The Amalfi diet is one of the best diets for weight loss, weight maintenance, and cardiovascular health. Unlike many diets, the Amalfi diet is a lifestyle diet that imposes only a few restrictions. Followers should limit the consumption of refined sugars and should eat red meat only once or twice a month. Other integral parts of the diet include eating smaller portions and exercising daily to mirror the Amalfi Coast lifestyle. Research studies demonstrate the benefits of the diet: reduced cholesterol levels, decreased chances of falling prey to a variety of diseases, such as Alzheimer's, diabetes, and even depression….

Summarize the first two sentences.

Practice with Direct Quotation, Paraphrase, and Summary, #4

Let's assume you are interested in writing a synthesis essay that deals with the eating for good health. One of the sources you decide to investigate is an article titled "The Amalfi Diet and Its Benefits" that appears in the June, 2014, issue of *Hospital Dietician's Newsletter*. Below is a passage from it, written by Dorothy Craig, which you believe to be important.

> …The Amalfi diet is one of the best diets for weight loss, weight maintenance, and cardiovascular health. Unlike many diets, the Amalfi diet is a lifestyle diet that imposes only a few restrictions. Followers should limit the consumption of refined sugars and should eat red meat only once or twice a month. Other integral parts of the diet include eating smaller portions and exercising daily to mirror the Amalfi Coast lifestyle. Research studies demonstrate the benefits of the diet: reduced cholesterol levels, decreased chances of falling prey to a variety of diseases, such as Alzheimer's, diabetes, and even depression….

Paraphrase the last sentence.

Composing a Summary of a Given Sentence

Compose a summary of the following sentence excerpted from "The Art of Political Lying," by Jonathan Swift, (1710).

> There is one essential point wherein a political liar differs from others of the faculty, that he ought to have but a short memory, which is necessary, according to the various occasions he meets with every hour, of differing from himself, and swearing to both sides of a contradiction, as he finds the persons disposed with whom he hath to deal. (61 words)

Sentences for Paraphrasing and Summarizing, #1

One of the requirements of AP English Language is to experience writing from various time periods. The more practice you have reading and understanding these writings with their strange subject matter, idiom, and syntax, the better prepared you will be when you meet unfamiliar texts in your course, in your personal reading, or on the exam.

Below is a sentence excerpted from the work of a well-known writer. Read it carefully and then either paraphrase or summarize it IN YOUR OWN WORDS.

> **There is also an artificial aristocracy founded on wealth and birth, without either virtue or talents... The artificial aristocracy is a mischievous ingredient in government, and provisions should be made to prevent its ascendancy.**   (34 words)

—Thomas Jefferson (1743–1826)

Sentences for Paraphrasing and Summarizing, #2

One of the requirements of AP English Language is to experience writing from various time periods. The more practice you have reading and understanding these writings with their strange subject matter, idiom, and syntax, the better prepared you will be when you meet unfamiliar texts in your course, in your personal reading, or on the exam.

Below is a sentence excerpted from the work of a well-known writer. Read it carefully and then either paraphrase or summarize it IN YOUR OWN WORDS.

> **What information consumes is rather obvious: it consumes the attention of its recipients. Hence a wealth of information creates a poverty of attention, and a need to allocate that attention efficiently among the overabundance of information sources that might consume it.**

—Herbert Alexander Simon, economist, Nobel laureate (1916–2001)

Sentences for Paraphrasing and Summarizing, #3

One of the requirements of AP English Language is to experience writing from various time periods. The more practice you have reading and understanding these writings with their strange subject matter, idiom, and syntax, the better prepared you will be when you meet unfamiliar texts in your course, in your personal reading, or on the exam.

Below is a sentence excerpted from the work of a well-known writer. Read it carefully and then paraphrase it. Good luck. This is a tricky one. Pay attention to the definition of *pilulous* and to the referent for *its*.

> **"Has anyone ever pinched into its pilulous[1] smallness the cobweb of pre-matrimonial acquaintanceship?"**

—George Eliot, *Middlemarch* (1871–1872)

––––––––––––––

[1]small, pill-like, insignificant

Sentences for Paraphrasing and Summarizing, #4

Below is a sentence excerpted from the work of a well-known writer. Read it carefully and then summarize it.

George Orwell, "Politics and the English Language," 1946

… It [English language] becomes ugly and inaccurate because our thoughts are foolish, but the slovenliness of our language makes it easier for us to have foolish thoughts. The point is that the process is reversible. Modern English, especially written English, is full of bad habits which spread by imitation and which can be avoided if one is willing to take the necessary trouble. If one gets rid of these habits one can think more clearly, and to think clearly is a necessary first step toward political regeneration: so that the fight against bad English is not frivolous and is not the exclusive concern of professional writers. …

Preliminary Evaluation of Your Sources

Assume you are doing the research for a synthesis essay about college expenditures on building athletic facilities. You have taken the preliminary position that the money spent to construct athletic facilities is too high. Your initial search includes the following possible source: http://www.stack.com/a/expensive-college-athletic-training-facilities. Take a close look at the site and answer the following questions.

1. Who created this page? ___ an academic ___ an advocacy group ___ a sales company ___ a specific interest group ___ a blogger

2. Can you identify the creator's credentials? ___ yes ___ no

3. The tone of this site is ___ informative ___ accusatory.

4. Based on the above information, this site is ___ objective ___ subjective

5 Minutes to a 5

Synthesis: Reading and Using Sources, #1

Assume you are considering writing a synthesis essay about the amount of money colleges spend on their athletic facilities. You have read an article written by Will Hobson and Steven Rich titled "The latest extravagances in the college sports arms race? Laser tag and mini golf" that appeared in *The Washington Post* on December 21, 2015.

Below is an excerpt from the article that really caught your attention.

> ...A decade of rampant athletics construction across the country has redefined what it takes to field a competitive top-tier college sports program.... Facilities spending is one of the biggest reasons otherwise profitable or self sufficient athletic departments run deficits, according to a *Washington Post* review of thousands of pages of financial records from athletic departments at 48 schools in the five wealthiest conferences in college sports.
>
> In 2014, these 48 schools spent $772 million combined on athletic facilities, an 89 percent increase from $408 million spent in 2004, adjusted for inflation. Those figures include annual debt payments, capital expenses and maintenance costs.

Underline what is most probably the thesis statement for the entire article.

Synthesis: Reading and Using Sources, #2

Assume you are considering writing a synthesis essay about the amount of money colleges spend on their athletic facilities. You have read an article written by Will Hobson and Steven Rich titled "The latest extravagances in the college sports arms race? Laser tag and mini golf" that appeared in *The Washington Post* on December 21, 2015.

Below is an excerpt from the article that really caught your attention.

> ...A decade of rampant athletics construction across the country has redefined what it takes to field a competitive top-tier college sports program.... Facilities spending is one of the biggest reasons otherwise profitable or self-sufficient athletic departments run deficits, according to a *Washington Post* review of thousands of pages of financial records from athletic departments at 48 schools in the five wealthiest conferences in college sports. In 2014, these 48 schools spent $772 million combined on athletic facilities, an 89 percent increase from $408 million spent in 2004, adjusted for inflation. Those figures include annual debt payments, capital expenses and maintenance costs.

Summarize this passage.

5 Minutes to a 5

Synthesis: Reading and Using Sources, #3

Assume you are considering writing a synthesis essay about the amount of money colleges spend on their athletic facilities. You have read an article written by Will Hobson and Steven Rich titled "The latest extravagances in the college sports arms race? Laser tag and mini golf" that appeared in *The Washington Post* on December 21, 2015.

Below is an excerpt from the article that really caught your attention.

> ...A decade of rampant athletics construction across the country has redefined what it takes to field a competitive top-tier college sports program.... Facilities spending is one of the biggest reasons otherwise profitable or self-sufficient athletic departments run deficits, according to a *Washington Post* review of thousands of pages of financial records from athletic departments at 48 schools in the five wealthiest conferences in college sports.
>
> In 2014, these 48 schools spent $772 million combined on athletic facilities, an 89 percent increase from $408 million spent in 2004, adjusted for inflation. Those figures include annual debt payments, capital expenses and maintenance costs.

Keeping in mind the difference between paraphrase and direct quotation, which of the two sentences in the second paragraph could easily be paraphrased? Which lends itself to direct quotation? Why?

Synthesis: Reading and Using Sources, #4

Assume you are considering writing a synthesis essay about the amount of money colleges spend on their athletic facilities. You have read an article written by Will Hobson and Steven Rich titled "The latest extravagances in the college sports arms race? Laser tag and mini golf" that appeared in *The Washington Post* on December 21, 2015.

Below is an excerpt from the article that really caught your attention.

> …A decade of rampant athletics construction across the country has redefined what it takes to field a competitive top-tier college sports program…. Facilities spending is one of the biggest reasons otherwise profitable or self-sufficient athletic departments run deficits, according to a *Washington Post* review of thousands of pages of financial records from athletic departments at 48 schools in the five wealthiest conferences in college sports.
>
> In 2014, these 48 schools spent $772 million combined on athletic facilities, an 89-percent increase from $408 million spent in 2004, adjusted for inflation. Those figures include annual debt payments, capital expenses and maintenance costs.

1. If you decided to directly quote the first sentence of the second paragraph as part of the introduction to your essay, which position on the amount of money spent on college athletic facilities would you be taking?

___Positive ___Negative ___Qualified

2. Compose the first draft of the thesis statement for your essay.

Synthesis – Drawing Conclusions

The following is a data-line from a national poll taken in September 2016, by Pollfish.[1]

Warming (Global): Do you agree that human behavior is substantially responsible for Global Warming? **D-Democrat R-Republican**

	USA D	USA R	Men D	Men R	Women D	Women R	18–24 D	18–24 R	25–34 D	25–34 R	35–44 D	35–44 R	45–54 D	45–54 R	55+ D	55+ R
%	44	17	40	22	47	13	44	12	48	11	46	14	43	20	43	19

---

[1]http://predictwise.com/politics/pollfish-public-opinion-polling

Based on the information cited in this chart, what are *two* conclusions you can logically make?

Synthesis – Evaluating Sources

The following is a data-line from a national poll taken in September, 2016, by Pollfish.[1]

Warming (Global): Do you agree that human behavior is substantially responsible for Global Warming? **D-Democrat R-Republican**

	USA D	USA R	Men D	Men R	Women D	Women R	18–24 D	18–24 R	25–34 D	25–34 R	35–44 D	35–44 R	45–54 D	45–54 R	55+ D	55+ R
%	44	17	40	22	47	13	44	12	48	11	46	14	43	20	43	19

_____

[1]http://predictwise.com/politics/pollfish-public-opinion-polling

Now that you've drawn a couple of conclusions on the above data, it's time begin to evaluate this source in order to determine whether or not the information is reliable and whether or not to use it. Go to the website cited in the footnote.

1. Who is the author of this chart? _____ individual's name _____ group's name

2. If a group, what is the purpose of this group? If an individual, what are the goals of this person?

3. What is the creation date of the chart?

4. Would this site be relevant to you if you were writing a synthesis essay about current issues of importance to Millennials?

Day 168

Synthesis – Close Reading of Sources

Assume you are closely reading this excerpt in order to decide whether or not to use this source in support of your thesis for a synthesis essay on the qualities of a good leader.

SOURCE F

Queen Elizabeth I – Speech to the Soldiers Assembled to Repel the Spanish Armada, 1588

My loving people, we have been persuaded by some, that are careful of our safety, to take heed how we commit ourselves to armed multitudes, for fear of treachery; but I assure you, I do not desire to live to distrust my faithful and loving people. Let tyrants fear; I have always so behaved myself that, under God, I have placed my chiefest strength and safeguard   5
in the loyal hearts and good will of my subjects. And therefore I am come amongst you at this time, not as for my recreation or sport, but being resolved, in the midst and heat of the battle, to live or die amongst you all; to lay down, for my God, and for my kingdom, and for my people, my honor and my blood, even the dust.   10

I know I have but the body of a weak and feeble woman; but I have the heart of a king, and of a king of England, too; and think foul scorn that Parma or Spain, or any prince of Europe, should dare to invade the borders of my realms: to which, rather than any dishonor should grow by me, I myself will take up arms; I myself will be your general, judge, and   15
rewarder of every one of your virtues in the field.

I know already, by your forwardness, that you have deserved rewards and crowns; and we do assure you, on the word of a prince, they shall be duly paid you. In the mean my lieutenant general shall be

5 Minutes to a 5

in my stead, than whom never prince commanded a more noble and worthy subject; not doubting by your obedience to my general, by your concord in the camp, and by your valor in the field, we shall shortly have a famous victory over the enemies of my God, of my kingdom, and of my people.

1. In Paragraph one, what does Elizabeth identify as her major (*chiefest*) strength?

2. What quality does she highlight in paragraph 2?

3. In paragraph 3?

Drawing Inferences

Carefully read the following pie chart.

Days per week students at an urban high school participated in 20 minutes of vigorous exercise or 30 minutes of moderate exercise in 2016.

High school students' physical exercise

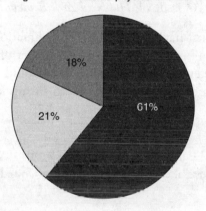

18%

21%

61%

1. List two inferences you can draw from this pie chart.

2. Based on the chart and your two inferences, if this pie chart were provided in a list of sources included in a synthesis essay prompt, what could you assume about the topic/subject of the essay?

Reading Footnotes, #1

After carefully reading the passage below AND its accompanying footnote, answer the question which follows.

Excerpted from: "Say What You Will" by David Luban, a review of *Free Speech: Ten Principles for a Connected World* by Timothy Garton Ash, which appeared in the September 29, 2016, issue of *The New York Review of Books*.

…Although laws against hate speech prohibit defamation of any racial or ethnic group, it is typically minority groups that face danger of public dehumanization. Jeremy Waldron, a defender of hate speech laws, would limit them to speech "directed at vulnerable minorities, calculated to stir up hatred against them."[3]

----

[3]Jeremy Waldron, *The Harm in Hate Speech* (Harvard University Press, 2014), p. 9, reviewed in these pages by John Paul Stevens, June 7, 2012. Waldron quotes examples of hate speech laws from several countries, including the United States, on pp. 8, 47, and 236–237.

Which of the following is an accurate reading of Footnote 3?

A. The author wants the reader to know that the U.S. is one among many countries that have documented hate speech laws.
B. The subject has been addressed before in this publication.
C. The author is aware of opposing viewpoints on this subject.
D. The author is in agreement with Waldron.
E. The author feels the need to explain the inclusion of minority groups.

Reading Footnotes, #2

After carefully reading the passage below AND its accompanying footnote, answer the question that follows.

> Excerpted from: "The Sorcerer of Jazz" by Adam Shatz, a review of *Bitches Brew* by George Grella Jr. which appeared in the September 29, 2016, issue of *The New York Review of Books*.

> …The music [Miles] Davis made from 1969 to 1975 was some of his blackest ever, sometimes directly based on bass lines and riffs he heard in James Brown and Sly Stone.[4]

> _____

> [4] The bass line in "Yesternow," the second side of *Jack Johnson*, the mesmerizing album he recorded soon after *Bitches Brew*, was lifted from James Brown's "Say It Loud, I'm Black and I'm Proud," and slowed down to a ghostly drone.

Taken as a whole, Footnote 4 suggests the author:

A. is a fan of James Brown.
B. is a music theorist.
C. implies that James Brown is owed credit for his contribution to Davis's music.
D. accuses Davis of plagiarizing James Brown's music.
E. is a jazz musician.

Reading Footnotes, #3

Excerpted from: "How to Eat Blue Crabs" by Joe Wenderoth, which appeared in the #18 issue of *Pen America*.

…To open a [blue crab] claw, lay it down flat so that its pincers are parallel with the table. Apply the dull blade of your weapon to the claw a little bit below the pincers. Then use the flat of your left hand to hammer the weapon into the shell. Ideally, your weapon should barely sink into the claw[2]…

_____

[2]…Here, in this one small instance, one of the tourist "crab hammers" might actually be useful, not only to apply to the crab directly, but to tamp down one's weapon into the claw. A billion other objects would serve just as well as a "crab hammer."

The purpose of this footnote is to

    A. provide further information about blue crabs
    B. enhance the authority of the author
    C. provide the reader with helpful information
    D. recommend further sources of information about shelling blue crabs
    E. acknowledge the author's opposition to the process being described

Methods of Incorporating Excerpted Text from a Source into a Sentence, #1

Remember that when using the paraphrase, summary, or direct quotation, it is possible to incorporate your attributed text into a sentence using a colon, *that*, or by interrupting the text.

Assume that you are involved in writing a synthesis essay around the topic of leadership. You have decided to incorporate the following excerpt from one of your sources into your essay.

Carefully read this original text:

> "A leader takes people where they want to go. A great leader takes people where they don't necessarily want to go, but ought to be."
>
> —Rosalynn Carter

Present this quotation in a <u>single sentence using a colon</u>.

5 Minutes to a 5

Methods of Incorporating Excerpted Text from a Source into a Sentence, #2

Remember that when using the paraphrase, summary, or direct quotation, it is possible to incorporate your attributed text into a sentence using a colon, *that*, or by interrupting the text.

Assume that you are involved in writing a synthesis essay around the topic of leadership. You have decided to incorporate the following excerpt from one of your sources into your essay.

Carefully read this original text:

> "My own definition of leadership is this: The capacity and the will to rally men and women to a common purpose and the character which inspires confidence."
>
> —General Montgomery

Present this quotation in a sentence <u>using *that*</u>.

Methods of Incorporating Excerpted Text from a Source into a Sentence, #3

Remember that when using the paraphrase, summary, or direct quotation, it is possible to incorporate your attributed text into a sentence using a colon, *that*, or by interrupting the text.

Assume that you are involved in writing a synthesis essay around the topic of leadership. You have decided to incorporate the following excerpt from one of your sources into your essay.

Carefully read this original text:

"A true leader has the confidence to stand alone, the courage to make tough decisions, and the compassion to listen to the needs of others. He does not set out to be a leader, but becomes one by the equality of his actions and the integrity of his intent."

—Douglas MacArthur

Present this quotation in a single sentence that *interrupts* the original text.

Methods of Incorporating a Direct Quotation into a Sentence

Carefully read this excerpt from George Orwell's *Politics and the English Language*.

> "Prose consists less and less of words chosen for the sake of their meaning, and more and more of phrases tacked together like the sections of a prefabricated hen-house."

You are writing an essay on political language and decide to use this sentence as a direct quotation. Paraphrasing or summarizing will not do it justice.

Incorporate this direct quotation into two different sentences that include both the quotation and the attribution.

1. Use a <u>colon</u>

2. Use *that*

Incorporating Sources into the Text of the Essay, #1

Let us assume you are writing an essay about famous writers' words of advice. Your first three sentences are:

So many renowned authors have written books or have given interviews about writing. I'm always looking for ways to make the writing process easier, and, if not easier, at least more fulfilling. A very special piece of advice comes from one of my favorite authors.

Following the directions, imbed all or part of the following quotation as part of your fourth sentence:

SOURCE D (Ray Bradbury, as quoted in *Advice to Writers* by Jon Winokur, 2000)

"You must write every single day of your life... You must lurk in libraries and climb the stacks like ladders to sniff books like perfumes and wear books like hats upon your crazy heads... may you be in love every day for the next 20,000 days. And out of that love, remake a world."

• Direct quotation: full citation provided at the beginning of the sentence
• Direct quotation: citation placed outside the text

Incorporating Sources into the Text of the Essay, #2

Following the directions, imbed all or part of the following quotation as part of your fourth sentence:

> SOURCE D (Ray Bradbury, as quoted in *Advice to Writers* by Jon Winokur, 2000)

"You must write every single day of your life... You must lurk in libraries and climb the stacks like ladders to sniff books like perfumes and wear books like hats upon your crazy heads... may you be in love every day for the next 20,000 days. And out of that love, remake a world."

- Combination of direct quotation and paraphrase: citation placed inside text
- Combination of direct quotation and paraphrase: Use citation outside of text

Incorporating Sources into the Text of the Essay, #3

Following the directions, imbed all or part of the following quotation as part of your fourth sentence:

SOURCE D (Ray Bradbury, as quoted in *Advice to Writers* by Jon Winokur, 2000)

"You must write every single day of your life… You must lurk in libraries and climb the stacks like ladders to sniff books like perfumes and wear books like hats upon your crazy heads… may you be in love every day for the next 20,000 days. And out of that love, remake a world."

- Paraphrase with citation inside of text
- Paraphrase with citation outside of text

A Self-Evaluation

Well, you've completed the AP English Language and Composition course, and you've probably taken the AP English Language exam. It's worth your while to evaluate how far you've come since the beginning of this course. What is your "takeaway" as an AP English Language student?

- What surprised you most as an AP English Language student?
- What did you find to be most interesting?
- How is your writing different from where you were at the beginning of the course?
- How is your reading different from where you were at the beginning of the course?
- What one thing covered in this course would you like to learn more about?
- Having taken this course, What is the most important outcome for you?
- How has participating in this AP English Language and Composition course prepared you to be a "citizen rhetor"?

Answers

Day 1

1. No matter what book you plan to read, it's always a good idea to peruse the table of contents to give yourself a general idea about the author's organizational plan and the topics that are covered in the text.

2. It's very easy to find the date of the AP English Language exam by going to the AP Central website at http://apcentral.collegeboard.com/apc/public/exam/dates_fees/index.html

3–4. The decision about which plan would work best for you is personal. Just make certain to be honest with yourself about your work habits and how you handle deadlines.

5. A quick scan of the Diagnostic/Master exam will give you an idea of what an AP English Language exam looks like. The more you know, the better able you are to plan and prepare.

Day 2

1. **A** This is strictly a **factual** question. You can go directly to the text and point to the answer. Just make certain you remember that, in our course, *antecedent* means the specific word in the previous part of the text that a pronoun refers to.

2. **C** **Analytical** question stems ask you to consider the author or speaker's purpose when using a specific rhetorical device, such as parallel structure. (In AP English Language, one type of analysis = using a rhetorical element for a specific purpose.)

3. <u>D</u> When you are asked about the effect of a specific rhetorical element, you are being asked an **inferential** question. You are required to draw a conclusion based on the given text.

4. <u>B</u> When asked about techniques, you are expected to look for **technical** elements, such as metaphor, juxtaposition, and hyperbole.

5. <u>D</u> Attitude requires you to draw a conclusion based on the author's subject, diction, organization, choice of details, syntax, etc. This is an **inferential** process.

6. <u>C</u> Function is part of **analysis**. You're asked to look for the parts that make up the whole and explain how each of the parts contributes to that whole.

7. <u>B</u> This is a **technical** question. When asked to locate a rhetorical device and to identify it, you are being asked to be technical. In a case like this, you are an AP English Language technician.

8. <u>D</u> *Context* and *interpreted* are the two words in the stem that tell you that this is an **inferential** question. You are being asked to draw a conclusion based on the specific text.

Day 3

1. <u>D</u> (FACTUAL) The antecedent of *it* is "the preservation of the means of knowledge" (11–12). As with all factual questions, the answer is actually given in the text. You can go to the text and point to it.

2. <u>A</u> (FACTUAL) In line 26, "that power" refers to "rulers" who are singled out in lines 6–7. The logic and sense of lines 26–27 will not support the other choices.

Day 4

1. <u>C</u> (TECHNICAL) Repetition can be found in lines 24–28 (A). Appeal to emotion is part of lines 18–20 (B). Line 31 contains a metaphor: "let every sluice of knowledge be opened and set a-flowing" (D). Adams appeals to authority (E) in line 3 ("Great Creator") and line 27 ("our forefathers"). **No simile appears in lines 10–27.**

2. <u>D</u> (TECHNICAL) The repetition of "Let us…" and "let" at the beginnings of sentences fits the very definition of **anaphora**. Every sentence in lines 24–30 begins with that phrase or word. Plus, the last sentence of the passage uses "let" after the introductory phrase.

Day 5

1. <u>A</u> (INFERENTIAL) The point-of-view in this passage is primarily that of a **patriot who is exhorting Americans to uphold freedom of the press.**

Lines 18–20 provide the clear evidence that this is the author's point-of-view. This statement follows Adams's stand in lines 11–13: "the preservation of the means of knowledge among the lowest ranks is of more importance to the public than all the property of all the rich men in the country."

2. B (ANALYTICAL) Lines 25–27 point out that the forefathers were led to fight for their liberty because of the cruel oppression under which they were living. Adams draws on that to compare with the current situation. This is made evident with the use of *their*, *our* and *us*.

Day 6

1. B (INFERENTIAL) As illustrated and supported in lines 10–14, lines 16–20, and in line 27, **Adams supported the education of individuals from all social classes.**

Day 7

This is a TECHNICAL question. **Personification** (1) is the only rhetorical device that Edward Abbey does not use in this passage. Metaphor is used in line 9 – "heart of the dead-still afternoon." Lines 1 and 9 contain examples of rhetorical questions. Examples of simile are embedded in lines 6, 9, and 10. Parallel structure can be located in lines 5 "Those pink …," 6 "… those diamondback …," 7 "… those unpleasant…," and 10 "… those sudden. …"

Day 8

This is an INFERENCE question. The most probable intended effect is **fear and loathing** (4). Remember that BOTH terms must be applicable to the text. All of the images created by Abbey contribute to EITHER **fear** ("sun roaring, pale cadaver of a ten-inch centipede, diamondback monsters thick as a truck driver's wrist, diamond-back monsters thick as a truck driver's wrist, sudden rockfalls, ubiquitous buzzard") OR **loathing** ("fetid, tepid, vapid little water holes, slowly evaporating under a scum of grease, unpleasant solpugids, diamondback monsters thick as a truck driver's wrist that lurk in shady places along the trail, crickets that scurry on dirty claws across your face at night.") Each of the other choices contains only one effect that could be inferred from the passage.

Day 9

The major rhetorical strategy used in this passage to define Cannery Row is **comparison/contrast** (4). For example, line 1 presents Cannery Row as a *poem* and as a *stink*. It is a *grating noise* and a *quality of light*. The definition goes from negative to positive throughout the passage.

There are no directions for the construction of an item (1). The definition of Cannery Row makes a claim, but there is no support (2). The author does not present cause/effect (3) in this passage, nor does he relate a story with a beginning, middle, and end (5).

Day 10

1. B The only rhetorical technique not used in this passage is **parallelism**. Metaphors (A) are found in lines 2, 3, and 4. A simile (C) is used in line 3, and exhortation (D) is easily recognized in the first and last sentences together with their ending with exclamation points. The two sentences: "Every spot of the old world is overrun with oppression. Freedom hath been hunted round the globe" located in lines 2 and 3 exemplify hyperbole (E).

2. E Remember that choices that are composed of two adjectives require that BOTH adjectives are found in the text. In this example, (A) Assertive could be used to describe the tone in certain circumstances, but there are no words or phrases that could be termed irreverent. The same holds true with (C). Indignant is a possibility, but not arrogant. Choices B and D have no descriptors that are appropriate to the given text. Looking carefully at the text, the exhortations in the first and last lines, plus the hyperbole and analogies, are all indications of **zeal** and **passion** for his subject.

Day 11

1. C The use of *Starbucks-guzzling* to describe a certain set of parents points to consumption meant to impress and announce their elitist qualities to all. This idea is supported with the specifics given throughout the passage. There is nothing in the text concerned with physical balance (A) or emotions (B). Education (D) is not mentioned in this excerpt nor is the concept of protection (E).

2. B The tone of the passage can best be described as critical and sarcastic. Remember that when each choice contains more than one item, each of the items MUST be correctly found in the text. With this in mind, harsh, ironic, or humorous could be part of the conversation, but the words that they are paired with negate their validity.

3. D The only rhetorical technique not used in this passage is **parody**. The use of *everybody* is an example of hyperbole (A). "cozy womb of noncompetition" and "Little Red Riding Hood" and "big, bad wolf" are metaphors/analogies (B). The entire excerpt is ripe with biting criticism (C). The idea of Little Red Riding Hood setting up a commune with the big, bad wolf is a nod to satire (E). Parody, a humorous, exaggerated imitation of a given action, person, or item, is not used in this text.

Day 12

1. C In line 17, *he* refers to **an antagonist**. Although lines 22–25 are rather convoluted, it is apparent that the author is referring to one antagonist deceiving the other antagonist in an argumentative situation.

2. D This passage can best be described as **argumentative and satirical**. Bierce makes it quite clear that he is aware of and quite displeased with how little people know or care about valid arguments. He is also making a case against those who engage in arguments and those who read or listen to arguments. His satire is evident in lines 6–8, lines 11–19, and lines 31–34.

Day 13

C In context *skein* means a length of yarn wound in a long, loose coil. The clues are found in lines 4 and 5 with *unravel, lengthening in curves*, plus *loosened*.

Day 14

B Deciphering the word *eminence* in line 3 demands a close reading of the situation pictured in the passage. Since he dismounted, Audubon is riding a horse, and this entails his being outdoors so that he can watch the flocks of birds. If he is going to count these flocks, he needs to easily and comfortably sit and hold paper and pen in hand. **A mound would provide both height and a kind of support as he sat and counted in his booklet.** A blind (A) must be built and assembled which Audubon make no mention of doing. (C) Ground does not indicate any height or back support. (D) Bench is a bit out of the time period, and (E) a blanket would not provide the height support.

Day 15

1. **E** In context, *puissance* in line 5 most probably means **power**. The major clues to the meaning are found lines 2 and 3: *most powerful military in the history of the world*, and *wealthiest economy in the history of the world*.

2. **B** In context, *ineluctably* in line 6 most probably means **unavoidably**. The major clues to the meaning are found in lines 8 and 9: *a zero-sum game*, and *all the potential for such games portend*.

Day 16

1. **E.** As defined in the *5 Steps to a 5* "Glossary," **metonymy** is a figure of speech in which a representative term is used for a larger idea. In this passage, the narrator stands on the shore of Chesapeake Bay looking out to the open water and the many ships sailing on it. By its very definition sail boats are powered by sails. So, not only do you need to know the definition of *metonymy*, you also need to closely read the text in order to infer the meaning of *sail* in context. There are no similes used in this excerpt (A). There are instances of hyperbole (B), but none in the underlined phrases. Nor are there any examples of antithesis or denotation (C, D).

2. **A.** A careful reading of this passage will lead you to infer that the narrator is giving a shout out to the multitude of ships sailing in Chesapeake Bay. Given the diction and syntax of the piece, the reader will not find any rhetorical devices that illustrate or support the ideas of silence, hope, helplessness, or cursing (B, C, D, or E). Again, this is an instance that not only calls for you to infer meaning from context, but it also requires you to know the definition of *apostrophe* as it applies to rhetorical/literary devices.

Day 17

The purpose of Footnote 4 is **C**, to **acknowledge the source of information**. The author gives what appears to be a factual/statistical statement. The idea that "residents living there are in fact less opposed to drones than the Pakistani population as a whole" has to have been located somewhere. This footnote provides that source. There is no support given, nor is there an explanation of the statement in the text. Since there is no obvious argument presented in the given text, there is no need to acknowledge an opposing position or idea. If a reader were interested in pursuing this topic further, the author cited in the footnote could be a new source, but this is NOT the primary purpose of this footnote.

Day 18

Footnote 2 is an example of **D**, an author's aside comment. Notice, there is no mention or citing of any sources nor other authors in the remaining choices. This footnote is the author speaking to any reader who is interested enough in the subject to seek his further background information.

Day 19

The purpose of Footnote 1 is **D**, to provide added information on the specific topic. Believing his audience to be fans of Miles Davis and interested in jazz, the author provides some interesting information that Davis fans would welcome. There is no indication of added support for the author's viewpoint (A) nor further explanation of a topic in the passage (B). No acknowledgment of a source is provided in this footnote (C). There is no opposition presented (E).

Day 20

Footnote 8 is **E**, a link to another source. The big clue here is the word *See* at the beginning of the footnote. This footnote is obviously a response to the question posed in the text. The authors are providing a further source to help answer the query.

Day 21

1. **B** The primary purpose of Footnote 15 is to indicate why Thoreau refers to *Mourt's Relation*. This passage is a narration of an episode that is not involved in presenting a position on a topic (A, C, E). While referencing *Mourt's Relation* does provide some further information (D), this information relates to Thoreau's illness, not on the specific subject of clams.

2. **D** The primary purpose of Footnote 16 is to provide further information on *sea-pearls* found in some clams to which Thoreau's reference to Cleopatra is an interesting piece of minutiae related to these mollusks.

Day 22

D The primary purpose of Footnote 19 is to provide further information on a specific topic, in this case broccoli. This, again, is a narrative about Thoreau's experiences while traveling in Cape Cod. The passage makes no argument about growing or eating broccoli.

Day 23

E Based on the context, *emetic* (line 5) most probably means that the clams caused Thoreau to experience a fit of vomiting.

Day 24

1. **C** **Description:** writing that appeals to one or more of the five senses

2. **A** **Exposition:** writing that explains or inform, widely used in non-fiction

3. **D** **Argument:** writing that presents a claim/position/assertion for acceptance by an audience

4. **B** **Narration:** writing that tells a story or retells a series of events

Day 25

1. **B** **Narration** This is the opening paragraph from Orwell's *1984*. It is the beginning of a story about the main character, Winston Smith.

2. **D** **Argument** This is the opening sentence of the Declaration of Independence that presents the argument for the right of the colonists to seek independence from England.

3. **C** **Description** These three sentences appeal to the reader's senses sight, smell, and touch.

4. **A** **Exposition** In this single sentence, the author begins to explain his thesis via examples.

Day 26

Diction is C. Your choice of words has a real impact on your presentation.

Connotation is E. The meaning associated with being called a *winner* is much more than only being the person or team that came in first in a specific competition.

Syntax is D. The types of sentences: type, how many of a type, when and where they are used are part of syntax. So is how, when, and where you use punctuation.

Imagery is A. A text that provides details about the colors, textures, sounds, aromas of a bakery is creating imagery so that you can almost experience the bakery as if you were there.

Denotation is B. The dictionary/literal definition of 13 is: a cardinal number, 10 + 3. But, this number can have many meanings other than the dictionary definition.

Day 27

1. The two items the prompt requires you to address in your essay are: Emerson's **purpose** and the **rhetorical devices** he uses to achieve that purpose.

2. It may not be specifically written in the prompt, but you must make certain to **include specific references** to the text that will illustrate or support your thesis.

Day 28

1. The two items you must address in your essay are: the <u>author's tone toward his subject</u> and <u>analyze how he rhetorically achieves this tone</u> (second sentence of the prompt).

2. The prompt is <u>NOT asking for an argument</u>; it is assigning a <u>rhetorical analysis</u> (second sentence of the prompt).

3. The prompt makes it very clear that the writer is <u>expected to incorporate specifics from the text to illustrate and support the thesis</u> (last sentence of the prompt).

4. Because you will be looking for clues from which you can deduce the tone that Reilly has toward his subject, you will be noting:
   - locate the thesis: assertion/claim about the subject
   - words and phrases that are related to constructing a tone
   - imagery that could provide clues
   - punctuation that adds emphasis or directs the reader's attention
   - specific examples or statements

Day 29

1. This prompt **does NOT** identify Tecumseh's reaction. It merely states what the subject of the speech was.

2. The prompt is **not asking** for your position on this issue. It is asking for analysis of Tecumseh's address.

3. As with question 2, your essay is to focus on Tecumseh's speech and the rhetorical strategies he uses to achieve his purpose. Your **personal experiences are not relevant** in this instance.

4. The two items that must be addressed in your essay are **Tecumseh's purpose** and the **rhetorical devices he uses to achieve his purpose**.

Day 30

1. The thesis statement is: "Nature provided for the communication of thought by planting with it in the receiving mind a fury to impart it."

2. Argue

3. Chronological: baby to adult

Day 31

The following is one example of a single sentence summary of the video:

> **This video shows school-aged kids trying to eat representative, typical brown bag lunches from the past 100 years.**

Day 32

S   The speaker is *Bon Appétit* (a food magazine)

O   The occasion is an experiment using students and attitudes toward different foods.

A   The audience would be people interested in the lunches, which students bring from home.

P   The purpose is to observe and record reactions to typical brown bag lunches from different decades from 1900 to 2000 and to get parents and schools thinking about what they give students for their lunches.

S   The subject of this video is school-aged kids trying to eat representative, typical brown bag lunches from the past 100 years. (This, by the way, is the sentence summary that you created for the first activity using this video.)

Day 33

Here is one example of a thesis statement that would use the video as the basis for an explanatory essay:

> **As illustrated in a recent YouTube video produced by *Bon Appétit* magazine, the lunches that students bring to school have changed over the past 100 years, for better or worse.**

This sentence is a valid thesis statement because of the following factors:

- The author's assertion is
  - clear
  - specific
- The reader has a sense of the essay's organization.
- The reader is made aware of the main point of the essay.

Day 34

Here is one example of a thesis statement that would use the video as the basic for an argument essay:

> **A recent YouTube video showed the reactions of several students to the changing brown bag lunches over the past 100 years, but, even though the students may have liked the more recent lunches better, they may not be healthier.**

This sentence is a valid thesis statement for an argument essay because of the following factors:

- The writer makes a definite claim/assertion about the subject.
- The statement is clear and focused.
- The reader has a sense of what to expect in the essay.
- The assertion is qualified. (...*may not be*...) This allows for the recognition of opposing ideas.

Day 35

1. informal, emotional, pretentious

2. informal, metaphorical

3. formal, patriotic, moralistic

4. informal, colloquial, aggressive

5. formal, moralistic, scholarly, esoteric

6. informal, slang, aggressive

Day 36

It's important to review the categories of sentence references in the activity.

- **Cumulative/Loose:** The main clause comes first, followed by other grammatical units/elements/structures.
- **Periodic:** The main clause comes at the end of the sentence preceded by other grammatical units/elements/ structures.
- **Inverted/Anastrophe:** The normal order of words in a sentence is reversed.

With this information in mind, these are the categories into which the sentences can be placed:

1. periodic
2. inverted
3. periodic
4. cumulative
5. inverted
6. periodic
7. cumulative
8. inverted
9. cumulative
10. inverted

Day 37

The underlined portions of Barbara Jordan's speech are **examples of parallel structure**. In the first paragraph, one notices the repetition of *At this*. The second paragraph includes the repetition of *It is possible*. The fourth paragraph contains two different examples of parallel structure: *The American Dream is* and *is slipping away*. These examples fit the definition of parallel structure as the repetition of grammatical structures.

Day 38

The predominant syntactical structure is **the rhetorical question**. There are 7 in all. This technique, while not really asking for a direct response to the author, involves the reader by asking her to consider the subject of the question.

Day 39

I wanted <u>to live deep</u> and suck out the marrow if life, <u>to live so sturdily</u> and Spartan-like as <u>to put to rout all</u> that was not life, <u>to cut a broad swath</u> and shave close, <u>to drive life</u> into a corner, and reduce it to its lowest terms.

The first of two syntactical strucuctures that you should notice is that this is a **cumulative sentence** (the main thought is at the beginning of the sentence, followed by a series of additional phrases). The second is the author's use of **parallelism** (see the underlined phrases).

Day 40

A careful reading of this passage reveals a **cumulative sentence** that begins with *It is an odious...* in lines 3–6. Beginning with *An oligarchy of learning ...* from line 6 through 12, you can find an example of a **periodic sentence.** The first part of the main clause is presented (*An oligarchy of learning*), followed by a series of phrases and clauses of additional information. The second part of the main clause is placed in lines 10 through 12 (*which ordains all men sovereigns...*). **Parallelism** is also part of the construction of this paragraph (*It is...* line 3).

Day 41

1. Sentences 1, 2, 3, and 4 are examples of **cumulative** sentences.

In each of these sentences, the subject is first, followed by the verb/predicate. This is our usual sentence format.

2. Sentences 5 and 6 are examples of **periodic** sentences.

Each of these sentences has its subject and/or predicate at the end preceded by descriptive and/or informative words, phrases, or clauses.

3. Sentence 7 is an example of a **cumulative** sentence.

Although quite long, the subject and verb are at the very beginning of the sentence, (*The texture and the color change in union*), followed by descriptive and informative words, phrases and subordinate clauses.

Day 42

Here is one example of a **cumulative** sentence:

> **Jessica always begins her writing sessions the same way by turning on her radio and setting it to the classical channel on Sirius XM, putting her phone on mute, opening her laptop, cracking her knuckles, and saying "alrighty then..."**

Remember that a cumulative/loose sentence begins with the main clause and is followed by a series that provides extra information to flesh out the main thought.

Day 43

Here is one example of a **periodic** sentence:

> **As always, after turning on the radio and setting it to the classical station on Sirius XM, muting her phone, and opening her laptop, then saying, "alrighty then," Jessica begins her writing session.**

The periodic sentence locates its main clause at the end of the sentence. In this example, the extra details are placed before the main thought.

Day 44

1. Here is an example of the **inverted** sentence: **Delivered in her email were all of the instructor's comments.**

2. Here is an example of the **inverted** sentence: **In the house next door lives a very famous writer.**

In each of these inverted sentences, the verb comes before the subject of the sentence.

Day 45

Below is one response which, because of diction, is informal/casual/relaxed:

> **87 years ago this country was founded on the principles of freedom and equality.**

(Notice that the archaic *four score and seven* is changed to a simple *87*. For today's audience, the formal, cumulative sentence and almost metaphorical words and phrases are replaced with a simple sentence that includes *principals of freedom and equality*.) Is your rewrite also shorter?

Day 46

You should have underlined **the last sentence of the paragraph**. Here the reader is notified that the purpose of the essay is to develop and support the statement *that something has gone badly wrong with the American male's conception of himself*. Aside from the rhetorical question in line 1, the remaining sentences are statements of specific observations that lead to the final sentence.

Day 47

You should have **underlined the sentence beginning with *If one gets rid of...* in lines 22–26.** As with any good thesis statement, this sentence informs the reader what the subject is and what the assertion of the author is.

Day 48

The ranking of the four statements is as follows:

C   My Dad thinks that *Huckleberry Finn* is Mark Twain's best novel.

B   *Huckleberry Finn* is Mark Twain's best novel.

A   Although some would argue that *The Adventures of Tom Sawyer* is Mark Twain's ultimate achievement, *Huckleberry Finn* has to be rated as his best because of its use of satire, imagery, and characterization.

D   *Huckleberry Finn* was written by Mark Twain in 1885.

Day 49

1. **A** **Argument** is the primary rhetorical strategy used to develop this paragraph. The first sentence which acts as the paragraph's topic sentence directly states Cather's position on the issue of what constitutes a good novel and its writer.

2. The sentence beginning in line 3 with "Writing ought either to …" and ending in line 7 with "standardized values." is an example of a **cumulative sentence**. In this sentence, the main clause is first, followed by a series of phrases and clauses that provide extra detail.

3. **D** According to Cather, a good novelist **does not compromise**. "… and he cannot compromise" in line 4 is the direct source of this answer.

Day 50

The thesis/topic sentence for this paragraph is situated in **lines 6–7**: *I still keep in mind a certain wonderful sunset which I witnessed when steamboating was new to me.* Lines 1–5 are set-ups for the topic of the paragraph to be introduced.

Day 51

"Something" in line 4 refers to: ***All the grace, the beauty, the poetry had gone out of the majestic river.***

This is one of those instances where the referent is AFTER the pronoun. Twain uses this technique as a buildup of a kind of suspense – What is this something?

Day 52

1. The purpose of this passage is to **inform**.

   As Twain says in the opening lines, he has lost something – the beauty of the Mississippi River. The remainder of the paragraph describes that beauty in a remembrance of a past sunset which he witnessed.

2. The primary rhetorical strategy employed in this paragraph is **description**.

   As a student of rhetorical analysis, your only choice for primary rhetorical strategy in this text is description.

3. The organization is **spatial**.

   Twain describes the scene from the "broad expanse ..." to "the middle distance..." to "upon of the water..." to "the shore on the left ..." to "woody heights ... soft distances ... over the whole scene."

Day 53

Here is one example that attempts to state the purpose of this particular sentence.

> **This long, undulating sentence is Twain's way of giving the reader a sense of the flow and pace of the river and what he sees and feels as he rides this river on a steamboat.**

Day 54

Using an argument of analogy, Thoreau's claim/assertion/thesis is that

> **an engine and its train is a powerful, almost mythological, man-made creation that can be of heroic help to humankind.**

Each of the analogies used in the text supports the image of a "demigod" that is "noble," a "cloud-compeller," a "race worthy" to inhabit the earth, "perspiration of heroic deeds," etc.

Day 55

1. The primary analogy developed in lines 1–3 compares a train to **comet** (line 2).

2. The primary analogy developed in lines 8–11 compares the locomotive to a **horse** (line 8).

3. The primary literary device Thoreau employs in the construction of this description of an engine and its train is **simile**, using "like" (lines 2, 4, 5, 9) and "as" (lines 7, 12, 13, 15).

Day 56

1. The thesis statement is: ***Our inventions are wont to be pretty toys, which distract our attention from serious things***. The first sentence in this passage could be included, but be aware that it is primarily a lead-in to the thesis.

2. Based on this paragraph, the reader can assume that the **primary purpose of the complete essay is to argue.** From the very beginning of the passage, Thoreau characterizes many inventions and improvements as toys, "not always a positive advance." Plus, the thesis makes it quite clear that Thoreau wishes to convince the reader to favor his position.

Day 57

Here is one possibility of a **bombastic rewording** of Twain's quotation:

> **When the happenstance of an altercation with a powerful or highly influential individual who vociferously opposes you presents itself, it is statistically more favorable to have judiciously prepared and to have committed oneself to confront your foe with unipeachable conviction and courage.**

We have gone from a statement of 19 words to one with 42 words. This revised "sentence" is lost in its own wordiness. It's just way too much. Twain gets right to the point using a clear metaphor. How did your "rewrite" compare?

Day 58

1. Here is the prompt with the key elements underlined:

In "<u>Message to President Franklin Pierce</u>," <u>Chief Seattle (chief of the Suquamish and Duwamish tribes of the Pacific Northwest</u>, also important to the "white man" as <u>Seattle was named after him</u>) <u>criticizes</u> and <u>cautions the attitudes and behaviors of the "white man."</u> After carefully reading the speech, compose a well-written essay <u>analyzing the rhetorical devices used by Chief Seattle to convey his message</u>.

This is a prompt in which almost every word/phrase is important. We are told what Chief Seattle's purpose is, and you are required to analyze rhetorical devices/strategies used by Seattle to achieve his purpose. Notice that you are NOT told which devices/strategies to analyze; that is your choice. But, remember that for each device/strategy you must do *two* things:

- Identify the rhetorical device/strategy/technique in the text.
- Discuss/describe *how* the device/strategy/technique works to further illustrate/support the author's purpose.

2. The **S**ubject is the "white man's" behavior toward Native Americans.

The **O**ccasion is Chief Seattle's message to President Franklin Pierce.

The **A**udience is the President of the United States.

The **P**urpose is to criticize the behavior and attitude of the "white man" toward Native Americans.

The **S**peaker is Chief Seattle.

Day 59

Carefully read <u>Judy Brady's essay</u> "I Want a Wife," originally <u>published in</u> *Ms.* magazine <u>in 1972</u> and <u>reprinted as "Why I [Still] Want a Wife" in the same magazine in 1990</u>. Then compose a well-written essay in which you <u>analyze</u> Brady's <u>use of rhetorical strategies to reveal what she believes to be society's attitude toward the role of husbands and wives in the United States.</u>

This is another prompt in which almost every word/phrase is important. Not only is it important to know the author and title of the essay, it is also important to know when and where the essay was written, and, in this case, when and where it was reprinted. The time period(s) could play an important role in diction, allusions, legalities, perceptions, etc. Don't overlook small details like this in a prompt. Notice that you are NOT told which devices/strategies to analyze; that is your choice. But, remember that for each device/strategy you must do *two* things:

- Identify the rhetorical device/strategy/technique in the text.
- Discuss/describe *how* the device/strategy/technique works to further illustrate/support the author's purpose.

2. The **S**ubject is society's attitude toward the role of husbands and wives in the U.S.

   The **O**ccasion is an article in *Ms.* magazine.

   The **A**udience is readers of *Ms.* magazine.

   The **P**urpose is to describe society's attitude towards the role of husbands and wives in the U.S.

   The **S**peaker is Judy Brady.

Day 60

During the hot summer of 1776, the Declaration of Independence <u>**was written by Thomas Jefferson**</u>, and the <u>bondage **was broken** between</u> Britain and the American colonies. The <u>Yankees **were at last separated** from</u> the dictatorial monarchy and its supporters. <u>The War of Independence **was fought** by</u> the joined colonies, and the <u>stars and stripes **were very soon unfurled**</u>.

Notice that each underlined set of words contains a form of the verb **to be + a past participle and in most instances a preposition, such as *by*.** That's the big clue. We are *not* told WHO broke the bondage, WHO separated the Yankees, nor WHO unfurled the stars and stripes.

Day 61

There is no one correct way to revise this sentence using active voice. Here are two examples:

> **Even though people <u>spend</u> a great deal of money on it, many others <u>wouldn't spend</u> a dime on hip-hop music.**

> **Many people <u>hate</u> hip-hop music even though others <u>spend</u> a great deal of money on it.**

In each of these sentences, the subject precedes the <u>verb</u> in each clause. It is clear who is doing the action.

Day 62

During the summer of 1776, Thomas Jefferson **wrote** The Declaration of Independence which **broke** the bondage between Britain and the American colonies. At last, the Yankees **separated** themselves from the dictatorial monarchy and its supporters. The colonies successfully **fought** the War of Independence and soon **unfurled** the stars and stripes. (49 words)

We've gone from 58 words to 49. It may not sound like much, but conciseness can greatly contribute to clear writing. With fewer words, the reader now knows that the Declaration of Independence broke the bondage, the Yankees separated themselves, and the colonies unfurled the stars and stripes.

Day 63

Here is an example of a summary of the first paragraph: **A group of bearded men and a few women gathered in front of a heavy, spiked wooden door.**

This sentence (18 words) states the bare bones of the original (43 words).

Day 64

1. *Gloomy* and *ominous* are two words that could be used to describe the tone of "The Prison-Door."

2. A throng of bearded men, in **sad-colored** garments and **gray, steeple-crowned hats,** intermixed with women, some wearing hoods, and others bareheaded, was assembled in front of a wooden edifice, the door of which was **heavily timbered** with oak and **studded with iron spikes.** The founders of a new colony, whatever Utopia of human virtue and happiness they might originally project, have invariably recognized it among their earliest practical necessities to **allot a portion of the virgin soil as a cemetery, and another portion as the site of a prison**. … Certain it is that, some fifteen or twenty years after the settlement of the town, the wooden jail was already marked with weather-stains and other indications of age which **gave a yet darker aspect to its beetle-browed and gloomy front.** The **rust** on the **ponderous iron-work** of its oaken door looked more antique than anything else in the New World. Like all that pertains to crime, it seemed never to have known a youthful era. Before this **ugly edifice**, and between it and the wheel-track of the street, was a grass plot, much **overgrown with burdock, pigweed, apple-peru, and such unsightly vegetation**, which evidently found something congenial in the soil that had **so early borne the black flower of civilized society,** a prison. But on one side of the portal, and rooted almost at the threshold, was a wild rosebush, covered, in this month of June, with its delicate gems, which might be imagined to offer their fragrance and fragile beauty to the prisoner as he went in, and to the **condemned criminal** as he came forth to his **doom**, in token that the deep heart of Nature could pity and be kind to him.

This rosebush, by a strange chance, has been kept alive in history; but whether it had merely survived out of the **stern old wilderness**, so long after the fall of the gigantic pines and oaks that originally overshadowed it – or whether as there is fair authority for believing, it had sprung up under the footsteps of the sainted Ann Hutchison, as she entered the prison door – we shall not take upon us to determine. Finding it so directly on the threshold of our narrative, which is now about to issue from that inauspicious portal, we could hardly do otherwise than pluck one of its flowers, and present it to the reader. It may serve, let us hope, to symbolize some sweet moral blossom that may be found along the track, or relieve the **darkening close of a tale of human frailty and sorrow**.

These words/phrases, together with the contrast with the wild rosebush, contribute to the creation of the gloomy and ominous tone.

Day 65

Here is an example of a thesis statement that addresses the prompt:

> **In "The Prison-Door," the first chapter of *The Scarlet Letter*, Hawthorne creates a picture of a village and its inhabitants that is somber, gloomy, and ominous.**

This sentence provides the reader with the writer's topic and assertion about this topic. It also gives a clear indication of the organization of the essay.

Day 66

1. The tone of the review is **critical, negative, disdainful, and sarcastic**.

2. Below are the underlined words/phrases that all work together to produce this negative review.

> The last of the summer's movie epics is a digitalized <u>eyesore hobbled</u> in every department by <u>staggering</u> incompetence. I'm talking about *Ben-Hur*, a remake of William Wyler's 1959 milestone (there was also a 1925 silent version) that won Charlton Heston an Oscar in the title role and put the climactic chariot race in the action-movie canon. No time capsule inclusion or little gold men for this <u>poor reboot</u>, however. Executive producers Mark Burnett and his wife Roma Downey have been pushing projects … aimed squarely at those moviegoers interested in religious themes…. <u>No harm in that, except the artistic kind</u>. The new *Ben-Hur,* directed [by] Timur Bekmanbetov (*Wanted*), stars Jack Huston (so dazzling on *Boardwalk Empire,* <u>so dreary here</u>)….
>
> The actors <u>rarely rise above the level of monotonous</u>, and that includes Morgan Freeman as an African sheik who sells horses for chariot races. To be fair, you can see a glint of mischief in Freeman's eyes. But the movie <u>soon blots out any hint of fun, ferocity or imagination</u>. *Ben-Hur* wants to preach, brother, preach, but it <u>lacks the essential quality to do that effectively</u>: soul.

Day 67

1. Sky, sea, beach, and village lie as still before us **as if** they were sitting for the picture. It is dead low-water. A ripple **plays** among the ripening corn upon the cliff **as if** it were faintly trying from recollection to imitate the sea, and the **world of** butterflies hovering over the crop of radish seed are as restless in their little way **as** the gulls are in their larger manner when the wind blows. But the ocean lies **winking** in the sunlight **like** a drowsy lion – its **glassy** waters scarcely curve upon the shore – the   5 fishing boats in the tiny harbor are all stranded in the mud – our two colliers (our watering place has a maritime trade employing that amount of shipping) have not an inch of water within a quarter of a mile of them, and they turn, exhausted, on their sides, **like** faint fish of an antediluvian species. Rusty cables and chains, ropes and rings, under-most parts of posts and piles and **confused** timber defenses against the waves lie strewn about in a brown litter of tangled seaweed and fallen cliff which   10 looks **as if** a family of giants had been making tea here for ages and had observed an untidy custom of throwing their tea leaves on the shore.

   Looking closely at the underlined and bold words and phrases, you can see the many varied similes (comparison using *like* or *as*) and metaphors (implied comparison) that Dickens uses to describe the mental painting he constructs in his mind's eye.

2. **C** Dickens' diction, syntax, and imagery create the over-all effect of **stillness and serenity**. You've already noted the similes and metaphors. Now, take a close look at Dickens' word choice and his long, wave-like, sentences.

Day 68

E Each of the statements is an example of **irony**. Each of the three situations/statements is an example of the unexpected or an incongruity between what is expected and what actually happens.

Day 69

1. The thesis is found in **lines 1–6**. Here Lamb tells his audience that those who watch and read Shakespeare are more interested in thinking about the characters than in being excited by their actions.

2. The purpose of Lamb's essay is **to argue** his thesis.

Day 70

1. Lamb's primary strategy to organize his presentation is **D comparison and contrast (c/c)**.

   The key to recognizing the c/c organizational strategy in this essay is the transitional word at the beginning of the second paragraph – *Whereas*. In the first paragraph Lamb states his thesis and examples of two plays whose main interest is, according to Lamb, the action of the characters. In the second paragraph Lamb contrast action with thought inherent in Shakespearean characters like Macbeth.

2. Lamb develops his primary organizational strategy using **A examples**.

   Lamb uses the examples of Shakespeare's Macbeth, Richard, Iago, plus the dramatic characters of Barnwell and Glenalvon to illustrate the c/c between the two types of characters.

Day 71

1. According to the second paragraph, the perspective that reading a Shakespearean play has in comparison to seeing it is that of **abstraction**. (line 24)

2. According to Lamb, the major difference between the effect of reading a Shakespearean play and seeing it is that when we read it we are **interested in the impulses of the inner mind of the character**, but when we see the character represented on the stage, actions are "**comparatively everything.**" (lines 14–19)

3. In comparing reading the play and seeing it performed, Lamb characterizes reading the play as "**nothing**" and seeing the play as "**everything.**" (lines 14–19)

Day 72

Although each of the choices has a connection to the original sentence, choices 1 and 3 leave out some important items that add meaning to the point of the sentence. Therefore, the best choice here is the second summary statement. It includes the character in question, the action of that character, and the effect of each type of involvement with the scene – reading and seeing.

Day 73

An objective/detached diction would require the elimination of those words and phrases that are metaphoric, emotional, connotative, etc. Here is one way to rewrite the excerpt using objective/detached diction:

> **This is the first time in history that this ceremony has been held on this West Front of the Capitol. I'm facing the mall that has the monuments to our nation's founders at its end.**

Day 74

There is not only one way to answer the question. There are many, but ask yourself: Have I included ideas such as:

- Trying to get across the passage of time?
- Some of the ways texture and color could fade?
- Trying to have the reader understand the creation of softness?
- Trying to have the reader really see the different shades of blue as it changes over time?
- Using only one l-o-n-g sentence makes the reader slow down and begin to feel the passage of time?
- The change in texture and the color are happening together and at the same time?

Day 75

1. This is an example of **direct** satirical style.

The subject is stated directly with no characters nor situational complications.

2. The passage can be classified as **Horatian**.

It reads like an average instructional or descriptive page from a manual. It does so in a mellow voice without anger or bitterness. It's just "there." It knows "you get the joke."

3. Here are examples of words/phrases you could have underlined:

The Mississippi State University English Department announces its <u>employment</u> of a <u>radically innovative technological device</u>, the BOOK.

BOOK is a <u>revolutionary breakthrough in technology</u>: no wires, no electric circuits, no batteries, <u>nothing to be connected or switched on</u>. It is so easy to use, <u>even a child can operate it</u>.

Compact and portable, it <u>can be used anywhere</u> – even when sitting in an armchair by the fire, yet powerful enough to <u>hold as much information as a [flash drive]</u>.

Here is how it works: BOOK is <u>constructed of sequentially numbered sheets of paper (recyclable)</u>, each <u>capable of holding thousands of bits of information</u>. The pages are locked together with a <u>custom-fit device called a binding</u>, which <u>keeps the sheets in their correct sequence</u>.

All of this is a direct imitation of a description of how one of our smartphones or computers operates.

Day 76

B Since the headlines have been identified as satire, they will (A) be related to issues that are familiar to the audience, (C) use irony when deliberately referring to something that the audience would not expect, (D) exaggerate using either hyperbole or understatement, (E) use incongruity for humorous effect. However, the only headline that has a literary allusion is "A Modest Proposal to Convert Shopping Malls into Prisons." But, not having read Swift's "A Modest Proposal" would not invalidate the satirical effect of this headline.

Day 77

1. The writer is satirizing the fashion industry and those who are interested in being stylish.

2. The author's purpose is to draw attention to the absurdity of always criticizing and wanting to "make-over" those who are not deemed fashionable.

Day 78

1. This is an example of **direct** satirical style.

In this text, the writer speaks directly to the reader. The writer does not use a narrative with characters to create his satire.

2. The passage can be classified as **Horation**.

The tone is light-hearted without bitterness or anger.

3. **D** In constructing the satire, the writer primarily uses **irony**. This text uses verbal irony that provides the unexpected/reversal of the norm. It is absurd. None of the other choices can be found in the excerpt.

Day 79

1. This 19th century political cartoon can be classified as **Juvenalian**.

It is accusatory, biting, angry, scolding, and with little or no humor.

2. Some of the items you could cite include:

* "Who stole the people's money?"
* The drawings of the figures
* The looks on the main figures in the center of the cartoon
* The pointing fingers
* The labeling/naming of the figures
* Tammany Ring

Day 80

1. This YouTube video which satirizes The Declaration of Independence can be classified as **Horatian**.

As with most Horatian satires, this tongue-in-cheek satire is light-hearted without the bitterness and anger present in Juvenalian satire.

2. **C** This satirical video relies primarily on **irony**.

The satire is constructed of verbal irony in which the expected language, subject matter, and references associated with an 18th century European monarch is turned on its head with modern idiom, syntax, and references.

Day 81

Take a look at your copy of FDR's Inaugural Address. Did you

* read slowly with a pen/pencil/highlighter in hand?
* underline the thesis statement?
* annotate any questions or remarks?

Remember, close reading requires you to be an ACTIVE reader.

Day 82

1. This type of initial analysis should be almost second nature to you now. Remember, it is only the first step.

   S – Franklin D. Roosevelt, U.S. President

   O – Presidential inauguration

   A – Those in attendance and those listening in the U.S. and around the world

   P – To let the citizens of the United States and the world know what he plans to do as President

   S – The current condition of the U.S. in relationship to the Great Depression and the world

   TONE – serious, authoritative

2. **The first three sentences (lines 1–5) of the speech comprise the thesis** for FDR's speech, with the first sentence being the central idea. Sentences two and three provide added emphasis and qualification.

Day 83

1. **Lines 14–21 appeal to logos.** In these lines FDR outlines what the problems are that face the U.S. This is an intellectual listing.

2. **Lines 9–13 appeal to ethos.** In these lines FDR identifies with the citizens of the U.S., and he encourages their support of him as their leader based on the history of the U.S.

3. **Lines 6–9 and 13–14 appeal to pathos.** Although we could make the case that all of the first two paragraphs appeal to pathos, the famous line: "the only thing we have to fear is fear itself…" is an outstanding example of an appeal to the emotions of the audience. So, too, are lines 18 and 19 with the comparisons of income and business to frozen water and withered vegetation.

4. **Two metaphors are found in lines 18–19:** "means of exchange are frozen in the currents of trade and withered leaves of industrial enterprise lie on every side."

5. **These two metaphors support the serious and dire tone** of the speech. *Frozen* and *withered* are both associated with that which is no longer growing or capable of growth.

Day 84

1. *Yet* functions as both a transitional element and to emphasize the contrast between the content of the current and the preceding paragraphs.

2. The purpose of inverting the usual word order (anastrophe) in the first two sentences is to place the emphasis on *no*. "NO failure of substance. NO plague of locusts." The failure is not biblical or a natural disaster. It is within our control.

3. *this* in line 6 refers to "Plenty is at our doorstep, but a generous use of it languishes in the very sight of the supply." (lines 5–6)

4. Throughout the second paragraph, *they* refers to the *money changers*.

5. Given the rhetorical structure of the two paragraphs, you can conclude that the purpose is to indict the *money changers*.

Day 85

1. Line **1** refers to **money changers** and line **2** compares **our nation to a temple**.

2. The primary rhetorical appeal of these three paragraphs is **pathos**. References to happiness, joy, mad chase, dark days, more noble, thrill of achievement, honor, honesty, faithful, unselfish, pride, all build an appeal to emotion.

3. **Anastrophe** is found in line **5**. **Metaphor** in lines **1** and **2**. **Personification** in lines **6** and **7**. **Parallelism/Anaphora** in lines **17** and **18**.

Day 86

There are many ways of stating the main thought of the three paragraphs. Here is one way: **Responsibility to ourselves and others is more important than just going after material possessions.**

The important thing is to make certain your single sentence contains elements related to self-reliance, caring for others, and the evils of chasing money and material goods.

Day 87

1. The purpose of the first paragraph in this passage is to **serve as a shift** from a general description of conditions in the U.S. to a call for immediate action.

2. *this* in line 9 refers to the **entire subject of paragraph 2, in general**, and, **specifically, to "put people to work" in line 3**.

3. **Parallelism is the syntactical technique** that is the basis of the sentences in line 16–22. (The repetition of "It can be helped.")

4. The two major tasks cited by FDR in this passage are **putting people to work** and **convincing more people to leave the crowded cities for farming**.

Day 88

1. *These* in lines 6 and 17 refers to "**a strict supervision of all banking and credits and investments; there must be an end to speculation with other people's money, and there must be provision for an adequate but sound currency**" in lines 2–5.

2. In line 9, *this* is referring to "**I shall presently urge upon a new Congress in special session detailed measures for their fulfillment, and I shall seek the immediate assistance of the several States**" in lines 6–8.

3. Parallelism is the predominant syntactical technique in paragraphs 12 (*there must be*) and 15 (*It is the...*).

4. The parallel structure in paragraphs 12 and 15 serves to emphasize the equal importance of each step of what must be done (paragraph 12) and to punctuate FDR's belief that the plan is the best course of action (paragraph 15).

Day 89

1. "this pledge" in line 12 refers to "**We are, I know, ready and willing to submit our lives and property to such discipline, because it makes possible a leadership which aims at a larger good**" (lines 6–8).

2. "Action in this image" refers to "**this great army of our people**" in line 13. "to this end" is referring "**to a disciplined attack upon our common problems**" in lines 13–14.

3. According to paragraph 18, FDR appoints himself the general in charge of the people's army ("**I assume unhesitatingly the leadership of this great army of our people…**")

4. The argument presented in this passage is based on an argument of analogy: an army attacking an enemy.

Day 90

1. Beginning paragraph 23 with **_But_** _in the event…_ is strong, emphatic, and, sounds almost unconditional in the face of what precedes this paragraph. Beginning the sentence with _If the Congress fails…_ indicates a conditional situation which is a weaker stance than that using _But. In the event…_ lacks the strength and determination of _But_ in this context.

2. Lines 5–7 continue to develop the extended analogy: armed warfare ("broad Executive power to wage a war against the emergency, as great as the power that would be given to me if we were in fact invaded by a foreign foe").

Day 91

1. You could have underlined the following to illustrate how FDR is building his emotional appeal:

For the <u>trust reposed in me</u> I will return <u>the courage and the devotion</u> that befit the time. I can do no less.

We face the <u>arduous days</u> that lie before us in the <u>warm courage</u> of the national unity; with the <u>clear consciousness of seeking old and precious moral values</u>; with the _clean satisfaction_ that comes from the <u>stern performance of duty</u> by old and young alike. We aim at the assurance of a rounded and permanent national life.   5

We do not distrust the future of essential democracy. The people of the United States have not failed. In their need they have registered a mandate that they want direct, vigorous action. They have asked for discipline and direction under leadership. They have made me the <u>present instrument of their wishes</u>. In the <u>spirit of the gift</u> I take it.   10

In this dedication of a Nation we humbly ask the blessing of God. May He protect each and every one of us. May He guide me in the days to come.

2. According to this passage, FDR is basing his authority on the will of the people and the help and guidance of God. (lines 8–16)

Day 92

1. **C** Based on a careful reading and analysis of FDR's first inaugural address, "A Time for Necessary Change" would be the best choice of a title for an essay based on this speech.

2. The basis for choosing **C** includes:
   - FDR is taking office in the middle of the Great Depression.
   - FDR points out the problems that need to be addressed.
   - FDR lists the changes he wants to make.
   - FDR describes how he will make those changes.

Day 93

There are many ways to create an appropriate thesis statement that addresses the given prompt. Here is one example:

> **Using powerful rhetorical strategies in his First Inaugural Address, FDR speaks to move the American people to accept him and his plan to fight and defeat the Great Depression.**

This is an economical statement that presents the general plan for the essay. Remember that the "main course" of your essay is in the body paragraphs.

Day 94

In her chapter "Serving in Florida," in *Nickel and Dimed*, Barbara Ehrenreich goes undercover to investigate the world of minimum wage jobs, in this case waiting tables at a restaurant in Florida. Ehrenreich learned that one of the dishwashers at the restaurant, a poor Czech immigrant named George, would be fired for taking a small amount of food. Ehrenreich states:

> "In real life I am moderately brave, but plenty of brave people shed their courage in POW camps, and maybe something similar goes on in the infinitely more congenial milieu of the low-wage American workplace. Maybe, in a month or two more at Jerry's, I might have regained my crusading spirit. Then again, in a month or two I might have turned into a different person altogether – say the kind of person who would have turned George in."

> Reflect on Ehrenheich's statement. Then, in a well-written essay, take a position on the author's assertion about the possibility of the environment affecting people's personalities and moral compass. Support your argument with appropriate evidence from your reading, observation, and/or experience.

1. The underlined sections are the important items that you, as the writer, need to be aware of in order to compose an essay that appropriately responds to the prompt. We've underlined:
   - The source
   - The name of the author
   - The author's circumstances
   - Needed background information
   - The major point of the excerpt
   - The assignment

Without an awareness of the specific assignment and its requirements, you, as the writer, are at a disadvantage when it comes to planning and composing a well-written essay.

Day 95

1. Thoreau's position is <u>yes to breaking unjust laws in order to bring about positive societal change.</u> ("...I say, break the law.")

2. Thoreau <u>does qualify his position</u>: Thoreau states, "Unjust laws exist; shall we be content to obey them, or shall we endeavor to amend them, and obey them until we have succeeded, or shall we transgress them at once?... <u>if [the law] is of such a nature that it requires you to be the agent of injustice to another</u>, then, I say, break the law."

Day 96

1. This prompt **does not require** you to use either of the quotations in your essay.

2. **Yes,** you could use material you've read or seen in your essay. But, make certain that it is appropriate to your subject and position as well as your audience.

3. **No**, there is no reason to fear the reader disagreeing with your position on an issue.

The reader is interested in your position in so far as *how well you present it*, not whether or not your position is agreeable.

Day 97

<u>3</u> You know, if this is the official car of the winners of the World Series, it's the one I'll buy.

<u>5</u> People who support allowing 16-year-olds the right to drive just want to give teenagers the right to drive any way they want without having to face any consequences.

<u>4</u> Do you want to get a college education or be poor all your life?

<u>1</u> We didn't publish Carrie's photograph because we don't think it was deserving of publication.

<u>2</u> That novel is obviously not worth reading because I don't recognize the author.

If you'd like to review the definitions and examples of these terms, go to Chapter 9.

Day 98

<u>2</u> A student writer cites experts in the field that's the subject of her research paper.

<u>5</u> Is that his brother? He's got to be a really good basketball player.

<u>4</u> An argument uses facts, statistics, and the opinions of experts to support a claim that a pitcher player deserves to be inducted into the Baseball Hall of Fame.

<u>1</u> During a speech the speaker says to the audience, "Don't you all just love this weather?"

<u>3</u> A commercial for the Animal Rescue League shows videos and still photos of dogs and cats in poor physical condition.

If you'd like to review the definitions and examples of these terms, go to Chapter 9.

Day 99

4 You can't believe him because he always lies.

1 Judge Carter's brother owns a supermarket; therefore, he's not able to impartially judge this case against Whole Foods.

2 Since I bought my new computer, I've been getting much better grades. It got to be the new laptop.

5 Obviously Tim's a really poor driver because he failed his first driver's test.

3 Carrie will do very well at Yale because her mother graduated from there.

If you'd like to review the definitions and examples of these terms, go to Chapter 9.

Day 100

1. logos

2. logos

3. logos

4. logos

5. logos/ethos

6. logos

7. logos

8. pathos

9. ethos

10. ethos

If you are in doubt about **logos**, **ethos**, and **pathos**, review these rhetorical appeals in Chapters 6 and 8.

Day 101

E. The statement "Give me liberty or give me death." is **NOT related to logos**.

The ending statement is not one that appeals to anyone's sense of reasonableness or logic. It is, however, an emotional appeal with an either/or stance that is based on exaggeration.

Day 102

1. Situation: A police car follows your car for several blocks.

   Inference: I'm probably going to be pulled over.

   Assumption: When a police car follows you, you are going to be pulled over.

2. Situation: Your cell phone rings in the middle of the night.

   Inference: Something awful must have happened.

   Assumption: Whenever the phone rings in the middle of the night bad things have occurred.

It is important to understand and realize that the inferences we make (rightly or wrongly) are products of our assumptions (correct or incorrect; rational or irrational) and our perspective or point-of-view. When writing or analyzing the writing of others, this is always going to be an important consideration.

Day 103

1. Here is one example of an inference that Brady will most likely support in her essay: **Wives are over-burdened with work and too easily discarded.**

2. Here are a couple of assumptions on which the inference is based:
   - **Wives are the ones who take care of the kids and the house.**
   - **Divorced husbands are happy and relaxed.**
   - **Men need a wife.**

Be aware that both the inference and the assumptions are based on the writer's perspective or point-of-view. Her purpose in writing the essay is to present and support her thesis in hopes that her audience will understand and accept her position.

Day 104

1. If you watch this campaign video there is no doubt about what three words/ phrases the producers of this video want you to remember: **hope, change, yes we can.**

   The words *hope* and *change* are shown on signs held by scores of people throughout the video; plus, the ad ends with Obama saying, "Yes we can."

2. **B** The tone of this video can best be described as **positive and hopeful.**

   The upbeat music and lyrics, together with smiling people of all ages and backgrounds, plus the numbers of people continuing to grow throughout the video create this optimistic tone.

Day 105

1. The argument being made in the ad is: Do not text while driving because there can be terrible consequences.

2. The ad uses **inductive** reasoning. Here is a presentation of the violent effects of a punch to the face. Two objects crashing into each other has a violent consequence. One vehicle crashing into another results in physical damage.

3. This entire ad is based on an **emotional response** to seeing the results of a punch to the face.

4. The ad argues from **analogy**. This is supported by the drawing of vehicle on the arm hitting a man's face on which is painted a large truck cab.

Day 106

1. Here is one example of a summary sentence for this campaign video.

This 1964 campaign video for LBJ shows a little girl picking the petals off a daisy, but her counting is interrupted with a nuclear bomb countdown and explosion with a voice-over warning that if LBJ is not elected nuclear Armageddon can result.

2. This campaign video appeals primarily to **pathos**.

Using the image of a little girl in a garden counting petals appeals to our emotions of love and caring, and the nuclear countdown and explosion appeal to the emotion of fear. The voice-over certainly reinforces the appeal to fear.

Day 107

The title of the cartoon is "Back to School." Two-thirds of the cartoon frame is taken up with a drawing of a large building labeled "Electoral College." The lower left corner of the cartoon shows two men wearing suits dragging a third man dressed in an Uncle Sam outfit toward the entrance to the building. Based on this information, one can conclude that the primary purpose of the cartoonist is to sarcastically indicate the need for the United States to revisit the Electoral College as it relates to presidential elections.

Day 108

Here is one example of a two-sentence summary of the passage:

In this passage, Montaigne argues against those who say that people should not make a profit off of others. For him, profit is the result of someone losing or giving up something, and he uses several specific examples to support his assertion.

Notice that with this summary, we have gone from 234 words in the original to 42. We have presented the essence of the passage.

Day 109

1. The topic of the graph is the number of those over the age of 16 employed in the information technology field.

2. The graph illustrates the number of over 16-year-olds employed in the information technology field between 1970 and 2014.

3. The obvious trend is upward. This is supported in both the bar and line graphs.

4. The U.S. Census Bureau published this chart in 2016. The date is located under the chart with the source information.

5. The source of the chart is the U.S. Census Bureau. This information is located at the bottom of the chart.

6. A major inference that is supported by this chart is that the employment possibilities in the Information Technology sector will continue to rise.

Day 110

1. There are any number of inferences that can be drawn from this bar graph. The important thing to remember is that an inference is a conclusion that is drawn from the given information. Here are two examples:
   - Watching TV and Internet streaming is a popular activity for high school students.
   - Activities that involve physical activity may be suffering as a result of the time teens spend in front of a TV or computer screen

2. Based on the two inferences above, here is an example of a thesis statement that could be the basis for an argument essay:
   - **Parental oversight is a necessary component of decreasing the amount of time teens spend on watching TV, gaming, and the Internet.**

Notice the use of information gathered from the bar graph and the stated position of the writer that provides the reader with an announcement of the subject of the essay to follow.

Day 111

The **subject** of this speech is the Japanese attack on Pearl Harbor. The **occasion** is a joint session of Congress on December 8, 1941. The **audience** is both the U.S. Congress and the American public. The **purpose** is to convince Congress to declare war on Japan. The **speaker** is U.S. President Franklin D. Roosevelt.

Day 112

The chronological organization of this speech provides compelling background and a sense of "being ambushed," together with a push to recognize the need for quick action.

Day 113

The parallel structure in lines 27–30 stacks one attack on top of the other so that the accumulation of these "night" attacks becomes a monumental sneak attack on the U.S. and its territories and allies that demands a quick response before other "night" attacks occur.

Day 114

The President changes from third person to first person in order to indicate that (1) he is joined together with all America, (2) all U.S. citizens are now in danger and in a state of war, and that (3) all Americans are going to be called on to work for victory.

Day 115

1. The topic sentence/thesis is found **in lines 2–3**: *I have learned that the swiftest traveller is he who goes afoot.*

2. The primary strategy Thoreau uses to develop/support his argument is **cause-effect**. In argument terms, Thoreau uses **if…then**.

Day 116

Deductive reasoning proceeds from a general idea/statement/proposal to specific examples of that generalization. **general→specific**

Inductive reasoning provides several specific instants/events/examples, and based on these examples, we draw a generalization/conclusion. **specific→general**

1. **Deduction.** This statement is based on the general idea that appendicitis is a serious illness. If Phil has appendicitis, he is seriously ill.

2. **Induction.** Observing album after album of classical music (specific) leads to the conclusion (general) that she would like to go to a classical concert.

3. **Induction.** Polls are specifics. Being a member of a particular party is a specific. Concluding that a member of the party in question will vote for the party's candidate is general.

4. **Deduction.** Icy roads are dangerous is the generalization. The traffic announcement reports icy roads. The conclusion is to not drive on the icy roads. (specific)

5. **Induction.** The amount of food and the daily exercise are specifics from which one can draw the conclusion about the poodle being overweight. (general)

Day 117

1. **Yes** The writer's authority is established in the information provided about the author under the title.

2. The claim/assertion/position is **stated in sentence two**: *Voting is just one of many ways to discharge the duties [of a citizen].*

3. **D** *The average auto mechanic does more good for society by fixing cars than by voting.* Is an example of a **hasty generalization**. As described in Chapter 9, a hasty generalization draws a conclusion about an entire group based little or no evidence.

Day 118

1. This is one example of a thesis statement for this campaign video:

   Given all of the improvements in the life and economy of America in the past four years, Ronald Reagan should be reelected President.

2. The main point of this campaign video is primarily developed using **induction**.

   The video presents a number of specific examples of the "good life" and specific numbers that indicate improving economic factors. All of this is given before the ending that states that Ronald Reagan is the reason all of this has come to pass; therefore, if America wants this to continue, he should be re-elected. (This ad proceeds from the specific to the general.)

Day 119

All three appeals are woven into the entire speech. But, we could point to each of the major emphases in the following manner:

The appeal to **logos** (logic, intellect) is developed primarily in **paragraphs 3, 4, and 5**. In these paragraphs, Sojourner Truth uses allusions to the Bible, juxtaposition, pinpointing the enemy, and if…then.

Ethos, using her experience and authority as a woman, a slave, and as a mother, plays a major part in **paragraphs 1 and 2**.

The appeal to **pathos** (emotions) is the key to development in **paragraph 2** which stresses Sojourner's life as a slave and as a mother in bondage.

Day 120

Sojouner Truth repeats "Ain't I a woman" in order to build up the emphasis on the fact that Sojourner is a woman like all other women and to build the case for equal treatment of all women, black or white.

Day 121

1. The **diction** of the passage can be described as **Homespun, colloquial, simple, plain** (slang and informal words/phrases)

2. The **overall effect of the passage can best be described as positive toward Sojourner Truth's argument** because of her appeals to logos, ethos, and pathos.

Day 122

1. **Logos** is the appeal that the writer uses in this brief argument. The reader is given no background on the writer that would establish is credibility (ethos), nor is there any emotional wording or examples (pathos).

2. The **first section of the second paragraph** contains the writer's assertion: *Yet isn't Mr. Dylan compromising that very artistic integrity by doing IBM TV commercials…*

   With his reference to the assertion made by Mr. Kirsch in the first paragraph, Mr. Bernstein clearly asserts his opposition to Kirsch's claim.

Day 123

1. The tone of the commercial is **sentimental**, **joyful**, and **slightly humorous**.

2. This tone is based on
- Action:
  - the father joyfully playing with his daughter and allowing himself to be made-up and dressed by his daughter
  - the father answering the door and slightly smiling at the two male strangers who look askance at him
  - the father shutting the going back to play with his daughter
  - the song played over the action
- Characters:
  - A young father
  - A young daughter
  - 2 rough looking male characters
- Setting
  - An apartment (rather than a luxurious house, or a busy street corner, or a public park, etc.)

Day 124

1. This Sprite commercial uses **inductive reason**. It shows the viewer several specific instances of the father actively and lovingly playing "make-up/dress-up" with his young daughter. From these specific examples, the viewer is led to conclude that this is an "ideal" father will not be bothered by negative glances of strangers who come to the door and see him "dressed-up." And, since this is an ideal father, drinking Sprite would be an ideal refreshment.

2. This commercial is based on an **appeal to emotions**. The music, lyrics to the song being sung in the background, the b/w film and soft focus, plus the loving father and daughter playing together ALL build up an emotional context.

3. The argument is **based on an analogy** that favorably compares the loving father with those who would drink Sprite.

4. This commercial hopes you will buy into a **hasty generalization** that equates drinking Sprite with being a loving/caring/sensitive person.

Day 125

1. The entire paragraph is made up of **4 rhetorical questions**.

2. The purpose of these rhetorical questions is: (1) to emphasize the point that the speaker does NOT take part in the benefits connected to the Declaration of Independence; (2) to push his audience to think about the conditions under which the speaker lives and was asked to speak.

Day 126

The thesis statement is located in lines 9–11: *My subject, then fellow-citizens, is AMERICAN SLAVERY. I shall see, this day, and its popular characteristics, from the slave's point of view.*

Day 127

D Each of the other choices names activities in which both black and white "free men" are engaged. There is no real philosophical discussion of "the Negro race" having abilities and potential for economic empowerment.

Day 128

1. **C** In the three sentences preceding the fourth, Douglass uses the diction of fire and brimstone to condemn the institution and continuation of slavery. The fourth sentence is a specific enumeration of the generalities of fire and thunder.

2. **B** *Quicken* as presented in context is synonymous with *to stimulate*. The other words do not illustrate nor support the context of a needed volcanic eruption of awareness and acknowledgment.

3. **E** It is important to remember that *all* parts of each choice must be correctly applicable to the text. **E** is supported by the diction and imagery of the text. In A, condemnation may be applicable, but there is no indication of forgiveness in this passage. With choice B, the political climate of the nation is not discussed in the excerpt. Regarding choice C, there is nothing in the text that relates specifically to immorality. For D, no discussion of the spiritual nature of the audience is present.

Day 129

1. A clearly developed thesis is evident _√_**yes** (*My subject, then fellow-citizens, is AMERICAN SLAVERY. I shall see, this day, and its popular characteristics, from the slave's point of view.*)

2. Facts are distinguished from opinions. _√_**yes**

3. Opinions are supported and qualified. _√_**yes**

4. The speaker develops a logical argument and avoids fallacies in reasoning. _√_**not applicable**

   The argument is not solely a logical one; rather, it is an argument developed also using the authority of the speaker and the appeal to pathos.

5. Support for facts is tested, reliable, and authoritative. _√_**yes**

6. The speaker does not confuse appeals to logic and emotion. _√_**yes**

7. Opposing views are represented in a fair and undistorted way. _√_**not applicable**

   There is only one side presented in Douglass's speech, and that is the side of those held in bondage as slaves in the United States. Douglass assumes his audience knows the viewpoint of those in America who uphold slavery.

8. The argument reflects a sense of audience. _√_**yes**

9. The argument reflects an identifiable voice and point-of-view. _√_**yes**

10. The piece reflects the image of a speaker with identifiable qualities –

    (honesty, sincerity, authority, intelligence, etc.). _√_**yes**

    Note: If you need further clarification of this checklist, go to Chapter 8 in the *5 Steps to a 5* text.

Day 130

Given the images, their positions and colors, in the ad, here is one sentence that states the argument being made. **Desertification is endangering Africa's elephant population.**

Day 131

1. The writer appeals primarily to logos. Examples of facts and logic can be found in lines 3, 4, 8–10, 11–12.

2. The claim/assertion/position is **stated in lines 8–10**: *Currently gas prices are low, so why not raise both federal and state gas taxes? This could fully fund the National Highway Trust Fund and its Mass Transit Account.*

3. **B** This is an example of a **hasty generalization**. As described in Chapter 9, a hasty generalization draws a conclusion about an entire group based little or no evidence. Is the price of gas the only criterion for raising or lowering gas taxes? Is it shown that raising gas taxes will fully fund the National Highway Trust Fund and its Mass Transit Account.

Day 132

1. This Gatorade commercial uses **inductive reasoning**. In a series of fast-paced action shots from a soccer match, plus close-ups of the famous soccer player Abby Wambach, and ending with a close-up of a bottle of Gatorade, the pitch goes from specific action to general conclusion.

2. The commercial is primarily based on an **appeal to pathos**. The dimly lit soccer field, the serious facial expressions, the perspiration, the intensity of the soccer players, ALL go to create a emotional effect that is tense, determined, and aggressive. Your opponents are like prey.

3. The **analogy** of opponents being like prey is the predominant strategy. Even though the main character is a soccer star, she is the predator in this commercial.

4. Given the choices, the best choice is a **bandwagon appeal**. Gatorade uses the soccer star as the central character/predator and the audience's recognition of her authority as a soccer player/athlete to sell their product. If Gatorade is good enough for Abby to recommend and use this, it's good enough for me.

Day 133

__√_A clearly thesis is evident. **The first sentence:** *[The] suggestion that the United States should adopt ranked-choice voting, just as in any other election, is long overdue.*

___Facts are distinguished from opinions. (Not really. The second paragraph is all opinion.)

___Support for facts is tested, reliable, and authoritative. (Reader must rely on the author.)

___Opinions are supported and qualified. (Only partially – Australia)

___The writer presents a logical argument and avoids fallacies in reasoning. (Use of either/or, over generalization…)

___The writer does not confuse appeals to logic and emotion. (use of hyperbole)

_√_The writer is aware of his audience.

___Opposing views are represented in a fair and undistorted way. (second paragraph is hyperbolic)

_√_The argument presents an identifiable voice and point-of-view.

_√_The piece reflects the image of a writer with identifiable qualities (**honesty**, **sincerity**, **authority**, **intelligence**, etc.) Note that the writer is a professor of economics at CUNY.

Day 134

1. The tone of this campaign ad is **negative and accusatory**.

2. Here are several specifics from the video that support the conclusion about the tone:

- Filmed in black and white
- Deep voice-over with heavy drum beats rumbling in the background
- Tower in shadow with what appear to be prison guards carrying guns
- Only negative statistics given at bottom of screen
- The revolving door that looks like a prison cell door
- The voice-over saying at the end of the video, "We can't afford that risk."

Day 135

The thesis statement is located in **lines 5–7**: *Forasmuch…what kind soever.*

With this statement, Montaigne announces what his position is on profit.

Day 136

1. This brief argument is primarily based on an appeal to **logos**.

As provided in this paragraph, Montaigne does not rely on his reputation/authority, nor does he appeal to the emotions of his audience. Montaigne does appeal to the intellect/logic by using example after example (lines 7–13).

2. **D** The primary method of development is **example**.

Montaigne sites eight examples from line 7 through 13. You could even include the last section of the last sentence: *for physicians hold, that the birth, nourishment and increase of every thing is the dissolution and corruption of another.*

Day 137

There are many ways to create an appropriate thesis statement that addresses the given argument prompt. Here is one example:

> **Fear can be a true motivator, and it can produce desired results – sometimes, but is the win or the grade worth the damage it can do to a person's sense of self-worth?**

The writer uses a rhetorical question to create the thesis statement. It's clear that the author's position is not going to be "yes" or "no" but rather one that looks at both sides.

Day 138

As an example, here are possible responses for a poster about leadership, voting, and parenthood.

- This poster will assert that leadership is present in the everyday, personal actions. It does not have to be earth shattering.
- The center of attention in this poster will be a voting table/desk surrounded by the privacy walls painted white with an American flag painted on each side. Below the bottom of the curtain are the legs of a woman wearing jeans with two small children standing on either side of her legs.
- The poster is a photo.
- The voting booth will begin slightly left of center and will take up all of the right side of the poster.
- The audience for this poster will be general adults of voting age.

Day 139

Using the idea presented in the first Build a Poster activity, here are possible responses for the second set of questions.

- Yes.
- In addition to the main object, there are the following: an American flag on the wall, a sign on the wall that says, "Your vote counts."
- These two items will be to the left of the booth and in the background. They will be smaller than the main item. The flag will take up the upper half of the background/wall, and the "Your vote counts" poster will be half that size and below the flag.
- There will be no predominant color, just the natural color of the photograph.

Day 140

Based on the responses to the first two set of questions, here are the answers to the questions above.

1. Leadership does not have to be just about governing a nation or commanding an army, it can be leading by example in the small, everyday actions and events.

2. This poster primarily appeals to PATHOS.

3. The primary rhetorical strategy will be EXAMPLE.

4. The tone of the poster is (Check all that apply.)

_√_positive___negative___formal _√_informal ___serious ___humorous

_√_inspirational ___accusatory ___satirical ___pompous ___laudatory

___preachy ___tense ___sad ___happy ___busy ___serene _√_hopeful

Day 141

Below is an example of a possible response to the given prompt.

This poster presents the photograph of one voter who has taken two children with her into the voting booth on Election Day. The most important and commanding visual in this poster is that voting table/desk with the woman and the two children standing with her behind the privacy wall. The American flag and "Your vote counts" sign mounted on the wall indicate that this is the United States. These images support this country's belief that leadership can be practiced in the ordinary, everyday actions and events by ordinary, average citizens.

Day 142

This is totally up to you. Do NOT try to impress anyone. No one will hold your position against you. Be yourself and honestly consider where you stand on the issue. As an example, **I favor a mandatory one year of national service.**

Day 143

With "I favor a mandatory one year of national service" as a starting point, here is an example of a list of reasons for holding this position.

- Could help bind people together
- Could be an opportunity to learn valuable skills
- Could build better citizens
- Could help a lot of people in need of aid
- Could help young people mature
- Could strengthen our military

Day 144

With "I favor a mandatory one year of national service" as a starting point, here is an example of the most important reasons checked off.

- Could help bind people together
- Could be an opportunity to learn valuable skills √
- Could build better citizens √
- Could help a lot of people in need of aid √
- Could help young people mature √
- Could strengthen our military

Note: The ones I did not check are actually included in those that I did check.

Day 145

With "I favor a mandatory one year of national service" as a starting point, here is an example of the completion of the SOAPStone information:

The <u>O</u>ccasion is going to be a letter to the editor of my local newspaper.

The <u>A</u>udience is general. The readers will be those who read a newspaper that is published in my hometown.

The <u>TONE</u> will be formal and serious.

Day 146

Below is one example of an introductory paragraph to the argument essay.

> **John F. Kennedy said in his 1961 inaugural speech, "Ask not what you**
> **country can do for you. Ask what you can do for your country." This**
> **still valid today, and that is why the United States should seriously**
> **mandating one year of national service for all 18-year-olds. With**
> **program in place, young adults would not only be given the opp**
> **to learn valuable skills, but they would also be helping where**
> **needed while maturing into better citizens.**

This introductory paragraph begins with the direct quotation that
statement. The last sentence of the paragraph provides the reader
the structure of the following essay and what to expect. With the
completed, you now have a structure firmly in hand. Each
follow will develop and support your position using the poin

This prompt could also be presented as a synthesis essay

Day 147

1. **D** This synthesis prompt is asking you to evalu
   a position on differing ideas.

2. The assignment given in the prompt is: ev
   if any, to solve the controversial issue o

3. If you checked off **every item**, you are ri
   sary to set up a framework to write your

1. The answer to this question is purely up to you. Just remember that to take a qualified position means you acknowledge that you believe there are positives AND negatives to be considered. Be honest. Don't try to play games with what you think the reader wants to hear.

2. Below are examples of each of the possible positions:

Negative: The amount of money that colleges are spending on athletic facilities is out of control.

Positive: If a college really wants to run an athletic program that successfully competes, it needs to spend money to construct and maintain sports facilities that will ~~attract~~ and keep top-notch athletes.

~~Qualified~~: At first glance, it seems that colleges spend an exorbitant amount of ~~money on sports~~ facilities, but it must be acknowledged that the sports program earns ~~enough money~~ for the college or university to spend in other areas.

~~Here are the conclusions~~ that can be made based on the given chart:

- ~~Women (22%) are more likely tha~~n Republicans (17%) to agree that ~~humans are the cause of~~ global warming.
- ~~Republicans (26%) are more likely than wo~~men (22%) to disagree that ~~humans are the cause of global~~ warming.

511

Day 169

1. There are any number of inferences that can be drawn from this pie chart. The important thing to remember is that an inference is a conclusion that is drawn from the given information. Here are two examples:
   - **High school students are active more than many people think.**
   - **The definition of exercise may have to be revised.**

2. Based on the chart and the two inferences, one could you assume the topic/subject of the synthesis essay to be: (two possibilities)
   - **the physical condition of the younger generation** or
   - **the responsibility of the schools to provide physical education to their students**

Day 170

<u>A</u> is the accurate reading of Footnote 3. Not only does the author provide publication information of the source of the quoted material in the text, but he also provides the page numbers where the reader can find other examples of hate speech laws both in this country and in several others. Mentioning that the subject has been addressed before in the publication is factual (B), but it is not applicable to the entire footnote. One could infer C and D, but that is not what the question is asking. There is no inclusion of minority groups in the footnote; therefore, E would not be correct.

Day 171

Taken as a whole, Footnote 4 suggests <u>C</u>, the author is implying that James Brown is owed credit for his contribution to Davis's music.

Given words like "mesmerizing album" when describing Davis's album, the reader can rightly infer that the author is a fan of Davis, but no such wording is found in this footnotes about Brown; therefore, A is not applicable here. Nor is B and E. Even though the reader could conclude that the author is a knowledgeable jazz fan, one could NOT conclude, therefore, that the author is either a music theorist or a jazz musician. D is much too harsh a characterization. "…lifted from" does imply, but it does not come out and accuse Davis of plagiarism.

Day 172

<u>C</u> The purpose of this footnote is to provide the reader with helpful information. There is no additional information about blue crabs (A), nor added authority of the author (B). There is no recommendation of other sources given (D), nor any indication of another process (E).

Day 173

Creating a sentence <u>using a colon</u> would look like this:

> **Rosalynn Carter's idea of leadership is quite straightforward: "A leader takes people where they want to go. A great leader takes people where they don't necessarily want to go, but ought to be."**

In this sentence the colon indicates that an example of straightforward is to follow.

Day 174

When asked to define leadership, General Montgomery said that it is "the capacity and the will to rally men and women to a common purpose and the character which inspires confidence."

This sentence quite clearly presents the original quotation using *that* after a brief introduction, which actually summarizes the very beginning of the original quotation.

Day 175

"A true leader has the confidence to stand alone, the courage to make tough decisions, and the compassion to listen to the needs of others," said five star general Douglas MacArthur who continued with the qualification, "He does not set out to be a leader, but becomes one by the equality of his actions and the integrity of his intent."

This sentence contains the complete quotation, but the writer *interrupts* it with a specific comment. This allows for a change in pacing and a way to interject an aside.

Day 176

1. <u>Using a colon</u>: As George Orwell states in *Politics and the English Language:* "Prose consists less and less of words chosen for the sake of their meaning, and more and more of phrases tacked together like the sections of a prefabricated hen-house."

2. <u>Using *that*</u>: In *Politics and the English Language*, George Orwell writes that "Prose consists less and less of words chosen for the sake of their meaning, and more and more of phrases tacked together like the sections of a prefabricated hen-house."

Day 177

Direct quotation: full citation provided at the beginning of the sentence

Ray Bradbury is quoted in the 2000 edition of *Advice to Writers* as saying, "You must write every single day of your life… You must lurk in libraries and climb the stacks like ladders to sniff books like perfumes and wear books like hats upon your crazy heads…"

Direct quotation: citation placed outside the text

Ray Bradbury said, "You must write every single day of your life… You must lurk in libraries and climb the stacks like ladders to sniff books like perfumes and wear books like hats upon your crazy heads…" (Source D) <u>or</u> (Winokur, *Advice to Writers*).

Day 178

Combination of direct quotation and paraphrase: citation placed inside text

In Jon Winokur's *Advice to Writers*, Ray Bradbury advised aspiring writers to write every day, spend time in libraries, read as much as possible, and to fall in love with what they read. "And," said Bradbury, "out of that love, remake a world."

Combination of direct quotation and paraphrase: Use citation outside of text

Ray Bradbury advised aspiring writers to write every day, spend time in libraries, read as much as possible, and to fall in love with what they read. "And," said Bradbury, "out of that love, remake a world" (Source D) or (Winokur, *Advice to Writers*).

Day 179

Paraphrase with citation inside of text

In Jon Winokur's *Advice to Writers*, Ray Bradbury advised aspiring writers to write every day, spend time in libraries, read as much as possible, fall in love with what they read. The result could be the making of a new world.

Paraphrase with citation outside of text

Ray Bradbury advised aspiring writers to write every day, spend time in libraries, read as much as possible, fall in love with what they read. The result could be the making of a new world (Source D) or (Winokur, *Advice to Writers*).

Day 180

This is totally up to you. It is our hope that your willingness to take risks as an AP English Language and Composition student has changed you. Changed you as a

- writer
- critical thinker
- close reader
- close and critical listener
- "citizen rhetor" with great potential

Abstract refers to language that describes concepts rather than concrete images.

Ad Hominem In an argument, an attack on the person rather than on the opponent's ideas. It comes from the Latin meaning "against the man."

Allegory a work that functions on a symbolic level.

Alliteration the repetition of initial consonant sounds, such as "Peter Piper picked a peck of pickled peppers."

Allusion a reference contained in a work.

Analogy a literary device employed to serve as a basis for comparison. It is assumed that what applies to the parallel situation also applies to the original circumstance. In other words, it is the comparison between two different items.

Analysis the process of taking apart a text by dividing it into its basic components for the purpose of examining how the author develops his/her subject.

Anecdote a story or brief episode told by the writer or a character to illustrate a point.

Annotate to make personal notes on a text in order to get a better understanding of the material. These notes can include questions, an argument with the author, acknowledging a good point, a clarification of an idea.

Antecedent the word, phrase, or clause to which a pronoun refers. The AP English Language and Composition exam often expects you to identify the antecedent in a passage.

Antithesis the presentation of two contrasting images. The ideas are balanced by word, phrase, clause, or paragraph. "To be or not to be . . ." "Ask not what your country can do for you, ask what you can do for your country . . ."

Argument a single assertion or a series of assertions presented and defended by the writer.

Attitude the relationship an author has toward his or her subject, and/or his or her audience.

Balance a situation in which all parts of the presentation are equal, whether in sentences or paragraphs or sections of a longer work.

Cacophony harsh and discordant sounds in a line or passage in a literary work.

Character those who carry out the action of the plot in literature. Major, minor, static, and dynamic are types of characters.

Colloquial the use of slang in writing, often to create local color and to provide an informal tone. *Huckleberry Finn* is written in a colloquial style.

Comic Relief the inclusion of a humorous character or scene to contrast with the tragic elements of a work, thereby intensifying the next tragic event.

Conflict a clash between opposing forces in a literary work, such as man vs. man; man vs. nature; man vs. god; man vs. self.

Connective Tissue those elements that help create coherence in a written piece. See Chapter 8.

Connotation the interpretive level of a word based on its associated images rather than its literal meaning.

Deduction the process of moving from a general rule to a specific example.

Denotation the literal or dictionary meaning of a word.

Dialect the re-creation of regional spoken language, such as a Southern dialect. Zora Neale Hurston uses this in such works as *Their Eyes Were Watching God*.

Diction the author's choice of words that creates tone, attitude, and style, as well as meaning.

Didactic writing whose purpose is to instruct or to teach. A didactic work is usually formal and focuses on moral or ethical concerns.

Discourse a discussion on a specific topic.

Ellipsis an indication by a series of three periods that some material has been omitted from a given text. It could be a word, a phrase, a sentence, a paragraph, or a whole section. Be wary of the ellipsis; it could obscure the real meaning of the piece of writing.

Epigraph the use of a quotation at the beginning of a work that hints at its theme. Hemingway begins *The Sun Also Rises* with two epigraphs. One of them is "You are all a lost generation" by Gertrude Stein.

Euphemism a more acceptable and usually more pleasant way of saying something that might be inappropriate or uncomfortable. "He went to his final reward" is a common euphemism for "he died." Euphemisms are also often used to obscure the reality of a situation. The military uses "collateral damage" to indicate civilian deaths in a military operation.

Euphony the pleasant, mellifluous presentation of sounds in a literary work.

Exposition background information presented in a literary work.

Extended Metaphor a sustained comparison, often referred to as a conceit. The extended metaphor is developed throughout a piece of writing.

Figurative Language the body of devices that enables the writer to operate on levels other than the literal one. It includes metaphor, simile, symbol, motif, and hyperbole, etc.

Flashback a device that enables a writer to refer to past thoughts, events, or episodes.

Form the shape or structure of a literary work.

Hyperbole extreme exaggeration, often humorous, it can also be ironic; the opposite of understatement.

Image a verbal approximation of a sensory impression, concept, or emotion.

Imagery the total effect of related sensory images in a work of literature.

Induction the process that moves from a given series of specifics to a generalization.

Inference a conclusion one can draw from the presented details.

Invective a verbally abusive attack.

Irony an unexpected twist or contrast between what happens and what was intended or expected to happen. It involves dialogue and situation and can be intentional or unplanned. Dramatic irony centers around the ignorance of those involved, whereas the audience is aware of the circumstance.

Logic the process of reasoning.

Logical Fallacy a mistake in reasoning (see Chapter 9 for specific examples).

Metaphor a direct comparison between dissimilar things. "Your eyes are stars" is an example.

Metonymy a figure of speech in which a representative term is used for a larger idea (*The pen is mightier than the sword*).

Monologue a speech given by one character (Hamlet's "To be or not to be . . .").

Motif the repetition or variations of an image or idea in a work used to develop theme or characters.

Narrator the speaker of a literary work.

Onomatopoeia words that sound like the sound they represent (hiss, gurgle, pop).

Oxymoron an image of contradictory terms (bittersweet, jumbo shrimp).

Pacing the movement of a literary piece from one point or one section to another.

Parable a story that operates on more than one level and usually teaches a moral lesson. (*The Pearl* by John Steinbeck is a fine example.)

Parody a comic imitation of a work that ridicules the original. It can be utterly mocking or gently humorous. It depends on allusion and exaggerates and distorts the original style and content.

Pathos the aspects of a literary work that elicit pity from the audience. An appeal to emotion that can be used as a means to persuade.

Pedantic a term used to describe writing that borders on lecturing. It is scholarly and academic and often overly difficult and distant.

Periodic Sentence presents its main clause at the end of the sentence for emphasis and sentence variety. Phrases and/or dependent clauses precede the main clause.

Personification the assigning of human qualities to inanimate objects or concepts. (Wordsworth personifies "the sea that bares her bosom to the moon" in the poem "London 1802.")

Persuasion a type of argument that has as its goal an action on the part of the audience.

Plot a sequence of events in a literary work.

Point of View the method of narration in a literary work.

Pun a play on words that often has a comic effect. Associated with wit and cleverness. A writer who speaks of the "grave topic of American funerals" may be employing an intentional or unintentional pun.

Reductio ad Absurdum the Latin for "to reduce to the absurd." This is a technique useful in creating a comic effect (see Twain's "At the Funeral") and is also an argumentative technique. It is considered a rhetorical fallacy, because it reduces an argument to an either/or choice.

Rhetoric refers to the entire process of written communication. Rhetorical strategies and devices are those tools that enable a writer to present ideas to an audience effectively.

Rhetorical Question one that does not expect an explicit answer. It is used to pose an idea to be considered by the speaker or audience. (François Villon [in translation] asks, "Where are the snows of yesteryear?")

Sarcasm a comic technique that ridicules through caustic language. Tone and attitude may both be described as sarcastic in a given text if the writer employs language, irony, and wit to mock or scorn.

Satire a mode of writing based on ridicule, that criticizes the foibles and follies of society without necessarily offering a solution. (Jonathan Swift's *Gulliver's Travels* is a great satire that exposes mankind's condition.)

Setting the time and place of a literary work.

Simile an indirect comparison that uses the word *like* or *as* to link the differing items in the comparison. ("Your eyes are like stars.")

Stage Directions the specific instructions a playwright includes concerning sets, characterization, delivery, etc.

Stanza a unit of a poem, similar in rhyme, meter, and length to other units in the poem.

Structure the organization and form of a work.

Style the unique way an author presents his ideas. Diction, syntax, imagery, structure, and content all contribute to a particular style.

Summary reducing the original text to its essential parts.

Syllogism the format of a formal argument that consists of a major premise, a minor premise, and a conclusion.

Symbol something in a literary work that stands for something else. (Plato has the light of the sun symbolize truth in "The Allegory of the Cave.")

Synecdoche a figure of speech that utilizes a part as representative of the whole. ("All hands on deck" is an example.)

Syntax the grammatical structure of prose and poetry.

Synthesis locating a number of sources and integrating them into the development and support of a writer's thesis/claim.

Theme the underlying ideas the author illustrates through characterization, motifs, language, plot, etc.

Thesis simply, the main idea of a piece of writing. It presents the author's assertion or claim. The effectiveness of a presentation is often based on how well the writer presents, develops, and supports the thesis.

Tone the author's attitude toward his subject.

Transition a word or phrase that links one idea to the next and carries the reader from sentence to sentence, paragraph to paragraph. See the list of transitions in Chapter 8.

Understatement the opposite of exaggeration. It is a technique for developing irony and/or humor where one writes or says less than intended.

Voice can refer to two different areas of writing. The first refers to the relationship between a sentence's subject and verb (active voice and passive voice). The second refers to the total "sound" of a writer's style.

SELECTED BIBLIOGRAPHY

The following is a select listing of both fiction and nonfiction writers, past and present, whose works include: essays, news articles, novels, short stories, journals, biographies, histories, autobiographies, diaries, satire, and political treatises. Each of these writers presents ideas in original, thought-provoking, and enlightening ways. Our recommendation is that you read as many and as much of them as you can. The more you read, discuss, and/or analyze these writers and their work, the better prepared you will be for the AP English Language and Composition exam. And, there is another wondrous benefit. You will become much more aware of the marvelous world of ideas that surrounds you. We invite you to accept our invitation to this complex universe.

Personal Writing: Journals, Autobiographies, Diaries

Maya Angelou
Annie Dillard
Frederick Douglass
Lillian Hellman
Helen Keller
Martin Luther King, Jr.
Maxine Hong Kingston

Mary McCarthy
Samuel Pepys
Richard Rodriguez
May Sarton
Richard Wright
Malcolm X

Biographies and Histories

Walter Jackson Bate
James Boswell
Thomas Carlyle
Bruce Catton

Winston Churchill
Shelby Foote
George Trevelyan
Barbara Tuchman

Journalists and Essayists

Joseph Addison
Michael Arlen
Matthew Arnold
Francis Bacon
Russell Baker
Harold Bloom
G. K. Chesterton
Kenneth Clark
Joan Didion
Maureen Dowd

Ellen Goodman
Pauline Kael
Garrison Keillor
John McPhee
N. Scott Momaday
Anna Quindlen
John Ruskin
Marjorie Sandor
Susan Sontag
Richard Steele

Nora Ephron
Anne Fadiman
William Hazlett
John Holt
Paul Russell

Henry David Thoreau
Calvin Trillin
Eudora Welty
E. B. White
Paul Zimmer

Political Writing and Satire

Hannah Arendt
Simone de Beauvoir
W. E. B. DuBois
William F. Buckley
Thomas Hobbes
Thomas Jefferson
John Locke
Machiavelli

John Stuart Mill
Sir Thomas More
Lincoln Steffens
Jonathan Swift
Alexis de Tocqueville
T. H. White
Tom Wolfe

Writers Known for Their Fiction and Nonfiction

Charlotte Perkins Gilman
Zora Neale Hurston
Norman Mailer

George Orwell
Virginia Woolf

Naturalists, Scientists, Adventurers

Edward Abbey
Rachel Carson
Charles Darwin
Loren Eisley
Stephen Jay Gould
William Least Heat-Moon

Verlyn Klinkenborg
Barry Lopez
Peter Matthiessen
Margaret Mead
Carl Sagan

Literally thousands of websites are, in some way, related to the study of college-level English. We are not attempting to give you a comprehensive list of all these websites. What we want to do is to provide you with a list that is most relevant to your preparation and review for the AP English Language and Composition exam. You can decide which websites may be of interest and/or offer you special benefits.

> *Note:* **These websites were available and online at the time this book was revised. Please be aware that we cannot guarantee that a site you choose to explore will be operating when you go to that URL.**

- Because this is an Advanced Placement exam you are preparing for, why not go to the source as your first choice: http://apcentral.collegeboard.com.
- McGraw-Hill has several sites that can be very helpful as you work your way through the AP English Language course and prepare for the exam in May: www.mhpracticeplus.com
- Dogpile: www.dogpile.com is a good search engine that finds topics via categories and other search engines.
- Search.com is one of the newest and best search engines that accesses the biggest of the search engines available at www.search.com.
- Bowling Green University Writer's Lab: http://www.firelands.bgsu.edu/library/writing_lab.html is chock full of information.
- Purdue On-Line Writing Lab (OWL): https://owl.english.purdue.edu/owl/section/1/ is a helpful online writing center with a huge set of links.
- A+ Research and Writing: http://www.ipl.org/div/aplus/ is a comprehensive guide to writing research papers.
- A portal site that links to the best of library and research sites is available at www.libraryspot.com. It consists of three sections: libraries (academic, film, government, and so forth), reference desk (almanacs, biographies, dictionaries, and so forth), and reading room (books, journals, newspapers, magazines).
- www.americanrhetoric.com has political speeches and speeches from movies.
- For terms, exercises, tips, and rules from a primate with attitude, go to Grammar Bytes: http://chompchomp.com.
- Two useful sites that provide help with rhetorical and literary terms are: http://andromeda.rutgers.edu/~jlynch/terms/index.html and http://humanities.byu.edu/rhetoric/Silva.htm
- You can compare coverage of major events in newspapers from around the world at www.newseum.org/todaysfrontpages.
- A website that provides access to the world of arts and letters—including newspapers, literary magazines, and blogs—is: https://www.aldaily.com/.

Each of these websites will lead you to many more. Take the time to explore the various sites and make your own evaluations about their value to you. You might even decide to set up your own AP Language website, or chat room!